Religion and the Struggle for European Union

RELIGION AND POLITICS SERIES

John C. Green, Ted Jelen, Mark Rozell, *Series Editors*

Religion and the Struggle for European Union

Confessional Culture and the Limits of Integration

BRENT F. NELSEN AND JAMES L. GUTH

Georgetown University Press / Washington, DC

LIBRARY OF CONGRESS CATALOGING-IN-PUBLICATION DATA

Nelsen, Brent F. author.
  Religion and the struggle for European union : confessional culture and the limits of integration / Brent F. Nelsen and James L. Guth.
    pages   cm
  Includes bibliographical references and index.
    ISBN 978-1-62616-070-5 (pbk. : alk. paper) — ISBN 978-1-62616-200-6 (hardcover : alk. paper) — ISBN 978-1-62616-071-2 (ebook)
    1. Religion and politics—European Union countries. 2. Christianity and politics—European Union countries. 3. Christianity and culture—European Union countries. 4. Group identity—European Union countries. 5. European Union countries—Politics and government. I. Guth, James L., author. II. Title.
  BL65.P7N45 2015
  322'.1094—dc23

                          2014038158

♾This book is printed on acid-free paper meeting the requirements of the American National Standard for Permanence in Paper for Printed Library Materials.

16 15   9 8 7 6 5 4 3 2 First printing

Printed in the United States of America
Cover design by Connie Gabbert Design and Illustration LLC.

To R. Booth Fowler

Contents

Illustrations

Preface

On June 9, 2014, a picture appeared in the *Financial Times*. Three men and a woman were seated in a rowboat in the middle of a Swedish lake. British prime minister David Cameron sat in the stern, Dutch prime minister Mark Rutte smiled in the bow, Swedish prime minister Fredrik Reinfeldt manned the oars, and German chancellor Angela Merkel sat just forward of Cameron. This staged—and cheesy—photo op drew attention to a "mini-summit" of "reformist leaders" called by Reinfeldt to discuss the choice of a new Commission president following the strong showing of anti-EU parties in the European parliamentary elections in May. The four leaders were calling for EU reforms and a president who would implement them. But these were not the familiar calls of many past European leaders to transfer more power from national governments to the EU's institutions in Brussels; they were not calling for "ever-closer union." On the contrary, they were advocating more "free trade and competition to try to push Europe in a more liberal direction."

What drew these four together to press for liberal reform, not deeper integration? True, they were all northern Europeans from the political center-right. But they were also Protestants. We believe that matters.

In this book we argue that religion—or what we call "confessional culture"—plays a powerful role in shaping ideas of Europe, attitudes toward integration, and felt identities—in both leaders and citizens. Catholicism has for centuries promoted the universality of the Church and the essential unity of Christendom, while Protestantism has valued particularity and feared Catholic dominance. These confessional cultures have produced two very different visions of Europe that have deeply influenced the process of postwar integration. Catholics have seen Europe as a single cultural entity that is best governed as a single polity. Protestants have never felt part of continental culture and have valued national borders as protectors of liberties that have historically been threatened by the Catholic powers. Catholics have pressed for a politically united Europe; Protestants have resisted sacrificing sovereignty to federal institutions, instead favoring pragmatic cooperation. This helps explain the four Protestants in the boat.

The following chapters explore the origins and continuing impact of confessional culture on the attitudes, behaviors, and identities of European elites, political parties, interest groups, and individuals. We demonstrate that despite the secularization of the Continent, religious culture still matters; cultural Catholics still favor integration, but Protestants resist it. These differences are not accidental; they are rooted in the religious struggles of the Reformation, which continue to reverberate across Europe. European elites must recognize the lasting importance of this cultural divide as the EU attempts to solve its slow-burning economic and political crisis. Failure to adjust, we fear, threatens decades of hard-won gains in security and prosperity for European citizens.

Acknowledgments

Scholarship is a communal activity. This book could not have been written without a community of friends who shared with us their knowledge, time, labor, and encouragement. We are in their debt, but we take full responsibility for the final product.

This book germinated in Cleveland Fraser's office at Furman University in the late 1990s. Several eager souls gathered around a computer as it ground through a large data set to see if the results would confirm a hunch. Would Catholics be more supportive of European integration than Protestants? The answer was yes; and thus we launched a series of studies that have finally culminated in this book.

Along the way many colleagues offered encouragement at crucial moments, whether they knew it or not. Several of these folks might be surprised to know how valuable they were: Mark Amstutz, Timothy Byrnes, François Foret, Ivy Hamerly, Ted Jelen, Bud Kellstedt, Paulette Kurzer, Leon Lindberg, Gary Marks, Janne Haaland Matláry, Catherine McCauliff, Steve Monsma, Craig Parsons, Daniel Philpot, Thomas Risse, Stuart Scheingold, Timothy Shah, Corwin Smidt, Christopher Soper, David Spear (our running partner and go-to medievalist), Kaare Strøm, Alexander Stubb, Michael Walzer, Carolyn Warner, Joseph Weiler, and Clyde Wilcox. We also both owe a debt to the teaching and scholarship of two giants in the field, Karl Deutsch and Leon Epstein.

Superb students at Furman provided valuable research assistance through the Furman Advantage Program, including Joe Biedlingmaier, Althea Deckrosh, Effie Fokas, Brian Highsmith, Klaudia Kruszynska, Joshua McKoon, Christopher Schoen, Stephanie Sillay, Stephen Tagert, Jodie Tillman, Robin Watson, and Noah Woodiwiss. Library assistance from Robyn Andrews, Laura Baker, Mary Fairbairn, Elaina Griffith, Jimmy Quinn, Steve Richardson, and Libby Young made the hunting down of resources so much easier. Library director Janis Bandelin always offered words of encouragement—and a secret scholar study! Additional thanks go to Jim and Carolyn Brown, Robert and Jan McClure, and Kirk and Lisa Redwine, who offered their lake or beach homes for extended writing stints. And, of course, we benefited from the expert logistical support—and good cheer—of our department assistants, Lori Schoen and Paige Blankenship. Thanks, too, to Jason Greer for help with the scholarly sources.

Generous financial support came from the Duke Endowment and the Knight Foundation, via Furman University's Research and Professional Growth and Furman

Advantage Programs. We also acknowledge the financial support of the William R. Kenan Jr. Endowment.

As ever, we thank our families—especially our wives, Lori Nelsen and Cydelle Guth—for their patience and encouragement.

Finally, both of us were inspired in different ways and at different times to explore the relationship between religion and politics by the same individual at the University of Wisconsin–Madison. We dedicate this book to the mentor who got us started, Booth Fowler.

PART I
The Framework

1

Culture and Integration

We . . . are heading for our objective, the United States of Europe;
and for us . . . there is no going back.
— Jean Monnet, *Memoirs*, 1976

We have not successfully rolled back the frontiers of the state in Britain,
only to see them reimposed at a European level, with a European
superstate exercising a new dominance from Brussels.
— Margaret Thatcher, Bruges Speech, September 1988

Two contrasting visions exist side by side in the European Union. One sees Europe as a single community that has suffered unnatural division and fraternal wars for so long that it will take generations to heal, but heal it shall. And heal it must, for global economic competition and shifting geopolitics demand that Europe face the world united. But a second vision challenges the first, resting on the judgment that a politically united Europe is dangerous—oppressive in the past, and very likely also in the future. In this view, the contemporary system of nation-states has guaranteed liberty for the peoples of Europe and should not be abandoned for a dream. European nations must cooperate in a competitive world, but cooperation is possible without undermining national sovereignty. To those with the first vision, the ideal Europe looks like a single people in a federal state, the United States of Europe; to those having the second vision, the European ideal is sovereign nations in an exceptionally close international organization.

This book explores the origins of these two conceptions of Europe, how they have divided European leaders and peoples since the early postwar years, and why the division is so persistent. It is also about the limits of European integration and the options facing a divided Europe as it looks to the future.

Our interest in this topic emerged from a simple observation: The two visions so pointedly summarized by Monnet and Thatcher in the quotations given above are not randomly distributed across the Continent, but tend to concentrate in cultural regions. Those with a federalist vision are often from areas that are now or once were strongly Catholic; those with an antifederalist vision often come from Protestant areas that broke from the Catholic Church during the Reformation. This should be no surprise. Even casual observers know that Belgium, Italy, and Spain have been full-throated integrationists, while Britain is Europe's "awkward partner" and the Scandinavians are "reluctant Europeans."[1] Most attribute British and Nordic orneriness to national idiosyncrasies and look no further. But we believe this pattern is a genuine puzzle that requires deeper investigation. Why are Britain and the Nordics so often the odd countries out—the integration party spoilers and the treaty opters-out? Why do they always resist deeper integration, never fully trust their EU partners, and frequently vote "no" in national referenda? This is systematic behavior that requires explanation.

We think that "culture" is the missing explanatory factor. Culture shapes ideas about what ties Europe together, who counts as "European," where Europe ends, and how national borders matter. These questions of identity inform and shape visions of European integration. In addition, we argue that *religious* culture has been crucial in shaping the main approaches to integration. Specifically, we contend that the Reformation and subsequent wars of religion divided Europe over the value of *political fragmentation*. Catholics rejected fragmentation and remained committed to a unified Europe—Latin Christendom—while Protestants found refuge in the separate and new European nation-states. Protestant national identities were forged in conflicts with Catholicism, making it difficult for Protestant leaders—even four hundred years later—to abandon their borders.

The Reformation continues to echo (perhaps more and more faintly) across Western Europe. Cultural divisions still keep Protestants wedded to their nation-states and emotionally disconnected from much of the Continent.[2] The EU has much to deal with as it tries to solve fundamental economic challenges without completely alienating Protestant-majority states. Britain is already contemplating a new relationship with the EU, and others may follow. In some ways the Reformation feels like only yesterday.

Culture has to be in the equation when explaining a social phenomenon as significant as the integration of former enemy countries. Religion is a central cultural ingredient, a powerful force that grips the human heart. It would be surprising if it did not influence the integration process and the evolution of identity in Europe. This book explores that role.

The Case against Religion

Most social scientists hesitate to give religion any role in the shaping of European integration. They assume that material interests determine political attitudes and behavior; ideas, norms, traditions, and identities have little or nothing to do with policy outcomes. Individuals and nation-states alike form their opinions and take action based on some calculation of economic interest. Theoretical orientations as diverse as Marxism, Realism, and rational choice theory take materialism as a basic starting point. Systems theories and pluralist (or "group") theories are less explicit, but also tend to focus on materially derived system functions or interests. Thus, most theoretical perspectives in the social sciences consider religious ideas and motivations as little more than window dressing, hiding the desire for greater power or wealth.

The study of European integration has followed this track, discounting the influence of religion on postwar decisions to integrate. Granted, scholars explaining the development of community law have sometimes identified religious influences on key legal principles. Joseph Weiler, for instance, points out the impact of Catholic social thinking on the development of subsidiarity and other doctrines.[3] Federalists and most legal theorists, however, are not usually seeking to identify the causes of integration but rather concern themselves with the building of its legal foundations. Rational choice theorists and institutional analysts, conversely, do try to explain European integration and explicitly adopt materialist assumptions. They model the behavior of the European Union's member states and governing institutions at all levels by assuming that rational actors make choices based on calculations of material benefit.

Perhaps the strongest challenge to the notion that religion matters to the European Union comes from "intergovernmentalists." These theorists often disagree about why European cooperation emerged after World War II, but they all conclude that national interests mattered most, and that such interests were primarily material. Alan Milward, for example, has insisted that integration, far from challenging the nation-state, actually saved it on the European Continent.[4] Milward claimed that idealism never influenced European leaders' decision to integrate. The economic crisis of the late 1940s had left Europe, particularly France, with no viable options except for "Franco-German association." He saw no evidence of an ideologically driven process and delighted in mocking the notion that "idealisms" could override "national interest."[5]

Andrew Moravcsik, drawing heavily on Milward, also contended that idealism explained very little about integration. Commercial interests, the bargaining powers of individual states, and incentives to lock in interstate commitments (sometimes by creating supranational institutions) explain "the form, substance, and timing of major steps toward European integration."[6] Although conceding that national preferences were sometimes shaped by ideas and by geostrategic interests,[7] Moravcsik adamantly rejected the possibility that such factors were decisive: "To be sure, technocratic imperatives, geopolitical concerns, and European idealism each played a role at the margin, but none has consistently been the decisive force behind major decisions."[8]

Such strong arguments cannot be easily dismissed. No credible analyst claims that economic interests had no role in decisions to integrate, or subsequent ones to expand and deepen cooperation. But the evidence presented in this book suggests a broader view. Ideas, social and political networks, and ideologically and religiously motivated groups also contributed to integration. To ignore them is to miss a big part of the story. Behind economic and geopolitical interests are cultures that shape the calculations of political elites—perceptions of who their friends and enemies are, and what options are "realistic." Understanding culture also helps us appreciate the impact of decisions on national publics—how they are received and how they shape popular opinion. Thus, we think integration theorists should reconsider culture as an explanatory factor.

Bringing Culture Back In

Admittedly, culture is suspect. Some social scientists ignore it because the concept itself is hard to define and measure—like air, it is everywhere, but hard to pin down. Other scholars studiously avoid it because using it is fraught with danger. Considering culture requires dealing with religion, and social scientists often find that their secular training and liberal sensibilities leave them unprepared or unwilling to take religion seriously. Even leaving religion aside, culture itself has become an emotionally charged political issue. In an age of both tolerance and terrorism, cultural identity is simultaneously encouraged and feared. On one hand, all cultures are to be positively evaluated; on the other hand, some cultures seem to encourage the darker angels of human nature. Students of culture find themselves caught in the middle—accused of promoting intolerance by casting some cultures in an unfavorable light or charged with minimizing dangerous cultural elements or trends.[9] Most social scientists choose to avoid the political minefield.[10] But culture *does* matter, and ignoring culture, especially its religious components, often means missing the deepest story.

Of course, some social scientists have taken culture seriously. Alexis de Tocqueville and Max Weber based their most profound insights on the notion that religious culture shaped the modern world.[11] Their contributions, however, were largely ignored during the social scientific revolution after World War II, as the behavioral revolution marginalized culture.[12] That changed as the twentieth century came to an end.

The fall of the Berlin Wall freed intellectuals from the stultifying ideological struggle between Liberals and Marxists. Important old questions—and some new ones—could now be addressed without eliciting Cold War ideological responses. Why does underdevelopment persist? Why does authoritarianism live on? What will drive international politics in a post-bipolar world? Why do nations cooperate after the Cold War? These questions received many answers, but one prominent theme was a renewed emphasis on cultural explanations. Lawrence Harrison, for instance, argued that Latin American countries remained poor because their societies lacked the values necessary for economic and political success. Their values were rooted in a "basic world view" that differed from those in Europe, North America, and parts of Asia.[13] David Landes applied the same insight in *The Wealth and Poverty of Nations*: "If we learn anything from the history of economic development, it is that culture makes all the difference."[14] Ronald Inglehart in *Culture Shift* and Robert Putnam in *Making Democracy Work* marshaled enormous bodies of evidence establishing the link between culture, economic development, and effective democracy.[15]

The study of world politics also witnessed a new emphasis on culture. Samuel Huntington's controversial *Clash of Civilizations* placed culture at the very center of international politics: "Culture and cultural identities, which at the broadest level are civilization identities, are shaping the patterns of cohesion, disintegration, and conflict in the post–Cold War world."[16] In a world no longer dominated by the clash of Cold War titans, nations regrouped around their cultural cores, partly as a reaction to the unsettling effects of rapid modernization, partly in response to the West's insistence that its civilization is universal. The Al Qaeda attacks of September 11, 2001, on New York and Washington, and the ensuing military actions by the United States and its allies, naturally focused attention on Huntington's thesis. Although President George W. Bush, and even Huntington himself, denied that the new war on terrorism was a civilizational war, few could deny that culture infused global politics.[17]

Although many scholars were beginning to take culture seriously, that was not generally true of those studying European integration. Journalists often identified a cultural divide between the "North" and the "South" during the euro crisis, but scholars were unconvinced.[18] Some of this skepticism, however, has begun to dissipate. Recent studies of European identities and a burgeoning literature on religion and politics in Europe have begun to fill this gap.[19] But no general cultural approach to European integration has yet emerged. In the rest of this chapter we outline a cultural approach to integration that highlights the role of religion in shaping a common culture and vision of unity.

Defining Culture

"Culture" defies a concrete definition. Anthropologists, who may think the most about these things, popularized the term in the mid–twentieth century. The anthropological pioneer E. G. Tylor defined culture as the "most complex whole," which includes "knowledge, belief, law, morals, custom."[20] Ruth Benedict's influential *Patterns of Culture* referred to culture as "custom," meaning "those physical characteristics and industrial techniques, those conventions and values, which distinguish one community from all others that belong to a different tradition."[21] Margaret Mead later defined it more generally as "the systematic body of learned behavior which is transmitted from parents to children,"[22] while Clifford Geertz saw culture as "webs of significance" that humans have spun.[23] More recently, the anthropologist Richard Shweder described culture as "community-specific ideas about what is true, good, beautiful, and efficient. To be 'cultural,' those ideas about truth, goodness, beauty, and efficiency must be socially inherited and customary; and they must actually be constitutive of different ways of life."[24] But here we run into a problem. Benedict and Mead define culture as observable behavior, but Shweder sees it wholly in terms of ideas that precede the behaviors that constitute "ways of life." So which is it—actions or ideas?

Perhaps the answer is both. Recently, Alan Patten has argued for a "social lineage" approach to culture that emphasizes the socializing effects of "formative conditions" setting one group apart from another: "Members of a group that can trace back through time a lineage of cultural continuity do share something that others do not share. They share with one another a common experience of socialization that is distinct from, because historically isolated from, the experiences of socialization undergone by others. . . . At any given moment, [a culture's] content consists in various beliefs, meanings, and practices, but what makes these the beliefs, meanings, and practices of a shared culture is that the people who hold them share a common social lineage."[25] This common social lineage produces what Huntington identifies as an "overall way of life of a people," including both ideas (values, norms, modes of thinking) and behaviors (customs).[26] In short, a culture is an interactive mix of ideas and behaviors passed from one generation to another. To the extent that individuals experience the same or very similar formative conditions, they belong to the same culture.

Culture and Religion

Few would deny that culture contains religious ideas and practices.[27] The real question is, how much of culture is religion? Huntington defines civilizations as "culture writ large."[28] And among "all the objective elements which define civilizations, . . . the most important usually is religion."[29] Lipset and Lenz argue that even in an irreligious age, religion remains "an important determinant of variation in larger secular cultures."[30]

Why is religion so central? The question is too large for a full treatment here, but the answer seems grounded in human nature. Van Til argues that human beings are religious by nature and, therefore, their cultures must be "religiously oriented."[31] Geertz sees religion shaping behavior and experience as it "tunes human actions to an envisaged cosmic order and projects images of cosmic order onto the plane of human experience."[32] Tocqueville, more boldly and more eloquently, fixes the source of nearly all behavior in notions of God: "There is hardly any human action, however private it may be, which does not result from some very general conception men have of God, of His relations with the human race, of the nature of their soul, and of their duties to their fellows. Nothing can prevent such ideas from being the common spring from which all else originates."[33]

Thus, to speak of culture is—in some deep, primal sense—to speak of religion. Often, we might employ "religion" and "culture" as interchangeable terms, but sometimes such usage lacks precision, especially when exploring causal connections. Huntington, for all his stress on religion, still sees nonreligious elements in Western civilization: European languages, classical legacy, separation of church and state, the rule of law, social pluralism, representative bodies, and individualism.[34] One could argue that all these elements were kneaded into shape by Roman Catholicism, and later Protestantism, but there is great value in disentangling them when exploring, for instance, the role of Western culture in forming international institutions or in promoting multiparty elections.

In sum, religion permeates culture, but there is little value in treating all cultural artifacts, customs, institutions, and values as "religious." Although all human culture may have its roots in religion, not all its elements are directly tied to religious beliefs, practices, and organizations. This distinction is particularly important in studying Europe, where formal religious practice is waning and many aspects of culture, especially pop culture, are far from recognizably religious. To say that Europe is increasingly secular, however, is not to say that it is unaffected by traditional religion. The long arm of religion, even when it seems to carry a dead hand, is still very powerful. It may govern the perceptions and life rhythms of people who have long ceased to believe. Norris and Inglehart assert that "the distinctive worldviews that were originally linked with religious traditions have shaped the cultures of each nation in an enduring fashion; today, these distinctive values are transmitted to the citizens even if they never set foot in a church, temple, or mosque. . . . Even in highly secular societies, the historical legacy of religion continues to shape worldviews and to define cultural zones."[35]Religious ideas may have lost their grip on European hearts, but they have been transformed into mores, customs, symbols, and institutions by individuals "working upon"—as Michael Walzer put it—their religious heritage.[36] Culture carries religious effects forward, if with losses as cultural forms flow away from their religious headwaters. Thus, the decline of traditional religion since the 1940s and 1950s should not stop our inquiry into religious influences on integration. European culture still displays its Christian heritage in languages and symbols, buildings, holidays, laws, and schools. Call it cultural inertia, but like the cosmic background radiation echoing the Big Bang, religion is still there for those who can tune it in.

In the following chapters we explore the role of culture in the postwar European integration process. Christianity has been at the heart of European culture for 1,500 years, but it has been far from monolithic. The division of Christendom into Eastern and Western versions came as early as the eighth century, but was ratified by the mutual excommunications of 1054 that led to the Great Schism. The West was divided further in 1517, when Martin Luther took a hammer to the Wittenberg door. Christianity thus fragmented into what we call *confessional cultures*—central to understanding European national identities, attitudes toward integration, and, most important, the visions of European unity pursued by national leaders.

Confessional Cultures

Confessional cultures are "overall ways of life" shaped by particular religious traditions that constitute powerful, common formative conditions. These confessional cultures in turn affect communities in three important ways. First, they provide important shared ideas. Confessional cultures specify the truths—often drawn from reflection on a sacred text or texts—around which people should order their collective lives. These truths may include but are not limited to notions of God or the gods, creation, humanity, good, evil, life, death, revelation, enlightenment, law, and the nature of the righteous community. They affect politics by influencing how leaders and ordinary citizens answer questions about who should rule, how nations should interact, and how the religious world should relate to secular authority. Second, confessional cultures provide shared behaviors: liturgies, rituals, prayers, recitations, holiday celebrations, righteous acts, and ceremonies that mark the passages of life. These behaviors reinforce beliefs and give communities distinctive rhythms. Finally, confessional cultures produce distinguishing institutions that embody and transmit religious beliefs and practices. Within the Christian world, ecclesiastical offices, churches, monasteries, missions, charities, schools, and universities shape, carry, and convey confessional cultures. How they are organized and how they influence society affect their impact on political and social outcomes. Confessional cultures thus provide Europeans with important identity markers and tools of socialization—ideas, behaviors, and institutions—that can be used by elites to distinguish "us" from "them."

Integration and National Identity

Confessional cultures helped form postwar Europe, especially as nations sought new ways to cooperate. Understanding the role of confessional cultures requires a grasp of the larger integration process. Thus, in this section we explore integration as a nation-building process. We will see that early students of European integration understood its social-psychological dimensions. Entire populations would have to stop considering people across national borders as enemies and accept them as compatriots, indeed fellow citizens. This process of constructing a new European identity and convincing whole citizenries to accept it as their own is the process of peaceful integration. Explaining this process has occupied some of the best minds in the field since World War II.

A Sense of Community and the Achievement of Stable Peace

Many students of European relations have emphasized the constitutional or bureaucratic aspects of integration, but others ask more fundamental questions about how leaders and citizens would have to change before nations moved from enmity to friendship. These early theorists and their successors are part of what we call the "stable peace school." Such scholars start with a simple observation: Some states that once fought each other have become close allies, and some—the cantons of Switzerland, for instance—have actually joined together to form a new state.[37] They want to know how and why this happens.

The stable peace school got its start in the 1950s, when Karl Deutsch dared suggest that the international system was not an unrelenting dog-eat-dog world.[38] Community among sovereign states was difficult but possible; enemies could become friends. So he set out to study peace while most political scientists studied Cold War conflict. He wanted to understand "peaceful change," how states could resolve social problems by "institutionalized procedures, without resort to large-scale physical force."[39] His team examined historical cases of "integration," where states in violent conflict came to see war between them as unthinkable, and "disintegration," where nations once again resorted to violence. Integrated states formed "security communities" that could, like Norway and Sweden, remain distinct nation-states ("pluralistic" security communities) or might, like the United States, move to full union ("amalgamated" security communities). Most of his major work, *Political Community in the North Atlantic Area: International Organization in the Light of Historical Experience* (1957), focused on the latter.

What Deutsch discovered was threefold. First, peace among neighbors required the emergence of a new community. Security communities were possible only when individuals at every level of society experienced a shift in perception. People across the border were no longer seen as fundamentally different, but instead as belonging to a group called "us." Deutsch argued that a security community could be established only when a new "sense of community" emerged, when everyone expected problems to be solved nonviolently.[40] But a sense of community meant more than expectations about acceptable behaviors. A sense of community affected individuals at an emotional level by shaping perceptions of who was safe, who was trustworthy, and who must be protected. For Deutsch, a sense of community must involve "mutual sympathy and loyalties; of 'we-feeling,' trust, and mutual consideration; of partial identification in terms of self-images and interests; of mutually successful predictions of behavior, and of cooperative action in accordance with it—in short, a matter of a perpetual dynamic process of mutual attention, communication, perception of needs, and responsiveness in the process of decision making. 'Peaceful change' could not be assured without this kind of relationship."[41]

Where did this new sense of community come from? Deutsch found that it was grounded in a distinct "way of life," which started with the "compatibility of the main values held by the politically relevant strata" in the region.[42] Deutsch was rather vague on the source of these values, offering examples drawn from political ideologies (the conservative / liberal split in nineteenth-century Germany), social structures (the slavery debate in the United States), and religion (the Presbyterian / Episcopal divide between Scotland and England).[43] He did not systematically identify the main sources, but acknowledged that politics influenced which values became the "main" ones shared among elites. In other words, leaders could emphasize some values while depoliticizing others. American leaders of the early nineteenth century, for instance, stressed representative government, while depoliticizing slavery.

Values are important, but Deutsch also stressed the necessity of living them: "Values were most effective politically when they were not held merely in abstract terms, but when they were incorporated in political institutions and in habits of political behavior which permitted these values to be acted on in such a way as to strengthen people's attachment to them."[44] Political institutions and behaviors structured by common values constituted, for Deutsch, a "way of life" that helped determine the formation of a security community. Such a way of life, especially if providing a foundation for amalgamation, had to constitute a "common culture" or "national character."[45] Ways of thinking and behaving had to be so similar that members of different communities would recognize themselves in the actions and attitudes of their cross-border neighbors. Thus, to Deutsch, similarity of culture and lifestyle was crucial to the integration process; the more similar these were, the more likely integration. As Philip Jacob summarized Deutsch's hypothesis in 1964, "Communities whose members are very different from one another will have a very hard time achieving or maintaining political integration. . . . The more that communities are similar, the more successful are attempts to build integrative relationships among them."[46]

Deutsch believed that developing a sense of community and a distinct way of life required certain raw materials in the values and cultures of regional communities. These raw materials were subject to manipulation, as political elites had some control over the values considered important. Leaders could emphasize what they shared in common or what divided them, they could find common elements of culture to create a security community, or they could stress differences to undermine peace. If this was true, it also meant that populations could change their own perceptions; they could learn to see certain groups differently.

Thus, Deutsch's third discovery was that a spirit of community and a distinct way of life could be acquired over time. He relied heavily on learning theory (learning through communication) to describe community formation: People came to think of themselves as part of a new community by experiencing the material and non-material benefits of their transactions with members of a broader group. He wrote colorfully of this community-building process in 1964:

> The classic reinforcement or learning theory describes what happens when there are many rewarding transactions in a community. When there is a significantly high level of important transactions, many of which bring joint rewards, the people who have experienced these mutual transactions will like them. When these transactions are highly visible, easy to identify and differentiate, people may form images of the community or of the group involved in the transactions. If these transactions were rewarded, the image of a community may be strongly positive. Liking this kind of community, people may say: We belong together. In their favorable reaction to the community, they might then also say, I can see myself as a member of this community; I will call it "we" if I speak of a group. I will call it "home" if I speak of a territory. I will express and experience love of country (patriotism) or love of a group of people (nationalism), but in any case I identify with this symbol or this group.[47]

Deutsch emphasized the interaction of people over time. Broader and deeper transactions, if reinforced by community-building messages from elites, will result in the gradual emergence of a new community bound together physically and emotionally. This hypothesis gave his theory a name, "transactionalism," but also seemed to doom its empirical project. Connecting the number and quality of transactions to attitudes toward members of other communities proved methodologically difficult and empirically unproductive. After a brief heyday, Deutsch's work on security communities drifted to the theoretical background.

Indeed, few scholars took up his challenge to study security communities until the late 1990s, when Deutsch again came into vogue. Constructivists, especially, were attracted to his emphasis on identity and international community.[48] "Constructivism" is rooted in approaches pioneered by John Ruggie, Alexander Wendt, and others.[49] As a group of theories, constructivism remains frustratingly amorphous and fragmented, but these theories are united by a "concern with how world politics is 'socially constructed.'"[50] Constructivism rejects the idea that states and other political actors perform like atoms in a mechanistic universe. Political interests are not derived wholly from the system in which they operate; nor are they the sole product of material forces. Constructivists want to know how actors formulate perceptions of themselves and others, and how they determine their interests. They want to explore the way cultures, norms, and ideas—in addition to material factors—shape, and sometimes change, the identities and interests of actors.[51] And they want to know how actors come to agree on certain "facts" about the world, and how "facts" are shaped by their social context. In short, the work of the constructivists, as

Ruggie puts it, "concerns the issue of human consciousness" and the role it plays in international relations.[52]

Deutsch was attractive to the constructivists. Emanuel Alder and Michael Barnett, for instance, placed Deutsch securely within a constructivist framework by emphasizing his willingness to challenge interest-based theories of international relations. He did so by raising the "possibility of international community," thus questioning the universality of anarchy.[53] Deutsch's theory, in contrast to the realism of his day, assumed that perceptions of reality were malleable; people could change their minds about enemies and friends. Changed perceptions could change behavior, as preparations for war ended and cooperation commenced. Moreover, the process was reciprocal: Perceptions changed behaviors; but behaviors, especially increased transactions, also taught trust and the benefits of cooperation, which created new perceptions of people once thought of as enemies. In short, Deutsch's theory suggested that something more than material interests was at work in relations between nations—placing him alongside others who saw interests as, at least in part, socially constructed.

The constructivists and their sympathizers have deepened Deutsch's work in several ways. One group has sought to refine his description of the pathway to peace, thereby elaborating on his explanation for why states move from being enemies to being friends. The two most important works here are Alder and Barnett's *Security Communities* and Charles A. Kupchan's *How Enemies Become Friends: The Sources of Stable Peace*.[54] Both generally follow Deutsch's model: Certain background conditions fall into place; transactions lead to greater trust; a new common identity emerges; and war between the participants becomes unthinkable.

For Alder and Barnett achieving a pluralistic security community involves three phases: nascent, ascendant, and mature. The process starts when an external threat or change to the technological, demographic, economic, or natural environment propels governments "to look in each other's direction and attempt to coordinate their policies to their mutual advantage."[55] In this *nascent phase* states will seek to cooperate with regional partners; new multilateral institutions designed to facilitate cooperation foster trust among governments and encourage transactions. As in Deutsch, transactions propel the process forward. The *ascendant phase* is characterized by a growing density of interactions among the partners, leading in turn to the emergence of a common "way of life." Political and cultural movements begin to tell the story of the region as though it possessed a single people with a single history; a collective identity begins to emerge. In the *mature phase* the expectations of peaceful change are institutionalized; regional actors now "share an identity"; a security community has been established. Borders go unfortified; security decisions are made collectively; populations move freely across borders; and people throughout the region use the language of community.[56]

Alder and Barnett, more explicitly than Deutsch, see stable peace as the outcome of a change in the way people perceive one another. Creating a new collective identity involves a reciprocal learning process that starts with a small shift in perception of the "other," followed by an increase in interactions, greater trust, then more interactions and so on, until an entirely new collective identity emerges. For Alder and Barnett, identities are almost entirely socially constructed; they do not need to be tied tightly to common values or culture. In a discussion about whether states had to be contiguous for a community to form, Alder and Barnett, quoting Ira Cohen, state that "recent technological developments can facilitate the development of a sense of community among people 'who are not physically co-present,'"[57] and go on to suggest that "individuals can organize and define themselves based on markers that are not necessarily tied to space, suggesting something of an 'imagined region,' or a 'cognitive region.'"[58] What these "markers" might be is left vague. Alder and Barnett hint at shared values as raw material for social construction, but leave the impression that identities are so malleable that under the right conditions any two or more countries can develop a common identity. Other scholars, however, have suggested that a sense of community must be rooted in something shared.

Like Alder and Barnett, Kupchan traces a more detailed route to stable peace than Deutsch did; but unlike Alder and Barnett, Kupchan ties the development of a sense of community to specific background conditions. Stable peace comes in three types, along a continuum of deepening peace: *rapprochement*, where states move away from armed conflict to peaceful coexistence; *security community*, which requires a shared identity and an institutionalized process of conflict management; and *union*, in which separate units merge into a single polity.[59] Kupchan says little about how states move from rapprochement to security community and on to union except to suggest that this progression requires "foresight and vision" from elites determined to establish a long-lasting zone of peace and, especially in the case of union, that the integrating units be "smaller in size and exhibit less diversity as to culture, language, and regime type."[60]

The end point for Kupchan is stable peace, but before states can begin this deepening peace process, they must experience four "phases of onset." The sequence begins at a crisis point with at least one state facing a strategic situation so threatening that it must "befriend an existing adversary."[61] This "triggering condition" is often accompanied by two others: the existence of a preponderant state ready and able to anchor a new zone of peace, and policy entrepreneurship that brings fresh ideas to the decision table, often after a major disruption such as a war or regime change. Once the process is triggered, the phases of onset then proceed:

> Phase one consists of *unilateral accommodation*. One party makes an initial concession to the other as an opening gesture of goodwill. It is then up to the target state to reciprocate with its own act of accommodation. . . . Phase two entails *reciprocal restraint*. Expectations of reciprocity promote successive rounds of mutual accommodation. . . . Phase three consists of *societal integration*. As the polities in question interact with increasing frequency and intensity, they come to attribute benign

qualities to one another's *political character*. Confidence builds, giving way to a sense of mutual *trust*. The final phase consists of the *generation of new political narratives*. Using the discourse of community as a vehicle, the polities in question embrace a compatible, shared, or common *identity* and expectations of peaceful relations come to have a taken-for-granted quality, producing a sense of social *solidarity* [emphasis in the original].[62]

In these phases of onset we see the strong influence of Deutsch and Alder and Barnett: Interactions lead to trust, which encourages more positive interactions, fostering a new sense of community and a common identity.

But why do some groups of states and not others take the route of peace? In other words, why does peace break out? Here Kupchan echoes Deutsch, but provides more detail. Three conditions favor the outbreak of peace: institutionalized restraint, compatible social orders, and cultural commonality. Institutionalized restraint is the presence within domestic governing structures of built-in checks on coercive power. It is an important condition, according to Kupchan, but not necessary to peace. The remaining two conditions are essential. First, the states must possess *compatible social orders*. Extensive interactions among peoples at all levels of society are necessary for a new sense of community to emerge. These interactions are far easier when societies have similar distributions of power across social classes and ethnic groups. In addition, commercial interactions are particularly facilitated if the integrating societies possess similar economic systems. Thus, the more similar the societies, the more natural the interactions and the more likely a common sense of community will emerge.

Second, stable peace will occur only under conditions of *cultural commonality*. For Kupchan, "culture refers to a repertoire of practices, significations, and symbols that arises primarily, although not exclusively, from ethnicity, race, and religion."[63] Indeed, it is "perceptions of cultural affinity" that "guide states toward each other": "When geopolitical necessity prompts states to seek to befriend an adversary, that state usually targets a party with which it enjoys an overlapping network of cultural practices and symbols."[64] Kupchan insists that perceptions of "cultural affinity" are open to political and social influence; identity is still socially constructed, just as Alder and Barnett argue.

National Identity in Early Integration Theory

Before we leave our discussion of integration and national identity, it is perhaps worth noting that Deutsch and his successors in the stable peace school were not the only integration theorists to suggest that the process required a social-psychological element. Nearly all the major schools of thought embraced as essential some manifestation of a new European identity. Early federalists, such as the Italian journalist, politician, and European activist Altiero Spinelli, spoke of a vague pan-European mass movement that would recognize the evils of nationalism and set aside national interests—and national leaders—in favor of a federal Constitution.[65] But the early federalists usually just *assumed* the existence of a European identity and moved on to propose legal changes that would facilitate supranational decision making. They seldom thought about how a new European *demos* would emerge to support a federal constitutional system.[66]

The functionalists, unlike the federalists, downplayed the role of political movements and national identities in favor of a global, technocratic approach to problems that had grown too large for small states to solve. David Mitrany, for instance, viewed integration as a process of administrative reorganization, albeit on a global scale. Other functionalists realized that integration involved more than bureaucratic planning. Indeed, Jean Monnet argued that peace in Europe would come about through a step-by-step coordination of activity in functional areas, regulated by "common rules which each member . . . committed to respect, and common institutions to watch over the application of these rules."[67] New laws made and implemented by new institutions would advance integration, but the process did not stop there. The goal of establishing "new procedures under common institutions" was to create "a silent revolution in men's minds," to generate "de facto solidarity, from which a federation would gradually emerge."[68] Unlike Mitrany, Monnet saw integration proceeding only if functional solutions broadened a European sense of solidarity, a European *identity*.

Monnet did not develop these ideas systematically, but Ernst Haas and his (neo) functionalist followers made the creation of a new community their theoretical focus. A key element was the psychological shift in loyalties that integration encouraged. According to Haas, in his often-quoted definition, political integration is *"the process whereby political actors in several distinct national settings are persuaded to shift their loyalties, expectations and political activities toward a new centre, whose institutions possess or demand jurisdiction over the preexisting national states.* The end result of a process of political integration is a new political community, superimposed over the pre-existing ones" (emphasis in the original).[69] Here is Monnet's revolution in men's minds—and, we might add, *hearts.* Haas believed that functional integration that included new institutions would change the way people *felt* about supranational political authority, in observable and measurable ways:[70]

> As the process of integration proceeds, it is assumed that values will undergo change, that interests will be redefined in terms of a regional rather than a purely national orientation and that the erstwhile set of separate national group values will gradually be superseded by a new and geographically larger set of beliefs. . . . As the beliefs and aspirations of groups undergo change due to the necessity of working in a transnational institutional framework, mergers in values and doctrine are expected

to come about, uniting groups across former frontiers. The expected overlapping of these group aspirations is finally thought to result in an accepted body of "national" doctrine, in effect heralding the advent of a new nationalism.[71]

Haas equated the process of integration with the creation of a new European political identity. Not surprisingly, he was in complete agreement with Deutsch on this point.[72] Thus, both the early transactionalists and the neofunctionalists saw the *need* for a new identity and the *mechanism* ("learning" or "socialization") for realizing it. The neofunctionalists, however, viewed increased cooperation in the context of new supranational institutions as crucial to identity construction. Everyday work in and around the new institutions would socialize people into a new sense of "we."

What we learn from the stable peace school, their constructivist allies, and various federalist, functionalist, and neofunctionalist theorists is this: Peaceful integration requires a fundamental transformation of perceptions and behavior among people who were once separated but who begin to move together psychologically, socially, and behaviorally. Separate national communities begin to form a single community that transcends international boundaries. The process is social; it involves active identity construction and learning. It also requires cultural raw materials—a new sense of community must be built on a common "way of life," which can be shaped by elites but only with reference to common beliefs, values, norms, and social structures. If integration is to proceed to its logical conclusion—some kind of union or amalgamated security community—the new sense of community that has made peaceful neighbors out of former enemies must produce a new national identity in which a loose "us" becomes a much tighter "my people" or "my nation." This transition requires greater exploration.

Constructing National Identity

How is national identity formed? The answer is hardly straightforward, and must be approached from several angles. We can start again with the stable peace school, where some attempt has been made to develop a theory of collective identity largely absent from the work of Deutsch, Alder and Barnett, and Kupchan. Bruce Cronin, for instance, in *Community under Anarchy*, grounds collective identities in sociological theories of the "self." "Parochial identities," he argues, "are rooted in a consciousness of difference; they emerge from an individual's understanding of oneself as being in many ways unique."[73] John Owen makes the point even stronger: "The essential mechanism at work in identity formation is negation. A thing only gains a determinate identity in the presence of an opposite."[74] As an individual moves from defining self to defining a group to which he or she belongs, he or she identifies a set of "reference others," and then uses them to form judgments about who he or she is like and who he or she is unlike. Thus, the very act of forming an identity is necessarily a social process; we construct who we are and to whom we belong by interacting with the "others" around us. Groups use the same process to arrive at a collective identity: they continually compare themselves to others to define "who they are and, equally important, who they are not."[75] Thus, nations, as large collectives, develop distinct identities as part of their social interactions with other nations; through a process of comparison they construct their own identities.[76]

If nations behave like individuals in forming identities, are they capable of developing group or "transnational" identities? Owen answers yes, but stresses again that group identity requires an "other." An "us" always requires a "them."[77] Deutsch, it seems, would have agreed: To be distinctive, a new way of life in a region would need to include "at least some major social or political values and institutions which are different from those which existed in the area during the recent past, or from those prevailing among important neighbors."[78] In short, groups of nation-states cannot develop a common identity without a common "other."

A national identity, however, is also formed around what is shared. Something other than an enemy must draw "us" together. A group of people must come to see themselves as a "nation." But where do nations come from? We draw on Anthony Smith to address this question, which in a broad sense pits primordialists on one side against modernists and postmodernists on the other.[79] Primordialists see nations as natural and fundamental to being human, whether in a biological or cultural sense. The nation, as an extended ethnic group, has existed from the beginning of history and remains an essential part of the human experience. National identity is thus grounded in human nature and the nature of society; we are born into our nations and thus our national identities. Nations are given, not created.

On the other side, modernists and postmodernists dispute the notion that national identity is somehow natural or "given," arguing that identity is socially constructed. Modernists, for instance, assert that nations and nationalism are the products of modernization. Industrialization, urbanization, secularization, and, most important, the rise of capitalism have dissolved traditional social ties and weakened the hold of culture and cultural institutions, including religion, on individuals and polities. This process, beginning in Europe in the eighteenth century, called for new systems of social control, including new ideologies to legitimize the state. For elites, the solution was to construct a people (nation), a national identity, and a mass movement fired by a mass ideology (nationalism). This strategy provided state elites with the tools needed to harness masses in support of the state. For the modernist, these constructed nations are "real": They constitute social communities comprising real people, institutions, cultures, and territories. Furthermore, they are glued together by "preexisting cultural material," such as language or religion, manipulated to serve the economic and political interests of social elites. But as a relatively new institution, constructed by elites who pick and choose from among cultural materials to fit the needs of the moment, nations are not simply premodern communities dragged into the modern era, as primordialists would have it. Nations are modern tools for modern purposes.[80]

In a similar way, postmodernists describe nations as constructed by elites for political purposes, but take this notion a step further to claim that all identities are essentially "imagined." As Benedict Anderson puts it, the nation is "*imagined* because the members of even the smallest nation will never know most of their fellow members, meet them, or even hear of them, yet in the minds of each lives the image of their communion."[81] The breakdown of sacral communities and divine dynasties and the rise of "print capitalism" and "national print languages" contributed to the creation of national consciousness in the late eighteenth and early nineteenth centuries.[82] Ultimately, however, a nation is "a fiction engineered by elites using 'invented traditions' for purposes of social control"; it is "a novel form of 'imagined community,' a discursive formation of linguistic and symbolic practices."[83] Preexisting cultural materials, which are of some importance to modernists, are irrelevant to postmodernists, who view even these resources as socially or linguistically constructed. What matters to the postmodernist is individual identity. In fact, postmodernists see the contemporary world moving away from the grand, national movements that dominated domestic and international politics in the nineteenth and twentieth centuries toward more fragmented, overlapping identities that are entirely constructed—by elites and nonelites alike.

Each position has its difficulties. Primordialists take cultural content seriously, but are too willing to apply "primordial" identities to modern communities and underestimate elites' ability to use cultural symbols to shape identity to their advantage. Modernists and postmodernists, conversely, understand the power of elites and others to construct identities, but downplay (modernists) or ignore (postmodernists) the grip subjective elements of culture have on "the masses."

We need a middle ground where culture matters but does not determine identity, and elites matter but are limited in their ability to construct identities de novo. "Ethnosymbolism"—the awkward term Anthony Smith uses for his analytic framework—attempts to stand on this middle ground. Such a posture requires ethnosymbolists to affirm the existence of nations as real as opposed to purely imagined communities and to take the cultural content of national identity seriously. They also must trace the cultural content back to its premodern roots and identify the limitations on elites in constructing a national identity.

Nations are, first of all, real communities with real consequences for the people who live in or with them. Smith defines a nation as "a named and self-defined human community, whose members cultivate shared myths, memories, symbols, values, and traditions, reside in and identify with a historic homeland, create and disseminate a distinctive public culture, and observe shared customs and common laws."[84] Not all members of a nation can possibly know each other; what binds them together is shared meanings derived from cultural artifacts and symbols.[85] Nations are observable social groups: They define themselves, cultivate a cultural heritage, claim a territory, engage in public ceremonies, and follow common laws and customs. People *identify* with these communities, often over long periods of time, and passionately defend them, sometimes with their lives. Nations, in Smith's view, must be more than "discursive formations" to attract such loyalty.

Second, the modernists would agree with Smith's critique of postmodernist approaches to national identity and assert the tangible reality of nations. But though the modernists ultimately ground their analysis in the rise of capitalism, secularism, and other characteristics of the modern world, Smith argues that this ignores the vital *content* of national identities and ideologies—and that content is cultural. Taking cultural content seriously means "analyzing communities, ideologies, and sense of identity in terms of their constituent symbolic resources, that is, the traditions, memories, values, myths, and symbols that compose the accumulated heritage of cultural units of population. . . . Against the modernist emphasis on material and political domains, ethnosymbolists highlight the role of subjective and symbolic resources in motivating ideologies and collective actions."[86]

Smith emphasizes the nonmaterial elements of culture and their enduring hold on humans in community. He does not discount elites' ability to use culture for economic and political purposes, but he is convinced that national identity rests on more than material foundations. Traditions, symbolic meanings, community values, and religious myths grip human minds and emotions. Understanding why these cultural resources can sometimes be employed to reinforce solidarity and sometimes manipulated to satisfy power-seeking elites requires us to consider subjective elements of culture and appreciate the perspective of those inside. As Smith puts it, ethno-symbolists "aim to enter the 'inner world' of the participants and understand their perceptions and visions."[87]

Third, Smith argues that historical antecedents matter. Nations may not have existed for all time, as primordialists assert, but nations and national identities often have deep roots in "earlier cultural and political forms of society."[88] These must be explored to understand the content of national identities. Moreover, making history matter means exploring "the social and symbolic effect of conflicts both within and between nations."[89] Internal conflict over the definition or purpose of the nation, or repeated clashes with a perceived "other," can lead to protracted rivalries that leave bitter legacies and deep scars. Thus, Smith explores the premodern history of a particular people as he looks for clues to illuminate modern identities.

Ethnosymbolists take us to the world of culture, with its symbols, myths, memories, values, and traditions. Cultural artifacts—the actual flags, ceremonies, stories, holidays, beliefs, heroes, coins, and so on—serve to define the nation, differentiate it from others, and tie it to the past.[90] Smith takes pains to identify and describe the cultural resources that maintain a sense of "national identity," which he defines as "the continuous reproduction and reinterpretation of the pattern of values, symbols, memories, myths, and traditions that compose the distinctive heritage of nations, and the identification of individuals with that pattern and heritage."[91] Territorial homelands, ethnohistories, ideals of sacrifice in the service of a national destiny, and myths of origins and divine election all provide resources for the construction of a felt community and national identity. Most important, some of these resources—and for some nations, *all* of them—are tied directly to religious belief and practice. They come "with a clear religious aura which imbues otherwise secular conceptions of the nation with a definite 'sacred' quality."[92] In this sense, "the cultural resources which maintain a sense of national identity in a population may also be regarded as 'sacred foundations' of the nation."[93] It is this sacred quality that gives the cultural resources their grip on human will and emotion. A territorial homeland is sacred ground; the people occupying the land are divinely chosen; history is the story of a "golden age," when the nation flourished religiously, politically, and economically; heroes who sacrificed their lives are martyrs; the nation's destiny is a divine mission.

The sacred foundations of national identity account for the enduring power of the "felt community," even into a secular age. Although religious belief and practice have eroded significantly in some parts of the world, "nationalism," the ideology based on national identity, has taken the functional place once held by religion. The symbols, ceremonies, myths, and traditions formerly exclusive to religion are now paralleled in the service of nationalism, and—in nations that have states—the state itself.[94] Thus, nationalism may be the *secular* religion of the modern nation-state, but according to Smith, "it draws on many of the motifs, beliefs, and rituals of traditional religions, not just for its forms, but also for some of its contents, such as myths of ethnic election, the sanctity of the homeland, and the messianic role of the leader."[95] We cannot miss this if we hope to understand national identities; we will find the keys to national identity in the religious belief and practice of the people, even if religious fervor has dissipated. In a secular age we are still right to see religion as wholly relevant to social and political life. National identity rests on sacred foundations.

Identity thus entails a connection with the subjective elements of human culture. These elements are, indeed, *subjective*, meaning that they can be interpreted and manipulated by political elites. But how far can they be manipulated? Smith admits that nations and national identities are constructed; they are "imagined, willed, and felt communities."[96] They are indeed constructed, but not in a straightforward manner. First, they are not the sole product of elites, but rather emerge from "the interplay between elites and different strata of society."[97] They "cannot be simply wished into existence by intellectuals or any other elite, without support from other sectors of the population."[98] Elites can and do *will* nations into existence, but are limited in their ability to construct identities by the willingness of other strata to go along. Second, the available cultural material limits the ability of elites to shape national identity. If, for instance, national elites wish to create a common identity among traditional ethnic enemies—as, for instance, in Sub-Saharan Africa in the 1960s—cultural materials that can bridge the gap, such as a common language, religion, or myth of ethnic origins, must be present.[99] In this Smith and the ethnosymbolists agree with the constructivists of the stable peace school. Elites work within boundaries; identities can be constructed, but the possibilities are not infinite.

To summarize, from an ethnosymbolist perspective, four points emerge:

- National communities are real, with measurable effects on those both inside and outside.
- National identity is based on cultural factors that have deep historical roots, traceable in many cases to premodern times.
- National identity is often built on "sacred foundations." Religion, even in a secularized form, will provide key elements of national identity.
- Elites can manipulate national identity, but within boundaries.

For the ethnosymbolist, national identities are both difficult to create and difficult to surmount once created. The transition from a sense of community to a new national identity must meet the challenge of entrenched identities in the merging states. A new national identity resting on its own sacred foundations must emerge strong enough to elicit deep emotional responses in the citizenry.

Multiple identities are, of course, possible.[100] Old identities do not have to disappear but must find a new place alongside a broader identity. Just as Virginians, Pennsylvanians, and South Carolinians learned to also be Americans, the Dutch, Italians, and Croats could (and often do) learn to fold or nest their national identities into a European one.[101] National identities do not disappear, just as local and regional identities remain, but make room for another identity that recognizes "Europe" as a community. And all this must be done without the use of force if the process is to remain democratically legitimate—something of a challenge, if the Civil War in the United States is any indication.

A Cultural Approach to Integration in Europe

We can now draw the pieces together. On the surface integration looks like diplomatic agreements on rules and institutions, but if observers from Karl Deutsch to Ernst Haas are correct, at its deepest level it is a shift in a collective state of mind toward a sense of community that results in behaviors encouraging common governance. Even Jean Monnet—the author of the "community method," which emphasized common rules and supranational institutions, the building blocks of regional government—knew that the step-by-step method of integration was effective only if it changed perceptions. Peaceful integration will include new forms of collective governance, but it is first and foremost the development of a new national identity by means of a growing "sense of community" (see figure 1.1). Conversely, disintegration is the loss of national identity by means of an evaporating "sense of community" that will eventually result in the erosion of collective institutions. Thus integration is not primarily about institution building, but rather the building of community. It is identity before organization.

New identities do not evolve naturally; they are constructed out of shared cultural raw materials and learned over time. Political, economic, and social elites will be most active in the construction of new identities, but they are not free to create ex nihilo. They must draw on a common culture to connect people emotionally. They are free to emphasize values, symbols, heroic myths, and traditions that support efforts to unite separated peoples, but they are limited in what they can manipulate for integrative purposes.

To say that identities are constructed out of common cultures, however, tells us little about how this process occurs. From our discussion above, however, we can describe in general terms the development of a new national identity. First, a crisis deep enough to threaten the existence or well-being of states in a region triggers the integration process. There is, of course, nothing inevitable about the choice of integration as a solution to an existential crisis as other less cooperative or peaceful options may be tried. Thus to strengthen the likelihood that elites will choose peaceful integration, a second development is needed: the rise of a transnational elite, with its own growing sense of community that predisposes members to choose integration over other policy options. These leaders must be convinced that they have much in common with counterparts across their borders and must value increased cooperation. Here a common culture—most powerfully, a common religion, especially one that values transnational cooperation—may emerge as a crucial factor.

Third, integration must become more than an elite project; publics must also embrace a new sense of community. Several mechanisms will be involved: Cross-border transactions will increase; civil society and the media will socialize citizens into backing integration; and new supranational rules and institutions will encourage support for more problem solving at the regional level. In short, whole societies will come to value deeper contact with their neighbors and expanded opportunities to interact. Facilitating this entire process must be a culture (often *made*) common enough for elites and masses to recognize the formerly "other" as "one of us." Finally, if the process is to reach the final stage of union, elites must first convince themselves, and then their populations, that what used to be separate nationalities have now become "one people," united by a common culture embodied in symbols that elicit deep emotions and called to a mission so important as to be considered sacred. Only then will a growing sense of community have resulted in a new national identity.

Figure 1.1   Integration as Identity Formation

Separate identities	Common national identity

Sense of community

$\longrightarrow$

Drawing on a common culture, elites can construct a transnational sense of community that through socialization and learning may evolve into a new national identity. But much can go wrong in this process. It can stall, or reverse, or, in fact, be hijacked by elites intent on creating a union by force. The pitfalls are manifest. Trouble can emerge if the ways of life in the separate nations are too different to create a new "we feeling." Or, perhaps, one or more of the cultures values separation more than integration. The ideological content of the cultures thus matters. Trouble can also emerge if transnational elite networks do not prove to be inclusive enough and cause divisions that fall along ethnic or religious lines. Various groups in civil society may reject the ideological basis for creating a new identity and refuse to socialize their members into a new, transnational sense of community. Finally, existing national identities may remain too strong to allow the emergence of an effective supranational identity, or elites simply fail to develop a new identity that adequately grips the hearts of people in the emerging polity. Peaceful integration can fail for any number of reasons. It can reverse and disintegrate. Or it may stall at some point on the integration continuum, with elites and masses in the several states experiencing a measurable sense of community with their neighbors but no new national identity. In short, integration does not move inevitably in one direction. Forging a new national identity is extremely difficult and never inevitable.

In the chapters that follow, we use this approach to help us understand why the European Union has failed to establish a true union or "amalgamated security community." The short answer is that it has thus far been unable to create a sense of community deep and broad enough to constitute a new European national identity. Why? Because at the heart of the European Union there exists a cultural division rooted in the Reformation that to this day makes it difficult to forge a sense of community between Catholics and Protestants. Furthermore, the confessional cultures produced disputes over the appropriate extent and shape of integration that undermine any common "vision" for a united Europe. Thus the content of these confessional cultures has also arrested the development of a deep sense of community.

To argue that Europe has failed to establish a United States of Europe as a result of cultural divisions is not to label the integration project a failure. Europe has developed enough of a sense of community to establish what Deutsch would surely recognize as a "pluralistic security community"—no small accomplishment on a war-torn continent. Nor is it to argue that Europe can never establish an amalgamated union. Cultures evolve. Europe may find the necessary "we feeling" to establish a federal union of some strength, but it will need to overcome Reformation animosities, now manifested not in arguments over the Eucharist but in disputes over austerity and solidarity, bank unions, and Eurobonds. The task is difficult, but not impossible. The European Union's hope, however, is not in the growing power of common institutions, but in a growing "we feeling" among its citizens.

Notes

1. Stephen George, *An Awkward Partner: Britain in the European Community*, 3rd ed. (Oxford: Oxford University Press, 1998); Sieglinde Gstöhl, *Reluctant Europeans: Norway, Sweden, and Switzerland in the Process of Integration* (Boulder, CO: Lynne Rienner, 2002).

2. So, too, to different degrees, do Orthodox and Muslim cultures, but we confine ourselves to the cultural divide that has characterized European integration from the beginning, leaving questions involving these cultures to future studies.

3. J. H. H. Weiler, "Federalism without Constitutionalism: Europe's *Sonderweg*," in *The Federal Vision: Legitimacy and Levels of Governance in the United States and the European Union*, ed. Kalypso Nicolaidis and Robert Howse (Oxford: Oxford University Press, 2001).

4. Alan S. Milward, *The European Rescue of the Nation-State*, 2nd ed. (London: Routledge, 2000).

5. Alan S. Milward, *The Reconstruction of Western Europe, 1945–51* (London: Routledge, 1984), 492.

6. Andrew Moravcsik, *The Choice for Europe: Social Purpose and State Power* (Ithaca, NY: Cornell University Press, 1998), 4.

7. Ibid., 23.

8. Ibid., 4.

9. For a defense of studying culture in the current intellectual atmosphere, see Clifford Geertz, *After the Fact: Two Countries, Four Decades, One Anthropologist* (Cambridge, MA: Harvard University Press, 1995), 42–63; and Lawrence E. Harrison, *Jews, Confucians, and Protestants: Cultural Capital and the End of Multiculturalism* (Lanham, MD: Rowman & Littlefield, 2013), 1–9.

10. As Landes put it, the study of culture has "the sulfuric odor of race and inheritance" about it. David S. Landes, *The Wealth and Poverty of Nations: Why Some Are So Rich and Some So Poor* (New York: W. W. Norton, 1998), 516.

11. Alexis de Tocqueville, *Democracy in America*, ed. J. P. Mayer and trans. George Lawrence (New York: HarperPerennial, 1966); Max Weber, *The Protestant Ethic and the Spirit of Capitalism*, trans. Talcott Parsons (Los Angeles: Roxbury, 1996).

12. Major exceptions included Gabriel A. Almond and Sidney Verba, *The Civic Culture: Political Attitudes and Democracy in Five Nations* (Boston: Little, Brown, 1965); and Ronald Inglehart, *The Silent Revolution: Changing Values and Political Styles among Western Publics* (Princeton, NJ: Princeton University Press, 1977).

13. Lawrence E. Harrison, *Underdevelopment Is a State of Mind: The Latin American Case*, updated ed. (Lanham, MD: Madison Books, 2000).

14. Landes, *Wealth and Poverty*, 516.

15. See Ronald Inglehart, *Culture Shift in Advanced Industrial Society* (Princeton, NJ: Princeton University Press, 1990); and Robert Putnam, *Making Democracy Work: Civic Traditions in Modern Italy* (Princeton, NJ: Princeton University Press, 1993). See also Jim Granato, Ronald Inglehart, and David Leblang, "The Effect of Cultural Values on Economic Development: Theory, Hypotheses, and Some Empirical Tests," *American Journal of Political Science* 40, no. 3 (1996): 607–31; and Jan W. Van Deth and Elinor Scarbrough, eds., *The Impact of Values*, vol. 4 of *Beliefs in Government* (Oxford: Oxford University Press, 1995). For a critique of the Inglehart and Putnam positions from a rational

choice institutionalist perspective, see Robert W. Jackman and Ross A. Miller, "A Renaissance of Political Culture?" *American Journal of Political Science* 40, no. 3 (1996): 632–59.

16. Samuel P. Huntington, *The Clash of Civilizations and the Remaking of World Order* (New York: Simon & Schuster, 1996), 20.

17. Samuel P. Huntington, "The Age of Muslim Wars," *Newsweek*, December 17, 2001.

18. Tara Brady, "Europe Is Being Split by North/South Economic Divide, Warns EU Chief Barroso as He Appeals for Solidarity among Nations," *Daily Mail Online*, April 4, 2013, www.dailymail .co.uk/news/article-2304134/Europe-split-north-south-economic-divide-warns-EU-chief-Barroso -appeals-solidarity-nations.html.

19. E.g., see Timothy A. Byrnes and Peter J. Katzenstein, eds., *Religion in an Expanding Europe* (Cambridge: Cambridge University Press, 2006); Liesbet Hooghe and Gary Marks, "A Postfunctionalist Theory of European Integration: From Permissive Consensus to Constraining Dissensus," *British Journal of Political Science*, 39 (2008), 1–23; Neil Fligstein, *Euroclash: The EU, European Identity, and the Future of Europe* (Oxford: Oxford University Press, 2008); Thomas Risse, *A Community of Europeans? Transnational Identities and Public Spheres* (Ithaca, NY: Cornell University Press, 2010); and François Foret and Xabier Itçaina, eds., *Politics of Religion in Western Europe: Modernities in Conflict?* (London: Routledge, 2012).

20. Quoted by Clifford Geertz, *The Interpretation of Cultures: Selected Essays* (New York: Basic Books, 1973), 4, 47.

21. Ruth Benedict, *Patterns of Culture, Sentry Edition* (Boston: Houghton Mifflin, 1959), 1.

22. Margaret Mead, "Preface," in ibid., vii.

23. Geertz, *Interpretation of Cultures*, 5.

24. Richard A. Shweder, "Moral Maps, 'First World' Conceits, and the New Evangelists," in *Culture Matters: How Values Shape Human Progress*, ed. Lawrence E. Harrison and Samuel P. Huntington (New York: Basic Books, 2000), 163.

25. Alan Patten, "Rethinking Culture: The Social Lineage Account," *American Political Science Review* 105, no. 4 (2011): 741.

26. Huntington, *Clash*, 41.

27. The Calvinist Henry R. Van Til does in *The Calvinistic Concept of Culture* (Grand Rapids: Baker Academic, 1972). At one point he states: "Culture, however, does not include religion" (27). What he seems to mean by this is that religion *precedes* culture; culture emerges from theological understandings of God, humanity, and the relationship between the two. In this sense, religion gives "culture its foundation, and serves as the presupposition of every culture" (39).

28. Huntington, *Clash*, 41.

29. Ibid., 42.

30. Seymour Martin Lipset and Gabriel Salman Lenz, "Corruption, Culture, and Markets," in *Culture Matters*, ed. Harrison and Huntington, 120.

31. Van Til, *Calvinistic Concept*, 27.

32. Geertz, *Interpretation of Cultures*, 90.

33. Alexis de Tocqueville, *Democracy in America*, ed. J. P. Mayer and trans. George Lawrence (New York: HarperCollins, 1966), 442–43.

34. Huntington, *Clash*, 68–72.

35. See Pippa Norris and Ronald Inglehart, *Sacred and Secular: Religion and Politics Worldwide* (Cambridge: Cambridge University Press, 2004), 17.

36. See Michael Walzer, *The Revolution of the Saints: A Study in the Origins of Radical Politics* (New York: Atheneum, 1970), 300.

37. We take the term "stable peace" from Kenneth E. Boulding's book: Kenneth E. Boulding, *Stable Peace* (Austin: University of Texas Press, 1978).

38. See Karl W. Deutsch, Sidney A. Burrell, Robert A. Kann, Maurice Lee Jr., Martin Lichterman, Raymond E. Lindgren, Francis L. Loewenheim, and Richard W. Van Wagenen, *Political Community and the North Atlantic Area: International Organization in the Light of Historical Experience* (Princeton, NJ: Princeton University Press, 1957). We identify Deutsch as the father of the postwar stable peace school, but his work on security communities is now considered one important focus

of a broader school that examines international communities not meeting the strict criteria of a security community. Alexander George's investigation of states experiencing "precarious peace" is a good example; see Arie M. Kacowicz and Yaacov Bar-Siman-Tov, "Stable Peace: A Conceptual Framework," in *Stable Peace among Nations*, ed. Arie M. Kacowicz, Yaacov Bar-Siman-Tov, Ole Elgstrøm, and Magnus Jerneck (Lanham, MD: Rowman & Littlefield, 2000), 17, 19–20. An important precursor to the stable peace school was the so-called English School, led by Martin Wight and others; see Herbert Butterfield and Martin Wight, *Diplomatic Investigations: Essays in the Theory of International Politics* (Cambridge, MA: Harvard University Press, 1966).

39. Deutsch et al., *Political Community*, 5.

40. Ibid.

41. Ibid., 36.

42. Ibid., 46.

43. Ibid., 46–47.

44. Ibid., 47.

45. Ibid., 57.

46. Philip E. Jacob, "The Integrative Process: Guidelines for Analysis of the Bases of Political Community," in *The Integration of Political Communities*, ed. Philip E. Jacob and James V. Toscano (Philadelphia: J. B. Lippincott, 1964), 18.

47. Karl W. Deutsch, "Communication Theory and Political Integration," in *Integration*, ed. Jacob and Toscano, 54.

48. See, e.g., Risse, *Community*. For a neofunctionalist revival of Deutsch, see Alec Stone Sweet and Wayne Sandholtz, "Integration, Supranational Governance, and the Institutionalization of the European Polity," in *European Integration and Supranational Governance*, ed. Wayne Sandholtz and Alec Stone Sweet (Oxford: Oxford University Press, 1998), 1–26.

49. For critiques of rationalism, see John Gerard Ruggie, *Constructing the World Polity: Essays on International Institutionalization* (London: Routledge, 1998); Alexander Wendt, "Constructing International Politics," *International Security* 20, no. 1 (1995): 71–81; Marlene Wind, "Rediscovering Institutions: A Reflectivist Critique of Rational Institutionalism," in *Reflective Approaches to European Governance*, ed. Knud Erik Jørgensen (New York: St. Martin's Press, 1997), 15–35; Janne Haaland Matlary, "Epilogue: New Bottles for New Wine," in *Reflective Approaches*, 201–13; Emanuel Adler, "Seizing the Middle Ground: Constructivism in World Politics," *European Journal of International Relations* 3, no. 3 (1997): 319–63; and Craig Parsons, *A Certain Idea of Europe* (Ithaca, NY: Cornell University Press, 2003), esp. chap. 1. Confusingly, constructivism can also be called "reflectivism." To our minds, however, reflectivism suggests a more critical approach to international relations that embodies a postmodern or deconstructivist ontology and epistemology. For a contrary view, see Knud Erik Jørgensen, "Introduction: Approaching European Governance," in *Reflective Approaches*, 3.

50. Wendt, "Constructing," 71.

51. Ruggie, *Constructing*, 4.

52. Ibid., 33.

53. Emanuel Alder and Michael Barnett, "Security Communities in Theoretical Perspective," in *Security Communities*, ed. Emanuel Alder and Michael Barnett (Cambridge: Cambridge University Press, 1998), 13.

54. Emanuel Alder and Michael Barnett, eds., *Security Communities* (Cambridge: Cambridge University Press, 1998); Charles A. Kupchan, *How Enemies Become Friends: The Sources of Stable Peace* (Princeton, NJ: Princeton University Press, 2010).

55. Emanuel Alder and Michael Barnett, "A Framework for the Study of Security Communities," in *Security Communities*, ed. Alder and Barnett, 38, 50.

56. Ibid., 50–57.

57. Ibid., 32n9.

58. Ibid., 33.

59. Kupchan, *How Enemies Become Friends*, 30–31.

60. Ibid., 69.

61. Ibid., 35.

62. Ibid., 35–36.

63. Ibid., 62.

64. Ibid.

65. See Sergio Pistone, "Altiero Spinelli and the Strategy for the United States of Europe," in *Altiero Spinelli and Federalism in Europe and the World*, ed. Lucio Levi (Milan: Franco Angeli, 1990). For a taste of more contemporary federalist writing, see John Pinder, *European Community: The Building of a Union* (Oxford: Oxford University Press, 1991); Michael Burgess, *Federalism and European Union: The Building of Europe, 1950–2000* (London: Routledge, 2000); Murray Forsyth, "The Political Theory of Federalism: The Relevance of Classical Approaches," in *Federalizing Europe? The Costs, Benefits, and Preconditions of Federal Political Systems*, ed. Joachim Jens Hesse and Vincent Wright (Oxford: Oxford University Press, 1996); and Guy Verhofstadt, *The United States of Europe: Manifesto for a New Europe* (London: Federal Trust for Education and Research, 2006).

66. See Weiler, "Federalism without Constitutionalism."

67. Jean Monnet, "A Ferment of Change," *Journal of Common Market Studies* 1, no. 1 (1962): 206.

68. Ibid.; Monnet, *Memoirs*, 367.

69. Ernst B. Haas, *The Uniting of Europe: Political, Social, and Economic Forces, 1950–1957* (Stanford, CA: Stanford University Press, 1958), 16.

70. "In part the existence of such sentiments can be tested by the regularity of popular compliance with fundamental government decisions; and in part it is subject to verification by the kind of attitude testing of perceptions of mutuality of aspirations made familiar by post-1945 surveys"; Haas, *Uniting of Europe*, 5.

71. Ibid., 13–14.

72. He disagrees with Deutsch, however, over the role of institutions in cementing new loyalties and in the role of group pressure as the engine of integration. See ibid., 7, 284–85.

73. Bruce Cronin, *Community under Anarchy: Transnational Identity and the Evolution of Cooperation* (New York: Columbia University Press, 1999), 24.

74. John M. Owen IV, "Pieces of Maximal Peace: Common Identities, Common Enemies," in *Stable Peace among Nations*, ed. Kacowicz et al., 76–77.

75. Cronin, *Community*, 25.

76. Ibid., 26.

77. Ibid., 77.

78. Deutsch et al., *Political Community*, 48.

79. For a concise survey of the field, see Anthony D. Smith, *Ethno-Symbolism and Nationalism: A Cultural Approach* (London: Routledge, 2009), 3–21.

80. See Paul R. Brass, *Ethnicity and Nationalism: Theory and Comparison* (New Delhi: Sage, 1991).

81. Benedict Anderson, *Imagined Communities: Reflections on the Origins and Spread of Nationalism*, 3rd ed. (London: Verso, 2006), 6.

82. Anderson, *Imagined*, 36, 46.

83. Smith, *Ethno-Symbolism*, 11–12.

84. Anthony D. Smith, *Cultural Foundations of Nations: Hierarchy, Covenant, and Republic* (Malden, MA: Blackwell, 2008), 19.

85. Risse, *Community*, 23.

86. Smith, *Ethno-Symbolism*, 15–16.

87. Ibid., 16.

88. Ibid., 17.

89. Ibid., 20.

90. Ibid., 25.

91. Smith, *Cultural Foundations*, 19.

92. Ibid., 40.

93. Ibid. See also Anthony D. Smith, *Chosen Peoples* (Oxford: Oxford University Press, 2003), 43.

94. See Smith, *Chosen Peoples*, 32–33.

95. Smith, *Ethno-Symbolism*, 77.

96. Smith, *Cultural Foundations*, 23.

97. Smith, *Ethno-Symbolism*, 19.

98. Ibid., 59.

99. Ibid.

100. Americans instinctively know this. One of the authors once observed the placement of flag stickers on a vehicle in Charleston, South Carolina. At the top of a flag "pillar" was a "Christian" flag (often seen in conservative Protestant churches), followed beneath by an American flag, then a South Carolina flag, a "Stars and Bars" flag (the official flag of the Old Confederacy), and at the bottom, a "Don't Tread on Me" flag (representing the Tea Party). This particular individual had a very clear sense of his multiple identities and their order of priority!

101. The notion of "nested identities" comes from Gary Marks, "A Third Lens: Comparing European Integration and State Building," in *European Integration in Social and Historical Perspective: 1850 to the Present*, ed. Jytte Klausen and Louise Tilly (Lanham, MD: Rowman & Littlefield, 1997), 34–35. See also Thomas Risse, "Neofunctionalism, European Identity, and the Puzzles of European Integration," *Journal of European Public Policy* 12, no. 2 (2005): 291–309.

PART II

Confessional Cultures

2

Common Roots

THE IDEA OF A united Europe is an echo from imperial Rome and Carolingian Aachen.[1] The notion that all Christendom should be united under one political and religious authority is rooted in the universal claims of Christianity and the Roman imperial ideal. Europe today has a sense of itself because Constantine once ruled Rome as emperor and priest and Charlemagne much later accomplished the same feat, but only in the West. Efforts at political union, whether carried out by emperors or popes, have met with limited success through the centuries, but a culture shaped by both Church and throne permeated the Continent and created a people with a common identity. As we demonstrate in this chapter, Christian universalism, imperial Rome, Frankish kings, and reforming popes all contributed to the creation of a people and a place we can call "Europe." These were the memories and cultural ties that the founders of the European Union drew on when seeking to reconcile a war-torn continent.

Christian Universalism

To be "Christian" is to be "catholic," or "universal." From the moment Jesus of Nazareth directed his followers to "go and make disciples of all nations" (Matt 28:19), Christianity became a religion with global intentions. Paul the Apostle put feet to this command and took the Kingdom of God to all when he preached: "There is neither Jew nor Greek, slave nor free, male nor female, for you are all one in Christ Jesus" (Gal 3:28). Despite their historical and practical failings, Christians have always stressed the relevance of the Gospel to *all* humanity and the spiritual unity of *all* believers who are "one in Christ." The importance of this claim cannot be overstated. Without a universal Gospel the early Christians would have remained a small Jewish sect in Palestine. The universality of the Gospel (coupled with local persecution) forced the early Church into "all the world" and forever stamped the religion with missionary zeal. Thus, Christianity emerged from the ethnic confines of Judaism to become the first global faith. And Jesus Christ became, in Jaroslav Pelikan's words, "the Man Who Belongs to the World."[2]

Christians established the universal reach of the Gospel very early in the history of the Church. Soon after the disciples began preaching the risen Jesus, anyone—Jew or Gentile—could join the Church (see Peter's encounter with Cornelius, a Roman centurion, in Acts 10). Although the Church was universal, it still had boundaries. The question was, where? The Church Fathers wrestled with the exact meaning of the "catholic" Church; initially, it indicated the "whole" Church, as opposed to particular local churches, but later came to mean the "orthodox" Church, as it came to be defined in the creeds and canon of Scripture through its struggles with heretics and schismatics. Saint Augustine extended "catholic" beyond the sense of comprehensive and orthodox to include geographic universality: "In Greek that is called 'catholic' which is spread through all the world."[3] And Saint Vincent of Lérins added that "catholic" meant "that which has been believed everywhere, always, and by all."[4] Thus the Church came to believe that "the holy catholic Church," as stated in the Apostles' Creed, meant that the "Church is to be disseminated through *all* nations, extended to *all* places, and propagated to *all* ages; that it contains in it *all* truths necessary to be known, exacts absolute obedience from *all* men to the commands of Christ, and furnishes us with *all* graces necessary to make our persons acceptable and our actions well-pleasing in the sight of God" (emphasis in the original).[5]

The universal Church did not remain united, of course. The division of Christendom—into East and West, Orthodox and Catholic—meant the emergence of slightly variant definitions of "catholic." The Orthodox Church came to define catholicity in mystical ways. It emphasized the work of God in Jesus Christ and the Holy Spirit, which unites believers by the "power of mutual love" and integrates them into the "mystical body of Christ." This qualitative catholicity overflows into quantitative catholicity as love crosses all boundaries, carried by the Church fulfilling its divine commission.[6]

The Roman Church has always defined catholicity more tangibly than has the Orthodox Church. Like most Christians, Catholics have affirmed the universality of Christian belief. The *Catechism*, for instance, declares, "Through the centuries, in so many languages, cultures, peoples, and nations, the Church has constantly confessed this one faith, received from the one Lord, transmitted by one Baptism, and grounded in the conviction that all people have only one God and Father."[7] But Catholics have made this universal faith visible. The Roman Church, at least before Vatican II, saw the boundaries of the Christian community and the Catholic Church as coterminous. The visible Church is "the sacrament of salvation, the sign and the instrument of the communion of God and men."[8] It reveals God's mysteries through the administration of the sacraments; it makes visible the rule of God through the actions of its ecclesiastical hierarchy.

The visible Church is the One True Church, the presence of Christ on Earth, Mother of all believers, and final authority over all who call themselves Christian. In the contemporary Catholic Church the pope, as the successor of Saint Peter, enjoys "supreme, full, immediate, and universal power in the care of souls" and, thus, rules—visibly—the spiritual society of believers.[9] Consequently, universality takes on an institutional dimension. The universal, catholic nature of the Church is not just a spiritual union with the timeless Body of Christ on Earth. Rather, it includes recognition that the universal Church has a universal head in the vicar of Christ, the pope. Including "church as organization" in the definition of universality has been challenged by other Christian traditions, and we will return to this topic in subsequent chapters.

The Universal Empire from Old Rome to Holy Rome

The medieval Latin Church emphasized the spiritual unity of all Christians in the *visible* Church, ordered by the *visible* representative of Christ on Earth. But for twenty-first-century observers, the pope's temporal rule in Vatican City reminds us that the visible universalism of the Church was once political as well as spiritual. This is crucial. All visions of European political unity have their roots in the medieval papal claims of universal temporal authority. Catholic political ideology is especially grounded in the concept of universal empire. In this section we explore the idea of universal empire as developed by the Romans and Christianized by the Church.

The Roman Empire from Augustus to Constantine

All the great empires of history, from Mesopotamia to pre-Columbian Mexico, were *universal* empires. These empires were universal in the sense that they recognized no other political community as their equal and claimed the right to rule the entire inhabited world, even the cosmos. They believed that all of humanity ought, by nature, to be subject to their imperial rule. If that power did not extend to the limits of the known world, they either treated the unconquered as barbarians unworthy of attention, or maintained elaborate ceremonial fictions to reinforce imperial ideology and disguise reality. A universal emperor who stood above the rest of humanity as a god or as God's representative headed all universal empires. These emperors ruled autocratically, uniting in their persons the legislative, executive, and judicial functions of the state.[10]

Rome was medieval Europe's model of universal empire, but Rome had inherited its imperial notions from the fountain of all its high culture: Greece. Alexander the Great's victories had brought Greece into contact with the imperial traditions of Asia and Egypt.[11] In the East Alexander adopted the provincial administrative structure of Persia and the awe-inspiring ceremonial of the Persian court. More important, he had learned to bind the disparate empire together with a single cohesive principle: a deified emperor. "The deified king," states Barker, "could claim the universality, and receive the universal worship, of a manifest god. On this ground Greek cities and Oriental nations could unite; and with the throne thus elevated to an altar, loyalty could become a religion."[12] This religion made conquerors and the conquered equals, bound together as friends sharing the same loyalty to empire and emperor. It created a culture of popular consent that stabilized the empire.

Alexander's universalism received philosophical backing from an additional gift of Greece to the Romans: Stoicism. Central to Stoic philosophy was the conception of the universe as a single intelligible unity, variously termed Reason, God, or Nature. Human beings were by nature equal, for all shared in the one substance; and they were equally governed by the universal law of nature. If the universe was governed by a common natural law, it reasonably followed that the best society would be one governed as a single whole under the law of nature: "one universal society, one state of the whole world; one law of nature, with which all its members must live in conformity."[13] Stoicism thus provided the Roman Empire with ideological legitimacy: universal empire was the natural government of equal human beings; to be a part of a world-state was to be at peace with God and all humanity. To be Roman was to be—quite literally—"at home in the universe."[14]

The unity of Rome was built on the work of Octavian, who emerged in 31 BCE as the one survivor of a titanic struggle for control of the crumbling Roman Republic and its empire. The machinery of government suitable to a city-state could not adequately govern the Italian Peninsula, much less the vast territories that Rome had recently acquired. A century of rapacious governors and devastating civil wars had created such insecurity that the people welcomed a single leader who could unite the state, restore peace, and control corruption. Octavian transformed a republic into a dictatorship by acquiring absolute power behind a republican screen. The forms of senatorial government remained in place, but the offices and titles amassed by Octavian allowed him to exercise autocratic control with few checks. He confirmed the wisdom of his imperial program by bringing peace to the Roman world. In return, his grateful subjects lavished him with genuine praise for their new peace and prosperity: "In him [Octavian] Providence has not only fulfilled, but even exceeded, the prayers of all—sea and land are at peace; cities flourish in order, harmony, and prosperity; there is a height and abundance of all good things; men are filled with hopes for the future and gladness in the present."[15]

Such praise naturally pointed toward emperor worship, with all its unifying benefits. However, Octavian was not eager to encourage Eastern-style emperor worship after watching his great uncle, Julius Caesar, sow the seeds of a personal cult only to reap assassination.[16] Thus Octavian proceeded slowly. He first accepted from the Senate the novel title of "Augustus," with its strong religious overtones. Although this rubric "indicated his superiority over the rest of humankind,"[17] and clothed Octavian "with a halo of sanctity, and the protection of religion and the gods," it left his divine status quite vague.[18] What the title left ambiguous, however, his grateful subjects clarified. From the provinces, to the cities of Italy, to Rome itself the people worshipped the *genius*, or soul, of Augustus, both in their homes and in public ceremonies. Roman hymns extolled him, and the eastern provincials hailed the "Savior," "Bringer of Glad Tidings," "God the Son of God," and the long-awaited "Messiah."[19]

Augustus did not encourage extreme forms of emperor worship, but he did recognize the value of a personal cult. The glory and sanctity of his person overwhelmed political opposition and overcame any limitations that his collection of official offices still placed on effective administration. Furthermore, as in the days of Alexander, the imperial cult served as patriotic glue cementing temple to state and uniting diverse religions in common worship.[20] Augustus, in fact, preferred to be honored in conjunction with the goddess Rome, thus encouraging the worship of the deified Roman state.[21] But he needed more than patriotism from religion—he also needed virtue. He lamented the virtual disappearance—particularly among the aristocracy—of the ordered Roman family and the solid values of the simple life, which he thought had provided the moral foundation for Rome's unprecedented success. The only antidote to moral decay was a revival of Roman religion—a return to the gods. Thus he promoted religion by rebuilding ruined temples, reviving and participating in ancient ceremonies, and endowing priestly colleges. In 12 BCE he solemnly assumed the office of *pontifex maximus*, chief priest and head of the Roman religion. In so doing, he united in his person all earthly political and religious authority. The union was unequal, however; religion was clearly the handmaiden of the state—*pontifex* served *imperator*.

The Augustan system proved resilient enough to outlast the series of clowns and madmen who succeeded to the purple between AD 14 and 96. When sanity returned in the second century under the emperors Nerva, Trajan, Hadrian, Antonius Pius, and Marcus Aurelius, the "vast extent of the Roman empire was governed by absolute power, under the guidance of virtue and wisdom."[22] The third century, however, was neither happy nor prosperous, as external pressure, internal strife, and economic decline strained the empire to the breaking point. What saved Rome from collapse was the transformation of the Augustan autocracy from a pagan principate into a Christian monarchy.

Diocletian was most responsible for ending the Augustan charade and creating the Roman imperial monarchy. The creative emperor's "tetrarchy" (collegial rule of four emperors) dropped the tattered republican veneer of the Roman Constitution and adopted the actual and ceremonial powers of the East's deified kings. Diocletian and his colleague Maximian became "gods and parents of gods,"[23] and declared themselves the companions of, respectively, the gods Jupiter and Hercules.[24] Moreover, they began wearing a diadem that symbolized a new source of imperial power. The purple worn by past Augusti had signified election by the Senate and thus represented the sovereign will of the people. But a crown indicated a bestowal of sovereign authority from above—from Heaven itself. If the fickle Senate could not guarantee peace and prosperity, perhaps the gods could. This ideological shift, of course, was risky. Any general failure to honor the gods who chose the emperors and inhabited their persons threatened the legitimacy of the state itself. The universal empire required a subordinate universal religion.

The Church threatened this new political and cultural order. From the time of the Apostles, the Christians had been remarkably willing, despite intermittent persecution, to submit to the Roman Empire as God's chosen authority on Earth. Jesus commanded his followers to "Give to Caesar what is Caesar's" (Matt 22:21); Peter urged a suffering Church to "honor the king" (I Peter 2:17); and Paul encouraged the Church in Rome to obey the "governing authorities" (Rom 13:1). But the Church could never acknowledge the Roman Empire as the final cosmic authority. God ruled the universe through his Son, Jesus Christ, the true emperor of the cosmos. Ultimate allegiance belonged to Christ and *his* kingdom.

The Church was under no heavenly obligation to challenge the Roman Empire for earthly superiority, but its moral critique of pagan culture angered Roman society and its growth and independence sparked frequent conflicts with the authorities. When its size and administrative capacity made it a virtual antistate within the state, it threatened to dissolve the glue holding the empire together. Roman rulers thus faced a choice: Eliminate Christianity from the empire, or convert the empire to Christianity. Diocletian and his colleagues chose the first option and declared war against Rome's internal enemy.[25] The Great Persecution of 303–11 began with the burning of churches. By 304 Christians were required to sacrifice to the gods or face execution. The state used every means at its disposal to destroy the Church, but failed. In 311 the emperor Galerius, sick and near death, agreed to the Edict of Toleration and asked the Christians for their prayers. The persecution would sputter on for two more years, but the conflict was essentially over: "Caesar and Christ had met in the arena, and Christ had won."[26]

The tetrarchy lost its kulturkampf; it also failed to guarantee peaceful succession. When the dust of civil war had settled in 323, Constantine I (the Great) ruled a converted Rome. Constantine's own conversion and the establishment of Christianity as an official religion of the empire was a monumental cultural revolution (as we will see below). However, this revolution altered very little in the world of practical politics. The tetrarchy's imperial Constitution and administrative reforms remained largely untouched. Constantine reigned absolutely as divinely appointed king and priest (he never renounced his position as *pontifex maximus* of the Roman religion); he regarded his person as sacred and accepted the "worship" of his subjects; and he looked to religion to unify the empire. In many ways, Constantine ruled as a baptized Diocletian.[27]

Christianity may not have altered the form of the Roman Constitution, but it profoundly changed the theory behind it. By establishing Christianity, Constantine had to accept the supremacy of the Kingdom of God over the Empire of Rome, but this did not mean the renunciation of Rome's universal ideal. Rather, it forced Constantine to redefine the empire in Platonic terms as the earthly reflection of a heavenly reality.[28] Runciman puts it this way: "[The Constitution of the empire] was based on a clear religious conviction: that it was the earthly copy of the Kingdom of Heaven. . . . It saw itself as a universal empire. Ideally it should embrace all the peoples of the Earth, who, ideally, should all be members of the one true Christian Church, its own Orthodox Church. Just as man was made in God's image, so man's kingdom on Earth was made in the image of the Kingdom of Heaven."[29]

In similar fashion, the theory of divine kingship also took a Platonic form. God the Father, the king of the universe, had conferred on Christ the Savior all authority in Heaven and on Earth. Christ was the rightful Lord of the world, but he had elected not to reign directly but to grant Constantine authority to rule as his representative.[30] Constantine was not divine, but he was godlike in nature. As a king in the pattern of Eastern monarchs, Constantine further encouraged the oriental court manners introduced by the tetrarchs. He wore a jeweled diadem and adopted the upward tilt of the face and eyes found in Alexander the Great's iconography. He referred to himself as "Our Clemency." All his possessions were sacred, and all his acts were praised. He surrounded himself with the splendor of the empire and the courtly trappings appropriate for Christ's earthly representative.[31]

Constantine was king and, like the emperors before him, also priest.[32] His role as ruler of the empire was matched by his new role as ruler of the Church. This role in the Church was justified from a Christian perspective by the same arguments made for divine kingship: The emperor, as Christ's representative, would naturally rule the Church. Pagan tradition also mattered. Just as Diocletian took it upon himself to intervene in religious matters in the interest of cultural and political unity, so Constantine needed to exercise firm control of the newly established Church. Early in his reign he made a concerted effort to settle the Donatist conflict in Africa that threatened to destabilize the West.[33]

Constantine's efforts failed, but they set a precedent that he followed at the Council of Nicaea, which he called to resolve a doctrinal controversy that threatened to split the very Church he needed to unify his empire. Was Jesus Christ, as Arius argued, created by God the Father and thus subordinate to the Father? Or was he "begotten" but not "made," and thus fully equal in substance and glory with the Father, as Athanasius maintained? Such a deep split over the nature of the Deity threatened the "settled uniformity" of religion and would, in fact, threaten the health of the empire.[34] He resolved to settle the dispute by calling a council of bishops of the entire Church, over which he would personally preside.

On May 20, 325, the emperor opened the council in Nicaea. His supreme interest was unity, and his interventions were designed to gain the support of the greatest number of bishops possible. Several issues besides the doctrinal question were decided during the proceedings, but the decision to reject the Arian position and declare Jesus Christ one in substance with the Father was by far the most important. In the end, only 2 out of 230 bishops refused to sign the declaration of the council; Constantine had his unity.

The emperor's actions at Nicaea had profound symbolic as well as practical importance. Constantine acted outside the Church as the supreme secular power intent on thwarting division and forcing religion to conform to the interests of the state by backing the decisions of the Council with coercive force.[35] But though the emperor played the role of secular authority outside the Church, he also had a significant role inside the Church. He seems to have naturally, almost unconsciously, presided over church officers as a divinely appointed shepherd of the shepherds. He took part in the Council of Nicaea by engaging in debate and making suggestions, but he did not vote. In short, he was *in* but not *of* the council.

For both the East and the West, Constantine at Nicaea represents an ideal type—almost an icon of temporal unity. For a brief moment this remarkable man united Earth and Heaven; the master of the known universe presided over the assembled Kingdom of God on Earth, wisely guided it to its inspired conclusion, and then judged the enemies of God. For the Byzantine East—which always considered itself "Roman"—Constantine represented the standard from which it dared not deviate. These Roman emperors reigned from Constantine's new Christian capital, Constantinople, in nearly unbroken succession for more than a thousand years, until the great city's overthrow in 1453. The empire was in chronic decline during most of that period, but never lost its conviction that it possessed a God-given obligation to rule all peoples.[36] Nor did it waver in its understanding of the emperor as ruler of both empire and Church. Occasionally, emperors ran into trouble with the Church, sometimes on theological grounds, as during the controversy over icons in the eighth century, but more often on moral grounds, as when Leo VI broke his own law by marrying a fourth time. But these times were rare. The Church accepted without objection the emperor's right to appoint patriarchs and call ecclesiastical councils. There was no separation of church and state in the East, because the separation of the terms had no meaning to the Byzantines.[37] The empire was the whole people of God, led by the viceroy of God. It could be no other way.

The Withering of Rome and the Rise of the Church

The conservatism of the East was a luxury that only Byzantine emperors—living in a kind of Constantinian time warp behind the great defenses of Constantinople—could afford in Late Antiquity. The Germanic migrations and the sackings of Rome fragmented the empire in the West. The Western Empire did not really "fall"; it withered. Like a dying tree, the Empire watched life drain first from its outermost twigs, then from its great branches, and finally, after long struggle, from its ancient trunk. The efforts of Diocletian and Constantine secured the troubled empire for a generation; but by the end of the fourth century, the Germanic tribes had inflicted enduring damage. They poured into the Balkans in 376 and across the Rhine River in 406. By 429, they were in Africa.[38] The barbarian migrations did not immediately end imperial rule in the West: German nobles gladly paid lip service to the emperor in Constantinople in exchange for a Roman title. But formal rule and practical governance are two different things. With the onset of migration from the east, the Latin West slowly drifted away from imperial control and broke up into a set of weak successor states.

Roman administration in the West had not collapsed, but it had fallen into the hands of Church officials, who struggled to maintain some sense of order. Pope Leo I (the Great), for instance, became the de facto ruler of Rome in 440 and negotiated with the Huns and Vandals, whereas Pope Gregory I (the Great), one hundred and fifty years later, ensured food supplies for Rome, paid the army, and bought off the Lombards. But most Western bishops found themselves performing more mundane civil tasks, such as ensuring water supplies and providing for the poor.[39] The Church, moreover, was not itself immune to fragmentation. Theological orthodoxy came under pressure from the German settlers, who came in two varieties: pagan and Arian. Furthermore, as the Western cities declined, the Roman Church moved to the countryside, often in the form of proprietary churches under the control of individual landowners and national rulers.[40] Thus Rome had little control over Church leadership, teaching, or practice.

Still, the Roman Church managed to survive the crumbling empire and carry its Latin cultural inheritance forward.[41] Three reasons stand out. First, monks, many from the Celtic fringes of the known world, swept into the post-Roman chaos in the sixth and seventh centuries and quietly built buildings, reclaimed land, taught Latin, copied ancient books, and baptized the population into the Roman Catholic faith. Monasteries dotted the devastated landscape with pockets of Roman religion and culture, and they eventually produced a new European elite that sought to reorganize Western society around the leadership of the bishop of Rome.[42] Second, the Roman Church was far better organized—despite tendencies toward fragmentation—than any other Western institution. The principle of apostolic succession created an ecclesiastical hierarchy that required obedience to the appointed bishops, the heirs to the Apostles. And the pope, by virtue of being the successor to Saint Peter, gradually gained preeminence among the bishops, especially in the West.[43] Thus the Church had (at least in principle, if not always in practice) an efficient decision-making structure centered on the pope.

Finally, the Roman See used its organizational skill to evangelize Europe. The program began, most noticeably, under Pope Gregory I, who in 596 sent Augustine to Britain to convert the Anglo-Saxons and organize the existing Church along Roman lines. The papal effort proceeded in the seventh and eighth centuries, with increasing support from the powerful Frankish kings.[44] Pope Gregory II, for instance, commissioned the Anglo-Saxon Benedictine monk Wynfrith—otherwise known as Boniface—in 719 as a missionary to the heathen, and then consecrated him a bishop of "peoples east of the Rhine." After securing papal backing, Boniface visited the Frankish court, where he acquired the support of the effective ruler, Charles Martel. Armed with papal and political power, Boniface left for religiously mixed Germany, where he established lavishly endowed monasteries, including Fulda (founded on royal property), and reorganized the Church along Roman lines. His efforts were enormously successful; the Frankish Church was extended and reoriented toward Rome, and where that Church went, so did Frankish arms and political influence. Boniface was binding the interests of the Franks and the popes together. Thus, Rome's missionary efforts resulted in a new Christendom, now united religiously and culturally not by the Roman state but by the Roman Church.

The Western Church, however, could not hold Christendom together by itself. External invasion and internal schism constantly threatened to splinter the Church. Unity required political power. According to Southern, "Religious unity could scarcely be thought of apart from political unity, if only because religious unity depended on some ultimate power of coercion."[45] The Eastern emperor was still, in theory, the ruler of all the Christians, but Rome feared the Lombards to its north and the popes were increasingly frustrated with imperial impotence. Although papal loyalty to the empire had not wavered, even into the eighth century, that position was becoming less tenable. Constantinople was in rapid decline after overextending itself against the Ostrogoths in Italy and in prolonged Balkan, Persian, and Islamic wars that effectively reduced the empire to little more than its core in Asia Minor.

A theological gulf was also opening with the West. The iconoclastic emperor Leo III drove a wedge between Constantinople and Rome in 729 by restricting the use of religious images in the West. The resulting controversy led Constantinople to restrict the ecclesiastical competence of the Holy See, stripping from it important territories in Italy and the Balkans. Still, the popes looked to the emperor to send relief against a renewed Lombard advance from the north. None came. In 739 the imperial capital of Ravenna fell, and Pope Gregory III begged Charles Martel to rescue him. Charles did not come either, but Rome had taken a decisive turn to the north.

Charlemagne and the Carolingian Empire

The Franks had already grown accustomed to working with the Roman Church, to their mutual advantage. Papal envoys—Boniface being the most prominent—had evangelized much of the territory east of the Rhine under Frankish protection. Not surprisingly, where the Roman Church went, so did Frankish political influence. But Frankish political life suffered from a legal dilemma: The Carolingian "mayors of the palace" rather than the Merovingian kings held real power, but with no legitimate way to replace the emasculated dynasty. With the papacy needing protection and the Carolingian family looking for legitimacy, a deal emerged, which Boniface himself may have negotiated. In 751, as the Lombards threatened Rome, Pepin the Short, the new Carolingian "mayor," asked Pope Zacharias if it was right "that a powerless ruler should continue to bear the title of king?"[46] Zacharias replied "that it was best that those be named kings who exercised the highest authority."[47] Pepin took the cue and deposed (perhaps violently[48]) the last Merovingian king—Childeric III—in a papally blessed coup.

This was more than a cynical power grab. Behind the political maneuvering was a new conception of Frankish kingship that better fit the reforming elements in Frankish society than the semipagan notions of kingship still clung to by the Merovingians. Boniface, as the pope's representative, presided over Pepin's coronation and symbolically initiated this new Carolingian kingship by anointing him with oil in a manner heavy with biblical imagery. Pepin, like the ancient kings of Israel, was appointed of God to rule a chosen nation as king and priest.[49] Frankish power would defend the one orthodox and catholic Church and its supreme bishop in Rome in exchange for papal backing of the Carolingians. It was left to Pope Stephen II to cross the Alps in 754 to reanoint Pepin and then, on his knees as before an emperor, to secure his assistance against the Lombards. Thus, with active papal support, the Frankish king was gradually assuming the honors and responsibilities of a Christian emperor. The culmination of this process, however, would have to wait for Charlemagne.

The outline of Charles' (Charlemagne's) life is familiar. He was born in 742 to Pepin and Bertrada, the first of two sons. Pope Stephen II anointed him with oil in 754 to designate him a divinely chosen successor to Pepin (along with his brother, Carloman). On the king's death in 768, both Charles and Carloman ascended to thrones of a divided realm, but Carloman's early demise in 771 made Charles the sole ruler of the united Frankish kingdom. He soon proved himself an able, if brutal, warrior. Year after year, his armies put down internal uprisings and aggressively expanded the kingdom, primarily to the east and south. Keeping his commitment to the Holy See, Charles defeated the Lombards in 774 and was crowned their king, thus adding most of Italy to his realm. Twenty-nine years of war—and countless cruelties on both sides—eventually brought the pagan Saxons to heel.[50] Additional victories added Bavaria and Carinthia and established buffer zones (*marches*) for protection against the Spanish Muslims and pagans east of the Elbe. By 800 Charles—now deservedly known as "Charlemagne," or Charles the Great—had defeated every major foe and had extended his rule over the heart of Europe, from the Latin west to the Germanic east (an area remarkably similar to that of the original six members of the European Economic Community).

Several factors made Christmas Day of 800 an opportune moment for Pope Leo III to boldly place the imperial crown on Charlemagne's head and to proclaim him emperor of the Romans.[51] The Franks were eager to see their dominance of the

West acknowledged in a grand fashion. In addition, Charlemagne, though he did not solicit the crown, seems to have seen the empire as a means to greater peace in his realm.[52] But more immediate concerns also encouraged a coronation. Leo found himself in a dispute with the Romans, who accused him of various misdeeds. Only the emperor could adjudicate this dispute, but this presented a problem, for the current emperor in Constantinople was, in fact, a woman. Thus in the eyes of the West, the imperial throne there lay vacant. To both Leo and Charlemagne, the Empress Irene ruled illegitimately because she was a woman and—because of the circumstances under which her son had died—a murderer,[53] with her sex a greater disqualification than her crime.[54] In sum, the time seemed right for the West to crown an emperor. And Leo believed he was qualified to place the crown on the new emperor's head.

Leo's confidence was fortified by a recently forged document called the Donation of Constantine. The forgery told the story of how Constantine the Great was cured of leprosy and in gratitude to Saint Peter granted to Pope Sylvester and his successors three privileges: preeminence over the universal Church, the right to wear imperial insignia, and full temporal authority over Rome and all the Western regions.[55] Based on the rights outlined in this Donation and the presumed vacancy of the throne, Leo felt fully justified in "translating" the empire from the East to the West, where it would be governed jointly by pope and emperor.[56]

The matter, of course, did not look quite so simple to Charlemagne. The Carolingian court also argued that Charlemagne's empire was the true Roman Empire, but the problem was how to convince the Byzantines. Charlemagne first decided to take advantage of the unmarried state of both imperial rulers and proposed to unite the empires by marrying Irene.[57] She briefly considered using the union to shore up her tottering regime, but before the plan could be carried out she was deposed on the last day of 802. With the marriage option closed, Charlemagne offered Irene's successor, Nicephorus I, an alliance on equal terms. Two or more emperors had often ruled without undermining the empire's theoretical unity, but Nicephorus was in no mood to accept this barbarian king as co-emperor. No reply came from Constantinople. Armed conflict between the two empires over control of Venetia and Dalmatia eventually led to a settlement in 812. In exchange for firm control of the disputed territories, Michael I, the new Byzantine emperor, yielded his claim to Croatia and acclaimed Charlemagne as *basileus*—emperor. The world was learning to live with two universal Roman empires existing side by side.[58]

Did the world also have to get used to two universal *emperors*? The short answer was yes; but there were complications. Charlemagne, even before his imperial coronation, had assumed the rights and responsibilities of sacral kingship by virtue of his anointing in 754. He ruled his expanding empire as God's chosen representative on Earth, much as David and Solomon had ruled Israel. It was his duty to bring peace and prosperity to his realm, to bring the heathen into the Church, to defend

Christian peoples from infidels and heretics, and to see to the religious health of his people. He exercised complete control over the Church in his realm through, for instance, the appointment of bishops and reform of the liturgy.[59] He also employed his religious authority by calling and presiding over the Council of Frankfurt in 794, further deepening the growing political and theological rift with the East.[60] In all these ways, Charlemagne followed the Constantinian pattern of divine kingship. His coronation as emperor of the Romans in 800 thus confirmed a role he had already come to play.

As emperor, however, Charlemagne was acknowledged as more than an extraordinary Frankish king. His reign was now universal; he was the one ruler of all humanity in the likeness of the Lord of Heaven. As one court poet put it: "There is only one who is enthroned in the realm of the air, the thunderer. It is proper that under him, one only be the ruler on Earth, in merit an example to all men."[61] Charlemagne claimed the same authority as Constantine, using the same theological justification. This did not, however, mean that he intended to rule as a Byzantine emperor. He set out to establish a worthy imperial capital, a "Second Rome," in Aachen (a task confined to the building of a church and palace), but he rejected the near deification customary in the East.[62] His court referred to him as "king and priest," but the latter title only gave him the right to preach and did not carry the same sacred connotations as it did in Constantinople.[63] Moreover, when Charlemagne built his chapel in Aachen, he underlined his humanity by placing his throne, not in the sacred east—in place of the altar—as Byzantine emperors did, but in the western choir reserved for the Christian faithful.[64] In sum, Charlemagne ruled his new Western Empire under a revived Constantinian Constitution, minus the Byzantine trappings of a near-deified monarch.

Latin Christendom and the Papal Triumph

Charlemagne set the standard for all subsequent Western emperors, none of whom could match his authority and stature. The division of the Carolingian inheritance among his grandsons destroyed the unity of the empire and undermined the authority of the emperor, leaving the Catholic episcopate as the "one guardian of Christian unity."[65] The Church "continued to insist on the need for a regime of 'fraternal concord' which would unite the separate kingdoms against the common enemy of the Christian name," but renewed barbarian invasions and steep Western decline in the ninth and tenth centuries made political unity impossible.[66] By the mid–tenth century, however, Western fortunes had revived and the vision of unity, kept alive by the Church, again became a realistic possibility.

This is not the place to recount in detail the history of the medieval Holy Roman Empire, because the German version of empire did not change the Carolingian imperial concept in any fundamental way. Suffice it to say that Otto I (the Great) revived a moribund empire by establishing a new power base in Germany and by appealing to the Carolingian ideal. He first evoked the memory of Charlemagne by holding his coronation as German king in the imperial chapel in Aachen in 936. Then after defeating the Magyars in 955, he—like his hero—traveled to Rome to receive the imperial crown from Pope John XII in 962, thus founding the Holy Roman Empire.[67] His realm and the realm of his medieval successors would be much smaller than Charlemagne's, containing little more than Germany and Italy, but that would not keep the Holy Roman emperors from claiming the rights of all universal emperors to rule the world as God's chosen representatives. The medieval emperors made much of their sacral kingship, but nothing in the new German version departed dramatically from the Carolingian model.[68]

The medieval emperors, in fact, were quite anxious to tie themselves personally to Charlemagne, and they often seemed intent on outdoing their predecessors in honoring his memory. Otto III, for instance, was so taken with his exemplar that he is said to have opened Charlemagne's tomb and recovered relics, including one of the emperor's teeth. Frederick I convinced a reluctant pope to canonize Charlemagne in 1165, then commissioned a golden reliquary for his remains and decorated Charlemagne's church in Aachen with a magnificent chandelier representing "the Celestial City, the eternal Jerusalem."[69] Frederick II, as part of his coronation ceremony, reburied Charlemagne in the new reliquary. And perhaps Charles IV outdid them all by adopting Charlemagne as his personal saint, building a castle in his honor, and, in the Golden Bull of 1356, naming Aachen as the imperial coronation site.[70]

The Holy Roman Empire, thus, picked up Charlemagne's imperial mandate. The Carolingian alliance of imperial and papal power was renewed, symbolized by the requirement that popes crown the emperors. But the seeds of conflict between emperor and pope had been sown in 800 at the very moment Leo placed the crown on Charles's head. Who would master the world, the chosen emperor or the crowning pope? The emperor could appeal to the traditions of Constantine and Charlemagne, but the popes also had reason to believe that they were the rightful heirs of the Roman Empire.[71] There was also, of course, the Donation of Constantine, which represented a developing papal ideology that stretched back to Leo the Great and forward to the papal monarchy. In the fifth century Pope Leo I had taken the discarded Roman imperial title of *pontifex maximus* and had asserted his right to rule all Christian peoples as Peter's ("the prince of the apostles") successor. Gelasius I expanded papal claims by asserting the superiority of the priestly power over the imperial power, while Nicolas I went even further, claiming "that the church was co-extensive with the Earth and that his office made him the rightful judge of terrestrial emperors and kings."[72] By 1059 the pope had acquired a second crown in addition to his diadem;[73] by 1075 he was wearing an imperial robe, so "that in his external appearance there was no difference between him and the former emperors."[74]

This tradition of papal supremacy undermined the Constantinian conception of universal empire by claiming for the Church authority that was independent of that of the emperor, the viceroy of God. Conflict was avoided, however, as long as the emperor remained strong relative to the pope; not coincidentally, both the Carolingian and Ottonian empires arose during eras of papal weakness. Charlemagne protected his imperial privileges by keeping the pope at arm's length after his coronation. Otto the Great, for his part, determined early in his reign to use the Church and its vast resources to help consolidate his hold on Germany. Thus he appointed bishops and abbots and even deposed Pope John XII (the pope who had crowned him!) for opposing his Italian policy. The Salian successors to the Ottonians continued this imperial policy of firm control of the German Church and intervention in messy papal matters when necessary. Henry III, the most powerful Salian emperor, enforced a broad peace in Germany; and by sorting through claimants to the papal throne, he brought order to the Holy See. The German emperors—perhaps contrary to their interests—could take some credit for cleaning up and strengthening a decrepit and debauched Roman papacy.

A reformed Church, however, was also a strong Church that grew resentful of imperial power. In the eleventh century the low-level conflict that had characterized relations between emperor and pope became the driving force in politics. Great battles—mostly of words, sometimes of swords—broke out over who controlled Western Christendom. The popes asserted their freedom. Gregory VII's *Dictatus Papae* (1075) claimed that he alone was "universal"—that he alone controlled the bishops, that he alone could wear the imperial insignia, that he alone could depose emperors, and that he alone could not be judged.[75] Boniface VIII, in *Unum Sanctam* (1302), declared the absolute spiritual and temporal supremacy of the Church and its pope:

> Both swords, . . . the spiritual and the temporal, are in the power of the Church. The former is to be used by the Church, the latter for the Church; the one by the hand of the priest, the other by the hand of kings and knights, but at the command and permission of the priest. Moreover, it is necessary for one sword to be under the other, and the temporal authority to be subjected to the spiritual. . . . We therefore declare, say, and affirm that submission on the part of every man to the bishop of Rome is altogether necessary for his salvation.[76]

The emperors, however, rejected these papal claims. Imperial defenders agreed with the popes that two swords governed the world, but they argued that the pope held only the spiritual sword, with the emperor, by order of the King of Kings, holding its temporal counterpart. The emperor defended and protected the Church—that is, all Christendom—and saw to it that everything within it was ordered with justice. His judgments were the judgments of God; his acts of mercy were the mercies of God. Thus, right government, in imperial ideology, meant emperor and pope ruling Christendom side by side as equals.[77] Papal claims to supremacy were acts of war against the balanced Constitution of God.

The war went badly for the emperors. The popes won the major battles—Gregory VII humiliated Henry IV at Canossa in 1077; Innocent IV deposed Frederick II in 1245—and, consequently, came to wield tremendous temporal power. Innocent III probably exercised the most earthly authority of any medieval pope as he chose between warring claimants to the imperial throne; raised up and advised kings; rallied Europe to the Crusades; played the role of feudal lord in the Papal States; accepted England, Aragon, Sicily, Denmark, and Bulgaria as vassals of the Holy See; collected taxes; sold indulgences; and made laws.[78] The Church had, in fact, become an imperial power capable of mobilizing large armies and successfully launching them against enemies as far away as Jerusalem and Egypt. During the first half of the thirteenth century, after more than a hundred years of crusading, papal rule extended—tenuously—to the Eastern Empire (after the sack of Constantinople in 1204) and much of the Holy Land. For a brief moment, a united Christendom under the universal rule of the Roman pontiff was no longer a papal pipedream but close to a political reality.

An imperial papacy, however, had altered the Constantinian Constitution. Medieval papal government—at least in theory—meant the universal rule of Christendom not by the divinely chosen emperor but by the pope: "one universal society, which is a Church, based utterly on the law of Christ and controlled ultimately by Christ's vicar."[79] In the eyes of the papacy, Constantinianism had failed to unify Christendom. Only the Church was capable of providing the benefits of universal empire. Only by drawing the world into itself could it bring peace. This was universal empire. This was its holy task.

To tell the story of universal empire in both East and West is to tell the political story of Europe. The East never wavered in its commitment to the Constantinian program, and it believed its visible empire to be the true Roman Empire and the Kingdom of Christ on Earth. Its story of universal empire was the story of successive emperors who ruled a unified, albeit shrinking, realm. The story of the West, however, is more complicated. Its universal goal remained elusive, and attempts at achieving unity were broken up by waves of violence and disintegration. The story of universal empire in the West was the story of the kings, monks, and popes who worked for Western unity but who generally failed to create an extensive, politically coherent, and lasting empire. It was the Church—the true successor of Rome in the West—that preserved the political notions of Western unity, and it was the Church that eventually came the closest to creating a durable empire. But this was never an empire in the traditional, political sense. The medieval popes' political power was real, but diffuse. The papacy established a system of supranational governance that was effective, but almost never without political challenge. Its echoes, however, can still be heard in Brussels today.

Papal Supranational Governance

The European Union is not the first attempt at supranational governance in Europe.[80] The medieval West was fragmented politically, but the Roman Church exercised authority above the local potentates in a manner not completely unlike that exercised today from Brussels. The purview of the Roman Church of the Middle Ages extended beyond—sometimes far beyond—the recognized Frankish or German imperial boundaries. As we have seen, the medieval popes were in theory to work in concert with the emperors, but the boundaries of the Holy Roman Empire required the papacy to acknowledge the temporal authority of kings in England, Ireland, France, Spain, and elsewhere. Thus, despite the chronic political fragmentation of feudalism, the weakness of the Holy Roman Empire, the growing power of the nascent national states, and the constant resistance from secular authorities, the Church managed to govern the whole of Western Christendom. As Morris puts it, starting in the mid–eleventh century, "Christendom was ruled by kings and princes under the supervision of the clergy, and especially of the Roman Church, which alone possessed the fullness of power."[81] The papacy acquired many characteristics of a state: a visible head, an extensive bureaucracy, an effective tax system, a uniform legal code, and a foreign policy. But despite its medieval growth, the papacy's authority remained unevenly enforced and often ignored.

Papal Government

The papal government was formally a monarchy patterned after the Roman imperium. Surrounding the pope was a permanent consultative body called the papal court, or Curia. Within the Curia was the College of Cardinals, which imitated the ancient Roman Senate as an electoral body and governing cabinet. The Curia also contained the Office of the Chamberlain—which managed papal financial matters—and the Papal Chancery—which handled the administrative and secretarial functions of the government, including the issuing of papal documents and written communications.[82] Popes exercised practical power throughout their realm through their legates (usually cardinals) who carried the pontiff's "presence and authority" to the far-flung reaches of Christendom. The wide use of legates made the papal court "the centre of a spider's web of activity that reached the whole of Christendom," allowing the popes to be directly involved in Church councils and synods, national and international negotiations, legal investigations, judicial judgments, the organization of crusades, and the collection of revenue.[83]

The medieval papacy also found itself at the center of a web of oaths of obedience and loyalty that bound the great political and social powers of medieval Europe to the person of the pope. Of course, bishops—the princes of the Church, and sometimes of their own temporal realms—swore personal obedience to the pope and pledged to defend the Roman papacy. In addition, certain monasteries—Cluny, founded in 909, being the most prominent—sought freedom from kings and local aristocrats by pledging fealty to Rome in exchange for the pope's protection. New internationally organized and highly disciplined religious orders, such as the Cistercians and Franciscans, and military orders, such as the Teutonic Knights, pledged allegiance to the medieval popes. Such vows were very similar to the feudal oaths that more and more involved the pope after eleventh-century reforms greatly strengthened the papacy over its secular rivals. Popes became feudal lords who were responsible for the protection of their vassals. As representatives of Saint Peter, however, the popes could offer a unique benefit, the Apostle's personal protection. To receive the protection of Peter, kings or princes were required to surrender their land to full papal ownership and receive it back as a fief in exchange for annual tribute and a pledge to place the kingdom's military power at the disposal of the Holy See. By entering into feudal relationships with the rulers of England, Sicily, Castile, Portugal, Aragon, and others, the pope became, at least in theory, the "strongest European feudal monarch," who could defend his loyal dependents with military force if necessary. The pope still claimed universal authority over all Christian rulers, not just the vassals of the Church, but the pontiff's feudal lordship over several great and small kingdoms of Europe made this authority tangible. In reality, the pope could muster an army.[84]

The popes could also harness vast financial resources. Before the twelfth century they found it difficult to raise the revenue needed to govern. Traditionally, local churches were financed by a tithe of 10 percent on most types of income.[85] Bishops were responsible for the distribution of this money, but it often fell into the hands of lay lords and little found its way to Rome.[86] Most revenue collected by the early medieval papacy came as rents from its Roman estates, tolls, and other income collected in the papal patrimony and gifts from the pious. These revenues increased, at least in theory, as monasteries and kings paid tribute for papal protection, but these payments were often late or were not made. Popes, to be sure, were not poor, but their responsibilities outpaced their resources.[87] New sources of funds were needed. Thus, in 1199 Pope Innocent III levied the first tax on clergy income to help pay for the Third Crusade. This income tax proved a success and soon became a permanent source of papal revenue. Additionally, the popes in the thirteenth and fourteenth centuries began to reserve vacated benefices for themselves, and soon whole classes of benefices (and their incomes) came under their direct control. Furthermore, the Papal Curia began charging fees for its services, including the confirmation of appointments and the rendering of judgments in judicial cases. Pope John XXII systematized and centralized the collection of papal revenues, so his successors could enjoy steady income from a wide variety of reliable sources.[88] Revenues still did not always meet desired expenditures, but the papacy had established its power to tax all of Latin Christendom.

Canon Law

The medieval papacy possessed the tools of effective government: efficient (by medieval standards) central institutions, available armed forces, and sufficient revenue. In addition, Rome ordered behavior and social relations through the implementation and enforcement of canon law, the truly supranational law of Christendom.[89] Church law originated in the late first or early second century as a series of moral precepts and basic rules concerning Church governance and the conduct of liturgical services. These rules represented the decisions of bishops or the consensus of Christian communities and were confined to the doctrine and discipline of the Church. And so it remained until Constantine elevated the Church to an imperial institution and called councils of bishops to rule on the great questions facing the Church. Thus Church councils and synods emerged as the legislative bodies of the Church, and their canons and decrees became the principal sources of Church law. By the fifth century the bishops of Rome had begun to assert their primacy over the other bishops, and their decretals (letters) and decisions became new sources of ecclesiastical law. Multiple sources made for profound confusion; so attempts were made as early as 380 to organize these laws into canonical collections. Authoritative legal texts were necessary because the recognition of Christianity by Constantine gave Church law the force of public law; the state backed episcopal decisions in matters of doctrine and morality with coercive force. As a consequence, the Church established its own courts—largely patterned after the Roman civil courts—to rule on matters within its jurisdiction.

The Germanic invaders disrupted the legal system of the West, just as they had every other Roman social institution. During most of the sixth and seventh centuries, in areas that preserved some practice of the rule of law, tribal, Roman, and ecclesiastical codes existed side by side in a confusion of jurisdictions. Moreover, canon law itself took on regional characteristics, thus undermining its universality. Carolingian reforms addressed part of this problem by recognizing an authoritative canon law (the Hadriana, used in conjunction with the Hispana) and by reinvigorating the Church courts, in part to enforce discipline on lax clergy. The application of canon law and the adjudication of disputes, however, remained haphazard. As in so many other areas, it was the papal reform movement that finally made canon law effective. First, reforming popes used canon law as a primary means of institutional reform, thus centralizing lawmaking power and increasing the papacy's legislative output. The popes made laws through their decretals, which often served (as appellate courts' opinions do today) to establish legal precedents and to address contradictions in the law. Second, new collections of canon law, culminating in the Liber extra (1234) and its subsequent additions, gave Christendom an updated authoritative body of ecclesiastical law. Third, new universities, such as the one established in Bologna in the twelfth century, began producing highly trained lawyers and detailed legal commentaries, increasing the quantity and quality of legal action and jurisprudence. Finally, ecclesiastical courts became more hierarchical and professional. At one end, the bishops and many lesser prelates handed over their judicial functions to trained specialists. At the other end, the pope maintained supreme judicial authority by exercising "both original and appellate jurisdictions over controversies from every part of Western Christendom."[90]

Although canon law officially pertained only to Church matters, in practice it regulated a breathtaking array of human activities.[91] It guarded the purity of the Christian community. Those who belonged to the Church in some special way—including priests, monks, nuns, canons, students, and others—were subject to canon law and to the Church courts. The remainder of Christian society was to conform to the pure doctrine of the Church and submit to its regulation of behavior. The responsibility for maintaining orthodoxy fell to local bishops before the early thirteenth century, but increased papal attention to doctrinal issues eventually led to the Curia's takeover of heresy investigations by means of the Roman Inquisition in 1231.

Regulation of Christian behavior was less centralized, but no less comprehensive. Canon law governed marriage and family life by bounding sexual conduct, defining legal marriage, and determining legitimate offspring. Church rules regulated economic activity by valuing private property and encouraging thrift and care for the needy, while prohibiting usury, unjust pricing, and work on the Sabbath and holy days. Legally mandated fasts influenced eating practices. And at the end of life canon law was there to direct Christian burial and divide the property. In short, "It would have been difficult, indeed almost impossible, for an individual, regardless of social status or occupation, to remain untouched from one year's end to the next by canonical regulations. . . . Canon law repeatedly touched the lives of practically every person from cradle to grave."[92]

Canon law also regulated the behavior of secular governments. Law governed the possession and use of legitimate authority—who rules, and how?—and determined where the authority of the Church ended and that of the civil authority began. Canon law even attempted to regulate the use of force in international relations. The devastating violence of the feudal period led the Church to establish restraints on warfare. First, the Church restricted the right to declare war to the highest authorities, those without superiors. Second, in a series of local initiatives that attracted wide attention, the Church attempted to curtail violence in Europe by restraining the conduct of war between Christian peoples.[93] The "Peace of God," for instance, emerged from the Council of Le Puy in 975 to address the rise in lawlessness in Anjou and Aquitaine. The council required knights and soldiers to take an oath to respect the property of the Church and protect peasants. The movement caught on in many parts of Europe and served to establish the principle of noncombatant immunity. A second canonical limitation on war, the "Truce of God," sought to proscribe warfare and all forms of violence on holy days. The Council of Toulouges promulgated the first Truce in 1027; additional eleventh-century councils expanded the number of proscribed days. Unfortunately, the Peace and Truce movements were both short-term failures—they did not immediately reduce violence—but their long-term effects were more substantial. Principles of just war were established and broadened; but more important for our purposes, the Church established its right to regulate the use of coercive force. The crowning achievement of the peace movement in Europe was, in fact, the rallying of all Christendom to the defense of the Holy Land. Pope Urban II's 1095 call to the First Crusade was in part an appeal for peace in Europe: "Let hatred, therefore, depart from among you; let your quarrels end; let wars cease; and let all dissensions and controversies slumber. Enter upon the road of the Holy Sepulcher."[94] This call to undertake the Crusade encouraged Christian princes and the European military classes to focus their violence against non-Christians not protected by the rules of war.[95]

The Crusades as Papal Foreign Policy

The Crusades offered an outlet to knights looking for glory and adventure; it also gave the medieval papacy a foreign policy. Popes did not lead crusades—kings and noblemen commanded the armed fighters—but the papacy was often the primary political force behind the endeavors. Urban II moved public opinion by touring northern Italy and southern France from March to October 1095 before making his public call to liberate the Holy Land at Clermont in November. The Second Crusade and Third Crusade were less directly inspired by the popes, but they still received strong Church backing. Saint Bernard of Clairvaux led the public campaign for the Second Crusade (1145–49) with the strong support of the less charismatic Pope Eugenius III, while the reports of the fall of Jerusalem from William, archbishop of Tyre, were instrumental in motivating the great kings of Europe—Emperor Frederick Barbarossa of Germany, Philip II (Augustus) of France, and Richard I (the Lion-Hearted) of England—to launch their unsuccessful effort to recover the city for Latin Christendom in the Third Crusade (1189–92).

After the failure of the Third Crusade, Innocent III returned the papacy to the center of the crusading movement. This visionary pope revitalized the Crusade by returning it to its original purpose: to purify and extend Christendom and thereby realize the dream of a united Christian society under papal rule.[96] Innocent enlarged the scope of the Crusades (especially to Spain and the Albigensians), reorganized their financial support (through taxation), strengthened their armies, and expanded and codified the spiritual benefits offered to crusaders and their supporters.[97] He also attempted to mobilize the whole of society behind the crusading effort—a prerequisite in his mind for success—by developing special liturgies that allowed participants to intercede for the crusaders.[98] And his efforts paid off. During his pontificate,

Christians made significant gains in Spain, Albigensians came under severe pressure in France, and, most important, Constantinople fell to the crusaders, who established a Latin kingdom in Byzantium. The Greeks, however, took back Constantinople in 1261, and the last Latin redoubts fell to Muslim conquerors in 1291. The grand international strategy of the reforming popes, the foreign policy of the Latin West, eventually failed. Western Christendom would be confined to Europe.

Papal governance in the Middle Ages—for all its centralizing tendencies—remained diffuse and relatively informal. Unlike the traditional empire of the Byzantine East, the Western medieval system never completely melded the spiritual and temporal powers; no single secular political authority governed all the areas loyal to the Roman Church, and temporal rulers remained the papacy's greatest competitors. But papal supranational governance was effective because it rested on a single culture that informed a common worldview. Faith and religious devotion allowed the Church to choose rulers, raise revenues, deploy armies, pass laws, and regulate private and public life. Resisting the will of the Church or breaking its canonical laws resulted in loss of office, payment of a fine, confinement to a monastery, public flogging, pilgrimage, maiming, or execution by any number of savage methods. Excommunication, the ultimate spiritual penalty, reserved its severest consequences for the afterlife. And all these powers and penalties carried weight as long as the European princes and their subjects believed that their security in this life and the next rested in the palm of the pope's hand. Power, however, corrupted the papacy, and Europe was soon awash in revolutionary political and religious movements that undermined the ideological basis for papal control. When faith—at least faith in the papacy—broke down, so did the powers of the pope.

The Common Culture of Christendom

Except for a few brief moments, political union in Europe was much more the ideal than the reality after the fifth century. But what the West lacked in political union, it made up for in cultural unity. The popes reigned, in fact, without opposition over a cultural empire that gave the papacy its supranational legitimacy and the West its true unity. In this section we describe the rise of the common Latin culture in Europe, beginning once again with Rome but dwelling on the Carolingian revival, the crucible of Christendom.

Europe's Roman Heritage

As we saw earlier in this chapter, the Roman emperors understood that military power alone could not prevent the fragmentation of the empire; disparate people had to be bound together by the ropes of a common culture. The cultic worship of the state and its emperor proved valuable as cultural glue until it was dissolved by determined Christian monotheists. The failure of Diocletian's fourth-century persecution, in fact, opened up a struggle for the soul of the empire. The civil struggle that followed the abdications of Diocletian and Maximian in 305 began as a competition for power and ended as a culture war. Constantine's identification of his cause with that of the Christians in 312 made his campaign for control of the West a war between Christianity and paganism. His victory over Maxentius at the Milvian Bridge guaranteed freedom for Christians in the western regions he controlled, but Christian liberties did not extend in practice to the East. Licinius, Rome's junior Augustus, resented the growing power of Constantine and launched a final persecution of Christian supporters of the Western emperor in the regions under his own rule. Constantine's victories at Adrianople and Chrysopolis in 323 rescued the Christians in the East and sealed Licinius's fate and that of paganism in the empire.

From a cultural point of view, Constantine's triumph changed everything. Christianity overthrew the hegemony of the ancient Roman religion, and paganism went into rapid decline. Imperial funds went to building monumental churches; clergy were recognized in official state capacities; crucifixion and branding were outlawed; slavery went into decline; and pagan Rome was abandoned for the new Christian capital at Constantinople. The sojourning Church on society's periphery became the established Church of the empire.[99]

The cultural change, however, went even deeper. As Christopher Dawson points out, Rome had been the political organ of Hellenism—"one of the greatest and most original cultures that the world has ever known."[100] Hellenism trained the mind and character of the Roman world and blessed it with a rich tradition of literature and learning, philosophy and science, art and architecture. Hellenism gave Rome the politics of the polis, "with its civic institutions, its ideal of citizenship and its ideas of democracy, liberty, and law."[101] But Hellenism lacked a unifying spiritual principle—a common religion—that united theology, philosophy, science, and the arts. The "unity" of Roman religion went no deeper than perfunctory ritual. Roman tolerance did not focus the mind or grip the heart. "The various modes of [Roman] worship," as Gibbon put it, "were all considered by the people as equally true; by the philosopher as equally false; and by the magistrate as equally useful."[102]

Christianity provided Hellenism with new passion and purpose. All cultural energy could now be focused on the glory of the one true God. The marriage of Christianity and classical culture, however, did not come easily. Tertullian's harsh second-century polemics against Roman culture and his rejection of philosophy as anti-Christian ("What does Athens have to do with Jerusalem?"[103]) set a counter-cultural tone for many Christians, especially in North Africa. In contrast, the late-second-century and early-third-century writings of the Church Fathers—particularly the Alexandrians Clement and Origin—reflected a deep willingness to embrace Greek philosophy (if not Roman culture) as consistent with divine revelation.[104] This trend continued in the fourth century, as Christian thinkers pushed the whole Hellenic philosophical tradition into distinctly Christian territory with their reflections on the Trinity. Equipped with the Scriptures and the tools of philosophy, Christians wrestled with the nature of Jesus Christ and what it meant for the Logos to be made flesh—the word, reason, structure, purpose, and power of the universe, in human form. In their minds Christ the Logos was the answer to all philosophical questions, the revealed mystery of the cosmos. As Pelikan writes: "By applying this title [Logos] to Jesus, the Christian philosophers . . . were enabled to interpret him as the divine clue to the structure of reality (metaphysics) and, within metaphysics, to the riddle of being (ontology)—in a word, as the Cosmic Christ."[105]

The synthesis of Christian teaching and Greek philosophy laid the groundwork for a full cultural union, but it was the political victory of Christianity that literally forced the whole of Hellenic culture through the doors of the Church. Architecture, literature, art, music, and drama were transformed and incorporated into Christian worship. Liturgy became the pinnacle of Christian culture—an art form in itself— and the Church's primary vehicle for cultural diffusion.[106] With the resources of the state at its disposal, the Church grew rapidly throughout the Mediterranean world, providing the adhesive for a fraying empire. Thus Constantine's cultural revolution created a new Christian society.

Christian Society

Constantine's Christian society survived in the Byzantine East, where it flourished largely intact until the fifteenth century. But the Roman version of Christian society did not survive the dark centuries of disintegration and anarchy in the West. As we have seen, the Catholic Church, primarily through the monastic movement, preserved classical culture and Christian orthodoxy in barbarian lands until the West could regain its balance under Frankish rule. Although the Carolingian period is important politically for making the old dream of universal empire a living reality in Germanic territories, it is perhaps more important for forging a uniform culture that extended beyond the Carolingian Empire and eventually encompassed the whole of Europe not under Islamic or Byzantine control.[107] To be sure, local customs governing language, food, dress, construction practices, and a host of other practical activities reflected the diversity of the peoples making up medieval Europe. But taken as a whole, the diversity of *Europe* was overwhelmed by the uniformity of *Christendom*. From Portugal to Poland, from Sicily to Scandinavia, and even in the Latin outposts of the Middle East, the whole of life, from birth to burial, revolved around the Roman Church.

The particular version of sacramentalism that developed in the Western Church provided the ideological support for a thoroughly Christian society. Sinful humanity needed the salvation offered to all people through Jesus Christ. As Mark Noll points out, this ancient conviction was interpreted by the medieval Church to mean "that saving grace comes to people through the sacraments in a social setting defined by the cooperation of church and state."[108]

Essential to this system was the universal Church, supported by the state. Only through the Church was life-giving grace dispensed to needy sinners. And, increasingly, Western Christians came to see that the only true Church was the one headed by the pope, the successor to Peter, the apostle chosen by Christ to lead his Church. The state's important but clearly subordinate role was to secure the spiritual health of its subjects by defending the purity of the Church against internal and external enemies, and by encouraging piety. Thus, together Church and state would so order society as to secure the grace and blessing of God for all Christians.

The Carolingian period proved crucial to the formation of a uniform sacramental culture.[109] For the first time the centralizing tendency of the Holy See, the scholarship and zeal of the monasteries, and the power of the Franks combined forces to shape religious practice throughout the West. Uniformity, of course, was not instantaneous, nor absolute; it was the result of a process that took generations to complete. Most of the elements, however, can be found in the actions of the Carolingian court, especially during the long reign of Charlemagne.

The Frankish rulers took seriously their responsibility to maintain the purity of the Church, and thus they launched a long-term program of religious reform. This was no easy task because organizational disarray and a mediocre, undisciplined, and often morally degenerate clergy plagued the Church. Carolingian legislation began to address the problems by first ordering the reorganization of the Frankish Church into archbishoprics and bishoprics along the lines advanced by Pope Gregory I in 601. In turn, the Carolingians imposed this hierarchical order on the nominally Christian and pagan realms that they conquered. In addition, they legislated specific duties of the priests and outlawed many immoral practices that undermined the moral authority of the Church. The monasteries also came under scrutiny. Charlemagne wished to bring uniformity to monastic practice and clearly favored the Rule of Saint Benedict, as opposed to the more severe Celtic rule attributed to Columbanus. But it was not until the reign of Louis the Pious that attempts were made—although not always successfully—to enforce the Rule across the empire. By the tenth or eleventh centuries, however, nearly every Western monastery adhered to some version of Saint Benedict's Rule.

Carolingian reforms also concerned the particulars of Church teaching and practice. Liturgy was of paramount importance because "uniformity and correctness in the performance of the services of the Church and the administration of the Sacraments was considered essential to the maintenance of divine favour."[110] Although unique local practices were never entirely eliminated, Charlemagne and Louis the Pious compiled a generally accepted service book (the expanded Gregorian Sacramentary) for the Frankish Church. Furthermore, the Carolingian passion for authoritative texts also extended to the Bible, circulating in a variety of Latin versions. The great scholar Alcuin seems to have assumed the task of revising the Vulgate biblical text, and he presented the finished product to Charlemagne at his imperial coronation. This text gained gradual acceptance in succeeding decades. Finally, Charlemagne understood the problems caused by a poorly educated clergy and attempted to compensate by issuing summaries of important doctrines and Church laws and by commissioning a homilary (book of readings) covering all the major feasts for use in churches.

Additional reforms made during the eighth and ninth centuries further homogenized Western culture and eventually aided its spread. Latin spellings were reformed, and a uniform script—the Carolingian minuscule—was widely adopted. Monasteries became important centers of learning, and highly trained monks crisscrossed Europe to assume important posts in the Church and in secular government. Latin-speaking monks and their Latin-speaking students thus ran Europe. Together they constituted a cosmopolitan elite that could, by the twelfth century, function as effectively in Toledo as in Canterbury or Rome.

Over time, the Carolingian reforms took root and spread throughout Western Christendom. Missionary thrusts to the outmost reaches of the West brought Catholic Christianity to areas untouched by Frankish rule, including Norway, Sweden, Iceland, the Baltic region, and re-Christianized Spain. By the mid–thirteenth century the cultural uniformity in the West was striking.[111] Feasts and fasts governed the rhythms of life—religious piety balancing its vicissitudes. Pilgrims from every Western land sought comfort and cure at sacred sites in Compostella, Amiens, Cologne, Rocamadour, Rome, Jerusalem, and a host of local shrines. These pilgrimages were often timed to coincide with certain holy days, and large crowds could descend on a single location; on one day in 1496, 142,000 pilgrims viewed Charlemagne's relics in the Aachen Cathedral.[112] Latin was the language of Scripture and liturgy, and it also dominated European libraries, scriptoria, cathedral chapters, law courts, universities, and bureaucracies, both secular and ecclesiastical.[113] Towns grew around churches, and cities around cathedrals. Art, music, and architecture, serving both didactic and liturgical purposes, bore distinctive common traits from Paris to Durham to Prague (so much so that students touring Europe today invariably protest that "all the cathedrals look the same"!). Feudal oaths, military service, peasant labors, and manufacturing and commerce also developed common Western characteristics—although more so in the core areas of the Continent than on the Celtic, Nordic, or Slavic fringes. In short, the many distinct customs of the Western peoples were subordinated to the one culture that had come to dominate the West.

The power of a common Western culture to order medieval life can also be seen in the identities of Europeans. Hay puts it succinctly: "Christendom was the largest unit to which men in the Latin west felt allegiance in the Middle Ages."[114] Medieval Europeans were first and foremost "Christians." But nested within this broad identification were additional identities. Latin Europeans identified with the Catholic Church and its pope. They also felt strong ties to their families, lords, and localities, while recognizing themselves as subjects of a king who ruled a "people" under a single law.[115] Individual identities were very complex—as they are in virtually every human society—but some order existed. In general the strength of medieval identities followed a flattened "U" shape.[116] The strongest identities stemmed from membership in families and clans on one end of the U and the Roman Church on the other. Identification with a king and nation (represented by the center of the U) was relatively weak—a relationship that would be reversed by the eighteenth century. The unity of Western culture gave medieval Europeans a strong supranational identity, matched only by the strength of local ties.

The West's unity and distinctiveness were most noticeable when set alongside the East.[117] Western Christendom between 500 and 1300 grew progressively distinct from Byzantium's version of Christian society. Deep common elements existed in theology, liturgy, ecclesiastical organization, monastic life, and iconography. But the growing differences overwhelmed the commonalities, as attested by Nicetas Choniates, who wrote during the reign of Emperor Manuel I: "The accursed Latins . . . between them and us there is a wide gulf of hatred, our outlooks are completely different, and our paths go in opposite directions."[118] Evidence for such an assessment abounds. The lingua franca of the East was Greek, not Latin; Eastern tastes were more cosmopolitan and refined; Eastern liturgical art and iconography were more devotional than educational; the Eastern churches were built on a square plan with domed roofs rather than on a cruciform plan with soaring spires; and in the East the finer points of theology were so important that they could bring down an emperor. Monasteries in the East were often located in urban areas, but the monks there were less intellectual, less likely to achieve secular influence, and more likely to be the party of political opposition than in the West.[119] And, of course, the East's refusal to take direction from the papacy guaranteed that the cultural differences would remain.

The West had, in fact, forged a new civilization out of the Classical, Christian, and Germanic elements that had so violently collided in the Western heartland in the fifth through the seventh centuries. The resulting culture was no longer Constantinian; it was rougher, cruder, and, ultimately, more creative than its Byzantine sister. It was initially fueled by Frankish power, but its political manifestation was not secular empire but sacred Church.

The Sacred Foundations of European Identity

We have reviewed in some detail the emergence of "Christendom" as a single political and cultural formation. The marriage of universal empire to universal religion in the Latin Church—most specifically and tangibly, in the person of the pope—created for the disparate peoples of Western Europe a common culture that formed the basis for a continental sense of community and identity. Europe, for all its ethnic and regional differences, was bound together by Roman history, orthodox beliefs, a common language of the literate, a sacred text, a holy liturgy, a style of art and architecture, an ecclesiastical law, and a system of taxation—all promoted and enabled by an organized, bureaucratic Church intent on ruling the world in justice and peace in the name of the One True King. Christendom was one in belief, practice, and governance—at least in theory, which in this instance is what really matters.

In his masterful little book *Europe: The Emergence of an Idea*, Denys Hay traces the identity built on this common culture. The common "European" identity was first based on the intertwining of Rome and the Church: "To be a Christian after Constantine was to be a Roman."[120] By the eleventh century "Christendom," or *Christianitas*, had become the domain of all Christians. By the fourteenth and fifteenth centuries "Christendom" had taken on a geographic meaning and had become identified with "Europe."[121] By the sixteenth century the two words were being used interchangeably to indicate that Christendom had clear geographical boundaries on the European Continent.[122]

European identity before the sixteenth century also required an "other." Pagans and heretics helped to define Christians; but nothing compelled a deeper "territorial view of Christianity" than the attacks on Christians carried out by Muslims.[123] Islam's military success in North Africa and the Middle East pushed the boundaries of Christendom back to those of the European Continent—and beyond, into Spain and France. Christendom's response, in the form of the Crusades, became a permanent feature of Christian activity and a critical element in European identity as it developed from the eleventh through the seventeenth centuries.[124]

We have also learned from our review of European history that medieval Christian identity—European identity, by the late Middle Ages—rested firmly on sacred foundations. Christendom was the Kingdom of God on Earth. Popes, emperors, and kings all claimed a sacred right to rule. Sometimes, their competing claims led to conflict; more often, they were content to live with the ambiguities. But no one doubted that God himself ruled through his chosen servants and that the people of Christendom were the chosen people of God. These happy tribes could trace their ancestry to the biblical Noah and his son Japheth, the father of Europe.[125] It was for them that Christ had died and through them that Christ made good on his promise to remain present on the Earth. Salvation was found in the orthodox Catholic Church, into which all were baptized. And it was to them that Christ would return to judge the Earth.

As the people of God, Christendom had a divine mission. The Christian rulers of the East had failed to protect the holy sites of Jerusalem. Heretics and infidels had overrun the very ground where Jesus and the apostles had walked. Moreover,

Muslims threatened to overrun all of Europe, spelling doom for Christendom in the Latin West. Europe would need to save Christendom. As Pope Urban II declared in his call for the First Crusade, it was up to the peoples of the Latin West to take hold of the cross of Christ and to pledge their fortunes and their lives to the holy task of freeing Jerusalem from the enemies of Christ—and protecting Latin Christendom in the process. God had appointed Europe to save his sacred lands and his Catholic Church.[126]

Finally, Christendom had its sacred heroes. Every pope was Saint Peter's successor; every emperor was a king and priest in the image of David and Solomon. But beyond the biblical archetypes were the historical figures who inspired the rulers of Christendom: Constantine, Charlemagne, Otto I, Leo the Great, Gregory the Great, Gregory VII, and Innocent III. And then there were the hundreds of saints whose lives and relics were revered across the Continent. These heroes were also stones in the sacred foundation of Christendom. The people of Christendom shared an identity grounded in a sacred common culture that gripped the heart and soul. Although parts of Europe were not always well incorporated into the dominant culture and governance structure, there was, nevertheless, an undeniable unity that covered Christendom like a sacred canopy.[127]

Then, one October day in 1517, everything changed.

Notes

1. We draw the term "common roots" from Robert E. Webber, *Common Roots: Call to Evangelical Maturity* (Grand Rapids: Zondervan, 1979).

2. Jaroslav Pelikan, *Jesus through the Centuries: His Place in the History of Culture* (New Haven, CT: Yale University Press, 1985), 221. See also Rodney Stark, *The Rise of Christianity: How the Obscure, Marginal Jesus Movement Became the Dominant Religious Force in the Western World in a Few Centuries* (New York: HarperCollins, 1997).

3. Quoted in "Catholic," in *Basilica-Chambers*, vol. 2 of *The New Schaff-Herzog Encyclopedia of Religious Knowledge*, ed. Samuel Macauley Jackson (Grand Rapids: Baker Book House, 1958), 457.

4. Ibid.

5. Ibid.

6. Erwin Gahlbusch, "Catholic, Catholicity," trans. Geoffrey W. Bromiley in *A–D*, vol. 1 of *The Encyclopedia of Christianity*, ed. Erwin Fahlbusch, Jan Mili Lochman, John Mbiti, Jaroslav Pelikan, and Lukas Vischer (Grand Rapids: William B. Eerdmans, 1999), 373.

7. *Catechism of the Catholic Church* (New York: Doubleday, 1994), 53.

8. Ibid., 224.

9. Ibid., 267.

10. Martin Van Creveld, *The Rise and Decline of the State* (Cambridge: Cambridge University Press, 1999), 35–52.

11. Sergio Bertelli, *The King's Body: Sacred Rituals of Power in Medieval and Early Modern Europe*, trans. R. Burr Litchfield (University Park: Pennsylvania State University Press, 2001), 10.

12. Ernest Barker, "The Conception of Empire," in *The Legacy of Rome*, ed. Cyril Bailey (Oxford: Clarendon Press, 1923), 48–49.

13. Ibid., 52.

14. Posidonius, as quoted by Barker, "Conception of Empire," 54.

15. This is a Greek inscription quoted in ibid., 59.

16. Ibid., 61.

17. Michael Grant, *History of Rome* (New York: Charles Scribner's Sons, 1978), 249.

18. Will Durant, *Caesar and Christ: A History of Roman Civilization and of Christianity from Their Beginnings to AD 325*, vol. 3 of *The Story of Civilization* (New York: Simon & Schuster, 1944), 214.

19. Ibid., 226.

20. Ibid., 226–27. See also Grant, *History of Rome*, 249–51.

21. Grant, *History of Rome*, 249–51.

22. Edward Gibbon, *The Decline and Fall of the Roman Empire*, vol. 1 (New York: Heritage Press, 1946), 61. Gibbon's rosy assessment would surely have been disputed by the victims of Hadrian's ruthless crushing of the Second Jewish Revolt in AD 132–35.

23. J. B. Bury, *From the Death of Theodosius I to the Death of Justinian*, vol. 1 of *History of the Later Roman Empire* (New York: Dover, 1958), 12. Before Diocletian the precise status of the living emperor was not entirely clear. Pliny the Younger wrestled with the problem and determined that while the emperor had a unique relationship with the gods that would lead to deification if he ruled virtuously, he was not a god until the Senate declared him such; Daniel N. Schowalter, *The Emperor and the Gods: Images from the Time of Trajan* (Minneapolis: Fortress Press, 1993), 5–80. Thus, in theory, an emperor did not join the Roman pantheon until his death. In practice, however, Romans, with the state's encouragement, worshiped the genius of the emperor in much the same way as they worshipped the gods. Pliny himself reported to the Emperor Trajan in 112 that he let those accused of being Christians go free if they "both worshipped your statue and the images of the gods, and cursed Christ"; Pliny the Younger, "Correspondence between Pliny and Trajan, 112," in *The Great Documents of Western Civilization*, ed. Milton Viorst (New York: Barnes & Noble, 1965), 11. For Pliny, worship of the emperor's statue may have been an act of loyalty and patriotism, while worship of the gods was purely religious, but in practice the difference appears trivial. A religious aura surrounded the emperor, making it impossible to separate his political and religious personas. Political honor was religious honor; religious honor was political honor.

24. Grant, *History of Rome*, 400–401.

25. For a detailed analysis of the causes of the Great Persecution, see W. H. C. Frend, *The Rise of Christianity* (Philadelphia: Fortress Press, 1984), 452–63.

26. Durant, *Caesar and Christ*, 652.

27. Constantine was not actually baptized until May 21, 337, the eve of his death. He did, however, clearly identify himself as a Christian by 323, when he took sole possession of the throne. Durant, *Caesar and Christ*, 655.

28. Steven Runciman, *The Byzantine Theocracy* (Cambridge: Cambridge University Press, 1977), 162–63.

29. Ibid., 1–2. See also Pelikan, *Jesus through the Centuries*, 54.

30. Frend, *Rise of Christianity*, 523.

31. Ramsay MacMullen, *Constantine* (New York: Dial Press, 1969), 197–98.

32. Constantine did not assume the sacramental functions of a priest, but he did refer to himself as a "bishop of those outside the church"; ibid., 236.

33. The Donatist controversy pit upper-class establishment bishops, who advocated reconciliation with those Christians who had renounced Christ under persecution, against generally lower-class Christians (eventually called Donatists), who had suffered as "confessors" and did not want to reconcile with unrepentant "betrayers."

34. Frend, *Rise of Christianity*, 497.

35. Ibid., 499.

36. George Ostrogorsky, *History of the Byzantine State*, trans. Joan Hussey (New Brunswick, NJ: Rutgers University Press, 1969), 28.

37. Runciman, *Byzantine Theocracy*, 4.

38. For a short history of this period, see J. B. Bury, *The Invasion of Europe by the Barbarians* (New York: W. W. Norton, 1967).

39. See Peter Brown, *Through the Eye of a Needle: Wealth, the Fall of Rome, and the Making of Christianity in the West, 350–550 AD* (Princeton, NJ: Princeton University Press, 2012); and Peter Brown, *The Rise of Western Christendom: Triumph and Diversity, AD 200–1000*, 2nd ed. (Malden, MA: Blackwell, 2003); Frend, *Rise of Christianity*, 728; Geoffrey Barraclough, *The Medieval Papacy* (New York: W. W. Norton, 1979), 26–27, 31–33.

40. See Isnard Wilhelm Frank, *A Concise History of the Mediaeval Church*, trans. John Bowden (New York: Continuum, 1996), 19–30.

41. See Christopher Dawson, *The Formation of Christendom* (New York: Sheed & Ward, 1967).

42. On the importance of the monastic movement, see Christopher Dawson, *Religion and the Rise of Western Culture* (New York: Sheed & Ward, 1950); Richard Fletcher, *The Barbarian Conversion: From Paganism to Christianity* (New York: Henry Holt, 1997); Thomas Cahill, *How the Irish Saved Civilization: The Untold Story of Ireland's Heroic Role from the Fall of Rome to the Rise of Medieval Europe* (New York: Doubleday, 1995); and Marjorie Rowling, *Life in Medieval Times* (New York: Paragon Books, 1968).

43. Constantine himself looked to Pope Miltiades to help him settle the Donatist controversy in 313.

44. Examples include Amandus, a seventh-century monk and bishop, who pursued his evangelistic activities from the Basque country to the Slavic regions as a representative of the pope and the Frankish king (Dagobert I). The latter backed Amandus's efforts with royal wealth, and—so it seems—coercion on occasion. See Fletcher, *Barbarian Conversion*, 147–54, 204–13; and Norman F. Cantor, *The Civilization of the Middle Ages* (New York: HarperPerennial, 1993), 167–71.

45. R. W. Southern, *Western Society and the Church in the Middle Ages* (New York: Penguin Books, 1970), 61.

46. C. Warren Hollister, *Medieval Europe: A Short History*, 8th ed. (New York: McGraw-Hill, 1998), 92.

47. Heinrich Fichtenau, *The Carolingian Empire: The Age of Charlemagne*, trans. Peter Munz (New York: Harper & Row, 1957), 18.

48. See J. M. Wallace-Hadrill, *The Barbarian West, 400–1000* (New York: Barnes & Noble, 1985), 92–93.

49. Louis Halphen, *Charlemagne and the Carolingian Empire*, trans. Giselle de Nie (Amsterdam: North-Holland, 1977), 17, 23–25.

50. See H. W. Carless Davis, *Charlemagne (Charles the Great): The Hero of Two Nations* (New York: G. P. Putnam's Sons, 1899), 123–25.

51. This is not the place to explore the many complex interpretations of Charlemagne's coronation. For excellent discussions, see Halphen, *Charlemagne*; Davis, *Charlemagne*; Roger Collins, *Charlemagne* (Toronto: University of Toronto Press, 1998); Heinrich Fichtenau, *The Carolingian Empire*; and Friedrich Heer, *The Holy Roman Empire*, trans. Janet Sondheimer (New York: Frederick A. Praeger, 1968).

52. Davis, *Charlemagne*, 209.

53. Irene killed her son, Emperor Constantine VI, in 797.

54. "And as the title of an emperor had then come to an end among the Greeks, since they had a woman on the imperial throne, it seemed to Pope Leo and the holy fathers assembled at the council as well as to the rest of the Christian people that they should give the title of emperor to Charles, King of the Franks." See "The Annals of Lorsch, c. 800," in *Medieval Europe: A Short Sourcebook*, 3rd edition, ed. C. Warren Hollister, Joe W. Leedom, Marc A. Meyer, and David S. Spear (New York: McGraw-Hill, 1997), 87; and John Julius Norwich, *A Short History of Byzantium* (New York: Vintage Books, 1997), 119.

55. For the text, see "The Donation of Constantine," in *Medieval Europe*, ed. Hollister et al., 79–82.

56. Barker, "Conception of Empire," 87.

57. Charles had earlier betrothed his daughter Rotrud to Irene's young son, the future Constantine VI, as a way of uniting his realm to the Empire. The plans came to naught after disputes over

Italian lands and a second Council of Nicaea (787) soured relations between the Franks and the Byzantines. See Collins, *Charlemagne*, 71–73.

58. This account of Charlemagne's eastern policy was drawn from Judith Herrin, *The Formation of Christendom* (Princeton, NJ: Princeton University Press, 1987), 464–66; and Davis, *Charlemagne*, 212–13.

59. Frank, *Concise History*, 27–30, 40. See also Geoffrey Barraclough, *The Crucible of Europe: The Ninth and Tenth Centuries in European History* (Berkeley: University of California Press, 1976), 23.

60. Herrin, *Formation of Christendom*, 434–44.

61. Fichtenau, *Carolingian Empire*, 47.

62. Herrin, *Formation of Christendom*, 446–47.

63. In the eighth century the pope actually forbade the use of the imperial title "king and priest" because it bordered on deification. See Fichtenau, *Carolingian Empire*, 57.

64. Ibid., 69.

65. Dawson, *Christendom*, 187.

66. Ibid.

67. The empire was designated "Roman" under Otto II and "Holy" under Frederick I; Heer, *Holy Roman Empire*, 39.

68. Artistic depictions of Otto III with his head in Heaven (being anointed by God) and his body on Earth make this point clear. See "Otto III in Majesty, From the Aachen Gospels, c. 1000," in *Medieval Europe*, ed. Hollister et al., 196–97.

69. Heer, *Holy Roman Empire*, 150.

70. Ibid., 117.

71. Much in this section is drawn from Barraclough, *Papacy*, 39–61.

72. Heer, *Holy Roman Empire*, 22.

73. The crown was added to the same conical-shaped cap to which a diadem had been added to the base sometime after the fourth century. By the fifteenth century, a third crown had been added, making the headdress a triple crown, or *triregnum*. In papal ideology the three crowns represented spiritual supremacy, temporal dominion, and suzerainty over all other monarchs. See Valérie Pirie, *The Triple Crown: An Account of the Papal Conclaves from the Fifteenth Century to the Present Day* (New York: Consortium Books, 1976), vii.

74. Walter Ullmann, *The Growth of Papal Government in the Middle Ages: A Study of the Ideological Relation of Clerical to Lay Power* (London: Methuen, 1970), 311; Colin Morris, *The Papal Monarchy: The Western Church from 1050 to 1250* (Oxford: Clarendon Press, 1989), 130.

75. Gregory VII, "Dictatus Papae, 1075," in *Great Documents*, ed. Viorst, 47–49. See also Brian Tierney, *The Crisis of Church and State, 1050–1300* (Englewood Cliffs, NJ: Prentice Hall, 1964), 45–52.

76. *Great Documents*, ed. Viorst, 72–73.

77. Heer, *Holy Roman Empire*, 76.

78. See James M. Powell, *Innocent III: Vicar of Christ or Lord of the World?* 2nd ed. (Washington, DC: Catholic University of America Press, 1994); and Jane Sayers, *Innocent III: Leader of Europe 1198–1216* (London: Longman, 1994).

79. Barker, "Conception of Empire," 88.

80. For interesting discussions of the EU as an empire, see Jan Zielonka, *Europe as Empire: The Nature of the Enlarged European Union* (Oxford: Oxford University Press, 2007); and Gary Marks, "Europe and Its Empires: From Rome to the European Union," *Journal of Common Market Studies* 50, no. 1 (2012): 1–20.

81. Morris, *Papal Monarchy*, 2; for a more detailed discussion of church rule, see Ullmann, *Growth*, 262–309.

82. Ullmann, *Growth*, 310–31.

83. Joseph H. Lynch, *The Medieval Church: A Brief History* (London: Longman, 1992), 173.

84. Ullmann, *Growth*, 331–43.

85. Charlemagne instituted the tithe in 779. The revenues it generated enabled the Church to expand rapidly and to meet better the needs of parishioners; James A. Brundage, *Medieval Canon Law* (London: Longman, 1995), 28.

86. Morris, *Papal Monarchy*, 61.

87. Lynch, *Medieval Church*, 178–80.

88. Barraclough, *Papacy*, 148–49.

89. Our main source for this section is Brundage, *Medieval Canon Law*.

90. Ibid., 123.

91. Ibid., 70–71.

92. Ibid., 96.

93. James Turner Johnson, *The Holy War Idea in Western and Islamic Traditions* (University Park: Pennsylvania State University Press, 1997), 102–12; Adriaan H. Bredero, "The Bishops' Peace of God: A Turning Point in Medieval Society?" *Christendom and Christianity in the Middle Ages: The Relations between Religion, Church, and Society*, trans. Reinder Bruinsma (Grand Rapids: William B. Eerdmans, 1994), 105n29.

94. "Pope Urban II Initiates the First Crusade, 1095, Document 12," in *Great Documents*, ed. Viorst, 43.

95. Bredero, "Bishops' Peace," 105–7; Hollister, *Medieval Europe*, 197.

96. Will Durant, *The Age of Faith: A History of Medieval Civilization—Christian, Islamic, and Judaic—from Constantine to Dante: AD 325–1300*, vol. 4 of *The Story of Civilization* (New York: Simon & Schuster, 1950), 586.

97. Christoph T. Maier, "Mass, the Eucharist, and the Cross: Innocent III and the Relocation of the Crusade," in *Pope Innocent III and His World*, ed. John C. Moore (Aldershot, UK: Ashgate, 1999), 351.

98. Ibid., 354.

99. See Frend, *Rise of Christianity*, 487–88. For a riveting account of the growth of the church in ancient Rome, see Stark, *Rise of Christianity*.

100. Dawson, *Christendom*, 119.

101. Ibid.

102. Gibbon, *Decline and Fall*, 22.

103. Tertullian, *On Prescription against Heretics*, quoted by Pelikan, *Jesus through the Centuries*, 64.

104. See Kenneth Scott Latourette, *Beginnings to AD 1500*, vol. 1 of *A History of Christianity* (New York: Harper & Row, 1953), 145–51.

105. Pelikan, *Jesus through the Centuries*, 58. See also Dawson, *Christendom*, 145–46.

106. Dawson, *Christendom*, 136–39.

107. Barraclough, *Crucible*, 20.

108. Mark A. Noll, *Turning Points: Decisive Moments in the History of Christianity*, 2nd ed. (Grand Rapids: Baker Academic, 2000), 122.

109. This discussion of the Carolingian reforms is drawn primarily from Collins, *Charlemagne*, 102–24.

110. Ibid., 114.

111. For a comprehensive view of medieval culture, see Rowling, *Medieval Times*.

112. Marianne Jungen, *A Small Guide to Aachen Cathedral* (Aachen: Alano Herodot Verlag, 1999), 38.

113. Latin was the language of the Western elite until French supplanted it in the Late Middle Ages; Rowling, *Medieval Times*, 99–100.

114. Denys Hay, *Europe: The Emergence of an Idea* (New York: Harper & Row, 1966), 56. Latins generously extended the term "Christian" to include Byzantine Greeks, thus indicating a broad conception of Christendom. Western Christians, however, referred to non-Latins as living "*outremer*" (overseas), hinting at the deepening divide within medieval Christendom; Hay, *Europe*, 56–57.

115. This identification with a king was not the nationalism of later centuries, but neither was it insignificant. See Susan Reynolds, *Kingdoms and Communities in Western Europe, 900–1300*, 2nd ed. (Oxford: Clarendon Press, 1997), 250–61.

116. We borrow the concept from Samuel P. Huntington, *The Clash of Civilizations and the Remaking of World Order* (New York: Simon & Schuster, 1996), 268.

117. See Herrin, *Formation of Christendom*, 390–444.

118. Quoted by Ostrogorsky, *Byzantine State*, 390.

119. Runciman, *Byzantine Theocracy*, 113–34.

120. Hay, *Europe*, 23.

121. Ibid., 61.

122. Ibid., 115. See also Benjamin J. Kaplan, *Divided by Faith: Religious Conflict and the Practice of Toleration in Early Modern Europe* (Cambridge, MA: Belknap Press, 2007), 10–11.

123. Hay, *Europe*, 24.

124. Ibid., 26.

125. Ibid., 43.

126. Ibid., 32.

127. Peter L. Berger, *The Sacred Canopy: Elements of a Sociological Theory of Religion* (New York: Anchor Books, 1990).

3

Reformation and Reaction

O NE CHURCH, one empire, one chosen people, one way of life—that was the medieval ideal. Latin Christendom never quite lived up to that ideal, but the commonalities of Western culture allowed the Church and temporal rulers to maintain the appearance of unity. The Reformation, however, shattered this visible union, as Protestants and Catholics struggled over theology, political ideas, and church structures. What eventually emerged were two confessional cultures—one Catholic, maintaining the core of the medieval ideal while adjusting to the rise of the nation-state; and one Protestant, legitimating the spiritual and temporal fragmentation of Christendom and fostering new national identities. This rupture was so catastrophic that the cultural and political shock waves still reverberate.

Theological Conflict and the Fragmentation of the Catholic Church

The great sixteenth-century reformers set out to *reform* the ancient Church, not to create a new one. Corruption and heresy had crept into the Roman Church, veiling the Gospel and leading the innocent astray. The goal of the early Protestants, particularly Martin Luther in Germany and Huldrych Zwingli in Switzerland, was profoundly conservative, calling the Church back to its roots.[1] When the Catholic Church rejected their charges and marked them as heretics, the reformers had no choice but to separate. But how could they justify the fragmentation of the Church?

Legitimating Fragmentation: Visible Division, Invisible Unity

Protestants retained key elements of Catholic ideology. Relying on Scripture to reconstruct the Church, they affirmed the universality of the Gospel. Moreover, the visible community of faith was still the universal—"catholic"—church of the Apostles' Creed. But here differences in interpretation emerged. Although the Roman Church claimed to contain all Christians, over whom it exercised full authority, the reformers denied that a Church so corrupt could include and rule the whole community of saints. Instead, the reformers drew on Saint Augustine's view that sinful humanity was incapable of participating in its own salvation; it was absolutely necessary for God, out of pure grace, to "elect" some to receive the gift of salvation and membership in his true church. This "doctrine of election" led the reformers to distinguish the *visible* and *invisible* church. The *visible* church is the Christian community gathered for worship. Because no human being can "distinguish between reprobate and elect," this church includes both saints and hypocrites.[2] The *invisible* church is the true universal church because the elect are united, not in a visible institution, but in a spiritual body. John Calvin put it this way:

> The church is called "catholic," or "universal," because there could not be two or three churches unless Christ be torn asunder—which cannot happen! But all the elect are so united in Christ that as they are dependent on one Head, they also grow together into one body, being joined and knit together as are the limbs of a body. They are made truly one since they live together in one faith, hope, and love, and in the same Spirit of God. . .
>
> Yet, to embrace the unity of the church in this way, we need not . . . see the church with the eyes or touch it with the hands. Rather, the fact that it belongs to the realm of faith should warn us to regard it no less since it passes our understanding than if it were clearly visible. And our faith is no worse because it recognizes a church beyond our ken.[3]

Although the invisible church could not be "torn asunder," the visible church certainly could. Yet Calvin conceded that even the Roman Church held a remnant of the elect: "Today we do not deprive the papists of those traces of the church which the Lord willed should among them survive the destruction."[4] The boundaries of the universal church were hidden from human eyes, but not from God's.

If the true church is invisible, then what is to become of the visible church? Luther hoped his movement would transform this church, but Rome rejected his reforms. Meanwhile, Reformation doctrine undermined church authority. Relying on the Bible as the sole guide for faith and practice meant rejecting church tradition as a source of truth. If justification (being made acceptable to God) was by faith alone, the pope no longer held the keys to Heaven and Hell. And finally, the reformers' "priesthood of all believers" meant that no priestly caste was required to mediate between sinners and God.[5]

The early reformers sought a sounder theological base for a reformed church, but more radical groups, now freed from Roman authority, began pushing to greater extremes.[6] Disorder threatened Luther's Wittenberg and Zwingli's Zurich, forcing both reformers to crack down. Luther ejected the radical Zwickau Prophets from Wittenberg in 1522 and set about drawing doctrinal boundaries around a new church; Zwingli and the Zurich City Council banned the Anabaptists, outlawed rebaptizing, and executed four men who refused to obey the law.

Luther, Zwingli, and, later, Calvin and Martin Bucer took steps to bring order to the Reformation, in part by reinforcing the visible church. Each held to the ideal of Christendom: a single church uniting all citizens, working in alliance with civil authority. Rooted in medieval conceptions of the unity of Christian society, the reformers could not conceive of a divided church within one polity. In any such case, at least one church would be apostate, and it would be the duty of both the civil and ecclesiastical authorities to punish the heretics and restore unity. Baptism was the key to church unity. Luther instinctively rejected the Zwickau Prophets' practice of believers' baptism (administered only to adults who confessed faith in Jesus Christ) without making it a major issue; but Zwingli fought a greater battle with the Anabaptists, who would purify the church by excluding unbelievers.[7] For them, church membership required a confession of faith and baptism (usually for a second time, because they did not consider an earlier infant baptism as legitimate), as mandated by Scripture.[8] Zwingli, however, recognized the danger to "Christendom" if citizens rejected or ignored the rite of baptism, for church membership would then become voluntary, undermining the church's universality and social authority. Heretical or godless citizens might then live freely apart from the church.[9] Society would be divided, purity compromised, and God displeased. Therefore, Zwingli enforced infant baptism, borrowing Luther's view that the rite was the church's equivalent of Hebrew circumcision, a practice by which *all* entered the community of faith. Inevitably, the visible church would include both the reprobate and the righteous. As Calvin put it, "In this church are mingled many hypocrites who have nothing of Christ but the name and outward appearance."[10] Still, the visible church was absolutely essential for nurturing and disciplining its baptized members.[11]

The reformers affirmed a vital role for the visible church—but which "church"? Luther's Augsburg Confession (1530) defined the church as "the congregation of saints in which the Gospel is rightly taught and the sacraments are rightly administered." The Gospel and the sacraments are thus the "marks" of the church. Calvin concurred; while Bucer, the First Scots Confession (1560), and the Belgic Confession (1561) added "church discipline" as a third mark.[12] By establishing these criteria for legitimate churches, the reformers rejected Rome's claim that the church headed by Peter's successor was, by definition, the only true church. Rather, the marks of the true church were established externally, and the church had to measure up or be declared apostate. Just as important, this standard created the possibility of multiple *legitimate* visible churches. Although none of the leading reformers considered Anabaptist communities "churches," and deep divisions existed between Lutheran and Reformed camps, they soon recognized the Protestant churches in different parts of Europe as legitimate. Churches were organized and visibly unified at the local or regional level, but they were divided by geography and political jurisdiction. The physical division of the Protestant churches proved politically difficult but posed no real theological problems.

More troubling were the reformers' quarrels over irritating doctrinal issues, which were exacerbated by the strong personalities of the reformers themselves. Repeated attempts between the late 1520s and the early 1540s to settle theological issues failed to produce a consensus. Emperor Charles V, desperate for peace in Germany, convened reconciliation talks between Rome and the evangelical rebels at Regensburg in 1541. As the basis for these talks, Charles accepted a version of the Augsburg Confession (the so-called Variata) that had been produced by Philipp Melanchthon and agreed to by Calvin and Bucer. Melanchthon, however, had not convinced the entire Lutheran community, most notably the furious Luther. Nor in the end could he agree with Catholics on the nature of the Eucharist.[13] The failure of the Regensburg talks ended any realistic hope of reconciling Catholics and Protestants or healing the splits within Protestantism. The visible Protestant church would need to accept both physical and doctrinal divisions.

Protestants joined Catholics in affirming the universal nature of the Christian Gospel and the universality of the church. But Protestants, inspired by the doctrine of election and the practical difficulties of unifying a church no longer held together by the authority of the pope, emphasized the universality of the *invisible* church while living with a divided *visible* church.

Defending Unity

Church reform was not restricted to Protestants; it had long been bubbling in the Catholic Church. Even before Luther, advocates for reforming doctrine, ecclesiastical organization, clerical morality, monastic orders, and popular piety were active, although not much heeded or appreciated.[14] But Luther's success in splitting the Church convinced many loyalists that the Roman Church had to reform or die. Ironically, the reforms in what Tracy calls the "Catholic Reformation" bore some similarity to those instituted by the Protestant rebels.[15] Indeed, many of the ideological, social, and political factors that triggered the Reformation were still at work in the Catholic Church and shaped its internal reformation. But the Catholic Reformation was in spirit conservative and reactionary—a "Counter-Reformation," responding to Protestants' deep critique: "The only way to counter the Protestants was to reform the Church."[16] Thus, though the Catholic Church already possessed reforming currents, the Protestant break forced the Church to get serious about change. As Evennett put it, "The spirituality of the Counter-Reformation Church, its roots deep in the past, developed nevertheless under the pressure of outward circumstances."[17]

The Council of Trent (1545–63) laid the foundation for the Counter-Reformation.[18] The intermittent council, presided over by three popes, considered nearly every aspect of Catholic belief and practice, from the place of Scripture to the operation of cathedrals. Its decrees set out the qualifications for bishops, clarified their role as pastors, and gave them effective powers in their dioceses—reforms that finally addressed the most grievous abuses and corruptions in the Church. On doctrine, the council's decrees and canons read like commentaries on Luther and Calvin. Although common ground with Protestants existed, on crucial issues the council underlined the differences. Responding to Luther's insistence on *sola scriptura* (by Scripture alone), the council affirmed the authority of both the Bible (including the Apocrypha) and the Church's unwritten traditions.[19] The council also decreed that faith required good works, writing into canon law a condemnation of anyone believing in justification by faith alone—in effect, any Protestant.[20] And the council emphatically declared—against strong Protestant opposition—that Christ, wholly present in the bread and wine, was sacrificed in each Mass and that "this sacrifice is truly propitiatory" for the forgiveness of sins.[21] And so it went through the thorny controversies that had been set off by Luther and the reformers. When it finished, the council had methodically countered the most critical challenges to Catholicism by reaffirming the very doctrines that Protestants found most offensive, drawing a clear line between orthodox Catholic faith and the heresies of the "schismatics."

The council's emphasis on right belief required—as it had for Protestants—new methods for ensuring that first the clergy, and then the people, knew the doctrines of the faith. Thus the council commissioned a catechism (1564) that informed clergy of the content of the Catholic faith as much as it trained parishioners. New energy was also directed toward clerical education through the establishment of universities and seminaries. Once educated, bishops and priests were expected to teach their flocks by preaching regularly and catechizing the young—like Protestant pastors.

Unlike most Protestant confessions of faith, Trent's doctrinal decrees stressed that individuals contributed to their own salvation through participation in the sacraments and good works. Indeed, the push to do good in the world unleashed a spiritual renaissance that had been gathering force even before Trent.[22] Ignatius of Loyola's Society of Jesus (the Jesuits) is the most obvious example. Obedience to the Church, spiritual discipline, self-control, education, acts of charity, mission—these were hallmarks of the Jesuits, the spiritual spearhead of the Counter-Reformation. But they were only the beginning. Teresa of Avila reformed the Carmelites; Francis de Sales founded the Order of the Visitation of Holy Mary to succor the sick and the poor; Pierre de Bérulle founded the French Oratory to give spiritual direction to individuals and found schools and seminaries; and Vincent de Paul began the Congregation of the Missions to preach to the rural poor and "charities" to distribute food and clothing. In addition, lay confraternities gathered students to participate in Ignatius's *Spiritual Exercises*.[23]

Catholic spirituality, much like Protestant practice, "took individual rather than corporate or liturgical expressions."[24] This was even true of the sacraments, especially the Eucharist. The Council of Trent brought the sacraments into clear focus for Catholics by declaring unequivocally that they were "necessary unto salvation."[25] Confession and attendance at Mass became regular for most, and frequent for some—there was no absolute rule. Veneration of the host outside of the liturgy—often by processing it through the streets, as suggested by the council—also became common.[26] Pilgrimages regained popularity as Catholics sought comfort, miracles, or an experience of God at holy shrines. Tridentine priests took greater care to root out fraudulent claims, but they still promoted local pilgrimage sites and miracles associated with the relics of the saints.[27]

The Counter-Reformation, of course, also had its dark side. The Council of Trent instituted far greater uniformity of belief and practice through its doctrinal decrees and institutional reforms. It identified the boundaries of the faith and labeled outsiders "heretics and schismatics." Pope Paul III revived the Roman Inquisition in 1542, and Pope Paul IV promulgated the *Index of Forbidden Books* in 1559. Catholic lands were to be purified of heretics, and Catholic rulers did their best to comply, with those on the Italian and Iberian peninsulas being the most successful. The Spanish also tried, through purges and war, to rid the Low Countries of heretics, but they ultimately failed; and repeated Spanish attempts to invade Protestant England proved disastrous. Queen Mary burned British Protestants, but any progress toward reuniting the Church of England with Rome was reversed by Elizabeth I. The Counter-Reformation was far more successful in Hungary and Poland, where state coercion was softened by Jesuit efforts to win hearts and minds.

These religious disputes had high stakes. Protestants were convinced that God had called them out from the heretical and corrupt Roman Church; Catholics were convinced of God's demand that they preserve ancient beliefs, traditions, and ecclesiastical structures—and purge the land of heretics. Both sides used violence; but there was a difference. As Kaplan points out, Protestants attacked "the paraphernalia of Catholic worship"—the images, relics, and wafers—anything that could be identified as an "idol."[28] These they smashed to show that the images were mere scraps of wood, glass, and metal. Natalie Davis points out that while the Protestants were "the champions in the destruction of religious property; . . . in bloodshed, the Catholics [were] the champions."[29] Certainly Protestants killed Catholics and Catholics smashed objects, but "Catholics seem to have feared with special intensity the bodies of 'heretics' as carriers of an infectious spiritual disease."[30] Catholics were indeed anti-Protestant. And they backed their rhetoric with deadly violence wherever they had political control.

During the sixteenth and seventeenth centuries, Europe gradually divided into separate but parallel confessional cultures. Doctrine, liturgy, spirituality, and church structure and discipline all responded to similar religious impulses—and to "other" confessional communities. Europeans desired religious conformity in their communities, but they also sought deeper spiritual lives, an individual connection to God. In this regard, Protestants were most affected, but Catholics were not far behind, transforming old traditions by giving ordinary parishioners responsibility for working out their own salvation. Both Protestants and Catholics turned their energies toward reforming religion and, ultimately, the societies these confessions shaped. The Counter-Reformation saved Catholicism in the Latin West—and in the world: "From its main basis in the Latin world, despite all its limitations, frustrations, and imperfections, the Counter-Reformation, by means of all its vigorous activities, ensured the survival into the post-medieval world of a still-persuasive, still-expanding, world form of Christianity."[31]

Political Conflict and the Victory of the Sovereign State

The Reformations fragmented Europe both theologically and politically. Protestants justified the breakup of Latin Christendom by appealing to the invisible nature of the church and by reconceiving of spiritual and temporal union at less-than-universal levels. They would establish Christian society wherever they could.

Securing Protestant Europe

The early Protestants were far from secure. Catholic Europe, like a wounded elephant, reacted slowly to the Protestant rebellion; but once awakened, it landed hard blows on the new enemy. A reformed Roman Church rolled back the Reformation in France, Southern Germany, the southern provinces of the Spanish Netherlands, Poland, Bohemia, and Hungary, drawing on the military might of Catholic princes and the evangelistic zeal of the Jesuits—often with great loss of life on both sides. Such efforts narrowly failed to return England, Scotland, Holland, and Scandinavia to the Catholic fold. Rome desperately wanted to reunite the Western church, but it refused to modify the Church's Tridentine theology or pope-centered structure. Reevangelization and military conquest were the only solutions for a disintegrating Christendom.

Faced with such a determined foe, the reformers needed political and military protection to survive. Some princes were willing to take up their cause, but medieval universalism left such allies, particularly in the Holy Roman Empire, vulnerable to external intervention.[32] The emperor had an ancient duty to enforce uniformity in the Latin West, but Protestants were keen to revoke that mandate. The battle was between mutually exclusive political positions.

Early during the Reformation, however, a possible solution to the religious crisis began to take shape. Hope appeared first in the Swiss Alpine valleys of the Graubünden, when as early as 1526 political and religious leaders allowed each town to choose which church, Catholic or Reformed, to maintain. Outside interference was proscribed. Remarkably, this plan worked. The Graubünden principle made its way to Augsburg in 1555 where, after the German Protestant forces achieved military supremacy over the bungling Emperor Charles V, the Catholic and Protestant negotiators agreed that each ruler would choose the religion of the land—either Catholic or Lutheran—without external interference.[33] Uniformity was expected within each realm, but dissenters could emigrate. Thus, the Peace of Augsburg established the principle of *cuius regio, eius religio*: "Where you come from decides your religion, and within that region no other can be tolerated."[34] Augsburg advanced religious freedom for princes, but did not give citizens the right to choose their church. This tied German Protestants inextricably to the state—the freedom of the prince guaranteed the freedom of the Protestants.

The Augsburg agreement, which neither side viewed as ideal, brought peace to Germany for fifty years, but it did not extend to the growing Reformed churches and much of the Continent. Both Catholic and Protestant leaders, fired by religious zeal, believed that the holy struggle between the forces of God and evil would soon reach an inevitable climax. The Protestant Union and the Catholic League each made plans for total victory. The Thirty Years' War (1618–48), Europe's first devastating world war, began as a spirited Bohemian revolt against the Hapsburgs and ended in exhaustion with the Treaty of Westphalia (1648). During this war, the Catholics made significant territorial gains; but through the treaty Protestants—both Lutheran and Reformed—achieved a protective settlement that extended to all of Europe.[35] The treaty and the norms of international politics developing from it established states as independent, sovereign entities that "never can or ought to be molested therein by any whomsoever upon any manner of pretence."[36] Religion was no longer a legitimate cause of war; Protestants were safe in their various states.

The arrival of the modern international state system marked a triumph for Protestants and a defeat for Catholics. Emperor Ferdinand III admitted his "substantial misgivings with regard to the confessional and dynastic concessions made during the peace [of Westphalia] negotiations." Pope Innocent X went further, dramatically condemning the Treaty of Westphalia as "null, void, invalid, iniquitous, unjust, damnable, reprobate, inane, empty of meaning and effect for all time."[37] From 1648 on, Catholics would see injustice and heresy at the heart of the new European system; Protestants would see liberty. This was not a struggle for freedom of conscience for the individual, but freedom for the Protestant community to conform to Scripture in belief and practice.[38] Religious freedom required political freedom to make decisions for the Christian commonwealth. Once political freedom was achieved, however, the church and state had to work out a new relationship.

From Single Empire to Christian Commonwealth

For Protestants, the church could be visibly fragmented but invisibly united. And what was true of the church could also be true of the empire. According to Calvin each church, appropriately constituted, was united in Christ; no earthly head was needed. Similarly, small groups needed single leaders, "but what prevails among the few is not to be applied directly to the whole Earth, over which no one person is competent to rule."[39] Protestants saw no scriptural or theological mandate for universal rule. Christ could rule his church and the world without the presence of a visible empire. A fragmented political system was justified, and even desirable, if division could prevent evil from ruling unchecked.

The early reformers all came to terms with political division. Luther initially dreamed of a reformed Latin Church supported by an equally reformed empire, but he later confined his vision of Christendom to the German nation as individual rulers declared for the Reformation, while the Hapsburgs and other German Catholic princes remained committed to Rome.[40] Zwingli's great ambition was to unite the Swiss cantons under the Reformation banner, but he died on a Kappel battlefield in 1531, leaving Switzerland forever divided between Catholic and Protestant cantons. Although Calvin and Bucer hoped that France might cut its ties to Rome and purify its church, they had to be content with establishing godly city-states in Geneva and Strasbourg.[41]

Christendom was important to Protestants, but preserving Christendom did not require the preservation of a *single* visible, worldwide church—or a *single* visible empire. Christian governance could survive at the local or national level; it was not political union that mattered, but spiritual union as ordered by divine providence. Thus, the Reformation gave ideological justification and support for ecclesiastical *and* political fragmentation in Europe.

Protestants justified the division of Europe, however, while simultaneously maintaining a commitment to Christendom, a commitment they shared with Catholics. In practice, Protestant Europe simply applied a refined set of characteristics of Christendom to smaller social and political units. Medieval Latin Europe had always been concerned with right belief, holy living, and loyalty to God's appointed spiritual and temporal authorities. The division of Europe, however, sharpened these characteristics, as religious and political leaders defined the boundaries of their (much smaller) confessional communities—whether villages, regions, or nations.

Medieval Christians knew very little doctrine. Their religion consisted of ritual prayers to honored saints and the Blessed Virgin Mary, feast and fast days, pilgrimages, parades, ribbons, and relics. Lay people received little instruction and heard few sermons from their priests. But all this changed after the Reformation. Protestants especially were bombarded with religious instruction through frequent sermons, instructional pamphlets, new liturgies and hymns, revamped rituals, and rigorous church discipline. Children received instruction at home, at school, and in special catechism classes. And much of this teaching was theological. Protestants identified themselves by their "confessions"—statements of fundamental doctrine—and thus they required that community members conform to the official system of belief.

Such a dispassionate account of the new ideological boundaries misses the emotion behind these new confessions of faith. Protestants believed that error had crept into the church; God's very honor was at stake. Purifying the church meant first establishing right doctrine by examining the Scriptures, then removing from the visible church those who deviated from the truth. Heretics were to repent. If they refused, they were to be handed over to the secular authorities for punishment. Sometimes the punishment was severe. *All* the Christian confessions—Catholic, Lutheran, and Reformed—affirmed the need to put unrepentant heretics to death. Calvin sums up the general sentiment: "Those who would spare heretics and blasphemers are themselves blasphemers."[42] The honor of God demanded a Christian Commonwealth zealous for the truth. Failure to maintain doctrinal purity would incur God's displeasure and his punishment of famine, pestilence, or war.

A Christian commonwealth also meant pure living. Again, the religious and secular authorities cooperated to ensure that society conformed to the laws of God. Acting as one, they built churches, appointed pastors and priests, established acceptable modes of worship, adopted liturgies, declared holidays, and enforced church discipline. In addition, religious considerations shaped the laws governing church attendance, moral behavior, business contracts, bank lending, public speech, and every other imaginable activity. The medieval authorities had, of course, governed Christendom in a similar fashion. But the difference after the Reformation was in the tightness of confessional communities. Western Christendom was sprawling and gangly; conformity was more an ideal than a reality. In fragmented Europe, where confessional communities were smaller, the authorities found it easier to enforce uniformity.[43]

Finally, in addition to pure doctrine and holy living, the Christian commonwealth meant a fusion of religious and political authority, making piety and patriotism one.[44] If God indwelt his church, ordered society according to his law, and appointed rulers to govern in his name, then religious dissent was treason and political rebellion heresy. Toleration of heresy was sure to bring on the wrath of God. And religious minorities with sympathies for coreligionists beyond the borders were suspected traitors. Huguenots in France, Catholics in England and the Netherlands, Lutherans in Poland—all were threats to the Christian commonwealth.

Clearly, the stakes were high for anyone challenging religious or secular authority. Where two or more confessional communities were in close contact—as in Germany, Switzerland, France, the Netherlands, Poland, and England—violence often erupted. Local riots might be sparked by a holiday, procession, or funeral. French Catholics engaged in an orgy of killing in 1572, starting with the Saint Bartholomew's Day Massacre. And a century and a half of war eventually devastated the Continent. More remarkably, perhaps, religious violence was not always the norm. Most mixed communities developed creative ways of preserving the fiction of confessional purity while tolerating the presence (if unofficially) of dissenting communities. Church buildings were sometimes shared with minority congregations, or offending churches were hidden away or moved outside the city walls.

Processions were routed around neighborhoods. Local political power was shared. But these were accommodations for the sake of peace. Confessional communities did not alter their commitment to purity, even as they sometimes acknowledged, perhaps grudgingly, the presence of the "other."

Ecclesiastical Conflict and the Rise of the National Church

Theological conflicts divided Western Christendom into confessional communities. The fragmentation of Christendom, however, raised disturbing questions: How would separated churches govern themselves while maintaining a commitment to the unity of the "body of Christ"? And how would both the new Protestant churches and the remaining Catholic Church order their relations with the secular authorities, especially in an age of ascendant nation-states? As this section shows, Protestant churches fortunate enough to find protection under a Protestant prince became the handmaids of temporal power, while their coreligionists in Catholic countries struggled for survival, often developing organizational strategies to counter state-sponsored persecution. The Roman Church, by contrast, fought both Catholic princes and, after the French Revolution, fought liberal states for control of national churches. Although the European powers succeeded in stripping the Roman Church of its temporal authority, the Church reacted to its loss of political influence by centralizing its structure and placing absolute spiritual authority in the hands of the pope.

The Protestant Churches and the European State

As we explain below, the early modern Catholic Church was a centralized, disciplined organization and was able, despite its diversity, to speak when necessary with one voice, the voice of the Holy Father. The Protestant churches could not have been more different. The Reformation, by nature, was fragmented. Rebellions broke out here and there—in the northern Empire, in Switzerland, France, Scotland, Poland, and Hungary—sometimes arising spontaneously under the influence of Luther's writings, which were often carried by refugees from a site of persecution to one of relative peace. Religious rebels faced different political situations in their scattered locations and often drew different conclusions from Scripture over the proper structure of the new church. There was absolute agreement on one crucial point: The reformed church had no room for an authoritative single voice. There would be no Protestant pope.

The fledgling Protestant churches, nevertheless, faced difficult questions. How would the reformed churches be organized? Was a reformed church possible if rejected by secular rulers? What role would secular authority play in ecclesiastical affairs? Who would discipline church members? Would Protestant organization be international? Answers to such questions emerged in the Reformation's early decades, but the answers were diverse. By the mid–sixteenth century three ecclesiastical models had emerged: episcopal, consistorial, and congregational. Each represented a different connection between state and church, but all encouraged Protestants to look to the nation-state for protection.

THE EPISCOPAL MODEL

The episcopal model retained bishops to rule the church. Most episcopal churches were also territorial, purporting to include all members of society. Most important, the episcopal churches came under the sway of nation-building states that placed ultimate ecclesiastical authority in the hands of a secular prince.[45] The churches needed state protection, both in the dangerous years of the Counter-Reformation and later, when sectarian Protestants threatened church unity and clerical privileges. The secular princes, conversely, wanted a single church to unify their realms and discipline their citizens. Loyalty to church and king became synonymous, and episcopal Protestantism became medieval Christendom with a prince as pope.

The episcopal model developed first in Germany, where fear of the peasants' revolt and Anabaptist fanaticism forced Luther to consider princes as "emergency bishops" to restore political and religious order.[46] German monarchs, enjoying such ecclesiastical powers, used the church to unify their polities and legitimate their absolute rule. Thus, in Germany Luther's "emergency" lasted well into the twentieth century. During the Second Reich the German Evangelical Church remained organized along regional (*land*) lines. The *Landskirchen* acted as government departments serving state interests; liturgies bound the nation to the ruling dynasty, and church officials enjoyed the status of civil servants. In return, the churches accepted state supervision of appointments, finances, property administration, taxation, and laws. In addition, the state had the right to summon synods, approve synod legislation, and appoint senior prelates.[47] The English Church followed a similar path. Henry VIII's Reformation was more a declaration of political independence from continental control than a religious rebellion. But reform took hold under Henry's son, Edward VI, and the result—after much strife—was an Anglican Church with the old ecclesiastical structure (and much of the ceremony) intact, and the politically charged task of choosing bishops and ordering worship left to the monarch and, later, Parliament.[48]

The episcopal model also characterized the less familiar post-Reformation Scandinavian churches. The monarchs in Denmark-Norway and Sweden-Finland eagerly adopted a state-led church model as a key to their nation-building strategies. Danish bishops were required to obey the king, not the pope, after 1526; by 1537 Christian III had assumed leadership of the new Lutheran Church and had extended the Reformation to Norway. A similar result occurred in Sweden-Finland, where Gustav

Vasa took control of the Church after dissolving the union with Denmark. Thus in Scandinavia the Protestant church became completely identified with the state, and adherence to Lutheranism became a requirement of citizenship.

The episcopal model most closely replicated the ideals of medieval Christendom among Protestants. Church and state were united under a sacred prince who ordered and protected the realm and ensured the salvation of his people. But there was a critical difference: The king could speak as a pope, but only to the borders of the realm. The episcopal model was employed by nation-building princes to legitimate their rule and unify their people. In a new era of nation-states, it worked remarkably well in bringing order out of religious and political chaos.

THE CONSISTORIAL MODEL

The *consistorial* model characterized most Reformed churches. Unlike the episcopal model, it dispensed with bishops and relied instead on "consistories," or councils (often elected by the laity), to oversee doctrine and enforce discipline. These consistories were often linked in a tiered system from the congregation through one or two regional levels to a national body. Furthermore, while the hierarchical episcopal model was always dominated by the state, consistorial churches sometimes linked church to state in a "territorial" fashion—as occurred in Zwingli's Zurich, Calvin's Geneva, the Rhine Palatinate, Nassau, and Scotland—but often had to organize without protection from the monarch when a hostile state opposed the Reformed church. Such was the case in France and among scattered refugees in Switzerland, the Low Countries, England, and Poland.

The primary issue facing the consistorial churches was how closely the state would be tied to the church. Calvin's Geneva chose to establish parallel administrative structures, with the civil authorities governing the community and elders overseeing the church. The two administrations were intertwined, as the City Council assisted in choosing church elders and the consistory often referred cases of moral wrongdoing to the magistrates. But Geneva clearly divided the responsibilities of church and civil government for the administration of Christian society. Zurich, conversely, followed Zwingli's rejection of Luther's and Calvin's notion of church and state operating in separate spheres. The city involved civil magistrates in the administration of the territorial church and required the government to punish religious offenders. Thus, church and state were more unified in Zwingli's Zurich than in Calvin's Geneva.

The Reformed churches in Zurich and Geneva were the official churches in their territories. But the consistorial churches in France, Scotland, and Holland were initially in rebellion against Catholic governments and faced the difficult question: How were churches to exist apart from the state? In France, where churches were first established "under the cross"—independent of secular authority—church leaders linked local congregations with a hierarchy of local, provincial, and national assemblies, composed of both lay and clerical delegates. Thus, French Protestants constituted the first "Presbyterian" system, whereby control over church doctrine and leadership did not involve civil magistrates. The French had, in fact, discovered the organizational recipe for an independent church.[49] They had also, incidentally, created an efficient system of communication to aid the raising of an army to resist government aggression.

Whereas Catholic forces eventually destroyed the Protestant Church in France, Scotland and Holland adopted a French-style, consistorial church. The Scottish Protestant Church first elected elders in 1558; by 1564 Scottish Protestant rebels, with English military assistance, had acquired political power and established a new church order. Initially, the church retained bishops, but eventually presbyteries were formed and—after much conflict—bishops were eliminated in 1690. The Scottish consistorial church proved far more willing than the episcopal churches (and most other Reformed churches) to call government authorities to account for moral shortcomings.[50] It also had a deep impact on legislation. Still, the church was unable to gain supremacy over the monarch; conversely, the monarch (particularly if a Stuart) was unable to dominate the church. Thus, a tense balance characterized religious politics in Scotland. Attempts by monarchs and local aristocrats to control the appointment of ministers caused constant irritation and eventually resulted in a major schism, with the creation of the Free Church of Scotland in 1843. In 1921 Parliament granted the Church of Scotland full independence in spiritual matters, ratifying its status as a "national" rather than "state" church.

The Dutch Reformed Church was also born in persecution. Unlike the Protestant Church in France, it survived; but its triumph as an established church was not as complete as the Protestant victory in Scotland. The Reformed Church was accorded privileges within the new United Provinces, and it even became the established church of the Kingdom of the Netherlands under royal control between 1815 and 1852. But it never achieved the "territorial" status of its German Lutheran neighbors. In their commitment to religious purity, church leaders limited full membership and access to the Communion table to those who professed the Reformed faith, lived uprightly, and submitted to the discipline of the consistory. By breaking the link between church membership and national citizenship, church leaders effectively abandoned Christendom; the church community would no longer be identical with the civic community.[51] To be sure, civic leaders still meddled in ecclesiastical affairs, often to the frustration of church elders.[52] But the restriction of the church to members in good standing opened up space for religious dissenters. Tolerance would have to be extended to the "alternatively" religious or nonreligious if the church refused to take them. Zwingli had been right; once citizens could live legally outside the church, church and state had to separate, with the church losing its universal authority.

THE CONGREGATIONAL MODEL

The congregational model developed outside the boundaries of post-Reformation ecclesiastical or political control. Congregational churches organized as local bodies without oversight or governance from religious or secular authorities. They selected their own clergy and determined their doctrine, liturgy, organizational structure, and means of discipline. Self-governing congregations popped up almost everywhere in Reformation Europe. Some were believers who simply banded together for worship in hostile environments. Others, such as the Anabaptists and other Reformation radicals, were congregational by conviction. The Anabaptists, for instance, tried at Nikolsburg (1526–27) and Münster (1534–36) to govern according to their particular principles, but both attempts ended in disaster and massive persecution. As a result, the Anabaptists denounced secular authority and withdrew from society into purified conclaves, often to suffer patiently and await the end of the world.

The mainstream reformers rejected congregationalism because it led to heterodoxy and questionable moral practices. Without collective or secular oversight, congregations could strike out in any number of dangerous directions, taking many innocents with them. Congregationalism, especially the Anabaptist variety, also undermined Christendom by denying the Christian vocation of the magistrate and by abjuring Christian involvement in governing. The traditional reformers were not willing to reject the world; God had ordained the magistrate to protect the church from enemies, both Protestant and Catholic. The church could survive only if its organization included a prominent role for the state.[53]

Ironically, it was the state churches that later drifted away from Protestant orthodoxy as Enlightenment rationality and democratic revolutions undercut biblical claims to truth and royal claims to authority. The dissenter churches that sprang up in England, Holland, and Scandinavia preserved the evangelical theology and religious enthusiasm of the Reformation, but they were often organized congregationally.[54] Zealous Protestants were, by the early twentieth century, prone to abandon the state churches for nonconformist communities. Thus, the guardians of Reformation theology were not the princes but the very congregations traditional reformers feared most.

INTERNATIONAL PROTESTANTISM

By now it should be apparent that Protestant organization never achieved an international dimension. Reformers such as Heinrich Bullinger of Zurich, Thomas Cranmer of England, and John Knox of Scotland had worked to unite the churches in grand, continent-wide alliances; but all such efforts failed.[55] Although transnational Protestantism did exist, as evidenced by the heavy correspondence among reformers across boundaries, it was informal and personal.[56] Churches so tied to their national governments simply could not organize internationally unless backed by the political will of the state. Without an international religious authority—a role only a pope or emperor could play—a transnational Protestant church was simply impossible. These churches had survived by organizing themselves as national bodies dependent on secular princes to defend them against powerful Catholic armies, both Hapsburg and Jesuit. The Protestant churches and states entered into mutually dependent relationships: The churches used the states to protect and defend their spiritual liberties; the states used the churches to unify and discipline their populations. The Protestant churches were not governed by any transnational spiritual authority; nor did they want to be. Consequently, they staked more on their ties to the state authorities and bound themselves more closely to the state than did the Catholic authorities, which usually saw relations with the civil authorities in diplomatic terms, with the Church assuming the rights of a nation-state. Church–state tensions existed, especially in Scotland and the Netherlands, and Protestant churches had of necessity developed organizational structures capable of standing independent of the state; but Protestantism was most successful politically when it was tethered to the nation-state. Protestant politics thus revolved around the defense of state sovereignty.

Catholic Centralization and Papal Supremacy

The Council of Trent redefined Catholic theology for a post-Luther era and cleaned up much of the corruption that had plagued the pre-Reformation Church. But the council also recognized that decisive leadership was required to overcome the external—and internal—challenges to the Church's authority. The shattering of Christendom by the Reformation led, ironically, to the strengthening of the papacy; but the story of papal ascendance must be told alongside that of ascendant state power and rising nationalism in Catholic countries.

THE RISING NATION-STATE

Even before the Reformation, the hold of the medieval popes on the Church had been loosened. The papacy's removal to Avignon in 1309 brought popes too close to the French monarchy, thus alienating the rest of Christendom, especially Germany. The result was conciliarism, an antipapal intellectual movement designed to establish the supremacy of general councils, representing the collective will of the whole people of God. Led by William of Ockham and Marsilius of Padua, this movement elicited from the Avignon pontiffs an emphatic assertion that they were second only to God in authority and on par with the Virgin Mary and the saints in the reverence due to them.[57] But the Papal Schism of the late fourteenth century so weakened the office that the College of Cardinals called a general council to settle the dispute. The Council of Pisa (1409) failed to end the schism, but it did change the constitution of the Church—at least for a time—by empowering the College of Cardinals to call a council.[58] Six years later the Council of Constance (summoned by the Holy Roman emperor) succeeded in reunifying the papacy and, in addition, extending conciliar powers. Its authority, claimed the council, came "directly from Christ," and thus "everybody, of whatever rank or dignity, including also the pope, is bound to obey this council in those things which pertain to the faith."[59] In effect, the council displaced the pope as the supreme ecclesiastical authority.

The rise of the state also weakened the papacy. The conciliarists naturally favored secular powers in their disputes with Rome. Marsilius had argued, in fact, that the pope should be subject to the emperor. Conciliarism thus provided a vehicle for the secular authorities to assert greater control over the Church's personnel and treasure in their territories. The state's new assertiveness began in France, where the clergy and King Charles VII agreed that necessary reforms could occur only if the Church were nationalized. In 1438 Charles called a council of the French Church, which issued "the Pragmatic Sanction of Bourges," declaring the supremacy of a council to the pope. The Pragmatic Sanction also asserted the right of local clergy to elect ecclesiastical offices (in consultation with the king) and prohibited legal appeals to Rome "until every other grade of jurisdiction shall have been exhausted."[60] In short, the council nationalized the French Church and placed the king at its head (in reality, although not in name—an important distinction), a move legitimized by the 1516 Concordat of Bologna.[61] France's successful nationalization, of course, paved the way for other monarchs—Henry VIII of England and Philip II of Spain—to carve off their own pieces of the universal church.

Thus, at the time of the Reformation, the papacy was already in a weakened state. Luther's revolt exacerbated the problem by removing a third of Western Christendom from papal control and by threatening to dissolve any remaining ties that bound Catholic Europe together. Eventually, the Roman Church met the challenge of the Reformation, albeit in two seemingly contradictory ways.

First, the Church turned to the pope for leadership and wholeheartedly endorsed his ecclesiastical primacy.[62] The Council of Trent ended the threat of conciliarism by granting the pope sole authority to call councils and confirm their conclusions. In addition, the council granted the pope—not councils or secular princes—the right to shape Catholic liturgical and devotional life by assigning him the tasks of producing the official Latin Vulgate Bible; controlling the content of the Catechism, Breviary, and Missal; and maintaining the *Index of Forbidden Books*.[63] The Counter-Reformation emphasized the organizational hierarchy and the pope's position at its pinnacle, while new religious orders, namely the Jesuits, pledged their absolute obedience to the pontiff. Much of this new attention to the pope as head of the visible Church hierarchy was a reaction to Protestant fragmentation and insistence on the invisible nature of the church, but it also reflected a recognition that Catholicism's survival in a fragmenting Europe depended on obedience to a single head.

Catholic Europe rallied to the spiritual leadership of the pope, but a second strategy for surviving the Reformation pointed in the opposite direction. The various national churches, aware that the pope's political position had deteriorated, instinctively drew closer to the Catholic princes who could protect them from their Protestant foes. In exchange for security, the churches aligned themselves with the interests of the state, wedding altar to throne. The French monarchy, for instance, defeated the Huguenots' attempts to pry the country away from Catholic Europe. Catholic victory, however, meant even tighter control of the Church by the French state. The Church still acknowledged the unity of Catholicism and the primacy of the pope, but in practice it pulled away from Rome. In 1682 the aristocratic clergy and the Crown codified the position of the French Church vis-à-vis the papacy in the Four Gallican Articles, which denied papal dominion over temporal things, affirmed conciliarism, insisted on the inviolability of the rights and liberties of the Gallican Church, and denied the infallibility of the pope.[64] Pope Alexander VIII annulled the Articles in 1690, and King Louis XIV solemnly withdrew them in 1693, but Gallican principles lived on until the Council of Pistoia in 1786 made them official again. In sum, the French Church survived religious conflict by adopting the interests of the state.

A similar union of throne and altar occurred in Spain, but there the state seemed to adopt the interests of the Church. Philip II took as his primary task the defense and expansion of Catholicism, but like his father, Emperor Charles V, Philip had universalistic tendencies, which were reinforced by Spain's conquest of the New World. He saw himself as "a kind of universal bishop" who supervised the worldwide church.[65] Political and religious authority united in his person, and he freely used Church institutions—especially the Inquisition—to enforce uniformity throughout his empire. Philip never wavered in his support for the papacy, but his control of the Spanish Church and willingness to censure papal pronouncements often frustrated Rome.

The Counter-Reformation Church thus experienced two seemingly contradictory trends: the rise of papal authority, and state capture of the national churches. The Tridentine papacy was a much stronger institution than its late medieval predecessor. The pope was the unquestioned leader of Catholicism. He defined orthodoxy, guided worship, and served as a powerful symbol of Catholic unity in the midst of religious fragmentation. He also led a reformed and strengthened bureaucracy that restored moral authority and administrative effectiveness to the office. But the pope's renewed spiritual authority could not completely mask the Church's loss of political power to European states. Papal supremacy was, in fact, a reaction to the loss of Catholic political unity: "The stress on the visible signs of the church and on the primacy of the pope . . . reflected the situation of a European Catholicism now split into isolated national churches whose sense of unity depended on papal primacy, since it no longer could be developed in a community of faith that transcended national borders."[66]

REVOLUTION AND THE MODERN WORLD

The Revolution of 1789 ranks below only Constantine's conversion and Luther's posting of the Ninety-Five Theses in its impact on the Catholic Church. Constantine gave the Church a share in earthly power, while the Protestant reformers ended the Roman Church's *religious* monopoly in the West. The French revolutionaries and their fellow travelers in Europe, however, took the Reformation a step further by stripping the Catholic Church of *temporal* power. Still, despite its best efforts, the Revolution did not destroy the Church.

The French Revolution and its aftermath had three major effects on the Catholic Church. First, it overthrew the national churches. This action was especially violent and thorough in France, where church privileges, at least those associated with feudal traditions, were swept away with the aristocracy. Church property was nationalized; priests were forced to swear loyalty to a new church constitution; and for the first time since Diocletian, rulers persecuted the church as an enemy of the state. Although such violence against the Church was not repeated across Europe—and, in fact, church and state would find ways to accommodate each other—the tide had turned decisively against the Catholic Church. The national churches, once quick to align with powerful nation-states for protection, grew distrustful of the new liberal (and nationalist) states. Their only option was to turn to Rome.

Second, the French Revolution first threatened, and then eliminated, the vestiges of papal temporal authority. The story is convoluted, but worth summarizing. Napoleon Bonaparte invaded the Papal States in 1796, stopping just short of Rome when Pius VI sued for peace. The killing of a French general by a Roman mob soon provided the pretext for a new conflict, and in February 1798 the French army occupied the city. Pius VI refused to renounce temporal authority over the Papal States, so the French took him prisoner and transported him to France, where he promptly died. In 1800 the Papal States were restored, and the new pope, Pius VII, was allowed back into Rome. Papal relations with the French government soon improved, reaching a high point in 1804, when Pius VII participated, uneasily, in Napoleon's coronation as emperor of France. Relations quickly deteriorated when the pope refused to end his neutrality in foreign affairs and incorporate the Papal States into Napoleon's Continental System. As a result, the French army occupied Rome again in 1808. The next year Napoleon annexed the Papal States to his empire and announced the end of the pope's temporal power. The pope responded by excommunicating the emperor.

The continental powers restored the Papal States after Napoleon's defeat, but liberal ideas had taken root in Italy. Revolutionary activity aimed at ending papal rule unsettled Rome in 1830, with the pope regaining control only after Austrian intervention. The election of Pius IX to the papal throne in 1846 elicited great excitement among liberals, who saw him as a reformer who might reconcile papal authority with democratic governance, perhaps as the constitutional monarch of a united Italy. But after a promising start, Pius IX failed to go to war against Austria on behalf of the Italian national cause and fled Rome in 1848 after the assassination of one of his ministers. The new Constituent Assembly stripped him of his temporal power and proclaimed a Roman Republic—which, however, was short-lived.[67] French troops defeated the republican forces and restored Pius IX to power in the Papal States in July 1849; they remained to prop up his temporal power even as the rest of Italy unified in 1861. A French military contingent remained in Rome until 1870, when Napoleon III called it away to fight in the Franco-Prussian War. The Italian army then overcame token resistance and marched into Rome to abolish the Papal States, uniting Rome and its environs with the rest of the country. Pope Pius IX refused to renounce his temporal authority and confined himself for the rest of his long pontificate in the Apostolic Palace as a "prisoner in the Vatican."[68] This situation would last into the twentieth century.[69] Ironically, the papacy's nineteenth-century political travails and the end of the pope's temporal reign only served to raise the papacy's stature among Europe's Catholics and to create a wellspring of sympathy for the pontiff.

Third and finally, the French Revolution created a democratic, latitudinarian ethos in Europe antithetical to the hierarchical, dogmatic culture of the Church. Sovereignty now rested with citizens, not monarchs; the rights of the ruled trumped the claims of rulers; and truth was no longer defined from above. The monarchical church was the cultural antithesis of the new liberal polity and reacted with some vehemence to the changed environment.[70] Catholic intellectuals such as Joseph de Maistre denounced the Revolution and the totalitarian tendencies of a secular state and called for a theocratic order under papal authority. Pius IX's *Syllabus of Errors* (1864) condemned religious toleration, secular philosophy, sovereignty of the people, secular education, separation of church and state, and divorce, refusing to "reconcile himself to, and agree with, progress, liberalism, and civilization as lately introduced."[71] And contrary to liberal skepticism, Pius X "told a group of priests that the love of the Pope was an important means of sanctification. That love should be manifested in deeds as well as words; the Pope and the Vatican bureaucracy which acted in his name should be obeyed without limit."[72]

Thus the defeat of the national churches, the stripping of papal temporal authority, and the rise of modernity drove the Church more deeply into the arms of the pope. Ultramontanism—the movement demanding greater papal authority in the church—triumphed over what remained of conciliarism and Erastianism (ecclesiastical nationalism).[73] The national churches, now greatly weakened, turned to the papacy for protection from a triumphant state. And the nineteenth-century popes, who were still accorded a dignity that surpassed their temporal authority, usually sought to provide that protection through diplomatic negotiations for concordats regulating church–state relations. Perhaps more important, the Church turned to the papacy for intellectual and spiritual guidance. The pope became the infallible teacher who could instruct the faithful how to think and act in the new world. In 1854 Pius IX defined as dogma (infallible truth) the Immaculate Conception of Mary, which the Council of Trent had refused to declare dogmatic. In 1870 the First Vatican Council (1869–70) proclaimed that the pope possessed "that infallibility which the divine Redeemer intended His Church to possess when defining doctrine concerning faith and morals."[74] Eighty years later Pope Pius XII infallibly defined the doctrine of the Assumption of Mary. Thus what the popes had lost in temporal authority they seemed to have transferred to their spiritual account.

As the focus of Catholic attention, the pope (and in Rome the powerful Curia, his complex bureaucracy that governed the Church; see chapter 2) acquired unprecedented power. The pontiff had complete authority over Church doctrine and exercised increasing control over teaching in Catholic schools and universities. He appointed and deposed bishops at will and had future bishops and leaders of the church come to Rome for their educations. As the Catholic revival swept Europe in the nineteenth century, a host of Ultramontane organizations sprang up. Some were old orders, such as the restored Jesuits, but others were new religious or lay groups conducting missionary activities or performing charitable tasks. All were absolutely loyal to the pope.

Perhaps the acme of papal dominance came in the mid–twentieth century, during the reigns of Pius XI and Pius XII. Pius XI rejected the defensive stand the Church had taken in the nineteenth century and directed its mission toward re-Christianizing modern society. By strengthening the Vatican bureaucracy, encouraging Catholic mass movements, exercising tight control over religious orders and social organizations, and negotiating dozens of concordats, Pius XI sought not merely to exercise moral authority over the spiritual life of the church but also to be its ruler.[75] He failed to re-Christianize Europe as envisioned, but he did regain temporal authority over a piece of Rome (Vatican City) by signing the Lateran Accords in 1929. By becoming head of state of the Holy See, the pope reclaimed the dignity of a temporal prince.

Pius XII continued his predecessor's policy. He had been trained as a papal diplomat and had been involved in many negotiations under Pius XI, and he preferred quiet diplomacy to public condemnations—a strategy that made him reluctant to attack totalitarian fascism.[76] For all its moral ambiguity, Pius XII's strategy of nonconfrontation allowed the Church to operate virtually intact throughout Europe during World War II. Moreover, Pius XII continued the process of spiritual and administrative centralization. As a result, the papacy emerged from the war remarkably undamaged and confident. Pius XII, despite criticism, expressed no remorse for his failure to vocally condemn fascism or the Nazis' treatment of Jews during the war.[77] He continued to exercise the full powers of his office in a self-assured manner: In 1949 he excommunicated all communists; and in 1950, as noted above, he invoked papal infallibility in declaring the Assumption of the Virgin Mary.[78] These were not acts of political or spiritual timidity. The nineteenth-century and early-twentieth-century papacy remained a resolute countercultural force in a liberal age.

Culture War and the Rise of Protestant Anti-Catholicism

Protestants built their confessional culture around the reformed church and sovereign state. They also based it on a deep anti-Catholicism that provided the movement with its popular energy—and a source of identity. Protestants thus identified themselves as the "not-Catholic" party—the antithesis of "Catholic." They were proud to be anti-Catholic, and especially antipapal. Anti-Catholicism permeated the highest and lowest rungs of society; it saturated community policy and foreign policy; it inspired laws and spawned holidays. Very early, anti-Catholicism became a mark of Protestantism that worked its way into every corner of Protestant confessional culture. Here we explore this ideology as it developed in the core areas of Germany, Switzerland, and France, and then as it settled into what became Protestant northern Europe: England, Scandinavia, and the Netherlands.

The Early Reformers

The early reformers—by definition—were anti-Catholic. Horrified by the sale of ecclesiastical offices, the immorality of the priesthood, the greed of the monasteries, the misuse of canon law, and the spiritual poverty of the laity, the reformers laid blame at the feet of the pope and the clerical establishment. For them, the pure Christian faith, derived from Scripture and affirmed in the great creeds of the church, had been obscured by the human-made policies and practices of an evil hierarchy. Thus Rome, and particularly the pope, became the focus of their increasingly harsh rhetoric.

Luther's 1520 treatise "To the Christian Nobility of the German Nation" accused the pope of serving the forces of evil. In a particularly vivid section on indulgences and absolutions (papal instruments used to absolve recipients of sin and its consequences, often for a price), Luther loosed a searing attack on Rome:

> . . . for payment of money they make unrighteousness into righteousness. . . . They assert that the pope has the authority to do this. It is the devil who tells them to say these things. They sell us doctrine so satanic, and take money for it, that they are teaching us sin and leading us to Hell.
>
> If there were no other trickery to prove that the pope is the true Antichrist, this one would be enough to prove it. Hear this, O pope, not of all men the holiest but of all men the most sinful! O that God from Heaven would soon destroy your throne and sink it in the abyss of Hell! Who has given you authority to exalt yourself above your God, to break and loose his commandments, and teach

Christians . . . to be inconstant, perjurers, traitors, profligates, and faithless? God has commanded us to keep word and faith even with an enemy, but you have taken it upon yourself to loose his commandment and have ordained in your heretical, anti-Christian decretals that you have his power. Thus through your voice and pen the wicked Satan lies as he has never lied before. . . . What else is papal power but simply the teaching and increasing of sin and wickedness? Papal power serves only to lead souls into damnation in your name and, to all outward appearances, with your approval![79]

By the end of his life, Luther was referring to the papacy as "an institution of the devil" and to Pope Paul III as the "Most Hellish Father."[80]

As Luther well illustrates, the reformers were virulently "antipapal." Committed to the universal (albeit invisible) church, they questioned the pontiff's assertion of divine authority and supremacy in Christendom.[81] Too often, in their view, the popes and "Romanists" had used this claim to defend corrupt and deceitful practices. The reformers had drawn back the veil to reveal Rome as the source of evil. As Calvin lamented, "The world today is flooded with so many perverse and impious doctrines, full of so many kinds of superstitions, blinded by so many errors, drowned in such great idolatry—there is none of these evils anywhere that does not flow from the Roman see, or at least draw strength there."[82] The pope was the human face of evil, the embodiment of all that was corrupt, false, and destructive in the Church, an enemy bent on the destruction of "the reviving doctrine of the Gospel."[83] Such a tool of Satan must be the feared enemy of the kingdom of God—the "Antichrist."

The Bible speaks of the "Antichrist" in two senses. The Antichrist in the first sense is any person who stands opposed to Christ and his kingdom. Such "Antichrists" may be outsiders attacking the church, or even church leaders whose false teachings eventually prove them to be enemies of Christ. The writer of II John says: "Many deceivers, who do not acknowledge Jesus Christ as coming in the flesh, have gone out into the world. Any such person is the deceiver and the Antichrist" (v. 7). Thus, the Antichrist is anyone who overtly or covertly undermines right teaching about the nature of Christ.

Both Luther and Calvin applied "Antichrist" to the popes and their defenders in this first sense. Speaking against "papists" who arrogantly "will not distinguish between God's word and human doctrine," Luther stated, "Here one sees so well how they have set themselves above God like blaspheming Antichrists."[84] Calvin, addressing the tyranny of the pontiff, accuses the papacy of masking heresy with a "semblance of Christ." But this cannot hide the fact that "all the heresies and sects which have been from the beginning belong to the kingdom of Antichrist."[85]

"Antichrist," however, also appears in the New Testament in a second, more apocalyptic sense. The Apostle Paul spoke of a coming "man of lawlessness" who would appear just before the Second Coming of Christ. This man, he said, "will oppose and will exalt himself over everything that is called God or worshiped, so that he sets himself up in God's temple, proclaiming himself to be God" (II Thess 2:1–4). To many interpreters of Scripture, this seemed to be the same man whom the writer of Revelation calls the "beast" who will receive the worship of the whole world (13:8) and whom I John calls *the* Antichrist who is to appear at the "last hour" (2:18). Identifying the last great Antichrist, therefore, was a key to unlocking the mystery of the Apocalypse and the coming Day of Judgment.

The reformers were cautious about such prophecies. They usually refrained from calling a particular pope the long-awaited Antichrist or the beast of the last days, but they drew heavily on the apocalyptic concepts to argue that it was from the papacy that the final Antichrist would emerge, perhaps quite soon. The pope's claim to divine authority and the pomp of his court deeply offended the reformers, who charged that the pope had done just what the Scriptures foretold of the Antichrist: elevating himself to a universal status equal with God.[86] In sum, the reformers spiced their critique of the pope with hints that their struggle with Rome might anticipate the Apocalypse—a view that subsequent Protestant generations would periodically elaborate.

The antipapalism of the early reformers, couched in the venomous language of vernacular books and pamphlets, drew on their personal experience of the Roman Church along with fourteenth- and fifteenth-century internal reform efforts. The Council of Trent later addressed many of these charges, especially concerning simony and other overt corruptions. But hatred of the pope as the monster at the center of a web of spiritual deception and material corruption entered the heart of Protestant confessional culture, even as Protestants lost contact with genuine Catholics. Exaggeration and distortion became the currency of Protestant propagandists. Still, Catholic military pressures in Germany, France, and the Low Countries and the persecution by Catholic rulers on the Continent and in Britain also hardened antipapalism. Protestants feared that the pope's "greatest ambition was to root out Protestantism with the maximum of bloodshed and cruelty."[87] Antipapalism and a more general opposition to Catholics as an enemy community became less and less distinguishable as the Reformation spiraled into religious warfare. As Counter-Reformation forces pushed embattled Protestantism to Europe's northern periphery, deep-seated anti-Catholicism emerged there, vilifying the pope and his "slavish minions."

Reformation England

The Reformation came to England only fifteen years after Luther posted his theses (1532), but under somewhat suspect conditions. Henry VIII's marital difficulties sparked the English secession from Roman Christendom, but the nation—at least large parts of it—took to its new independent status with considerable vigor.[88] Special antipathy toward Rome developed soon after the break.[89]

England was, in fact, justified in its fear of Catholic power. Rome wanted England back in the fold, and Catholics had taken up the challenge. England's own Catholic Queen Mary I tried to wrench her kingdom out of Protestant hands by executing hundreds of Protestant leaders. Her widower, Phillip II of Spain, launched his unsuccessful armada against Elizabeth I in 1588. Homegrown Catholics later attempted a coup d'état against James I in the Gunpowder Plot of 1605. And, of course, the Stuart kings, especially Charles II, who converted to Catholicism on his deathbed, and the openly Catholic James II, caused so much consternation among Protestants that Parliament overthrew James in the Glorious Revolution of 1688 and banned Catholics from the throne. For Protestants, these miraculous deliverances proved that God favored the English. To commemorate these confessional and national triumphs, English Protestants instituted a cycle of holidays, each with its own antipapal traditions, such as burning the pope in effigy on the anniversary of Elizabeth I's accession.[90]

In response to the external threat, as well as the popular desire for uniformity, Parliament passed a series of harsh penal codes between 1559 and 1610 that made it unlawful, and indeed treasonable, to engage in Catholic rites. Catholics could not hear Mass, join a profession, hold office, own a weapon, or come within 10 miles of London. Priests were banned from the country, and anyone harboring them could be condemned to death. The list of prohibited activities was very long and the penalties were harsh, but rarely enforced; the laws were designed more to deter than to punish.[91]

Throughout the seventeenth century, fear motivated English anti-Catholicism. Protestants believed that a Catholic takeover would result in arbitrary and tyrannical rule. A Catholic monarch, whether imposed from the outside or raised up from within, would inevitably hand England over to the pope, whose rule would mean disorder, persecution, torture, heavy taxation, and the confiscation of lost monastic property. Popular writers wittingly or unwittingly stoked such fears. John Foxe, for instance, extolled the virtues of those Protestants martyred by Catholics in his best-selling *Acts and Monuments*, while pamphleteers such as John Pym and William Prynne whipped up anti-Catholic sentiment by accusing "papists" of various acts of treason.[92] Some pamphlets were more graphic than others. According to Henry Care (1680), a Catholic takeover would see English Protestants

> forced to fly destitute of bread and harbour, your wives prostituted to the lust of every savage bog-trotter, your daughters ravished by goatish monks, your smaller children tossed upon pikes, or torn limb from limb, whilst you have your own bowels ripped up, . . . or else murdered with some other exquisite tortures and holy candles made of your grease (which was done within our memory in Ireland), your

dearest friends flaming in Smithfield, foreigners rendering your poor babes that can escape everlasting slaves, never more to see a Bible, nor hear again the joyful sounds of Liberty and Property. This, this gentlemen is Popery.[93]

Protestants feared that a Catholic monarch would collude with Rome to strip them of their property, dissolve Parliament, end representative government, and move to wipe out their faith, just as Louis XIV was doing in France. The struggle with Catholicism was thus a struggle for English liberties against the threat of continental tyranny.[94]

For the English Protestants, this struggle constituted a final stage in history. John Foxe depicted the fight "as the final cataclysmic conflict of the forces of Christ and the forces of Antichrist which was to end only on the Day of Judgment."[95] Puritan writers, both before the Civil War and during the Commonwealth, readily identified the pope as the Antichrist and proclaimed the imminence of the coming millennium (the earthly reign of Christ) based on their reading of Daniel and Revelation.[96] Restoration writers also made frequent references to the Antichrist and to "Babylon" (which usually meant the papacy).[97] Millennial agitation subsided, however, as the seventeenth century wore on. As Miller puts it, "The Puritan failure to build a new godly society during the Interregnum and the obstinate failure of the world to come to an end greatly reduced the attractiveness of prophecies about the immediate future based on the books of Daniel and Revelation and, incidentally, also reduced the attractiveness of an apocalyptic interpretation of the conflict of Catholicism and Protestantism."[98] Thus, the apocalyptic tradition receded, only to reemerge a century later.

The early eighteenth century saw a new form of Protestantism—"Evangelicalism"—arise out of the open-air revival preaching of George Whitefield and John Wesley. Out of this "Great Awakening" came the Evangelical movement, which placed new emphasis on personal conversion to faith in Jesus Christ and the Bible as the sole guide for Christian doctrine and practice, an emphasis Wesley seems to have absorbed during his travels among the German Pietists in 1738.[99] These were the true heirs of the Puritans, whose churches—which included dissenting Presbyterians, Congregationalists, and Particular Baptists—had experienced recent declines.[100] They were active and zealous for the "Gospel," and their energy revitalized old denominations (including the Church of England) and led to the creation of new ones, most notably Methodism. By the mid–nineteenth century the movement had dramatically revived church attendance across many denominations and had achieved a level of religious influence in Victorian Britain not seen since the seventeenth century.[101]

The eighteenth-century Evangelicals were quite free of anti-Catholic rhetoric, but this was due more to the Catholics' status as a small minority on the fringes of British society than to any strong commitment to tolerance. As the nineteenth century dawned, however, Catholics became more visible and the Evangelicals, like their Puritan ancestors, reacted against a perceived threat to the nation. They responded sympathetically toward Protestants in Ireland under pressure from Catholics angered by Methodist preaching. They also created anti-Catholic propaganda organizations to oppose Catholic political rights when the cause of emancipation gained steam in the 1820s. And finally, they decried the growing influence of "papist" doctrine and practice in the Church of England (to which most still belonged) through the Oxford Movement, a High-Church conduit for significant conversions to Catholicism such as those of John Henry Newman and Henry Edward Manning. The main factor, however, was the massive influx of Catholic refugees from the Irish Potato Famine (1845–49) into England, which added a hearty dose of ethnic prejudice, class stereotyping, and fear of revolution to existing anti-Catholicism, fermenting into a "heady and distasteful brew."[102] With the survival of Protestant Britain at stake, Evangelicals established organizations such as the influential Protestant Association (1835) to combat Catholic influences.[103]

Such anti-Catholic efforts among Evangelicals persisted well into the twentieth century. The sectarian struggle in Ireland over Home Rule continued to excite anti-papal sentiments among British Protestants, as did sectarian conflict in Scotland. And controversies over the "papistical" Revised Prayer Book (which was rejected by Parliament in 1928), the centenary celebration of the Oxford Movement in 1932–33, and the establishment of the World Council of Churches in 1948 (which many expected—wrongly—would include the Catholic Church) all involved Evangelicals taking anti-Catholic stands.[104] Thus Evangelicals preserved the anti-Catholic traditions of the English Reformation that not only opposed the teachings and practices of the Roman Church but also vilified Catholics for a host of shortcomings that included disloyalty to the nation. But what set Evangelicalism apart from run-of-the-mill British anti-Catholicism was its rediscovery in the early nineteenth century of the role of the Roman Church in the "last days." Evangelicalism's particular fascination—bordering on obsession—with prophecies of the Apocalypse injected new emotion into its anti-Catholicism.

The Premillennial Shift in British Evangelicalism

As we saw above, the early reformers sometimes attempted to connect their struggle with Rome to the biblical Apocalypse. Such apocalyptic thinking was not new to Christendom. Anticipation of a return of God to Earth in judgment had been an important element of the Christian religion from the first century, based on the witness of the Jewish prophets, Jesus, Paul, and the writer of the Revelation.[105] Christians through the centuries, however, had often paid little attention to difficult scriptures dealing with the last days, content simply to affirm with the Apostles' Creed that Christ will come to "judge the living and the dead." But in crises Christians often sought to make sense of mystifying events by fitting them to particular interpretations of prophecy.[106]

The Reformation itself brought on much speculation about the timing of the events depicted in prophetic passages. Many in Latin Europe believed that the split in the church was clear evidence that the great final struggle between good and evil had begun and that Christ was soon to return. The early reformers, apart from their references to the Antichrist, tried to downplay apocalyptic speculations for justified fears of radical (mainly Anabaptist) attempts to hurry the millennium. But as the Reformation passed into its seventeenth-century adolescence, apocalyptic speculation took hold of the Protestant imagination—inspiring some to flee Europe for a millennial kingdom in America; others to execute King Charles I in favor of a holy Commonwealth; and still others to back the young Elector Friedrich in his bid to block the Habsburg and papal powers from recapturing central Europe for Rome, thus igniting the Thirty Years' War.[107] Each side in these great conflicts believed themselves to be Christ's agents and their enemies to be in camp with the Antichrist. But the Protestants in particular thought the end was at hand and that Christ was preparing to return to claim his chosen faithful.

As the Enlightenment took hold of Protestant Britain in the eighteenth century, apocalyptic speculation declined, along with virulent antipapalism. The French Revolution, however, encouraged Evangelicals to reconsider biblical prophecy, as they sensed that such a cataclysmic event might signify the imminent return of Christ.[108] In the first three decades of the nineteenth century, numerous Evangelical writers—usually Anglicans, and often prominent scholars—returned to the books of Daniel (chaps. 2, 7–8) and Revelation (chap. 13) to interpret the times and predict the future.[109] Much speculation centered on exactly when Christ would return. The Roman Church, following Saint Augustine, had been content to view itself as the embodiment of Christ's present reign and to abjure speculation as to when he might return in the flesh (*amillennialism*). The early reformers did not challenge such thinking, although some argued that the struggle with Rome signaled the imminence of Christ's return. Those Protestants who did speculate on the Apocalypse usually assumed that at some point the world would be Christianized and an age of peace would settle on humanity for a thousand years, after which Christ would return to reign (*postmillennialism*). The new nineteenth-century prophecy teachers, however, rediscovered a neglected reading of Revelation 20 that called for Christ's return *before* the millennial peace.[110] This *pre*millennial view envisioned a time of general spiritual, moral, and material decline in Christendom, ending in a series of divine judgments and the glorious return of Christ to Earth as supreme judge of all, visibly and in the flesh. After the final judgment, his reign of peace would last a thousand years.[111]

The British "premillennial shift" in the early 1800s had profound effects on Evangelical Protestantism. First, it added a sense of urgency to preaching the Gospel that fueled Evangelicalism's sometimes frenetic activism. If judgment was near and Christ's return was imminent—literally, could occur "at any moment"—preachers must traverse the globe to warn of impending doom and map the way of escape.[112] Heightening the urgency was the emphasis placed by some premillennialist teachers, most notably the Anglo-Irish clergyman John Nelson Darby, on the "secret rapture" of the saints—a literal flight to Heaven of Christians—that would come before the worst of the predicted suffering. Many responded in faith, for fear of being "left behind" and forced to endure the horrors of sinful society's death throes.

Second, premillennialism encouraged the Evangelicals to watch closely for signs of social decay and divine judgment. Thus the premillennial Evangelicals became profoundly pessimistic about the course of human history, believing that the times had to get worse before they could—after Christ's intervention—get better. They also were fascinated by constant attempts to fit current events to biblical prophecy, seeing in political and economic developments the fulfillment of various Scriptures.

Finally, the premillennialists remained staunch anti-Catholics, but their anti-Catholicism took a new direction, given the papacy's waning political authority. The pope was still an Antichrist, but after the French Revolution he was more likely to represent the decadence and godlessness of the present age than the Great Evil feared by the reformers. As Sandeen observes, "Millenarians [premillennialists] without exception were stoutly anti-Catholic and viewed every agitation by English and Irish Catholics as confirmation of the increasing corruption of the world and thus of the increasing likelihood of the second advent."[113]

Premillennialism steadily gained ground among Evangelicals in the nineteenth and early twentieth centuries, with John Nelson Darby credited for this success.[114] Not only did he preach the secret rapture, but he also developed an entire system of biblical interpretation called "dispensationalism," dividing God's intervention in human history into "ages" or "dispensations." Although he failed to draw most Evangelicals out of their apostate churches to join his Plymouth Brethren, Darby did disseminate his doctrine widely through extensive writings and many travels, including seven lengthy tours of North America between 1862 and 1877. His teaching converted a prominent American preacher, James H. Brookes, who taught the system to Cyrus Scofield. The latter's *Scofield Reference Bible* (first published in 1909) deeply influenced British and American Evangelicals through its notes and commentary supporting a dispensational interpretation of biblical texts.

By World War I "dispensationalism was the dominant form of the advent hope."[115] Trench warfare silenced the postmillennialist Evangelicals; they could no longer expect a peaceful Kingdom of God on Earth before Christ's return. Premillennial dispensationalists now dominated conservative Christian circles in Britain. Some actively looked for signs of fulfilled prophecy in past and current events, while others thought all prophecy was yet to be fulfilled. Some remained virulently anti-Catholic; others, less so.[116] Mid-twentieth-century Evangelicalism in Britain, however, remained anti-Catholic and wary of Rome. Many believed that cosmic events were unfolding as tyrants rose to power and nations flew headlong into war. These certainly looked like the "end times."

Apocalyptic thinking reinforced the old British Protestant sense that God had intervened in history to save his church from the evil grip of the papacy. Protestant peoples were chosen peoples, none more so than the English, who had stood up to Catholic power and by the hand of God had escaped destruction and preserved English liberties. The English Evangelicals, like most British Protestants, saw in these events a cosmic struggle between good and evil, but they went one step further by predicting that history was soon to climax. The premillennialist shift encouraged the Evangelicals to scan current events for signs of the Antichrist and the coming Tribulation. And where were they to look for these signs? Without question, they looked toward Rome.

The Netherlands

Evangelical premillennialism did not stay in Britain, but also influenced Protestants elsewhere in Europe. Calvinists on the Continent were also prone to such antipapal and apocalyptic ruminations: "It was a particular mark of Reformed Protestantism to conceive itself as a crusade against the papal Antichrist."[117] Such sentiment was certainly evident in the Netherlands.

The Reformation started slowly in the Netherlands. But it picked up steam in 1566, when open-air "hedge preaching" (much of it "Reformed") led to the spontaneous cleansing of the churches by mobs intent on smashing images and other accoutrements of Catholic worship. This iconoclasm, which began in West Flanders in August 1566 and spread east and north through much of the autumn, did not target the rulers or the symbols of the Habsburg regime. Rather, it "was purely and simply an attack on the Church and not anything else."[118] Local leaders who opposed the cleansings were powerless to stop the destruction when the civic militia sided with the mob, as they did in Middelburg, where the militiamen declared, "We will not fight for church, pope, or monks."[119]

The brutal Spanish reprisals, led by the duke of Alva, only hardened Protestant—now mostly Reformed—attitudes toward the Roman Church. When the great Revolt broke out in 1572, the rebel states quickly moved against Catholics, seizing churches, driving out clergy, and prohibiting Mass. Despite the efforts of William I of Orange to institute toleration of both Catholic and Reformed worship in the new States of Holland, popular pressure prevailed, and Catholic worship was outlawed in early 1573. But the established Reformed Church of the new United Provinces was not the Church of England. Unlike the English Church, the Dutch Church brought in only a minority—in most places, less than a third—of the population as full members.[120] The Reformed Church controlled the levers of political power, but the nature of the Church—with its strong emphasis on purity of worship, righteous living, and church discipline—made it less suited than the very broad English Church for a public role. Thus, many Dutch citizens remained outside, either as nonattenders or as Lutheran, Mennonite (Anabaptist), Catholic, or Jewish dissenters. The religious communities competed for converts in a slow process of confessionalization that lasted until the mid–seventeenth century. When Spanish armies and other Counter-Reformation forces no longer threatened Reformed Protestantism and Dutch independence, confessional tensions eased, leaving well-defined and very stable confessional communities in the United Provinces.[121] Law and custom separated religious communities, with the non-Reformed groups particularly closed out due to official threats and occasionally violent suppression that often forced them underground, or at least out of sight. But the reality of religious pluralism forced a degree of toleration—if unofficial—on civic and church leaders. Not everyone in the United Provinces, however, agreed that toleration should be extended to the non-Reformed, making tolerance *the* fundamental issue for the Dutch republic in the post-Reformation period.

Given the intellectual nature of the Reformed faith, theological controversies were at the heart of church conflicts spilling into Dutch society. The theological struggles between Arminians and Gomarists, Remonstrants and Counter-Remonstrants, Voetians and Cocceians, Calvinists and Socinians, Collegiants, Cartesians, Spinozists, Bekkerites, and more all boil down to a battle between Reformed orthodoxy—and its desire to create and maintain the pure society—and liberalizing elements intent on opening up both the church and society. When the orthodox were ascendant, Catholics, Lutherans, Mennonites, and Jews were harassed and prevented from worshiping. Orthodox control also meant tighter enforcement of Sabbath regulations and public morals. In contrast, when "Libertines" were dominant, non-Reformed groups were allowed greater—although not complete—freedom to practice their religions.

The orthodox Reformed were the most ideologically anti-Catholic group in the United Provinces, but events sometimes evoked a latent fear of Catholicism and papal conspiracies that permeated all non-Catholic communities. Like their English brethren, Dutch Protestants of all stripes feared that Louis XIV would extend his relentless war against Protestants to their own territories and feared religious isolation as the Catholic James II took the throne in England. These events put pressure on William III of Orange (and later of England) to permit the expulsion of the Jesuits and other "regular clergy," and the suppression of Catholic schools as protective measures. William prevented such actions and, in fact, did much to promote religious tolerance in the Dutch Republic and in England after 1688, despite his own conservative perspective.[122] But insecurity lingered, and Dutch Protestants kept a wary eye on Catholics, both near and far.

During the nineteenth and twentieth centuries, Dutch society realized the benefits of tolerance—even if "tolerance" meant the creation of tight confessional communities that acknowledged the right of other communities to exist but had little contact with them. Nineteenth-century confessional communities developed a full range of social organizations—such as labor unions, business associations, political parties, social clubs, and newspapers—that united coreligionists and separated them from people of other faiths. This "pillarization" was most evident among Catholics, but it also took hold among Protestants, most conspicuously among the conservative (in Dutch, *gereformeerd*) groups that left the increasingly "modernist" Dutch Reformed Church, first in 1834, and then again in 1886.[123] These conservative movements reinforced separation from Catholics, seeing cooperation with papists as a "sellout of national history, political freedom, and Protestant principles."[124]

Reformed Protestantism clung to anti-Catholicism primarily to protect the distinctive Calvinist nature of the Dutch nation; but some of this resistance can also be attributed to apocalyptic thinking. Dutch Protestants were certainly caught up in the apocalyptic rhetoric of the Thirty Years' War, but it was the French Revolution that excited interest in biblical prophecy, as it had in Britain. Abraham Kuyper saw the Revolution bringing much benefit in the form of political rights, but blamed it for unleashing a "spirit that stole into the historical life of nations and fundamentally set their heart against Christ as the God-anointed king."[125] He believed, along with the British premillennialists, that the Revolution's results fit well with prophetic passages that foresaw an "anti-Christian power [that] will manifest itself in all its naked brutality only *toward the end*" (emphasis in the original).[126] Christians who discerned this "great apostasy" and knew that the end was approaching were to love their enemies, but not "accede to their counsel."[127] Rather, all those who loved Christ and awaited his return should "heartily unite with all sincere believers in the land to resist their [enemies'] philosophy and to rescue the country from their pernicious influence" so that "the spirit of apostasy [could] be arrested."[128]

Scandinavia

In Scandinavia the kings, not the clergy or the laity, led the revolt against the Roman Church. The Reformation was a top-down affair that took several decades to permeate the newly independent kingdoms of Denmark (including Norway) and Sweden (including Finland). Once reform took hold, however, it achieved total victory. So thorough was the transformation in Scandinavia that by the end of the sixteenth century, Catholicism had been completely eliminated for all practical purposes. Thus—unlike their German, English, and Dutch counterparts—Scandinavian Protestants had no contact with Catholics, domestic or foreign. Lutheranism—the Protestant form chosen by the monarchs of both Denmark (Fredrick I) and Sweden (Gustav Vasa)—had no competition from, or even much contact with, other forms of Protestantism until the nineteenth century.

Scandinavian Lutherans were anti-Catholic like their Protestant brethren everywhere, but their opposition to the Roman Church was a national assumption that virtually never needed defending. The law in both Denmark and Sweden reflected the anti-Catholic nature of state and society. In Denmark Christian III abolished Catholicism in 1536, expropriating Church property in the process; the Royal Law of 1665 pledged the Crown to tolerate only the Lutheran faith in the Kingdom of Denmark-Norway; in 1705 the police were ordered to prohibit the practice of foreign religion, including Protestant alternatives to Lutheranism and Catholicism; and in 1736 Lutheran rites were made compulsory for every citizen.[129] When Norway wrote its 1814 Constitution, it kept the official faith: "The Evangelical-Lutheran religion shall remain the official religion of the state."[130] Furthermore, Catholic orders were explicitly prohibited from entering the country. As for Sweden, the Reformation was not complete until the early seventeenth century, when the threat of royal reimposition of Catholicism by force had passed. By 1593, however, Sweden, like Denmark, had prohibited Catholic practice—except by foreigners who promised not to proselytize. The Church law of 1686 went further, demanding that all Swedish subjects assent to the Lutherans' Augsburg Confession of 1530 and Book of Concord of 1580.[131]

In sum, once the Reformation dust settled in Scandinavia, only Lutheranism remained; all non-Lutheran religions, especially Catholicism, were banned. The state compelled the teaching and practice of Lutheranism and occasionally sought to purify the national religion of vestigial "papism."[132] And the evidence indicates that the population was more than willing to follow the state's lead.

The strict religious conformity required by the state in Denmark and Sweden resulted in a particularly impersonal religious experience for most people, especially in sparsely populated rural districts. A shortage of priests made church attendance difficult; class differences between clergy and peasant parishioners hindered pastoral care; and state-mandated restrictions on theological content and the educational differences between clergy and illiterate congregants made religious instruction arid and impractical. The resulting spiritual hunger opened many Scandinavians to the German pietism of Philip Spener and August Francke. The Pietists taught the need for personal conversion, the study of Scripture in small groups, private devotions, Christian behavior, practical preaching, and lay participation in church government—all of which gained them a ready hearing in many rural communities. The Lutheran establishment objected to the dispensing of religion by unsanctioned individuals and opened a new religious conflict in Scandinavia that pit the religious establishment against unauthorized, but otherwise orthodox, religious communities that had no intention of withdrawing from the state churches, only of purifying them. Both Sweden (1726) and Denmark (1741) passed Conventicle Acts prohibiting small, unauthorized gatherings for prayer and Bible study. If caught, participants could be fined, imprisoned, or even banished from the kingdom.[133]

Official opposition did not eradicate Pietism from Scandinavia. Pietism, instead, laid the foundation for the larger Evangelical revival of the early nineteenth century—one similar to the British awakening. The new revivals were more enthusiastic than the sincere but rather staid Pietistic movements, and were more popular among peasants than their more intellectual predecessors.[134] The Scandinavian Evangelical revival began in Norway with Hans Nielsen Hauge, a farmer's son who became an unordained, itinerate preacher after his conversion in 1795. He preached a simple message of salvation by faith in Jesus Christ and called newly awakened believers to study the Bible and live holy, productive lives.[135] He traveled to Denmark in 1804, but had little impact. The Danes, however, began their own revival—first in Jutland, where the peasants objected to new devotional books; and then more forcefully and successfully after 1811, under the leadership of Christen Madsen.[136] The revival in Sweden was ignited after the British Methodist George Scott arrived in 1830. Typically, the Evangelicals were not angry rebels; their focus was on changing individual hearts. But they were critical of the worldliness of the state church, and they sometimes angered fellow citizens by refusing to take Communion with the "unregenerate." They criticized the clergy's lax morals, inattentiveness to the laity's spiritual needs, and ostentation, which some could only describe as "popishness."[137] They were no more anti-Catholic than the religious establishments of Denmark and Sweden, but they saw themselves as the carriers of the authentic national religious tradition.[138]

Improved transportation in the nineteenth century and mass migrations from Scandinavia to America—encouraged by pressure put on the revivalists by the Swedish and Norwegian states—soon connected the Evangelical revivals in Europe and North America. Across the two continents, the revivalists shared a belief in personal salvation by faith in Jesus Christ, reliance on the Bible for guidance in doctrine and practice, and, in many cases, premillennial interpretations of biblical eschatology.

Dispensationalism reached Scandinavia by midcentury and took hold of the revivalist elements. For instance, in 1871 a dispute over school textbooks in Jarlsberg, Norway, led an Evangelical congregation to charge that the state Church's unwillingness to fight the new texts revealed the power of the Antichrist and pointed to the imminent return of Christ.[139] One of the most influential evangelists and missionaries of the late nineteenth century, Fredrik Franson, a Swedish immigrant to America, carried the message of Christ's imminent return back to Scandinavia during several evangelistic forays, the last from 1898 to 1900.[140] Premillennialism did not affect the majority of Scandinavian Lutherans; but for the revivalists, both inside and eventually outside the state churches, end-times thinking, with its strong dose of anti-Catholicism, remained a central article of faith well into the twentieth century.

The Sacred Foundations of National Identity

The Protestant Reformation shattered the religious, political, and cultural uniformity of medieval Christendom. It also shattered Christian identity. Who were you if not a baptized member of the Roman Catholic Church? Who were you if you did not acknowledge the pope as the head of all Christendom?

For some, these very questions were incomprehensible. Consider, for example, the case of Sir Thomas More. More refused to acknowledge Henry VIII as the "supreme head" of the English Church in 1532, and he was sentenced to death. When his friends urged him to change his mind in light of English elite opinion, he wrote from the Tower: "I am not . . . bounden to change my conscience and confirm it to the council of one realm, against the general council of Christendom."[141] He could not understand how "one realm" could stand against the whole of Latin Christendom. He could not condone the secession of the English Church, because his highest loyalty remained to the universal church. As Greenfeld points out, however, More was behind the times: "Sir Thomas More was a Christian; this was his identity, and all his roles, functions, and commitments that did not derive from it (but were implied, for example, in being a subject of the king of England) were incidental to it. . . . Sir Thomas' perspective was that of a pre-nationalist era. He found the position of his judges incomprehensible. He failed to realize that they were already transformed, that being Englishmen, for them, was no longer incidental to their allegiances, as it was for him, but had become the very core of their being."[142] The Reformation replaced loyalty to Christendom with loyalty to "nation," and it also replaced Christian identity with national identity. More could scarcely comprehend such a transformation, and he could never condone it.

Protestant National Identity

But on what did Protestant national identity rest? We saw in the last section that anti-Catholicism permeated the Protestants' confessional culture and provided them with a clear "other." Their identity, in part, was shaped by who they were not; but Protestant religion also proved a deep source of positive identity. Protestant populations viewed themselves as God's chosen people called out of exile to accomplish a divine mission, led by a sacred monarch. Chosen-ness and mission, exile and martyrdom, sacral kingship—these became the sacred foundations of the Protestant states of Europe.

GOD'S CHOSEN PEOPLE

According to Smith, "The central concept of the political religion of nationalism is that of a *sacred communion of the people* . . . that unites its adherents into a single moral community of the faithful, . . . a community that sees itself as holy and prizes its uniqueness, its special bond of intimacy with the divine and its separation from surrounding communities" (emphasis in the original).[143] Protestantism provided communities with a treasure trove of resources to mark out a particular people by placing a new emphasis on the importance of the Old Testament scriptures as both revelatory and instructive. Reformed Protestants, in particular, viewed the whole

Bible as a single story of God's redemption of the human race. They drew a direct line from the covenants God made with ancient Israel to the call of the church to live out the Kingdom of God on Earth. As God called Israel to be "a kingdom of priests and a holy nation," so God called special people to fulfill a holy mission in the world. Ancient Israel, time and again, proved to be an instructive example for the Protestants. God rescued Israel from the yoke of Egyptian slavery, gave it a holy law, led it to a promised land, and raised up priestly kings. He blessed the people when they obeyed the law and sent them into exile when they disobeyed. The Protestants scattered across Europe saw themselves in these stories. They were all chosen people.

Protestants' belief in their chosen-ness in particular characterized the Scottish Calvinists, and to a lesser degree the Welsh Protestants.[144] German and Scandinavian Lutherans were less inclined than their Reformed coreligionists to see themselves as chosen by God for a cosmic mission, but they too saw their alliance of state and church as a guarantee of righteous purity. The English and the Dutch, however, best exemplified the Protestant sense of chosen-ness and mission.

Before the Reformation the English were well on their way to developing a sense of divine election. Gildas, for instance, drew close parallels between the punishments of sinful Israel and the sufferings of Britons at the hands of the Saxon invaders, whereas the Venerable Bede considered the English—the gens Anglorum—to be "a people of the Covenant" as early as the eighth century.[145] The early sixteenth century only heightened the awareness of the English "that they were a people somehow different to all others, called to a special destiny."[146] Protestantism—which walked through the door opened by Henry VIII's break with Rome—gave this greater sense of "nation" and national destiny a voice. Greenfeld summarizes this role: "Though Protestantism cannot be said to have given birth to the English nation, it did play the crucial role of a midwife, without whom the child might not have been born."[147]

John Foxe's immensely popular *Book of Martyrs* (the shorthand for *Actes and Monuments*) best articulated this vision of English chosen-ness for every stratum of society, for the growing number of Protestant readers and for the illiterate, who looked at the plentiful graphic illustrations. England had always been faithful to the true religion. The break with Rome and the consequent suffering under Queen Mary was only the most recent example of England's staunch defense of the truth. God had made a covenant with England and given it a mission to lead the Reformation in the world: "Being English in fact implied being a true Christian; the English people was chosen, separated from others and distinguished by God; the strength and glory of England was the interest of His Church; and the triumph of Protestantism was a national triumph."[148] In 1559 John Aylmer, the future bishop of London, in an often-quoted passage from *An Harborow of True and Faithful Subjects*, stated this theme with unabashed directness: "God is English. For you fight not only in the quarrel of your country, but also and chiefly in defence of His true religion and of His dear son Christ. [England says to her children:] God hath brought forth in me the greatest and excellentest treasure that He hath for your comfort and all the worlds. He would that out of my womb should come that servant of Christ John Wyclif, who begat Huss, who begat Luther, who begat the truth."[149]

God had chosen England to preserve his truth. But England was now required to take this truth to the world. The explorer John Davys expressed this mission: "For are not we only set upon Mount Zion to give light to all the rest of the world? . . . It is only we, therefore, that must be these shining messengers of the Lord, and none but we."[150]

Puritan England, with equal fervor, took up the cause of God's new chosen people. Oliver Cromwell equated England with the biblical kingdom of Judah when he spoke to the Little Parliament in 1653: "Truly you are called by God as Judah was, to rule with Him, and for Him." The English were the chosen people of God, whose divine mission was to bring truth and liberty to a world drenched in Catholic superstition and Roman slavery. As Linda Colley has pointed out, British identity assumed the mantel of English chosen-ness after the Act of Union in 1707, and was reinforced at every point.[151] Foxe's *Book of Martyrs* saw new editions in 1732 and (in cheaper form) several times later in the century. The book proved wildly popular and could be assumed to be in almost every household in Britain.[152] George Frederick Handel's oratorios drew explicit parallels between Britain and Israel. And in the early nineteenth century William Blake penned these famous lines:

I will not cease from Mental Fight
Nor shall my Sword sleep in my hand:
Till we have built Jerusalem,
In England's green and pleasant land.[153]

Wars in the eighteenth century also solidified Britain's Protestant identity; most were against Catholic powers, primarily France and Spain. Furthermore, Jacobin attempts to retake the British throne for Catholic rulers in the same century brought the conflict with the so-called papists nearer to home and whipped up Protestant patriotism. Much more than religion was at stake in these struggles, but the national perception that Britain was fighting for the truth against the papal foe never hurt the war efforts. Without doubt, Protestantism encouraged a British sense of independence and separateness from the Continent with a good dose of bombast and chauvinism. It "gave the majority of men and women a sense of their place in history and a sense of worth. . . . It gave them identity."[154] Protestantism made Britain a nation.

Protestantism did the same for the Dutch. Unlike the British, however, the Dutch had little to build on when their union with the Holy Roman Empire dissolved in the sixteenth century. None of the usual markers of national consciousness were present—territory, language, tribe, or dynasty. What they did have was a new religion that rushed in to fill the void. The Reformed faith provided the people of the Low

Countries—or at least *enough* of them, in a religiously divided territory—with the answers to the key questions of identity. As Schama summarizes Protestantism's influence on a new Dutch identity: "Who were they [the Dutch]? They were the new/old Batavians, guardians of the *waare vrijheid* (the true liberty). They were reborn Hebrews, children of the Covenant. Where had they come from? From slavery and idolatry, through ordeal, to freedom and godliness. Whither would they go? To reveal God's design for the world through their destiny and to swell in honor, prosperity and glory, so long as they obeyed His commandments."[155]

The Eighty-Years' War with Spain that ended only with the Treaty of Westphalia offered many occasions for the Dutch Calvinists to see contemporary events in the stories of the Old Testament. Their dwelling places were Zions or Jerusalems; their leaders were Gideons, Joshuas, Davids, or Hezekiahs; and their enemies were Amalekites, Canaanites, Sodomites, or Philistines.[156] God had called them to carry out his will and defeat his enemies, and to obey his law if they were to experience peace and prosperity. More than the English, the Dutch agonized over exactly what God required of a holy people. Few doubted that God was watching.

As we have seen, the Reformed Church never attracted a majority of the Dutch, but Calvinism defined the nation. So deeply rooted was this identity that Abraham Kuyper, the founder of the Anti-Revolutionary Party (the leading Protestant party of the nineteenth and twentieth centuries) and Dutch prime minister from 1901 to 1905, could still appeal to the Calvinist nature of the Netherlands. Arguing in favor of political but against cultural cooperation with Catholics, he reminded his followers: "You have the Christian name in common with Rome, but only in Calvinism lies your fundamental and historically distinguishing Dutch characteristic."[157] We see in Kuyper the Dutch Calvinist identity in stark relief. Calvinism defines the nation—a people separate from the Catholics, who in some real sense are not part of the nation. The Dutch possessed a destiny that tied them to God's movement in history. They were part of God's plan for the world, which would one day climax in the return of Christ. They, too, were God's chosen people.

EXILE AND MARTYRDOM

The dark side of being God's chosen people is that suffering is always part of the divine mission. Again, for Protestants, the Old Testament provided the model. Suffering could sometimes be God's discipline of his unfaithful children. Repentance and a return to holy living were the appropriate responses. Thus, the Netherlands "Anthem of Commemoration," which was popular in the seventeenth century, includes these words: "O Lord you have performed wondrous things for us. And when we have not heeded you, you have punished us with hard but Fatherly force so that your visitations have always been meted out as a children's punishment."[158]

Of course, the suffering of God's elect could also have another cause: the forces of evil arrayed against God himself and his righteous people. Just as the Egyptians enslaved the Hebrews and the Assyrians and Babylonians carried Israel and Judah away into exile, so the armies of the Antichrist persecute and enslave the chosen people of God. For the English, the Scots, and especially the Dutch, exile was the "nursery of nationalism."[159]

Protestants in England found in Queen Mary's persecution both their "Egypt" and their "Babylon." For those trapped by Mary in England, it was Egypt. Mary burned 275 people for heresy between 1555 and 1558—a minuscule number by modern standards, but one of huge importance at the time. Great lions of the English Reformation—including Archbishop Thomas Cranmer, Bishop Hugh Latimer, and Bishop Nicholas Ridley—were executed, as were common people who knew very little about the theological issues at stake.[160] But the suffering was temporary. Queen Mary's early death in 1558 was for English Protestants a true miracle of God's deliverance; God had freed his people from Egyptian slavery. Foxe, of course, recorded in graphic detail each of the Marian burnings and developed the theme of deliverance. By the end of the sixteenth century a copy of his book could be found alongside the Bible in every cathedral church.

For those who escaped England—including Foxe—the reign of Queen Mary was spent in "Babylon"—Switzerland, France, Germany, Denmark, or the Low Countries. While these Marian Exiles were engaged in the great theological debates of the age, they also began to understand that the nation could be separated from the Crown. As John Poynet wrote from exile, "Men ought to have more respect to the country than to the prince, to the commonwealth than to any one person." For "kings and princes, be they never so great are but members, and commonwealths may stand well enough and flourish albeit there be no kings."[161] These exiles returned from Babylon to England, their promised land, with a new sense that a Christian commonwealth was an enterprise of the whole nation, not just of the prince and the clerical elite.

For the English, the Exodus was a metaphor used throughout the seventeenth century to justify radical separation from idolatry and sin. For the Dutch, the Exodus was less a metaphor than a historical occurrence. One hundred and fifty thousand refugees "had physically left the fleshpots of the south, crossed formidable water barriers and reached a land of abundance."[162] Phillip II was often depicted as Pharaoh and William I of Orange as Moses in the art and literature of the era. In fact, the Dutch Exodus and the sufferings of the long war with Spain became the justification for the rupture with Christendom. The resulting prosperity of the Dutch Republic was proof that God was with his people in their time of pain.

SACRAL KINGSHIP

The biblical images of chosen people, exodus, and martyrdom were rounded out for Protestants with a vision of earthly headship that also had roots in Old Testament archetypes. As we saw above, William of Orange was Moses leading his people to the Promised Land and giving them the laws of God. William was also depicted as King David, who slew giants and ruled a mighty kingdom.[163] Such explicit reference to biblical heroes was common in Protestant states. Practically all the Protestant monarchs were depicted as Davids and Solomons, renowned for their might, wisdom, and godly leadership. Sometimes the list of champions was broadened. England's Edward VI, the boy king who succeeded Henry VIII, was compared with Israel's boy king Josiah in Archbishop Cranmer's coronation address.[164] It was his sacred duty to rid the land of idolatry and to see that God was truly worshipped. Queen Elizabeth I, by virtue of her sex, was depicted as Deborah from the book of Judges, who was a "virtuous and virginal creature."[165]

Sacral kingship, much like its medieval predecessor, united in the monarch both spiritual and temporal roles. Denmark's Christian II, for instance, accepted upon his coronation the obligation "to promote true Christian worship and to guarantee the existence of a just society."[166] The difference in the Protestant countries was that the monarchs were obliged to uphold the *Protestant* religion and to give no credence to the pope. The crowns of Denmark and Sweden could only pass to Lutherans; the Dutch would have only Reformed princes. In Britain, after 1688, the monarchs swore to rule according to the "true profession of the Gospel, and the Protestant reformed religion established by law." Once crowned, the new monarchs were—and are—handed a Bible to remind them that the Scriptures, not the pope, are the religious authority of the land.[167]

The Protestant religion was the center of the new national identities that emerged after the Reformation. The provincialism of Protestantism allowed *all* the separate Protestant peoples to believe that *they* were God's elect, the new Israel. Protestants never seemed to be bothered that other nations were also claiming God's special calling. Protestant national identity was the consequence of a fragmented world— resting on new national myths of chosen-ness, exile, and martyrdom—and sacral kingship that pledged the whole society—prince and people—to worship in truth and live as the people of God. This was true Christian commonwealth. The ethos of these nations was a sense of righteousness, and even of self-righteousness, that caused them to look askance at those who were not of them. Other Protestant nations did not quite measure up, but they were far more acceptable than the popish states of the Continent, which remained the distrusted opponents of God and his people.

The religious fervor and intensity of the Reformation faded in the eighteenth century—in some places, even sooner. Nevertheless, what Colley said about late-seventeenth-century Britain was surely true of Protestant Europe generally: "The Protestant worldview was so ingrained in this culture that it influenced peoples' thinking irrespective of whether they went to church or not, whether they read the Bible or not, or whether, indeed, they were capable of reading anything at all."[168] Protestant confessional culture, the national identities it spawned, and the nation-states that protected both were now fixed on the European continent.

National Identity in Catholic Nation-States

As we have seen, the Catholic Church responded to the challenges of Reformation and the French Revolution by forcefully, even aggressively, articulating its theological and ideological differences with Protestantism and Liberalism, by centralizing its ecclesiastical institutions, and by establishing the pope as the focus of Catholic loyalty. These responses to the end of medieval Christendom saved the Catholic Church as a viable European, and even global, religious institution. Europe, however, had taken a decisive turn away from universalism. The conclusion of the religious wars in the mid–seventeenth century ended any hope of reestablishing Christendom under the tutelage of Rome; independent churches had taken root, and the nation-state, largely modeled on Britain, was on its way to becoming the new norm.[169] How would the Catholic states construct national identities if their religion remained dead set against the nation-state?

Predictably, there was tension between the European trend toward national identity and Catholic universalistic instincts. Protestants held a distinct advantage over Catholics when it came to forming national identities. Having overthrown the visible universal church, Protestants were free to establish their particular identity supported by a national church that did not need to give as much as lip service to a universal head. Catholics were never so free. And those nationalists who remained Catholic would need to bridge the particularism of Westphalia and the universalism of Rome.

The French and the Spanish found ways to foster national identities while remaining vociferously Catholic. In the late medieval era both monarchies developed royal cults that emphasized the Catholicity of the monarchs and their absolute loyalty to the Church and the pope—ironically, even as they grew more independent of Rome. The monarchs accumulated Christian titles that were often used as covers for independent action. Pope Alexander VI bestowed on Ferdinand II and Isabella I the title los Reyes Católicos (the Catholic monarchs), a title Spanish rulers cherished until forced into exile in 1931.[170]

The more striking case, of course, was the French monarchy's appropriation of the title Rex Christianissimus (the most Christian king)—to which French kings claimed exclusive rights by the fifteenth century. And the late medieval popes did not seem to object. They were simply acknowledging the close alliance between the papacy and the French Crown—not to mention Rome's frequent reliance on the French for protection. In the fifteenth century the papal nuncio had told Charles VII: "To you the most Christian of kings we entrust the common salvation, for by hereditary right you are the head of the Christian army, and it is to you that the other princes look up for the salvation of all."[171] The French people were also singled out for special recognition. Pope Clement V said of the French: "The kingdom of France, as a peculiar people chosen by the Lord to carry out the orders of Heaven, is distinguished by marks of special honour and grace."[172]

At first blush France's designation as a "peculiar people chosen by the Lord" looks remarkably similar to the English sense of chosen-ness, but there is a key difference. Whereas the English were a special people with a king, the French were a special king with a people. As Adrian Hastings observes, "The unity of the French nation depended upon the mystique of its monarchy in a way that of England never did, and the monarchy's mystique was an intensely Catholic one."[173] Greenfeld rightly calls the mystery surrounding the French throne a "Christian cult of royalty" and ties to that cult any kernel of national identity in the consciousness of the French people. The French language and other elements of culture were beginning to bind the French together by the fifteenth century, but "the key point of allegiance, the *source* of the French identity, however, was still the royal person, the high priest of a unique religious cult. One became French through the relationship to the 'most Christian' king. . . . Nothing French could conceivably exist at this time outside this relationship."[174] The rise of absolutism and the doctrine of the Divine Right of Kings in effect deified the French monarch and equated loyalty to the king with loyalty to God. As a popular apology for royal absolutism stated, "The ancients who were not flatterers called you [kings] *corporeal and living gods*, and God himself has taught men the same language and desires that you be called gods." It went on to say "the enemies of our kings are the enemies of God."[175]

The cult of royalty was not enough, however, to give rise to a truly national identity, so Catholic princes employed a second strategy: exclusion.[176] The process was dramatic and forceful in Spain, but only partially successful. Ferdinand and Isabella's unification project included the reconquest of areas ruled by Moorish infidels, accomplished by defeating Granada in 1492, the same year they expelled the Jews. Nevertheless, the Inquisition perhaps did the most to forge a nation. Its relentless search-and-purge activities in the name of religious purity may have started as a purely religious exercise, but its effect was political. The most efficient arm of the state enforced a Catholic identity and bound the people to their monarchs.[177] Dynastic instability and the problems of a far-flung empire, however, plagued Spain throughout the sixteenth century, making it difficult for a true national identity to emerge. And Catholicism was little help. As Anthony Marx puts it, "Most of the people whose descendants would become Spaniards did not yet think of themselves as such and often resisted efforts to force such coherence. The major potential focus of cohesion, widespread Catholic religious faith, remained largely 'other worldly,' not harnessed to the project of nation building. Catholic Spain did avoid religious schism within Christianity . . . But such relative religious uniformity may have produced less secularized identity formation than elsewhere."[178]

The French were more successful in using religious conflict to forge an identity. The initial success of the Reformation undermined the image of France as an undefiled Catholic country, but the outpouring of anti-Protestant violence during and after the Saint Bartholomew's Day Massacre demonstrated the depth of Catholic identity across all social strata. Catholic France engaged in a nearly four-decade purge of Protestants that, ironically, opened the possibility of a non-Catholic French identity. Catherine de' Medici—certainly no Huguenot—pleaded with her countrymen during the religious conflict: "Frenchmen should not think of other Frenchmen as Turks . . . There should be brotherhood and love between them." And the Huguenot leader Henry of Navarre, the future King Henry IV, pleaded with Henry III, "In the name of all I beg peace from my Lord the King, for me, for all the French and for France."[179] The effort to forge a non-Catholic identity, however, failed. Henry converted to Catholicism before taking the crown, and his attempt to create a religiously diverse (although still officially Catholic) France through the Edict of Nantes failed, with the reestablishment of Catholic uniformity and a renewed cult of royalty under Louis XIV in 1685. The revocation of the edict made it clear that to be French meant being first and foremost a Catholic. The Huguenots fled the country.

Religious conflict forged a heightened sense of national identity in France and (somewhat less so) in Spain. But Catholicism across Europe did not offer the same range of raw materials for identity formation as did Protestantism. Catholicism's commitment to a visible universalism made it difficult for people sharing a common language, for instance, to employ religious symbols to support a theory of divine chosen-ness. The Protestant emphasis on the whole Bible as the repository of revelation encouraged Protestant populations to see their national narratives as continuations of chosen Israel's story. Catholics, as a rule, did not use the Old Testament to undergird their sense, if one existed, of chosen-ness. They were perhaps "chosen" for a mission to defend the True Church, but this was, in Hastings's term, a "focused universalism" rather than a straight claim to being a defined people exclusively chosen by the Lord.[180] Perhaps the strongest evidence for this lack of raw material for national identity formation comes from the Catholic lands without an unusually strong Erastian tradition of independence from Rome—such as the borderlands of the Rhine River, or the fragmented statelets of Germany and Italy. In these heavily Catholic areas, no genuine national identity emerged in the seventeenth and eighteenth centuries.[181] Some areas, such as Belgium and Luxembourg, still lack strong national identities. Catholicism could not provide the sacred foundations of *national* identity. It was not until the secular revolutions of the late eighteenth and nineteenth centuries that a true sense of national identity emerged in Catholic lands.[182] Even in France and Spain, it took the secularization of the state to accomplish this task.

In France the doctrine of Divine Right deified the king and the state that served as his extended body. But as Greenfeld points out, this royal cult, far from increasing the Church's influence over the French government, actually moved the state farther from Rome. According to the Divine Right doctrine, kings were responsible directly to God alone—not to the Catholic Church as the presence of God on Earth. Once the king was extricated from the iron grip of Rome, it took very little to remove God completely from the chain of authority, granting the state absolute sovereignty unfettered by men or gods.[183] The French could now overthrow the deified state and replace it with a deified nation—"a super-human collective person."[184] Where once the French had worshipped the king, they now worshipped the nation. After the Revolution, France was a nation, and its citizens identified as part of that nation—revolution, not religion, made France.

Once France became a nation, the French Catholic Church became the opposition to the nation and its government. As a result Catholics suffered at the hands of a brutal republican government.[185] Across Catholic Europe, to be Catholic was to oppose the nation and republican government. A "Catholic nationalist" was considered an oxymoron—or, as the nineteenth-century French republican Léon Gambetta put it, "It is rare for a Catholic to be a patriot."[186] On the Italian Peninsula the pope had to be shut up in the Vatican before the Italians could unify. In Germany Catholics watched while Protestants forged a united nation-state. As Hastings expressed it, "For the new world of constitutional government, the very nature of government and of state legitimacy required an organic unity of its citizens which is what being a nation signifies."[187] Catholicism could not supply an organic unity on such a limited scale; its only option was to go into opposition. The messy histories of Spain, France, Italy, and Austria in the nineteenth and early twentieth centuries can in part be attributed to the struggle between secular national identities and reactionary Catholic universalism. Catholicism could not legitimize a particularistic identity process. National identity in Catholic areas of Europe would need to be republican, not Catholic.

Catholics eventually came to terms with liberalism and nationalism, as we shall see. Still, they never quite bridged the gap between Westphalian particularism and Catholic universalism. At the end of a long struggle, Catholics accepted the secular state and joined the nation on secular terms—but they did so with their fingers crossed.

Notes

1. Owen Chadwick says of Luther: "He was a conservative, not by intellect but by temperament. Throughout his life he resented unnecessary change. He intended no revolution, he aimed at purifying the Catholic Church and preserving its truth." Owen Chadwick, *The Reformation* (Harmondsworth, UK: Penguin Books, 1964), 51. See also Jacques Barzun, *From Dawn to Decadence: 500 Years of Western Cultural Life, 1500 to the Present* (New York: HarperCollins, 2000), 4–7.

2. John Calvin, *Calvin: Institutes of the Christian Religion, Vol. 2*, trans. Ford Lewis Battles, vol. 21 of *The Library of Christian Classics*, ed. John T. McNeill (Louisville: Westminster John Knox Press, 1960), 1015.

3. Ibid., 1014–15.

4. Ibid., 1051.

5. A good summary of Protestant teaching is given by James D. Tracy, *Europe's Reformations, 1450–1650* (Lanham, MD: Rowman & Littlefield, 1999), 13–29.

6. Diarmaid MacCulloch, *Reformation: Europe's House Divided 1490–1700* (New York: Viking, 2003), 144.

7. Ibid., 145.

8. Anabaptists noted that most baptisms recorded in the New Testament were of adults who had publicly repented of their sins and/or confessed faith in Jesus as Messiah; see Matt 3:6, Jn 4:2, Acts 2:38.

9. Philip Benedict, *Christ's Churches Purely Reformed: A Social History of Calvinism* (New Haven, CT: Yale University Press, 2002), 28.

10. Calvin, *Institutes*, 1021.

11. Note Calvin (*Institutes*, 1016) who stated: "Let us learn even from the simple title 'mother' how useful, indeed how necessary, it is that we should know her [the visible church]. . . . Away from her bosom one cannot hope for any forgiveness of sins or any salvation."

12. Ibid., 1023n18.

13. MacCulloch, *Reformation*, 221–24.

14. Tracy, *Europe's Reformations*, 4–5.

15. Ibid., 97.

16. Chadwick, *Reformation*, 264.

17. H. Outram Evennett, *The Spirit of the Counter-Reformation* (Notre Dame, IN: University of Notre Dame Press, 1968), 29; and see 1–22 for a fuller description of the definitions of the Counter-Reformation.

18. A readable history of the Counter-Reformation is given by Marvin R. O'Connell, *The Counter Reformation, 1559–1610* (New York: Harper & Row, 1974).

19. Council of Trent, Fourth Session, *The Canons and Decrees of the Sacred and Oecumenical Council of Trent*, trans. J. Waterworth (London: Dolman, 1848), 17–21, available at http://history.hanover.edu/texts/trent/ct04.html.

20. "If any one saith, that by faith alone the impious is justified; in such wise as to mean, that nothing else is required to co-operate in order to the obtaining the grace of Justification, and that it is not in any way necessary, that he be prepared and disposed by the movement of his own will; let him be anathema." Council of Trent, Sixth Session, *The Canons and Decrees of the Sacred and Oecumenical Council of Trent*, trans. J. Waterworth (London: Dolman, 1848), 30–53, http://history.hanover.edu/texts/trent/ct06.html.

21. Council of Trent, Twenty-Second Session, *The Canons and Decrees of the Sacred and Oecumenical Council of Trent*, ed. and trans. J. Waterworth (London: Dolman, 1848), 152–70, http://history.hanover.edu/texts/trent/ct22.html.

22. Evennett, *Counter-Reformation*, 31–32.

23. Tracy, *Europe's Reformations*, 272–74.

24. Evennett, *Counter-Reformation*, 41.

25. Council of Trent, Seventh Session, *The Canons and Decrees of the Sacred and Oecumenical Council of Trent*, trans. J. Waterworth (London: Dolman, 1848), 53–67, http://history.hanover.edu/texts/trent/ct07.html.

26. Benjamin J. Kaplan, *Divided by Faith: Religious Conflict and the Practice of Toleration in Early Modern Europe* (Cambridge, MA: Belknap Press, 2007), 80; Evennett, *Counter-Reformation*, 37–38.

27. Tracy, *Europe's Reformations*, 280.

28. Kaplan, *Divided by Faith*, 77.

29. Natalie Zemon Davis, "The Rites of Violence," in *Society and Culture in Early Modern France*, ed. Natalie Zemon Davis (Stanford, CA: Stanford University Press, 1975), 153; as quoted by Kaplan, *Divided by Faith*, 77.

30. Kaplan, *Divided by Faith*, 77.

31. Evennett, *Counter-Reformation*, 21–22.

32. Areas outside the empire were also threatened by Hapsburg forces, as England and Scotland discovered in 1588 when King Philip II of Spain launched his Armada.

33. Charles won the Battle of Mühlberg in 1547, but he had prematurely disbanded his army and lost the war.

34. MacCulloch, *Reformation*, 160.

35. Daniel Philpott, *Revolutions in Sovereignty: How Ideas Shaped Modern International Relations* (Princeton, NJ: Princeton University Press, 2001), 82.

36. Quoted in ibid., 85.

37. Both quotations are in ibid., 87.

38. See Kaplan, *Divided by Faith*, 22–28.

39. Calvin, *Institutes*, 1109.

40. The most important of these individual rulers were Duke Albrecht of Prussia, Duke Johann of Saxony, and Landgraf Philipp of Hesse. See MacCulloch, *Reformation*, 158–59.

41. See esp. Calvin's 1536 dedication of the *Institutes* to King Francis I.

42. Quoted by Kaplan, *Divided by Faith*, 19.

43. Ibid., 45.

44. Ibid., 102.

45. Thomas M. Linsay, *A History of the Reformation* (New York: Charles Scribner's Sons, 1949), 9.

46. To label the German Church "episcopal" is somewhat misleading. The German Church has adopted varied church structures over time and between regions. Synods and consistories have been as prevalent as superintendents. But the structure has always remained hierarchical, with top-down decision making and little to no involvement by congregations in ecclesiastical affairs.

47. J. R. C. Wright, *"Above Parties": The Political Attitudes of the German Protestant Church Leadership, 1918–1933* (Oxford: Oxford University Press, 1974), 4–5.

48. See Diarmaid MacCulloch, *The Boy King: Edward VI and the Protestant Reformation* (New York: Palgrave, 1999); and Paul Johnson, *A History of the English People* (New York: Harper & Row, 1972), 153–67.

49. See Benedict, *Christ's Churches*, chap. 4.

50. Ibid., 172.

51. Ibid., 194.

52. Andrew Pettegree, "Coming to Terms with Victory: The Upbuilding of a Calvinist Church in Holland, 1572–1590," in *Calvinism in Europe, 1540–1620*, ed. Andrew Pettegree, Alastair Duke, and Gillian Lewis (Cambridge: Cambridge University Press, 1994), 160–80.

53. For Calvin's defense of the Christian vocation of the magistrate, see *Treatises against the Anabaptists and against the Libertines*, ed. and trans. Benjamin Wirt Farley (Grand Rapids: Baker Academic, 1982), 78.

54. See Hugh McLeod, *Religion and the People of Western Europe, 1789–1989* (Oxford: Oxford University Press, 1997).

55. Scottish Presbyterians in 1578 called for a Protestant church structure that included an international council, but the transnational aspects of the plan never came to fruition. See Benedict, *Christ's Churches*, 168–69.

56. See ibid., 37, 111 (maps).

57. Will Durant, *The Reformation: A History of European Civilization from Wyclif to Calvin: 1300–1564*, vol. 6 of *The Story of Civilization* (New York: Simon & Schuster, 1957), 8.

58. See the "Declaration of the Council of Pisa, 1409," in *The Great Documents of Western Civilization*, ed. Milton Viorst (New York: Barnes and Noble, 1965), 74.

59. "The Council of Constance, 1415," in ibid., 76.

60. "The Pragmatic Sanction of Bourges, 1438," in ibid., 78.

61. Liah Greenfeld, *Nationalism: Five Roads to Modernity* (Cambridge, MA: Harvard University Press, 1993), 104.

62. According to Evennett, the concentration of authority in the pope preserved the Catholic Church in Europe; Evennett, *Counter-Reformation*, 95–96.

63. See Robert Birely, *The Refashioning of Catholicism, 1450–1700: A Reassessment of the Counter Reformation* (Washington, DC: Catholic University of America Press, 1999), 58–59.

64. Derek Holmes, *The Triumph of the Holy See: A Short History of the Papacy in the Nineteenth Century* (London: Burns and Oates, 1978), 4.

65. Christopher Dawson, *The Dividing of Christendom* (New York: Sheed & Ward, 1965), 181.

66. Hans Maier, *Revolution and Church: The Early History of Christian Democracy, 1789–1901*, trans. Emily M. Schossberger (Notre Dame, IN: University of Notre Dame Press, 1965), 76–77.

67. On the events of 1846–49, see Owen Chadwick, *A History of the Popes, 1830–1914* (Oxford: Oxford University Press, 1998), 61–94; and Holmes, *Triumph of the Holy See*, 101–26.

68. Chadwick, *History of the Popes*, 226.

69. "For fifty-eight years no pope after his election put a foot down outside the precincts of the Vatican." Chadwick, *History of the Popes*, 227.

70. See Maier's important discussion of the relationship between the revolutionary state and the church; Maier, *Revolution*, 127–41.

71. "The Papal Syllabus of Errors," in *The Creeds of Christendom*, vol. 2, ed. Philip Schaff (Grand Rapids: Baker Book House, 1919), 233.

72. Holmes, *Triumph of the Holy See*, 263.

73. And according to Owen Chadwick, Ultramontanism also demanded much more: "But its ardour included love of the Pope, support of the Pope, desire for Roman liturgy or habits or architecture . . . supporting the Syllabus, distrusting representative government, attacking liberty of the press or of conscience; standing in short against 'the Revolution.'" Owen Chadwick, *The Secularization of the European Mind in the Nineteenth Century* (Cambridge: Cambridge University Press, 1975), 123.

74. Holmes, *Triumph of the Holy See*, 158.

75. Martin Conway, *Catholic Politics in Europe, 1918–1945* (London: Routledge, 1997), 40.

76. Pius XII's role during the Nazi period is, of course, the subject of great controversy. For a taste of the debate, see John Cornwell, *Hitler's Pope: The Secret History of Pius XII* (New York: Viking Penguin, 1999); and Frank J. Coppa, *The Life and Pontificate of Pope Pius XII: Between History and Controversy* (Washington, DC: Catholic University of America Press, 2013).

77. István Deák, "The Pope, the Nazis, and the Jews," *New York Review of Books*, March 23, 2000, 44.

78. Martin Conway, "The Age of Christian Democracy: The Frontiers of Success and Failure," in *European Christian Democracy: Historical Legacies and Comparative Perspectives*, ed. Thomas Kesselman and Joseph A. Buttigieg (Notre Dame, IN: Notre Dame Press, 2003), 47.

79. Martin Luther, "To the Christian Nobility of the German Nation Concerning the Reform of the Christian Estate," trans. Charles M. Jacobs and rev. James Atkinson, in *Luther's Works*, vol. 44, ed. James Atkinson (Philadelphia: Fortress Press, 1966), 193–94.

80. Martin Luther, "Against the Roman Papacy an Institution of the Devil," trans. Eric W. Gritsch, in *Luther's Works*, vol. 41, ed. Eric W. Gritsch (Philadelphia: Fortress Press, 1966), 263.

81. See Martin Luther, "On the Papacy in Rome: Against the Most Celebrated Romanist in Leipzig," trans. Eric W. Gritsch and Ruth C. Gritsch, in *Luther's Works*, vol. 39, ed. Eric W. Gritsch (Philadelphia: Fortress Press, 1966), 57–58.

82. Calvin, *Institutes*, 1143–44.

83. Ibid., 1144.

84. Martin Luther, "Against Hanswurst," trans. Eric W. Grisch, in *Luther's Works*, vol. 41, 211.

85. Calvin, *Institutes*, 1144.

86. Luther, "Nobility," 194–95; Calvin, *Institutes*, 1145.

87. John Miller, *Popery and Politics in England, 1660–1688* (Cambridge: Cambridge University Press, 1973), 67.

88. Roman Catholicism did not collapse, but remained remarkably strong in parts of Britain. See Eamon Duffy, *The Stripping of the Altars: Traditional Religion in England, 1400–1580* (New Haven, CT: Yale University Press, 2005).

89. Reformation thinking was not new to Britain. John Wycliff developed many ideas in the fourteenth century that were later taken up by the Reformers, including the notion that the pope was the Antichrist himself. See Robert C. Fuller, *Naming the Antichrist: The History of an American Obsession* (Oxford: Oxford University Press, 1995), 37.

90. Kaplan, *Divided by Faith*, 88–91.

91. See Miller, *Popery and Politics*, 51–55.

92. Ibid., 72–73, 83–84.

93. Henry Care, quoted by Miller, *Popery and Politics*, 75.

94. See Anthony W. Marx, *Faith in Nation: Exclusionary Origins of Nationalism* (Oxford: Oxford University Press, 2003).

95. Miller, *Popery and Politics*, 72.

96. See the discussion of the "Fifth Monarchy Men" in *Messianic Revolution: Radical Religious Politics to the End of the Second Millennium*, ed. David S. Katz and Richard H. Popkin (New York: Hill and Wang, 1998), 65–80.

97. Miller, *Popery and Politics*, 88.

98. Ibid., 87–88.

99. See W. R. Ward, "Power and Piety: The Origins of Religious Revival in the Early Eighteenth Century," *Bulletin of the John Rylands University Library of Manchester* 63, no. 1 (1980): 231–52.

100. David Bebbington, *Evangelicalism in Modern Britain: A History from the 1730s to the 1980s* (Grand Rapids: Baker Book House, 1989), 20–21, 34–35.

101. Ibid., 107–9.

102. Ibid., 102.

103. The information and all quotations are from Bebbington, *Evangelicalism*, 101–2.

104. Ibid., 221–22, 255.

105. See, e.g., Malachi's (4:1) day that "will burn like a furnace," Jesus' teaching on the unexpected coming of the "Son of Man" (Matt 24), Paul's discussion of the "day of the Lord" (II Thess 2:2), and the "great white throne" of Revelation (20:11).

106. A good discussion of apocalyptic agitation at the turn of the first millennium, see Richard Erdoes, *AD 1000: A World on the Brink of Apocalypse* (Berkeley, CA: Seastone, 1998).

107. For an excellent summary of Protestant apocalyptic motivations, see MacCulloch, *Reformation*, 532–37; and Anthony F. Upton, *Europe, 1600–1789* (London: Arnold, 2001), 37–46.

108. Ernest R. Sandeen, *The Roots of Fundamentalism: British and American Millenarianism* (Chicago: University of Chicago Press, 1970), 6–7.

109. The title of the Reverend George Stanley Faber's early (1804) contribution illustrates the flavor of this literature: *Dissertation on the Prophecies That Have Been Fulfilled, Are Now Fulfilling, or Will Hereafter Be Fulfilled, Relative to the Great Period of 1260 Years*; cited by Sandeen, *Roots*, 8.

110. One important source of this premillennial revival was, ironically, the Chilean Jesuit Manuel Lacunza's *The Coming of Messiah in Glory and Majesty*. Lacunza finished the book around 1791 but he died before it was published in 1801. It appeared in Spanish in about 1812, and in English in 1826. Its English translator was the popular London pastor Edward Irving, who deeply influenced the development of British Evangelicalism. See Sandeen, *Roots*, 17–18.

111. Sandeen, *Roots*, 21–22.

112. Dewey M. Beegle, *Prophecy and Prediction* (Ann Arbor, MI: Pryor Pettegill, 1978), 160.

113. Sandeen, *Roots*, 17.

114. On Darby, see ibid., 60–80; Ernest R. Sandeen, *The Origins of Fundamentalism: Toward a Historical Interpretation* (Philadelphia: Fortress Press, 1968), 3–9; Beegle, *Prophecy and Prediction*, 157–59; and Bebbington, *Evangelicalism*, 192–93.

115. Ibid., 192.

116. Ibid., 192–93.

117. MacCulloch, *Reformation*, 536.

118. Jonathan I. Israel, *The Dutch Republic: Its Rise, Greatness, and Fall, 1477–1806* (Oxford: Clarendon Press, 1995), 148.

119. Benedict, *Christ's Churches*, 182.

120. Ibid., 199.

121. Israel, *Dutch Republic*, 389.

122. Ibid., 646–47.

123. See Thomas R. Rochon, *The Netherlands: Negotiating Sovereignty in an Interdependent World* (Boulder, CO: Westview Press, 1999), 26–29; and Rudy B. Andeweg and Galen A. Irwin, *Governance and Politics of the Netherlands* (New York: Palgrave Macmillan, 2002), 21–26.

124. James D. Bratt, "Introduction to 'Maranatha,'" in *Abraham Kuyper: A Centennial Reader*, ed. James D. Bratt (Grand Rapids: William B. Eerdmans, 1998), 205.

125. Abraham Kuyper, "Maranatha," in ibid., 212.

126. Ibid.

127. Ibid., 213.

128. Ibid., 213–14.

129. Peder A. Eidberg, "Norwegian Free Churches and Religious Liberty: A History," *Journal of Church and State* 37, no. 4 (1995): 869–85; Martin Schwarz Lausten, "The Early Reformation in Denmark and Norway 1520–1559," in *The Scandinavian Reformation: From Evangelical Movement to Institutionalization of Reform*, ed. Ole Peter Grell (Cambridge: Cambridge University Press, 1995), 32.

130. Eidberg, "Norwegian Free Churches." See also Frederick Hale, "Anticlericalism and Norwegian Society before the Breakthrough of Modernity," *Scandinavian Studies* 52, no. 3 (1980): 247.

131. Olaf Severn Olsen, "Civil Religion and Christianity in Sweden," *Fides et historia: Official Publication of the Conference on Faith and History* 7, no. 2 (1975): 42–43.

132. The pietist Erik Pontoppidan, whose text explaining Luther's *Shorter Catechism* (1737) was a standard in Denmark for nearly forty years and Norway for a hundred and fifty years, wrote a short tract on the occasion of the bicentenary of the Reformation (1736) that called for a "sweeping out" of the active remnants of paganism and Catholicism. See Henrik Horstbøll, "Pietism and the Politics of Catechisms: The Case of Denmark and Norway in the Eighteenth and Nineteenth Centuries," *Scandinavian Journal of History* 29, no. 2 (2004): 145.

133. For the pietist movement in Scandinavia, see B. J. Hovde, *The Scandinavian Countries, 1720–1865: The Rise of the Middle Classes*, vol. 1 (Boston: Chapman and Grimes, 1943), 303–47; Horstbøll, "Pietism"; and Olsen, "Civil Religion," 44–45.

134. Hanne Sanders, "Peasant Revivalism and Secularization: Protestant Popular Culture in Denmark and Sweden, 1820–1850," in *Individualisierung, Rationalisierung, Säkularisierung: Neue Wege der Religionsgeschichte*, ed. Michael Weinzierl (Munich: R. Oldenbourg Verlag München, 1997), 220.

135. Hovde, *Scandinavian Countries*, 315–18.

136. Ibid., 312–13.

137. Ibid., 331.

138. John Madeley, "Religion and the Political Order: The Case of Norway," in *Secularization and Fundamentalism Reconsidered: Religion and the Political Order*, vol. 3, ed. Jeffrey K. Hadden and Anson Shupe (New York: Paragon House, 1989), 292.

139. Hale, "Anticlericalism," 252.

140. David B. Woodward, *Aflame for God: Biography of Fredrik Franson* (Chicago: Moody Press, 1966), 147–49.

141. Greenfeld, *Nationalism*, 29–30.

142. Ibid., 30.

143. Anthony D. Smith, *Chosen Peoples* (Oxford: Oxford University Press, 2003), 32.

144. Ibid., 123–29.

145. Ibid., 116–17; for thorough examinations of the medieval origins of English nationalism, see Adrian Hastings, *The Construction of Nationhood: Ethnicity, Religion and Nationalism* (Cambridge: Cambridge University Press, 1997), 35–65; and J. C. D. Clark, "Protestantism, Nationalism, and National Identity, 1660–1832," *Historical Journal* 43, no. 1 (2000): 267.

146. Johnson, *English People*, 174.

147. Greenfeld, *Nationalism*, 63; see also 52.

148. Ibid., 61.

149. Quoted by Johnson, *English People*, 176–77.

150. Quoted in ibid., 179.

151. Linda Colley, *Britons: Forging the Nation 1707–1837* (New Haven, CT: Yale University Press, 1992).

152. Ibid., 25–26.

153. Quoted by Colley, *Britons*, 30.

154. Ibid., 53.

155. Simon Schama, *The Embarrassment of Riches: An Interpretation of Dutch Culture in the Golden Age* (New York: Alfred A. Knopf, 1987), 68.

156. Ibid., 95.

157. Kuyper, "Maranatha," 219.

158. Quoted by Schama, *Embarrassment of Riches*, 98.

159. Smith, *Chosen Peoples*, 19.

160. Greenfeld, *Nationalism*, 54–57.

161. Quoted by Greenfeld, *Nationalism*, 58.

162. Schama, *Embarrassment of Riches*, 104.

163. Ibid., 103.

164. MacCulloch, *Boy King*, 62.

165. Johnson, *English People*, 177.

166. Lausten, "Early Reformation," 33–37.

167. Colley, *Britons*, 47–48.

168. Ibid., 31.

169. See Greenfeld, *Nationalism*, 14; Hastings, *Construction of Nationhood*, 28.

170. The current monarch, King Felipe VI, does not use this title.

171. Quoted by Greenfeld, *Nationalism*, 94.

172. Quoted by Hastings, *Nationhood*, 98.

173. Ibid., 99.

174. Greenfeld, *Nationalism*, 102.

175. Quoted in ibid., 114. The intense focus on the French king's body and blood was eventually taken to absurd lengths—see ibid., 95–96; and Simon Schama, *Citizens: A Chronicle of the French Revolution* (New York: Alfred A. Knopf, 1989), 211.

176. Marx, *Faith in Nation*.

177. Ibid., 82.

178. Ibid., 44.

179. Both quotations are from Greenfeld, *Nationalism*, 106–7.

180. Hastings, *Nationhood*, 98.

181. Ibid., 122.

182. Chadwick, *Secularization*, 134.

183. See Greenfeld, *Nationalism*, 111.

184. Ibid., 167.

185. Schama, *Citizens*, 789.

186. Quoted by Chadwick, *Secularization*, 131.

187. Hastings, *Nationhood*, 119.

4

Political Movements

MODERNITY, TO NINETEENTH-CENTURY Catholics, was foreign and hostile. The triumph of sovereign states over Christendom, the emergence of secular liberal states after the French Revolution, and the growth of democratic forms had all challenged the rights and privileges of the Church. Nineteenth-century Protestants, by contrast, felt far more comfortable in the new Europe of sovereign states, welcoming liberalism and democracy as beneficial manifestations of Protestantism. Catholics and Protestants thus pulled away from one another in the nineteenth century, both culturally and politically. They sometimes lived side by side, but they existed in different worlds. And they viewed their surroundings differently. Catholics became defensive and resisted changes in politics and society while protecting the privileges of the Church. Lay and clerical Catholics first created mass movements and then confessional political parties to protect their communities and to press for policies consistent with the views of the Catholic hierarchy. And when it was clear that Europe would never permit restoration of the Catholic Church to supremacy in a reconstituted Christendom, Catholic intellectuals and politicians set aside their specifically religious goals and developed a vision for a united Europe that would move the Continent away from a destructive reliance on nation-states. A federal Europe became the aim of Catholics.

Protestants perceived the world through different glasses. They identified—fervently, even religiously—with their nation-states, and they usually embraced the liberal and democratic changes brought by the French Revolution. Needless to say, European political unity never became a Protestant goal. Furthermore, Protestants (outside the Netherlands) felt no need to organize political parties to challenge the state, resorting to confessional politics only when threatened by secularizing forces. Anti-Catholicism, however, remained a potent motivator for Protestants.

In this chapter we examine the divided world of post-Reformation Europe. Catholics and Protestants in nineteenth- and twentieth-century Europe lived in distinct confessional communities characterized by different cultures, ideologies, and political organizations. The debates surrounding post–World War II integration emerged from these distinct confessional cultures.

Confessionalism in Europe

The Reformation and subsequent religious wars brought down an "Iron Curtain" that divided Western Europe for centuries.[1] The Tridentine Catholic world was bound together by doctrine and ritual, ecclesiastical centralization, Jesuit education, and—most of all—loyalty to the pope. After the French Revolution the Catholic community built confessional walls even higher to repel secularism, liberalism, and democracy. Catholics created a full range of exclusive organizations—schools, labor unions, political parties, newspapers, youth groups, women's societies, athletic clubs, and more—that maintained the cohesion of their communities. Only in the mid–twentieth century, when secularization finally penetrated the European Catholic world, did "closed Catholicism" begin to open. Protestant Europe, conversely, never attained the transnational cultural unity of the Catholics, but it had also developed its own distinct, albeit somewhat fragmented culture.

Catholic Confessional Culture

The Catholic confessional culture emerging from the Counter-Reformation could trace its lineage to Latin Christendom—as a cultural expression more than a political unity. Christendom as a political community extended far beyond the borders of the Holy Roman Empire, but the pope's temporal authority, though in theory enforceable wherever the Roman Church was present, was in practice unevenly distributed, even in the High Middle Ages. Culture, in fact, defined Christendom.[2] As Europe emerged from the chaos of the barbarian invasions, the Frankish warriors, Roman popes, and Celtic monks forged a new civilization tied together by a liturgy that ordered the whole of life; by a language shared by a cosmopolitan monastic elite; by laws governing most public and private activities of both clergy and laity; by common art, music, and architecture; and by a supranational identity as Latin Christians. Latin culture did not eliminate local distinctions, but it employed them to serve a sacred community that stretched from Portugal to Poland, Sicily to Sweden, and even to the Latin outposts in the Middle East.

The Reformation, however, divided Latin Europe into two cultural communities.[3] Catholic Europe remained unified around Tridentine orthodoxy and papal authority. The Society of Jesus and a host of other new religious orders—through education, charity, and new forms of personal spirituality—aggressively defended Catholic belief and practice internally, and then helped Catholic princes claw back much of the territory that had been initially lost to Protestants in France, Germany, and Eastern Europe. With a baroque flourish, Catholic culture retained its hold on most of Europe, as magnificent churches adorned with elaborate sculptures, paintings, and woodcarvings visually tied this realm together. New feasts and popular cults focusing on the Sacred Hearts of Jesus and of Mary—along with elaborate processions—also united Catholics visually. But these common cultural cords were far more than visual. A new uniformity of ritual united Europe's Catholics. The Roman Church revised its liturgical books in the early seventeenth century, made them "nonreformable," and established the Congregation of Rites to enforce "central control."[4] The Reformation split Christian Europe, but ironically it worked to unite Catholics through art and ritual as never before.

The Catholic community, of course, took another blow from the French Revolution. But Catholic culture was resilient. Revolutionary experiments with secular cults, despite their crass imitations of Catholic rituals, were utter failures. Even nonbelievers recognized that the rhythms of secular life—from weekly work schedules to holiday traditions—would continue to follow Christian patterns. Kings could be overthrown in a day; but culture possessed an inertia that could not be reversed by political will. The Continent's Catholic nation-states, even those most influenced by the secularizing forces of the Revolution, would remain heavily influenced by Catholic culture well into the twenty-first century.

The continued influence of their common culture, however, did not mean that the Catholics always felt comfortable in traditionally Catholic parts of Europe. The French Revolution caused antirevolutionary Catholic communities in France and Germany to withdraw into self-contained worlds behind ideological and institutional walls. Nineteenth-century Catholics were increasingly conscious of having made a choice to join a distinct social group that transcended ethnic, class, and national divisions. The Revolution thus birthed "closed Catholicism," with unique beliefs, behaviors, and institutions as a distinct culture within the broader European civilization. Papal efforts, religious revival, lay activism, and participation in electoral politics in the 1920s and 1930s heightened the "shared purpose and common identity" among Catholics, not just within nation-states but also all across Europe. National boundaries—so fundamental in a Westphalian world—by necessity remained important within Catholicism, but the "Catholic horizons had broadened, and with this change came a sense of membership of a spiritual community that transcended secular boundaries."[5]

Protestant Confessional Culture

The Protestant world built its own walls of separation from the so-called papists. But with no centralizing authority to unify these opponents of Rome, Protestants threw up smaller barriers dividing Lutherans, Calvinists, Anabaptists, Anglicans, Methodists, and Baptists from each other. Doctrine was primary, as the various camps lobbed competing interpretations of Scripture at each other in the form of confessions of faith and an occasional catechism.[6] Forms of worship were also important. Lutherans and Anglicans preserved much of the ceremony of the old Church, and tolerated some images. But the Reformed sects eschewed images and cere-mony—some even forsook instrumental music—for a stripped-down, austere worship life.

These divisions in doctrine and worship, however, did not prevent the Protestants from developing distinctive cultural characteristics common to all. For instance, the reformers encouraged lay participation in worship, which no longer focused exclusively on the sacraments and instead became a corporate expression of praise and an opportunity to hear the Word of God preached. The reformers had encouraged prayers in the common tongue during worship, bringing the laity directly into communication with God. Music, including congregational singing (with or without instruments), became a central part of every service.[7] Above all, the Protestants elevated the vernacular Bible to prominence. In the place of images, saints, relics, pilgrimages, holy days, and processions, there was the preaching of the Word. Luther said "that a Christian congregation should never gather together without the preaching of God's Word and prayer."[8] Few Protestant congregations ignored his instruction.

Along with the preaching of the Word came a new Protestant emphasis on personal righteousness. Each believer, now justified by faith, stood free from condemnation and in a direct, unmediated relationship with God. Each person was responsible to live, by the power of the Spirit, a new, regenerated life according to God's law revealed in the Scriptures—not because he or she *had* to, but because as lovers of God, they *wanted* to. In short, the Reformation asked of all what pre-Reformation Catholics required only of those in religious orders: strict personal piety and moral perfection.[9] In practice it was the duty of the clergy, the civil authorities, or some combination of the two to enforce godly discipline. Reformed and Anabaptist communities, more than their Lutheran or Anglican counterparts, emphasized rules governing conduct, but some measure of discipline was found in all Protestant churches.[10] This "revolution of manners" had a profound, often astounding effect, especially in Reformed communities. In Calvin's Geneva during the late 1500s—not typical of all Protestant communities, but held up as an ideal—illegitimacy fell to just over 1 percent, and public manners in a city full of refugees were dramatically improved. One Italian Jesuit, no friend of Calvinism, remarked in 1580: "What caused me some surprise was that during the three days I was in Geneva I never heard any blasphemy, swearing, or indecent language."[11] In non-Reformed areas, such as Britain and Germany, the church hierarchy, more like civil servants than religious leaders, spent little time cultivating parishioners' spiritual life, but periodic revivals fostered individual conversion, personal piety, and upright living.[12] Thus Protestant communities across northern Europe upheld high standards of personal conduct and social responsibility—enforced externally by the state, and internally by conscience. These standards, in effect, were the foundations of a new European Protestant culture.

This new Protestant culture was most obvious where Protestants lived side by side with Catholics, as in the Netherlands, Germany, and Northern Ireland. In these countries, especially the Netherlands, a state-supported pillarization of society eventually arose in the late nineteenth century, characterized by "a series of discrete subcultures, each living a life largely separated from that of the others, each represented by its own political parties, and each having its own characteristic religious institutions."[13] Catholics tended to form tight pillars; Protestants often split between a more theologically and politically conservative pillar and a liberal one.[14] Though this pillarization promoted cultural cohesion within the confessional communities, it widened the gap between them.

Protestant culture, unlike Catholicism, did not produce a transnational community. The Protestants certainly joined political and military alliances in the sixteenth and seventeenth centuries to fight off the militant Counter-Reformation, but these alliances were often frustrated by theological disagreements and the realpolitik of the Protestant princes. Protestants, for instance, were hopeful that a great alliance of Protestant nations stretching from Scotland to Transylvania would ultimately defeat Catholic armies in the Thirty Years' War. But this plan failed when James I and the British refused to fully commit to the war effort, leaving much smaller Sweden to lead the Protestant forces.

Although the Protestant nations had difficulty forging an international political community, a recognizable Protestant culture did emerge, in part due to the mass migration of religious refugees, such as the Huguenots, to Britain, the Netherlands, and the American colonies, where they found other breakaway traditions.[15] Protestants across Europe exhibited certain commonalities: a spirit of moral rectitude, individualism, entrepreneurialism, and skepticism; a commitment to the written word; a shunning of earthly pleasures; an austere artistic style; and, everywhere but Germany, a growing trust in democratic decision making.[16] At a more popular level, Protestants had their beer, and Catholics had their wine.[17] Protestantism, however, never achieved the cultural coherence found in Catholic Europe. Northern Germany, Scandinavia, the Netherlands, Britain, and parts of Switzerland were linked by common sensibilities, but without an institutionalized common cultural link like the Roman Church, these countries never achieved the transnational community spirit found among Catholics.

Catholicism and Protestantism divided what was once Latin Christendom into two large camps, which by the nineteenth century had developed different cultures. Catholics' cultural uniformity, which centered on the papacy, surpassed even the unity of medieval Christendom, while Protestants created a "Protestant ethos" but little more. These separate cultures, not surprisingly, resulted in different ideologies and political movements. In the next section we begin to trace the ideological and political implications of Europe's division into confessional cultures.

Catholic Politics

The French Revolution had accelerated the Tridentine movement of giving greater spiritual and ecclesiastical authority to the pope, even as his temporal power waned. But this ecclesiastical centralization in the pope's hands did not also achieve a homogeneous Catholic politics. The Revolution created a new political world of separated churches and states and mobilized masses, one that caught the Roman Church off balance. For a century it floundered about for a viable political strategy, often at odds with itself.

The Church hierarchy rejected the liberal state and developing democracy, but its official position masked deeper complexities. Tension existed, for instance, *within* the eighteenth-century French Church. Its high prelates were divided between proponents of the liberty of the Church from both Rome and Paris and partisans of the monarchy's attempts to control it for "reasons of state." The aristocratic upper clergy enjoyed the luxuries of a wealthy Church, while the impoverished lower clergy resented its inequalities. In addition, the growing middle class came to see the Church as restrictive and increasingly irrelevant, prompting many to remain in the Church but not of it—or to leave it altogether.[18] Thus, when the Revolution finally erupted, some Catholics were active supporters. An alliance of middle-class Catholics and the lower clergy proved essential to the success of the revolt. Surprisingly, a third of the clergy swore allegiance to the Civil Constitution in the early days of the Republic, but when the liberal state turned totalitarian, the tenuous union of Revolution and religion was over.[19] Liberal Catholics again made common cause with the revolutionaries in 1830 and 1848, but without papal support or great political success.[20] Catholicism and liberalism would not be reconciled in the nineteenth century.

In fact, Catholicism and liberalism grew further apart. Liberal attacks heightened the Church's need for an effective strategy to protect its rights, especially in sensitive areas such as education. The hierarchy underlined its rejection of liberalism by discouraging or even prohibiting Catholics from participating in democratic politics. Prelates instead preferred to lobby governments directly. Nevertheless, the age of mass politics had arrived, and Church leaders were powerless to stop Catholics—lay and clergy alike—from creating organizations of workers, farmers, former soldiers, women, youths, and others. Although the tactics of such groups were decidedly liberal, their ideologies were not. Almost all of them, often encouraged or led by the clergy, were aggressively antiliberal and antidemocratic. The goal was to create a Catholic movement so large, monolithic, and comprehensive that it would, as Kalyvas puts it, "swallow the Liberal state and reestablish the Church in its former glory."[21]

Although the Church rejected electoral politics, the bishops soon learned to play the democratic power game. They decided to combine the political potential of the Catholic mass movements with Conservative parties that pledged to defend the Church's interests. These alliances proved successful, and thus Catholics in liberal states tasted political power for the first time and—against the wishes of the Church—began to accept parliamentary democracy. This Conservative–Catholic alliance, however, proved uncomfortable, especially for workers, who disagreed with the Conservatives on most political issues other than the rights of the Church. This prompted some Catholic politicians to found independent political parties against the wishes of Church leaders, first in Germany (1871), and then in Belgium (1884), the Netherlands (1888), and Austria (1890). Soon these parties had adopted programs that went beyond defense of the Church to address broader social and political problems. Catholic party leaders remained deferential to the Church hierarchy, but they did not always take orders. When in 1887 the pope and bishops negotiated an agreement with German chancellor Otto von Bismarck requiring the Catholic Center Party's vote in favor of the chancellor's military budget, the party refused, exhibiting just the kind of independence that Rome had feared.[22]

The construction of a distinctive Catholic social policy in the late nineteenth century provided these Catholic political parties with an ideology that appealed to Catholics across the social spectrum, including workers. In 1891 Pope Leo XIII's encyclical *Rerum Novarum* gave Catholics a radical political and social program that challenged secular ideologies. The pope rejected both the extreme individualism of liberalism and the tyranny of socialism, outlining a middle-ground program of worker benefits, private property, family, and class unity.[23] In 1901 he labeled the program "Christian Democracy" in another encyclical (*Graves De Communi Rè*).[24] The Catholic parties championed this social program, particularly after World War I, coupled with a commitment to democratic institutions that buried any remaining nostalgia for the ancien régime.[25] This development was encouraged by a postwar religious revival that swept Catholic Europe, bringing pious and stridently countercultural young people into the Church. A vibrant Catholic intelligentsia, centered in the Catholic universities, began publishing newspapers and journals that promoted discussions of democracy and human liberties. Although these discussions included the antimodernist approach of the French literary critic Henri Massis, who called for a revived medieval Catholicism to avert the calamity facing the war-torn West (the "Occident"), most of the young Catholic intellectuals looked forward, not back.[26]

The most important influence on Christian Democracy between the world wars was the "personalism" of Emmanuel Mounier, Jacques Maritain, Denis de Rougemont, and others.[27] The personalists made it the first duty of every society to protect the inherent worth of every human "person," both body and soul, by setting the person at the center of political, economic, and social life. Liberalism stripped humans of their dignity, by wrenching them from their natural social groupings and reducing them to atomized producers and consumers. Socialism created a deified super state that crushed their freedom and dignity beneath a powerful, dehumanizing bureaucracy. The personalist solution was to create a society built on laws that protected human dignity, upheld the natural rights of human beings, nurtured the whole person in natural communities (particularly families), and supported the Church in its spiritual mission. Personalism rejected the tendency of both socialism and nationalism toward a totalitarianism that subordinates the interests of human beings to the interests of the state. Human dignity transcends the state's interests, and also national borders; states, to be of any use, must serve the interests of persons.

Personalists prepared the way for a Catholic embrace of democracy by giving Catholics the intellectual tools needed to construct a political philosophy that legitimated government by popular will. Personalism, in short, made democracy safe for Catholics. But that did not make all Catholics democrats—or, indeed, all personalists democrats. Interwar Catholicism continued to distrust liberal notions of individual rights, preferring to see individual rights in the context of social groups, above all, in families. Furthermore, following Pius XI's *Quadragesimo Anno* (1933), Catholics came to distrust the economic individualism (and materialism) that seemed to accompany political individualism, preferring to order economic activities through corporate structures—most important, labor unions—that would protect the social rights of persons. Thus, many interwar Catholics still rejected liberal parliamentary democracy. Jacques Maritain, for instance, was active in Action Française, a Catholic monarchist group with anti-Semitic undertones, until Pius XI condemned it in 1926.[28] Maritain, like the Church itself, moved slowly toward liberal democracy as the century wore on.

In the 1920s Catholic political parties regularly participated in coalition governments in Austria, Belgium, Italy, Germany, and the Netherlands, but all was not well. Despite the obvious electoral advantages of multiclass parties, the divisions between working-class and middle-class Catholics eventually took a toll. Class conflict contributed to the electoral decline of Catholic parties, starting with the collapse of the Italian People's Party in 1926.[29] In addition, the revival that energized Catholics to work toward the "Christian society" also diverted many young people toward more explicitly religious activities. Finally, the hierarchy itself undermined the Catholic parties, because Church officials continued to prefer direct diplomacy to electoral participation, bypassing the parties. They also created "Catholic Action" movements across Europe to compete directly with socialist organizations. These lay movements sought to re-Christianize Europe by raising awareness of Catholic teaching and by conducting campaigns—through demonstrations, parades, and rallies—in favor of Catholic virtues and against vices. Catholic Action—not parties in Parliament—was the hierarchy's favored means of transforming Europe.

The Catholic electoral slump of the late 1920s persisted into the 1930s, as the Great Depression and political instability discredited Catholic parties in government. Meanwhile, the radicalization of Catholic laity in the 1920s and the hierarchy's natural authoritarianism made autocratic means attractive for pursuing the

Church's social and political ends. As a result, fascism drew many Catholics into its ranks during the 1920s, particularly in Spain and Mussolini's Italy. And although Nazi paganism repulsed many Christians, many German Catholics supported right-wing movements. Pius XI eventually condemned anticlerical fascism in 1931, but Catholics were quick to back Catholic authoritarianism in Austria and Slovakia. By the end of the 1930s, however, Catholics had to choose: fascism or liberal democracy. They continued to insist on a third way, but their pleas were swallowed up in the onslaught of World War II.

Catholics eased—reluctantly, at best—into electoral politics in the nineteenth and early twentieth centuries as liberalism took hold in countries with large Catholic populations, such as France, Germany, Italy, Austria, Belgium, and the Netherlands. Christian Democracy as an ideology, with its unapologetic defense of the rights of the Church and its centrist mix of support for private capital and concern for the laboring masses, gave Catholic political parties a coherent political map to guide them through domestic policy debates. But Christian Democracy also incorporated an international strategy that drew directly on Catholic universalism and its distrust—and often outright rejection—of sovereign nation-states and the Westphalian system. In the next section we explore the influence of this universalism on the "idea of Europe" and on the development of federalism as a core ideological commitment of European Catholics.

Catholicism and the "Idea of Europe"

The "idea of Europe"—the notion that Europe ought to be politically united—is rooted in Christian universalism and ancient notions of universal empire. Although the Protestants contributed to the discussion of European unity, Catholics were the primary drivers of the debate. For Catholics, the idea of Europe helps reconcile the realities of a Westphalian system with what Denis de Rougemont (himself a Swiss Protestant) identified as a longing for a "universal peace" that would end internal conflict and external threats, ensure economic prosperity, and establish a "spiritual community."[30] This has been the European dream—stretching back to the Middle Ages.

The Idea of Europe before World War I

For most of Europe's turbulent history, the unity of Christendom, indeed, has been a *dream*. But plans to realize this dream appeared as early as the thirteenth century and continued to surface after World War II. All were rooted in distinctly Christian—mostly Roman Catholic—ideas.

Pre-Reformation unity proposals were consciously Christian, and naturally Roman Catholic, although not always acceptable to the Church. Dante Alighieri, for instance, called for a world government—a new universal Roman Empire—that would be governed temporally by an emperor and spiritually by the pope: "Thus the reins of man are held by a double driver according to man's twofold end; one is the supreme pontiff, who guides mankind with revelations to life eternal, and the other is the emperor, who guides mankind with philosophical instructions to temporal happiness."[31] Dante's French contemporary, Pierre Du Bois, rejected arguments in favor of universal empire, but he granted the pope important powers to mediate disputes among princes, who would be constituted as a Christian Council. In both cases, these dreamers' plans were heavily influenced by medieval theories of Christendom: one Church, one state.

The Reformation and the subsequent protracted religious wars produced a flurry of new proposals from both Catholics and Protestants. No great ideological wall divided the Catholic from the Protestant proposals; all were concerned with peace, and many with religious reconciliation. Some Catholics still envisioned a reunited Catholic Christendom; but by the end of the sixteenth century, most serious thinkers had come to see this goal as unattainable. Catholics and Protestants both began devising arbitration schemes that started with the reality of a religiously and politically divided Europe. Many plans were rather similar, calling for a gathering of princes to resolve conflicts—often with the pope presiding. This was true for Catholics, such as Émeric Crucé, as well as for Protestants, such as the Lutheran Gottfried Wilhelm von Leibnez.[32]

Although great differences in approach to unity did not open up between Catholics and Protestants, distinctions in tone can be discerned. Central to the Protestant proposals were (not always subtle) commitments to the sovereignty of nation-states. Two examples illustrate the point. First, the Calvinist Duc de Sully, who had served Henry IV of France as a loyal and able minister until Henry's assassination in 1610, based his "Grand Design" on a reorganization of Europe into fifteen states of equal power. Each state would have the right to decide its own national religion. The emperor and—surprisingly for a Protestant, although writing for a Catholic monarch—the pope would preside over a dispute settlement structure. But the primary mechanism for maintaining peace, according to Sully, would be the "equilibrium of power," which would make it impossible for one state to gain advantage over another. In the Grand Design states would remain sovereign, but their ambition would be checked by the political power of their neighbors and the moral power of the emperor and the pope.

A second Protestant example comes from William Penn, a Quaker, who in 1693 offered a plan to create an "Imperial Parliament" that would meet regularly to settle disputes. This system would include weighted parliamentary voting and a rotating presidency, but Penn made it clear that the internal sovereignty of each nation would not be compromised: "[The states] remain as Sovereign at Home as ever they were. . . . It may be the War Establishment may be reduced, which will indeed of

Course follow, or be better employed to the Advantage of the Publick."[33] Penn's system would reduce the freedom of states to make war in exchange for better protection from aggressive nations seeking influence over domestic politics in smaller states—hardly a recipe for ending the state system.

In contrast to the Protestants Sully and Penn, the French Abbé de Saint-Pierre called for a "Treaty of Union, and a Perpetual Congress, much after the Model . . . of the seven Sovereignties of *Holland* . . . [to] form an *European Union*" (emphasis in the original).[34] His radical vision of union included a European Senate with equal voting, and courts to adjudicate economic and political disputes. Though his plan was not specifically Catholic, giving no role to the pope or the Church, it went much further than Sully's and Penn's in creating a truly federal structure.

The Enlightenment saw the rise of a more self-conscious Europe. The Age of Exploration had brought new cultures into view, which only served to underline European cultural unity. As Jean-Jacques Rousseau put it, "The nations of Europe form a kind of closely knit society."[35] This awareness of Europe's unique culture inspired the brightest stars of the Age of Enlightenment and the Romantic Era to reflect on the possibility of European peace—and thus Bentham, Burke, Vico, Comte, Constant, Fichte, Goethe, Hegel, Kant, Schelling, de Staël, Voltaire, and others all offered their proposals for a peaceful Europe. Some, such as the Comte de Saint-Simon, provided detailed plans for a federated Europe; others suggested, often vaguely, some assembly of princes or diplomats to adjudicate disputes in an early version of the League of Nations; and still others followed Victor Hugo's passionate belief in a coming "United States of Europe." Immanuel Kant, in his optimistic 1795 essay *Perpetual Peace: A Philosophical Sketch*, offered the most influential proposal. Drawing on social contract theorists, such as Thomas Hobbes and John Locke, Kant argued for a society of nations—what he called "a federation of free states"—that would leave behind their perpetual state of war and establish a community of law ("covenant of peace"), "which will be ever increasing and would finally embrace all the peoples of the Earth."[36]

In many of these proposals—though not Kant's—Christianity was seen as a binding cultural force, but the plans of the Enlightenment rationalists were not designed to restore Christendom. Nor did they aim to create a universal empire, despite (or in many cases, *because of*) Napoleon's Carolingian attempt to force Europe into what he called "a single national body."[37] Enlightenment intellectuals instead called for a united Europe based on law and cooperation, not conquest.

Not everyone agreed with the rationalism and secularism of Enlightenment thinkers. Some Catholic intellectuals were deeply troubled by Europe's spiritual bankruptcy, which they attributed to the division of Christendom by the Reformation and the overthrow of throne and altar by the Revolution. Count Joseph de Maistre of France, one of the most popular reactionaries, argued in his widely read *The Pope* that the nations of Europe must unite in humble submission and form "an universal republic, under the measured supremacy of the supreme spiritual power."[38] His defense of papal supremacy and appeal to Protestants (starting with the English!) to "return to the common father" was a startling call to restore medieval Christendom.[39] In a similar vein, several Germans, often Catholic converts, lamented the Revolution and called for restoration of the old order. Johann Joseph von Görres—in his later years as an Ultramontane—called for a revived Germanic Holy Roman Empire, and Frederich von Schlegel decried the loss of a "Christian Empire" resting on "the perfect unity of religious principles."[40] But perhaps the most passionate Catholic romantic was Friedrich von Hardenberg, otherwise known as Novalis, who in 1799 called for a European religious revival and the reestablishment of church government: "Only religion can awaken Europe again, and reassure the peoples, and install Christendom with new splendor visibly on Earth in its old peace-establishing office. . . . Christendom must come alive again and be effective, and, without regard to national boundaries, again form a visible church which will take into its bosom all souls athirst for the supernatural."[41]

These romantics swam against the liberal intellectual current of the era, but they captured the antiliberal, antidemocratic sentiment of the Church hierarchy and Catholic mass movements. The Catholics of the nineteenth century, who were often walled off socially from people of other confessions, saw no hope for Europe save in the restoration of the authority of the Church over all of Christendom. Achieving this end, however, would require accommodation to the emerging liberal order; at the very least, Catholics must participate in existing political parties, or begin forming their own. They did both, but they came more and more to favor distinctively Catholic electoral vehicles. Thus, the rise of Catholic political parties in Germany, Belgium, and elsewhere during the late nineteenth century gave closed Catholicism a voice in government. But the formation of these parties required a shift away from the political pursuit of an unrealistic medieval dream and toward a more realistic political ideology.

The Idea of Europe in the Interwar Period

The uneasy interwar years between 1919 and 1939 witnessed a surge in "federalist" thought and activity. This surge—which was due first to international cooperative efforts through the League of Nations, and then to the return of aggressive nationalism—was not particularly strong and attracted little public attention.[42] Ironically, part of the problem was disunity among those calling for federalist unity: Some advocated European federation, some world government, and others Marxist solidarity, and still others were working for simple economic cooperation. Furthermore, those nations that engaged in serious attempts to establish customs unions and integrated economies, such as the countries in the Danube River region and the Low Countries, or those pursuing defense alliances, such as the Scandinavian nations, found it difficult to overcome nationalist sentiment.[43] In the end, all these interwar integration efforts failed.

The prospect of European unity seemed most attractive in the 1920s, but it faded in the early 1930s. Ideas of European union were rooted both in the secular Enlightenment and in Catholic notions of Christendom, but Catholics were often the most prominent advocates of a democratic European union.

THE CHRISTIAN DEMOCRATS

The Catholic interest in European unity received a boost from the Vatican at the height of World War I. In August 1917 Pope Benedict XV offered a peace plan: Replace "the material force of arms" with "the moral force of law," and settle international disputes with an "institution of arbitration." Once international law had been made supreme, the pope suggested that all obstacles "to the ways of communication between peoples be removed," in order to "open new sources of prosperity and progress to all."[44] This plan went nowhere; but later, in a May 1920 encyclical, *Pacem, Dei Munus Pulcherrimum*, the pope urged the peoples of Europe to "clear their hearts of bitterness," "abandon hatred and . . . pardon offenses," and "draw together in the bonds of Christian charity." Moreover, he called on the world's nations to "establish a true peace among themselves and join together in an alliance which shall be just and therefore lasting."[45] Again, the European powers did nothing, but the proposal to establish multilateral organizations and international institutions to mediate disputes caught the attention of some Catholic politicians.

In response to the pope's encyclical, the Italian People's Party drew up a political program calling for an "international society with characteristics deriving from a juridical organization of international life."[46] Led by Don Luigi Sturzo, a charismatic Catholic priest and political theorist, the party set out to unite Catholic political groups in an international organization of Christian parties as a "means of achieving a world order based upon peace and justice."[47] Sturzo's activity between 1920 and 1925 brought him into contact with Catholic leaders in many countries. (On a visit to Germany, for instance, he included in his delegation another leader of the Italian People's Party, Alcide De Gasperi. At a stop in Cologne, De Gasperi, the future postwar Italian prime minister, met Mayor Konrad Adenauer, the future German chancellor.) In 1925 Sturzo's work came to fruition with the creation of the International Secretariat of Democratic Parties of Christian Inspiration (SIPDIC). Prominent European Catholics took part in SIPDIC's proceedings, including German chancellor Karl Wirth, Dutch prime minister Ruys de Beerenbrouck, and Robert Schuman of France.[48]

The European Catholic political parties were conscious of the need to defend "Christian civilization." However, they rejected widespread notions of reviving Christendom by authoritarian means, arguing instead for democratic governments based on "Christian principles."[49] Their first political priority was the international program inspired by the pronouncements of Benedict XV and the principles of personalism. This program was straightforward: Law must replace force as the basis for international relations; international institutions must adjudicate disputes; borders must be opened to foster peaceful exchanges; and enemies must be reconciled. At the Congress of Cologne in 1932, SIPDIC adopted a resolution strikingly similar to later actual postwar integration efforts, calling for a European "common market."[50] This market would produce "a freer circulation of products, capital, and persons" as a necessary first step to "complete assimilation," presumably of the separate European economies into one. And, even more important, "interpenetration of the economy and politics must lead to an examination and to the liquidation, in a spirit of mutual understanding, of all the obstacles that have hitherto been set against political cooperation."[51] These Catholic political leaders had staked out a clear position: National borders were obstacles to peace and prosperity. But their program for overcoming borders and for integrating European political and economic life stalled; the Great Depression and the rise of fascism ended any hope among Catholics that their plans for Europe would take more than paper form. But these plans remained in the minds and hearts of two men present in Cologne: Adenauer and Schuman.[52]

PAN-EUROPA

The Christian Democrats were not alone in developing a program for European unity between the wars. Politically independent efforts were also under way to convince leaders that unification was the only way out of the European crisis. One of the most prominent advocates for federation was Count Richard Coudenhove-Kalergi, a Bohemian aristocrat who worked tirelessly for a European union.[53] His widely read *Pan-Europa* (1926) and the popular Pan-Europa movement he founded appealed to a broad range of European intellectual elites. He was born to an Austrian father and Japanese mother but was raised and educated as a devout Catholic in his father's tradition. He did not take a distinctly Catholic perspective on European unity, but he did see the Continent "bound together by the Christian religion, by European science, art and culture, which rest on a *Christian-Hellenic* basis."[54] Such unity ran deeper than religious and language divisions, thus justifying the creation of a single European political order.[55]

Coudenhove-Kalergi's political strategy reflected his elite background, as he relied primarily on extensive interaction with politicians to argue his case against suicidal nationalism and to encourage steps toward unity. He had some effect on elite opinion, as a number of democratic politicians signed up for his plan, but the movement was not particularly powerful. Only once did he come close to influencing political decision making. The French Socialist prime minister Aristide Briand, with whom Coudenhove-Kalergi developed a close personal relationship in the 1920s, did offer a 1930 plan for a European confederation, loosely following the staged approach proposed in *Pan-Europa*.[56] The Briand Plan, however, ran into opposition from nearly every quarter and was soon overtaken by events. As with the Christian Democratic ideas, the Great Depression and Hitler's rise made implementation of the Briand Plan unthinkable.

The Pan-Europa movement lacked genuine political muscle and—it must be said—theoretical depth, but it held the attention of those on the Continent who were interested in moving beyond the balance-of-power system. Of course, Coudenhove-Kalergi was not the only continental European writing about unity. Other proposals came from Maurice Renoult, Bertrand de Jouvenel, Roger Manuel, Max Waechter, Kerman Kranold, Edo Fimmen, and Edouard Herriot, among others.[57] But these writings did not inspire the creation of a transnational pressure group, as did *Pan-Europa*, and Coudenhove-Kalergi must be credited with moving the idea of unity out of the intellectual ghetto and into the minds of elites.

BRITISH FEDERALISM

Surprisingly, the Continent was not the only place where a European unity movement took shape. Britain also had its own, quite separate "federal" movement. For more than a century, the bulk of the British political class has been allergic to the word "federalism," yet the federal idea has deep roots in British political theory. British intellectuals, especially in the interwar period, produced works that were later influential in the postwar integration movement. The British federalists were hardly united; but two broad streams stand out, both influenced by British Catholics.

The first stream—which was not strictly a federalist school—emerged as a distinctly Catholic movement that focused on Western Europe as a cultural entity unified by its common experience of Latin Christianity.[58] The intellectual and spiritual successors to Cardinal Newman and Cardinal Manning saw in the Church the glue that held Europe together. The prolific twentieth-century Catholic writer Hilaire Belloc, whose mother converted from Unitarianism to Catholicism under the tutelage of Manning and attended Newman's Oratory School, asserted rather belligerently that Europe was a cultural and religious unity and that only Catholics could fully understand its essence. He wrote in *Europe and the Faith* (1920): "A Catholic as he reads that story [of Europe] does not grope at it from without, he understands it from within. He cannot understand it altogether, because he is a finite being; but he is also that which he has to understand. The Faith is Europe and Europe is the Faith. . . . The Church is Europe: and Europe is the Church."[59]

The English historian Christopher Dawson, who was raised Anglo-Catholic but converted to Rome in 1914, took a more sober line that proved influential. In *The Making of Europe: An Introduction to the History of European Unity* (1932), he argued that Europe was in fact forged during those same centuries that were considered by Enlightenment thinkers to be the "Dark Ages," when the Catholic Church came to dominate the West. Dawson, rather than seeing the establishment of Western Christendom as a disastrous diversion on a triumphant march to modernity, credits the Church with fashioning a new civilization, built from the remnants of Rome and the customs and ambitions of the Teutonic tribes. For Dawson, the Church was essential to making Europe Europe; the Roman Church, he argued, made Latin Europe a cultural family and a single community. This was the starting point for any discussion of European political unity.[60]

British Catholics were in the forefront of scholarship examining the cultural basis for European unity, but they also took a leading role in deepening the theory of federalism and placing it in a European context. Philip Kerr, after 1930 known as Lord Lothian, was arguably the most important intellectual and political figure in the British federalist movement. He was raised in a staunchly Catholic aristocratic family, and like Belloc, was educated at the Oratory School. He seems to have thought of entering the priesthood; but in the years before World War I, he experienced a crisis of faith that led him to abandon Catholicism for a deep devotion to Christian Science.

Before World War I, Lothian worked in South Africa as a civil servant and joined a group of young men gathered around a former British high commissioner for Southern Africa, Lord Milner. The Milner group, known as the Kindergarten, drew on American federalism and the writings of Hamilton, Madison, and Jay in *The Federalist* to work out an elaborate plan for a federal South Africa. The Kindergarten's efforts were not entirely successful in South Africa; but its members had caught the federalist bug, and so they now turned to reforming the British imperial system. They eventually developed a full-fledged political program for transforming the British Empire into a federal union, which its members carried back to Britain. When Lothian returned home in 1909, he helped establish the Round Table, a pressure group dedicated to an imperial federation. He edited the group's publication for several years, before accepting a position as Prime Minister David Lloyd George's private secretary, thus launching a successful political and diplomatic career. His premature death in 1940 while serving as British ambassador to the United States cut short his life, but not his influence.[61]

Lothian's writings drew heavily on American federal thought and experience, as well as on the Enlightenment idealism of Immanuel Kant, but they also bear the marks of his thoroughly Catholic training, and, perhaps, the influence of Catholic historians. Lothian's solution to the problem of war was to abolish national sovereignty and to create federal institutions at a global level to enforce supranational law. His 1937 lecture "The Demonic Influence of National Sovereignty" embedded this theme in a distinctly Christian context: The "worship of national sovereignty" is at the heart of the international crisis; and this idolatry produces "demonic evils" that lead to war.[62] The solution is a global federal system.[63]

Lothian's vision was universal and grounded in the historical experience of Christendom, which for him became the ideal. Evil emerged from the Reformation's creation of nation-states demanding absolute loyalty. Overcoming evil required common people to love God more than the state. Only then would a federal system be both practical and just.

Lothian's ideas gained only a small audience. Three young Oxford graduates—Charles Kimber, Patrick Ransome, and Derek Rawnsley—issued an invitation in 1939 to selected individuals to form an advocacy group dedicated to world federation. The group adopted the name "Federal Union" and quickly added to its membership a long list of prominent academics and political leaders.[64] Lothian was one of the first to respond to the invitation, and he wrote an early pamphlet for the group. Federal Union, however, contained several individuals who believed that European federation would precede world government. Lothian hesitated to back such a plan, preferring instead a British–American partnership better suited to forging the way. Lothian seems later to have accepted the idea that Europe would federalize first, but maintained that Britain *should* not and *would* not participate.[65] He did not live long enough to see if he was right.

The British federalist movement peaked in 1940–41, and it then succumbed to internal division between world and European federalists—and general apathy. It failed to seriously affect British decision making or popular opinion, but Lord Lothian's writings influenced federalist thinking on the Continent.[66] Altiero Spinelli and Ernesto Rossi read Lothian's Burge Memorial Lecture, "Pacifism Is Not Enough (Nor Patriotism Either)," on the prison island of Ventotene before writing a federalist manifesto that became the political program of most of the noncommunist resistance movement on the Continent.[67] Thus, though Lothian's work had little discernible impact in Britain, it offered resistance fighters in Nazi-occupied territory a political alternative to a discredited international system. [68]

For Catholics in modern Europe, the nationalistic wars of the nineteenth and twentieth centuries were evidence enough that the nation-state system had utterly failed. A new form of unity in Europe was the only way out of the Continent's destructive cycle. Protestants, however, saw things quite differently.

Protestant Politics

Protestant politics in modern Europe differed from Catholic politics in several ways. First, Protestants for the most part were not alienated from the state in the nineteenth century, as were the continental Catholics. The revolutions that began in France overthrew the Catholic Church when they toppled national monarchs. Catholics were forced to enter electoral politics in states they did not accept as legitimate and in opposition to liberals and socialists who were committed to undermining any attempt by the hierarchy to reestablish the temporal authority of the Church. Most Protestants faced a very different situation.

First, the Protestant churches relied on their princes for protection from Counter-Reformation forces, and as a consequence they never gained or lost their independence and were "subsumed into the apparatus of the state."[69] Moreover, the revolutions did not sweep away Protestant monarchs or their established churches; instead, Protestantism nurtured the rise of liberalism and democracy in Britain, Denmark, Norway, and Sweden—although less so in Germany. Protestant resistance to the French Revolution—in particular, its secularizing elements—did motivate antirevolutionary political action in the Netherlands.[70] But the Dutch Protestants embraced the representative aspects of liberal government while rejecting the secularism of radical liberalism and socialism. In short, except in the Netherlands, Protestants were never forced to organize politically as a bloc against the state. They largely embraced liberal and democratic politics.

Second, Protestants did not usually establish confessional parties. In the religiously homogeneous nation-states of Scandinavia, social cleavages—especially along class lines—accounted for most of the political tension.[71] Britain's diversity of Protestant sects did give rise to political conflict, with Anglicans supporting the Tories and most nonconformists siding with the Liberals.[72] But, again, class divisions contributed more to political party formation. The same was largely true in Switzerland, where Protestants divided politically by class rather than confession and did not establish sectarian parties. There were exceptions to this rule, however. Where Protestants and Catholics still rubbed shoulders, Protestants formed confessional parties in opposition to Catholics, as well as to secular liberals and socialists. These parties sprang up prominently in the Netherlands and Northern Ireland, as one would expect, but only sputteringly in pre–World War I Germany. In the twentieth century confessional parties emerged in Scandinavia, not in response to Catholic pressure but rather as a countercultural challenge to secularization.

Third, European Protestants remained anti-Catholic, even where few Catholics existed. In Britain the Gordon Riots of 1780 and strong popular opposition to the Catholic Emancipation Act of 1829 showed the depth of anti-Catholic feeling. Britain, however, was comparatively tolerant. Not until the mid–twentieth century did all the Nordic countries pass laws guaranteeing religious liberty. Norway allowed Catholic services in 1843, and in 1845 it permitted dissenter congregations to organize. But its prohibitions against the Jesuits remained until 1956.[73] Sweden continued to restrict Catholics and the existence of monasteries until 1951.[74] For Scandinavians to be Catholic was to be truly "foreign"; few Catholics lived in Scandinavia, and fewer were native born. Scandinavians saw their Lutheran religion and their nationality as completely intertwined. As for religiously mixed areas, including the Netherlands and Northern Ireland, anti-Catholicism continued to run deeply in some particularly conservative circles. Looking at hard-line Dutch and Northern Irish Protestants in the late twentieth century was a bit like peering back into the sixteenth century.

Finally, few Protestants believed that a European federation was necessary or desirable. National identity rested on sacred foundations that had been laid during the

Reformation. Nationalism and lingering anti-Catholicism made Protestant countries lukewarm at best and often more openly hostile to the "idea of Europe."

Protestant politics demonstrated transnational similarities, but national particularities remained significant. A brief survey of religious politics in the important Protestant regions will help place national approaches to European integration in context.

Germany

German Protestants drifted in a Conservative, Liberal, or Socialist direction, depending on class location rather than religious affiliation. Most German Protestants (especially Prussians) supported the nation-building strategies of Otto von Bismarck, even though the churches remained organized along state lines.[75] Small Protestant fringe parties made occasional appearances but never lasted long or made much of a political impact. A Protestant court chaplain, Adolf Stöker, founded the Christian Social Party in 1878 to provide a home for religious workers dissatisfied with the Social Democrats. The party never won more than one seat in the Reichstag, and it folded after Stöker undermined its credibility with his anti-Semitism.[76] During the Weimar Republic the nationalist Christian Social People's Service formed in response to developments on the political right, but it was dissolved by the Nazis in 1933.

Support for nationalism, however, made German Protestants vulnerable to Nazi cooptation. The Nazi takeover of the Protestant state churches and the formation of the Protestant Reich Church as a vehicle of control and transmission belt for Nazi propaganda prompted the creation of the underground "Confessing Church," some of whose leaders, including Dietrich Bonhoeffer, participated in plots to overthrow Hitler. The overall failure of the Protestant Church to resist Nazism, however, discredited Church leaders and made it difficult for Protestants to exert much influence over policy after the war.[77] Protestants did join with Catholics to form the Christian Democratic Union, but far from being a Protestant confessional party, the union was dominated by Catholics in its early years.

Britain and Northern Ireland

Protestant politics in Britain were not as conservative as those in Germany. The Church of England supported the Crown, but Puritans in the seventeenth century accused the Anglican Church and the Stuart monarchy of "papism" and sought to purify both. The nineteenth-century Evangelicals tended to side with the reformers, abolitionist William Wilberforce being one of the most prominent. Later, as the country's modern political parties emerged, the nonconformists often supported the Liberals or the Labour Party.[78]

Anti-Catholicism remained a hallmark of nineteenth-century Protestant politics. The Liberal politician and four-time prime minister William Gladstone, himself a committed High-Church Anglican, spent time in the opposition during the 1870s writing pamphlets critical of the Vatican. As he informed Lord Granville, his purpose was to defeat the worldwide Catholic conspiracy "to direct European war to the re-establishment of the temporal power; or even to bring about such a war for that purpose."[79] His pamphlet *The Vatican Decrees in Their Bearing on Civil Allegiance* (1874) attacked papal infallibility as inconsistent with freedom of thought and questioned whether British Catholics could be loyal to both the Crown and the pope. The following year, in *Vaticanism: An Answer to Reproofs and Replies*, he described the Catholic Church as "an Asian monarchy: nothing but one giddy height of despotism, and one dead level of religious subservience."[80] The papacy would destroy the rule of law, establish tyranny, and hide these "crimes against liberty beneath a suffocating cloud of incense."[81] Gladstone's pamphlets sold well.

British Protestants avoided creating explicitly religious political parties everywhere but in Northern Ireland, where conflict with Catholics made religion the most politically salient social cleavage. Protestantism and support for union with Great Britain went hand in hand in Northern Ireland from its founding in 1921 as an administrative unit within the United Kingdom. Fear drove Protestants to cling fiercely to the British state as their protector from the Catholic-dominated Republic of Ireland. The Ulster Unionist Party and the mainline Protestant churches led the Northern Irish Protestants through most of the twentieth century, but the theological and political conservatives perceived a drift toward modernism and ecumenism in those churches (a "Romeward trend" in conservative rhetoric[82]), and in the party's reformist wing (toward accommodation with Catholics). In response, conservatives launched a religious and political counter movement in the 1960s.[83] Various small parties, such as the Protestant Unionist Party and Protestant Action, pushed back against modernist and reformist tendencies, but an explicitly religious Protestant political movement did not reemerge in Northern Ireland until Ian Paisley, a fiery preacher and leader of the small but growing Free Presbyterian Church, created the Ulster Democratic Unionist party (DUP) in 1971. The DUP's close ties to the Free Presbyterians, through overlapping leadership and a shared ideology, sometimes made party and Church indistinguishable. Early on, the DUP relied heavily on Paisley's leadership and rhetoric and the activism of Free Presbyterian Church members.

The political Protestantism of the DUP was raw. The party and the religious movement behind it represented well-preserved remnants of nineteenth- and early-twentieth-century evangelical Protestant Britain, products of the frozen sectarian politics of Irish independence. The DUP represented a minority of Ulster Protestants who believed that the Protestant way of life in Northern Ireland was under threat from a Catholic conspiracy being masterminded by the Antichrist in the

Vatican, who was intent on curtailing their liberties and ultimately returning all of Britain to the Roman fold.[84]

Long before the creation of the DUP, Paisley acquired a reputation for articulating the combination of religion and politics characteristic of conservative Ulster Protestants. In one episode Paisley, who supported the holding of an anti-Catholic meeting in the Ballymoney Town Hall, found himself at odds with a priest named Father Murphy and some mainline Protestant leaders. The local council eventually canceled the meeting, causing Paisley to vent his fury:

> Priest Murphy, speak for your own bloodthirsty persecuting intolerant blaspheming political religious papacy but do not dare to pretend to be the spokesman of free Ulster men. You are not in the South of Ireland. . . . Go back to your priestly intolerance, back to your blasphemous masses, back to your beads, holy water, holy smoke and stinks and remember we are the sons of the martyrs whom your church butchered and we know your church to be the *mother of harlots* and the abominations of the Earth [emphasis in the original].[85]
>
> We repudiate the lies of Priest Murphy, bachelor agent of a foreign power and brand as traitors all those associated with him and those who hastened to do his will. We affirm Article 31 of the Church of our Gracious Lady Queen Elizabeth II that "Masses are blasphemous fables and dangerous deceits."[86]

Here we see conservative Irish Protestantism's no-holds-barred anti-Catholicism, fear of a Roman conspiracy, and reliance on the protection of the Protestant British state against Catholic "traitors." Protestant Unionists believed that their liberty—indeed, all liberty—depended on the Protestant state's resistance to Catholic tyranny.

Paisley's religious movement, beginning on the fringes of Ulster Unionism, entered politics and gained support, even from the less religious Protestants, because the Unionists perceived a weakening of state protection. The DUP was committed to defending Protestant identity and to strengthening the state in its fight against the Catholic insurgency. But Paisley and his followers saw the Protestant struggle against Catholicism in more apocalyptic terms. The conflict in Northern Ireland was a small but significant battle in a worldwide conflict against the forces of darkness in these "last days." Paisley's conservative Presbyterianism drew its premillennialism from nineteenth-century British Evangelicals, but it shared this theological ancestry with American Fundamentalists, with whom he had strong ties.[87] Paisley's premillennialism, however, differed significantly from that of most American Fundamentalists; it did not include a belief in the Rapture, and it focused almost exclusively on the papal Antichrist and the Roman Church.[88] The Catholic Church was viewed by Paisley's movement as the only institution with "the power, influence, and reach to be the sort of comprehensive anti-Christian force suggested in prophecy," the evil "Babylon" of Scripture.[89] Boosted by a general fear of Catholics in unionist Ulster and by a conviction that they were fighting a cosmic battle, more Protestants turned to the DUP to represent their interests.[90]

The Netherlands

Protestant political movements in the Netherlands, like those in Northern Ireland, struggled against the forces of Catholicism and liberalism. But unlike Northern Ireland, most of the Dutch Protestant parties came to terms with both.

Protestants in the Netherlands organized politically in the nineteenth century in reaction to the liberalism and secularism of the French Revolution. Abraham Kuyper's Anti-Revolutionary Party (ARP), which he founded in 1879, drew heavily on orthodox factions within the Dutch Reformed Church, which eventually broke away to form the Reformed Churches in the Netherlands. These conservatives resisted liberal tendencies in both religion and politics, preferring a Protestant theocracy to the tolerant liberal state that developed after 1815. Kuyper argued for a confessional alliance with Catholics (although not a party merger) to resist secularizing tendencies.[91] The ARP joined with Catholics (who did not form a true democratic party, the Roman Catholic State Party, until 1926) to form a government in 1888.

The first Protestant political schism occurred in 1894, when upper-class leaders broke with Kuyper and his "little people" over the extension of suffrage and its implied notion of *popular* as opposed to *divine* sovereignty. In 1904 they formed the Christian Historical Union (CHU), which continued to oppose extension of the franchise, while also taking a harder line against the Catholic Church. In 1918 another split of the ARP gave rise to the Political Reformed Party (SGP), a permanent opposition party that refused to cooperate with the Catholics. In 1944 a theological spat within the Reformed Churches in the Netherlands produced, in 1948, yet another Protestant party, the Reformed Political Alliance (GPV), which required all party members to be members of the new Reformed Churches in the Netherlands (Liberated). This process of increasing Protestant political divisions went into reverse in 1980, when the ARP and CHU joined with the Catholic party to form the Christian Democratic Appeal (CDA). This merger resulted in a disgruntled ARP faction forming its own party, the Reformatory Political Federation (RPF), joining the GPV and SGP as one more small orthodox party. In 2000 the GPV and RPF merged to form the Christian Union, and the combined party entered a CDA-led government for the first time in 2007.

Theology has always mattered to the Protestant parties, often being the only difference between them. The ARP, though seldom attracting more than one-fifth of the electorate, regularly participated in government with other political forces, including Catholics. It defended Protestants' rights, especially in education, but its appeal was broad and tolerant compared with the other Protestant parties. For the most part, the small Reformed parties were content to advocate "biblical principles" while winning no more than a few seats in Parliament. The SGP, for instance, refused to accept women in church or party leadership, making the party unattractive to most orthodox Protestants, much less secular voters. All these small parties were strongly anti-Catholic, and their rhetoric was quite apocalyptic—with frequent mentions of the papal Antichrist.[92] The Protestant parties, both large and small, were strong supporters of the monarchy and Dutch nationalism. After World War II the CHU's manifesto still called the Netherlands a Protestant nation and extolled God's liberation of the land from Catholic Hapsburg domination.[93] The ARP, for its part, resisted decolonization of the East Indies because it would undermine Dutch sovereignty. The Dutch Protestants, for all their factional fighting, were strong nationalists.

The division of Dutch Protestantism, however, was not the big religious story of the twentieth century. That story in the Netherlands (as in other parts of Europe, if less dramatically) was the collapse of traditional religious belief and behavior among both Catholics and Protestants.[94] Church attendance remained high among conservatives, but the majority of Dutch citizens lost their taste for religion.

Scandinavia

As we saw above, commitment to Protestant religion and loyalty to the state became synonymous in Protestant Europe. The Scandinavian states, however, were more successful in driving out the Catholics and other non-Lutherans than, say, the British or Dutch, and thus they achieved greater sectarian purity than the other Protestant countries. At the first sign of religious deviation, the state—often with popular support—moved quickly to crush the rebellion, even when the deviants were committed to orthodox Lutheranism and the state churches. The eighteenth-century Pietists, for instance, and the nineteenth-century Norwegian Haugeans were victims of such drives for purity. Revivalism in Norway and Sweden did eventually produce Free Church movements that broke from the state churches, but the state churches remained fixtures of Scandinavian society. The question of how to treat dissenters continued to be a problem throughout the twentieth century. The Danish state Church faced similar issues with the rise of Nicolai Frederik Severin Grundtvig, whose popular religious teachings ran afoul of the religious authorities in the 1820s. But the Danish state found in Grundtvig and his movement a safe way of transforming the distant and hierarchical state Church into the "people's Church," thus depriving free church advocates of a grievance. So powerful was this sense of unity in Denmark that even in today's secular society, the reactions to the presence of Islam, according to Jespersen, "can hardly be attributed to Danes feeling threatened in their own faith, but relate to the perception that any attack on the Church is an attack on the entire basis on which Danish society is built."[95]

The Scandinavian Protestants, as noted above, did not organize as religious blocs until the twentieth century. The new religious parties that sprang up beginning in the 1930s represented those revivalist and morally conservative elements that had long been repressed. Their electoral support was centered in the geographical areas that were associated with anticlericalism and Evangelical enthusiasm.[96] The Norwegian Christian People's Party (KrP) ignited the Christian movement in the Nordic region. And the revivalists, beginning with Hauge in the early nineteenth century, considered politics a noble calling and sought to achieve many social goals by political means. Their struggle against the religious and political establishment in their strongholds in the south and west of Norway led them into an alliance with the Liberals in the nineteenth century. That alliance pressed for liberal and nationalist causes: parliamentary supremacy over the Swedish king (Norway was in a union with Sweden after 1814), defense of the language and culture of rural areas, and, eventually, Norwegian independence (which came in 1905). The religiously conservative Norwegians, who formed an important faction in the nationalist alliance, were increasingly concerned with the growing modernism in the state Church and the secularism of Norwegian society. Revivalist support for the Liberals continued to weaken in the first decades of the twentieth century, but in 1933 conflict over teetotalism (the revivalists were in favor) and the opening of a blasphemous play at the National Theater in Oslo (the revivalists were against) inspired religiously conservative leaders in western Norway to start the independent Christian People's Party, which became a national party in 1945.[97] The party's first program stated its commitment "to protect Christian and national values in the Church, the school, the workplace, and in our cultural life as a whole."[98]

Other Christian parties have followed the Norwegian model. The Finnish Christian League was formed in 1958 and adopted a nearly verbatim translation of the KrP program.[99] The Finnish party was most concerned about the "proliferation of politically motivated secularism and atheism," along with the strong influence of communism on national politics.[100] The Swedish Christian Democratic Union appeared in 1964 after a series of moral issues rose to national prominence. Conservative Swedish Christians were concerned about the rising abortion rate, an increase in sexually transmitted diseases, sexual instruction in schools, public warnings against sending young children to religiously "ecstatic meetings," the public showing of sexually explicit films, and a proposed reduction in religious instruction in public education. The story was similar in Denmark, when the Christian People's Party formed in 1970 as a reaction to the moral laxity of Danish society and changes to religious instruction in the schools.[101] Unlike the Norwegian KrP, which led governments, the Finnish, Swedish, and Danish Christian parties were mostly small, socially distinct protest groups, although all eventually participated as junior coalition partners in national governments. Like the KrP in Norway, these parties did not represent the views of the liberal state Lutheran churches, but instead spoke for the church-attending laity in the state churches and for free church members, who believed that they represented the genuinely Protestant perspectives on politics and society.

The Protestants founded distinctly confessional political parties in response to the opening of a religious social cleavage in the Protestant nations. But only in Northern Ireland, and to a lesser degree in the Netherlands, were the Protestant parties designed to counter Catholic influence. The confessional parties, for the most part, arose in response to the secularization of society and to the religious and social liberalism *within* official, state-supported Protestantism. Less fervent Protestants in Germany and the Netherlands supported Catholic–Protestant political alliances, but devout believers, often from revivalist traditions, created parties to represent their countercultural movements.

Conclusion

Europe in the mid–twentieth century was divided into two distinct confessional cultures rooted in the Reformation. Catholicism remained culturally opposed to modernity, and it sought, often successfully, to insulate its devotees from the perceived excesses of the fast-changing industrialized world. Moreover, Catholic clerics and politicians were still struggling to come to terms with the modern liberal state. Some held out for an authoritarian solution to the problem of declining Church influence in Europe. But others saw the value of democratic politics as a means of defending Catholic interests, with some going so far as to embrace democracy as the only form of government capable of defending human dignity. Most midcentury Catholics were still committed to a cultural and political role for the supranational Roman Church, but they were divided as to how best to defend the Church's interests. Some were willing to let the Catholic confessional parties fight for Church privileges through the democratic process; others preferred the traditional diplomatic method, whereby Church officials negotiated with political leaders, resulting in state–church pacts. In fact, both methods were pursued in the twentieth century, but in most of Western Europe, the Christian Democratic parties emerged as the most effective representatives of Catholic cultural and political interests. On the domestic front, they sought to build societies free from the excesses of radical collectivism and individualism. On the international front, they hoped to free the Continent from the excesses of nationalism and the nation-state system that had nurtured it. They even began to think seriously about building a new European federation. Catholics had a theological and cultural vision of modern European society that transcended national borders and united in purpose Europeans who shared a common culture, a spirit of community, a "we feeling." Moreover, Catholics were not afraid to use their political parties in legitimate, democratic ways to achieve their political goals.

Protestants in Europe shared a confessional culture, but one that developed very differently from its Catholic counterpart. Protestants did not have a supranational church to serve as their cultural focal point. Nor did their churches resist the modern liberal states; quite the contrary, they helped create them. Protestant churches willingly submitted to the state and supported its modernizing vocation—even when, as in Germany, the state took a totalitarian form. Protestant culture was individualistic and was increasingly tolerant of alternative religious perspectives—as long, of course, as they were not "papist." Most important, Protestantism did not advocate a common comprehensive vision of society—certainly not one that included a Catholic-dominated European federation. Protestants found liberty in independence and diversity.

The Catholic and Protestant visions of European society, which developed over four centuries, were simply incompatible. This mismatch was grounded in religious differences that evolved into different cultures with conflicting visions of what constituted an appropriate political community for Europe. Identifying these differences thus helps to explain the shape of European integration efforts after World War II.

Notes

1. Christopher Dawson, *The Dividing of Christendom* (New York: Sheed & Ward, 1965), 160.

2. For a classic statement on this subject, see Christopher Dawson, *The Making of Europe: An Introduction to the History of European Unity* (Washington, DC: Catholic University of America Press, 1954; orig. pub. 1932). For a similar perspective, see Jacques Le Goff, *The Birth of Europe*, trans. Janet Lloyd (Malden, MA: Blackwell, 2005).

3. See Dawson, *Dividing of Christendom*, 139–40.

4. James F. White, *Protestant Worship: Traditions in Transition* (Louisville: Westminster John Knox Press, 1989), 30.

5. Martin Conway, *Catholic Politics in Europe, 1918–1945* (New York: Routledge, 1997), 3–4.

6. The most notable examples include the *Sixty-Seven Articles* (Zwingli, 1523); the *Schleitheim Confession* (Anabaptist, 1527); the *Augsburg Confession* (Lutheran, 1530); the *Smalcald Articles* (Martin Luther, 1537); the *French Confession* (John Calvin, 1559); the *Scots Confession* (John Knox, 1560); the *Belgic Confession* (Guido de Bres, 1561); the *Thirty-Nine Articles* (Church of England, 1562); the *Heidelberg Catechism* (Reformed, 1563); the *Canons of Dordt* (Reformed, 1618–19); and the *Westminster Confession of Faith* (Presbyterian, 1647). Also see Michael H. Anderson, "Creeds of Christendom," www.creeds.net.

7. White, *Protestant Worship*, 41–42.

8. Quoted by Stephen J. Nichols, *Martin Luther: A Guided Tour of His Life and Thought* (Phillipsburg, NJ: P&R, 2002), 198.

9. Luther, in fact, laid out a daily schedule of three preaching services per day, beginning at 5 AM, for every member of the congregation; ibid., 197–99.

10. Lutherans, unable to exercise discipline through consistories, relied more on private confession to pastors; Diarmaid MacCulloch, *Reformation: Europe's House Divided 1490–1700* (New York: Viking, 2003), 575.

11. Quoted by Philip Benedict, *Christ's Churches Purely Reformed: A Social History of Calvinism* (New Haven, CT: Yale University Press, 2002), 103.

12. See Hugh McLeod, *Religion and the People of Western Europe, 1789–1989* (Oxford: Oxford University Press, 1997); and David Bebbington, *Evangelicalism in Modern Britain: A History from the 1730s to the 1980s* (Grand Rapids: Baker Book House, 1989).

13. McLeod, *Religion*, 17.

14. See McLeod, *Religion*; J. R. C. Wright, *"Above Parties": The Political Attitudes of the German Protestant Church Leadership, 1918–1933* (Oxford: Oxford University Press, 1974); Daniel R. Borg, *The Old-Prussian Church and the Weimar Republic: A Study in Political Adjustment, 1917–1927* (Hanover, NH: University Press of New England, 1984).

15. Alastair Duke, "Perspectives on International Calvinism," in *Calvinism in Europe, 1540–1620*, ed. Andrew Pettegree, Alastair Duke, and Gillian Lewis (Cambridge: Cambridge University Press, 1994), 4.

16. See MacCulloch, *Reformation*, 580–86; Benedict, *Christ's Churches*, 532.

17. "In Catholic Ireland, the Protestant Guinnesses were accused [in the late eighteenth century] of signing an anti-Catholic petition, and Guinness [stout] was boycotted as 'Protestant porter'"; *Time*, March 26, 1951, www.time.com/time/magazine/article/0,9171,805967-1,00.html.

18. Hans Maier, *Revolution and Church: The Early History of Christian Democracy, 1789–1901*, trans. Emily M. Schossberger (Notre Dame, IN: University of Notre Dame Press, 1965), 85–93.

19. Ibid., 97–141.

20. René Rémond, "The Case of France," in *Concilium, The Church and Christian Democracy*, ed. Gregory Baum and John Coleman (Edinburgh: T. & T. Clark, 1987), 73–74. See also Maier's discussion of the life and thought of Hugues Felicité Robert de Lamennais, the influential Catholic cleric of the early nineteenth century; ibid., 181–201.

21. Stathis N. Kalyvas, *The Rise of Christian Democracy in Europe* (Ithaca, NY: Cornell University Press, 1996), 23.

22. Michael P. Fogarty, *Christian Democracy in Western Europe, 1820–1953* (Notre Dame, IN: University of Notre Dame Press, 1957), 312–13.

23. Pope Leo XIII, *Rerum Novarum*, Vatican, May 15, 1891, www.vatican.va/holy_father/leo_xiii/encyclicals/documents/hf_l-xiii_enc_15051891_rerum-novarum_en.html.

24. See Pope Leo XIII, *Graves De Communi Re*, Vatican, January 18, 1901, www.vatican.va/holy_father/leo_xiii/encyclicals/documents/hf_l-xiii_enc_18011901_graves-de-communi-re_en.html.

25. Conway, *Catholic Politics*, 39.

26. Jan Ifversen, "The Crisis of European Civilization after 1918," in *Ideas of Europe since 1914: The Legacy of the First World War*, ed. Menno Spiering and Michael Wintle (London: Palgrave, 2002), 18–19.

27. Fogarty, *Christian Democracy*, 27ff.

28. Alan Paul Fimister, *Robert Schuman: Neo-Scholastic Humanism and the Reunification of Europe* (Brussels: PIE–Peter Lang, 2008), 106–13.

29. Conway, *Catholic Politics*, 31.

30. Denis de Rougemont, *The Meaning of Europe*, trans. Alan Braley (New York: Stein & Day, 1963), 66–67. See also Anthony Pagden, "Introduction," in *The Idea of Europe: From Antiquity to the European Union*, ed. Anthony Pagden (Cambridge: Cambridge University Press, 2002), 14.

31. Dante Alighieri, *On World-Government, or De Monarchia*, trans. Herbert W. Schneider (Indianapolis: Liberal Arts Press, 1957), 79.

32. Derek Heater, *The Idea of European Unity* (New York: St. Martin's Press, 1992), 17.

33. William Penn, "An Essay towards the Present and Future Peace of Europe," in *The Political Writings of William Penn*, ed. Andrew R. Murphy (Indianapolis: Liberty Fund, 2002), 412.

34. Quoted by Denis de Rougemont, *The Idea of Europe*, trans. Norbert Guterman (Cleveland: World, 1968), 115.

35. Quoted in ibid., 150.

36. Immanuel Kant, *Perpetual Peace: A Philosophical Essay*, translated, with introduction and notes, by M. Campbell Smith (London: George Allen & Unwin, 1917), 136; reprinted by Liberty Fund, http://oll.libertyfund.org/title/357. Kant seems to contradict himself on the nature of the

federation. At one point he declares that the demands of states seeking release from the state of war "would give rise to a federation of nations which, however, would not have to be a State of nations" (129).

37. Quoted by de Rougemont, *Idea*, 216.

38. Count Joseph de Maistre, *The Pope* (New York: Howard Fertig, 1975), 193.

39. Ibid., 347.

40. Quoted by de Rougemont, *Idea*, 238, 240.

41. Novalis, *Hymns to the Night and Other Selected Writings*, trans. Charles E. Passage (New York: Liberal Arts Press, 1960), as quoted by de Rougemont, *Idea*, 236–37. See also Liah Greenfeld, *Nationalism: Five Roads to Modernity* (Cambridge, MA: Harvard University Press, 1992), 357.

42. See Peter M. R. Stirk, "Introduction: Crisis and Continuity in Interwar Europe," in *European Unity in Context: The Interwar Period*, ed. Peter M. R. Stirk (London: Pinter, 1989), 11; and Walter Lipgens, "General Introduction," in *Continental Plans for European Union 1939–1945*, vol. 1 of *Documents on the History of European Integration*, ed. Walter Lipgens (Berlin: Walter de Gruyter, 1985), 4–7.

43. Anthony Upton, "The Crisis of Scandinavia and the Collapse of Interwar Ideals, 1938–1940," in *European Unity in Context*, ed. Stirk, 170–87.

44. "Pope Benedict XV's Peace Proposal," World War I Document Archive, August 1, 1917, wwi.lib.byu.edu/index.php/Pope_Benedict_XV%27s_Peace_Proposal. See also Philip Jenkins, *The Great and Holy War: How World War I Became a Religious Crusade* (New York: HarperCollins, 2014), 65–66.

45. Pope Benedict XV, *Pacem, Dei Munus Pulcherrimum*, Vatican, www.vatican.va/holy_father/benedict_xv/encyclicals/documents/hf_ben-xv_enc_23051920_pacem-dei-munus-pulcherrimum_en.html.

46. Quoted by Roberto Papini, *The Christian Democrat International*, trans. Robert Royal (Lanham, MD: Rowman & Littlefield, 1997), 20.

47. Elisa A. Carrillo, *Alcide De Gasperi: The Long Apprenticeship* (Notre Dame, IN: University of Notre Dame Press, 1965), 59.

48. Papini, *Christian Democrat International*, 27.

49. See, e.g., the discussion of early Italian Christian Democracy by Fogarty, *Christian Democracy*, 319–22. See also Papini, *Christian Democrat International*, 28.

50. See Wolfram Kaiser, *Christian Democracy and the Origins of European Union* (Cambridge: Cambridge University Press, 2007), 107. See also Michael Gehler and Wolfram Kaiser, "Toward a 'Core Europe' in a Christian Western Bloc: Transnational Cooperation in European Christian Democracy, 1925–1965," in *European Christian Democracy: Historical Legacies and Comparative Perspectives*, ed. Thomas Kselman and Joseph A. Buttigieg (Notre Dame, IN: Notre Dame Press, 2003), 240–45.

51. Papini, *Christian Democrat International*, 43–44n63. See also Kaiser, *Christian Democracy*, 117.

52. Kaiser, *Christian Democracy*, 214.

53. See Ralph White, "The Europeanism of Coudenhove-Kalergi," in *European Unity in Context*, ed. Stirk, 23–40.

54. Richard N. Coudenhove-Kalergi, *Pan-Europe* (New York: Alfred A. Knopf, 1926), 162.

55. Pan-Europa's emphasis on the Christian nature of Europe has remained a central tenet of the movement. The "Fundamental Declaration of the International General Assembly of the Pan-Europa Union in Strasbourg 1995" states: "Christianity is the soul of Europe. Our mission is characterized by the Christian image of man and the rule of law. By calling on European community values, the Pan-Europa Union opposes all tendencies which erode the intellectual and moral force of Europe"; "Programm," Paneuropa, www.paneuropa.org.

56. Wim Roobol, "Aristide Briand's Plan: The Seed of European Unification," in *Ideas of Europe since 1914: The Legacy of the First World War*, ed. Menno Spiering and Michael Wintle (London: Palgrave, 2002), 43; Cornelia Navari, "The Origins of the Briand Plan," in *The Federal Idea: The History of Federalism from Enlightenment to 1945*, ed. Andrea Bosco (London: Lothian Foundation Press, 1991), 216.

57. For a bibliography of interwar writings on European unity, see Andrea Bosco, "National Sovereignty and Peace: Lord Lothian's Federalist Thought," in *The Larger Idea: Lord Lothian and the Problem of National Sovereignty*, ed. John Turner (London: Historians' Press, 1988), 119n19.

58. See Peter Bugge, "The Nation Supreme, the Idea of Europe, 1914–1945," in *The History of the Idea of Europe*, ed. Kevin Wilson and Jan van der Dussen (London: Routledge, 1993), 132–34.

59. Hilaire Belloc, *Europe and the Faith* (London: Burns and Oates, 1962), 24–25. See also the commentary on this quotation given by Fiminster, *Robert Schuman*, 94–100.

60. Christopher Dawson, *Making of Europe*, 9, 251–55.

61. For the details of the life and thought of Lord Lothian, see John Pinder and Andrea Bosco, "Introduction: Lothian's Contribution to the Federal Idea," in *Pacifism Is Not Enough: Collected Lectures and Speeches of Lord Lothian (Philip Kerr)*, ed. John Pinder and Andrea Bosco (London: Lothian Foundation Press, 1990); *Larger Idea*, ed. Turner; and Richard Mayne and John Pinder with John C. de V. Roberts, *Federal Union: The Pioneers, A History of Federal Union* (New York: St. Martin's Press, 1990).

62. Philip Henry Kerr Lothian, "The Demonic Influence of National Sovereignty," in *Pacifism Is Not Enough*, ed. Pinder and Bosco.

63. Ibid., 192.

64. John Pinder, "Federalism in Britain and Italy: Radicals and the English Liberal Tradition," in *European Unity in Context*, ed. Stirk, 207; Clemens A. Wurm, "Great Britain: Political Parties and Pressure Groups in the Discussion on European Union," in *Plans for European Union in Great Britain and in Exile, 1939–1945*, vol. 2 of *Documents on the History of European Integration*, ed. Walter Lipgens (Berlin: Walter de Gruyter, 1986), 637.

65. John Pinder, "Prophet Not Without Honour: Lothian and the Federal Idea," in *Larger Idea*, ed. Turner, 138–42.

66. See Pinder, "Federalism."

67. Andrea Bosco, "National Sovereignty and Peace: Lord Lothian's Federalist Thought," in *Larger Idea*, ed. Turner, 116.

68. For a summary of resistance thinking on postwar Europe, see Lipgens, "General Introduction"; and Derek W. Urwin, *The Community of Europe: A History of European Integration since 1945* (London: Longman, 1991), 7–12.

69. Knud J. V. Jespersen, *A History of Denmark*, trans. Ivan Hill (Houndmills, UK: Palgrave, 2004), 90.

70. R. B. Andeweg and Galen A. Irwin, *Governance and Politics of the Netherlands* (Houndmills, UK: Palgrave Macmillan, 2002), 43–45; Ken Gladdish, *Governing from the Center: Politics and Policy-Making in the Netherlands* (DeKalb: Northern Illinois University Press, 1991), 15–32.

71. For a discussion of social cleavages and the rise of political parties in Europe, see Seymour Martin Lipset and Stein Rokkan, "Cleavage Structures, Party Systems, and Voter Alignments: An Introduction," in *Party Systems and Voter Alignments: Cross-National Perspectives*, ed. Seymour M. Lipset and Stein Rokkan (New York: Free Press, 1967), 1–64.

72. Kenneth D. Wald, *Crosses on the Ballot: Patterns of British Voter Alignment since 1885* (Princeton, NJ: Princeton University Press, 1983).

73. Peder A. Eidberg, "Norwegian Free Churches and Religious Liberty: A History," *Journal of Church and State* 37, no. 4 (1995): 869–85. Denmark guaranteed religious freedom in 1849 and permitted the Roman church to organize soon after.

74. Franklin D. Scott, *Sweden: The Nation's History* (Carbondale: Southern Illinois University Press, 1988), 359.

75. Wright, "Above Parties," 2.

76. William Carr, *A History of Germany, 1815–1985*, 3rd ed. (London: Edward Arnold, 1987), 136–37.

77. Frederic Spotts, *The Churches and Politics in Germany* (Middletown, CT: Wesleyan University Press, 1973), 165.

78. Wald, *Crosses*, 162–201; David Seawright, "A Confessional Cleavage Resurrected? The Denominational Vote in Britain," in *Religion and Mass Electoral Behaviour in Europe*, ed. David Broughton and Hans-Martien ten Napel (London: Routledge, 2000), 46–47.

79. Quoted by Philip Magnus, *Gladstone: A Biography* (London: John Murray, 1963), 235.

80. Quoted in ibid., 236.

81. Ibid.

82. Steve Bruce, *God Save Ulster! The Religion and Politics of Paisleyism* (Oxford: Oxford University Press, 1986), 90.

83. See Peter Brooke, *Ulster Presbyterianism: The Historical Perspective, 1610–1970* (Dublin: Gill and Macmillan, 1987).

84. Bruce, *God Save Ulster!* 91–92, 222–23.

85. *Revivalist* 3, no. 11, 1–2, as quoted by Bruce, *God Save Ulster!* 67.

86. As quoted by Bruce, *God Save Ulster!* 67.

87. Paisley was particularly close to the fundamentalists associated with Bob Jones University in Greenville, South Carolina, where Paisley was given an honorary doctorate in 1966; Bruce, *God Save Ulster!* 168–69, 183.

88. Ibid., 206–7, 221–31.

89. Ibid., 228.

90. Three-quarters of Unionists expressed a general "fear of the power of the Roman Catholic Church" in the early 1980s; Edward Moxon-Browne, *Nation, Class, and Creed in Northern Ireland* (Aldershot: Gower, 1983), 38, as cited by Bruce, *God Save Ulster!* 123.

91. Kuyper argued that unlike secular liberals, Catholics confess the Christian faith: "Whereas all the parties of the Revolution ignore, if not ridicule, the Second Coming of our Lord, our Roman Catholic countrymen confess with us: 'Whence he will come again to judge the living and the dead.'. . . They, like we, acknowledge that all authority and power on Earth flows from God and is rooted in the reality of creation. They say as do you that this God has sent his only Son into the world and as a reward for his cross has placed on his head the mediator's crown. And they testify with you that this divinely anointed King now sits at the right hand of God, [and] controls the destiny of peoples and States"; Abraham Kuyper, "Maranatha," in *Abraham Kuyper: A Centennial Reader*, ed. James D. Bratt (Grand Rapids: William B. Eerdmans, 1998), 218.

92. Hans Vollard, "Protestantism and Euro-Scepticism in the Netherlands," *Perspectives on European Politics and Society* 7, no. 3 (2006): 287.

93. Ibid., 280.

94. McLeod, *Religion*, 146–48.

95. Jespersen, *History of Denmark*, 112.

96. See Stein Rokkan, "Geography, Religion, and Social Class: Crosscutting Cleavages in Norwegian Politics," in *Party Systems*, ed. Lipset and Rokkan, 415–25; Lauri Karvonen, "In From the Cold? Christian Politics in Scandinavia," *Scandinavian Political Studies* 16, no. 1 (1993): 35–37; John T. S. Madeley, "The Antinomies of Lutheran Politics: The Case of Norway's Christian People's Party," in *Christian Democracy in Europe: A Comparative Perspective*, ed. David Hanley (London: Pinter, 1994), 142–54.

97. Madeley, "Antinomies," 142–50. The Norwegian word *kristenfolket*—literally translated "Christian people"—came to mean "revivalists" or "fundamentalists."

98. John T. S. Madeley, "Religion and the Political Order: The Case of Norway," in *Secularization and Fundamentalism Reconsidered, Religion and the Political Order*, vol. 3, ed. Jeffrey K. Hadden and Anson Shupe (New York: Paragon House, 1989), 298.

99. Karvonen, "In From the Cold?" 30.

100. Ibid., 31.

101. Ibid., 31–32.

PART III

Constructing a New Europe

5

Postwar Preparation

EUROPE IN 1945 was ruined but not destroyed.[1] The Allies and the Resistance had defeated fascism, but exactly what would emerge in its place was not immediately clear, beyond a commitment to build some form of parliamentary democracy in each country. New political movements would surely appear, but the most likely scenario was for the major prewar political groups to compete again for power. In the West, the socialists seemed likely to benefit from their resistance to fascism and their pledges to deploy state power to alleviate the suffering of working people. Few observers gave the small Catholic parties of the interwar era much chance of challenging the left for control of the state and, thus, of leading the rebuilding of Western Europe. Nevertheless, the Catholic Christian Democratic movement developed a strong following, allowing it to dominate the politics of Europe west of the Elbe River for over two decades.

The Christian Democrats were successful in what Michael Gehler and Wolfram Kaiser call "core Europe"—France, Germany, Italy, and the Benelux countries—because they organized quickly and honed a message that resonated with a conservative but evolving electorate.[2] The Christian Democratic elites also reconstituted their transnational community, finding unity in an attractive ideology that drew on Catholic confessional culture without being stridently sectarian. And they quietly cooperated with the Catholic Church to secure a solid electoral base. Achieving overwhelming political success after the war enabled the Christian Democrats to shape core Europe, especially its efforts to integrate politically and economically.

The Postwar Christian Democratic Community

Christian Democratic leaders emerging from their hiding places or from exile found a physically and emotionally devastated Continent. But they were confident they could lead Europe out of its cycle of violence, and thus wasted no time preparing their movement for political leadership. Through a series of uncoordinated and overlapping meetings among movement elites, Catholic and some Protestant political leaders reestablished a transnational Christian Democratic network. Through this network flowed ideas and norms that socialized a new generation of leaders who were united around a broad Christian Democratic ideology.[3] As Catholics came to power in country after country—much to their own surprise[4]—these meetings became serious forums where the Christian Democrats hammered out common positions and coordinated policies.[5] The network also rebuilt and extended a sense of community among the elites in the areas free from Soviet control. In short, the Christian Democratic elites, who were mostly Catholics sharing a confessional culture, created a web of interaction and exchange across borders that proved essential to the success of both their parties and the integration process.

Restoring the Christian Democratic network, which had been ripped apart by fascism and war, proved far from easy. The crisis of the 1930s and wartime disruptions made it impossible for Catholic politicians to maintain an effective movement. Soon after the 1932 Congress in Cologne of the International Secretariat of Democratic Parties of Christian Inspiration (SIPDIC), the organization experienced an identity crisis.[6] SIPDIC existed primarily to reconcile France and Germany through cooperation among political parties inspired by Catholic social teaching. In 1933 the German Center Party disbanded in response to Hitler's rise to power and the conclusion of a Concordat between the Vatican and the Nazi regime. German participation in SIPDIC was no longer possible, leaving the organization without its primary Franco-German purpose.[7] SIPDIC scaled back operations but continued to function until January 1939. By the mid-1930s, however, several member parties had turned to the authoritarian right and could no longer be regarded as "democratic": Some leaned toward clericalism, and others carried a strong whiff of anti-Semitism.[8] Thus, with SIPDIC moribund and suspect, the Christian Democrats, especially those with leftist leanings, had few opportunities to cooperate.

A small but important exception was the People and Freedom Group founded in 1936 in Britain and later expanded to the United States. Virginia Crawford was its founder, but its "catalyst" was a priest and politician, Luigi Sturzo, who was living in exile from fascist Italy.[9] The organization numbered only about a hundred persons (no accurate membership rolls were kept), but it provided British and continental Catholics with a forum to discuss Christian Democratic ideas. Its publication, *People and Freedom*, became an important showcase for Sturzo's own writings; his opinions—the most distinctive being his support for European unity—came to define the organization's point of view.[10] Most important, Sturzo's ideas spread "via 'capillary action' to other exiles and thinkers," including Alcide De Gasperi, who read *People and Freedom* in the Vatican Library.[11] He recorded his thanks to the group later when, as the Italian prime minister, he visited London in 1945.[12]

The end of World War II presented Catholic politicians with difficult challenges. Communication and transportation across Europe were not easy, making transnational contacts somewhat tricky. Right-wing authoritarianism had been thoroughly discredited, rendering out of the question a revival of the politically tainted SIPDIC, or its anemic successor, the International Christian Democratic Union

(ICDU). So Christian Democracy was faced with the challenge of starting over as a political movement.[13]

The process of stitching Catholics back together as a political force began personally, informally, and in ad hoc fashion. Robert Bichet, secretary-general of the French Popular Republican Movement (Mouvement Républicain Populaire, MRP), toured the European capitals in 1945 and 1946, seeking to establish ties with the Christian Democratic parties in Austria, Belgium, Italy, Luxembourg, and the Netherlands.[14] Barbara Barclay Carter, a close associate of Sturzo in the People and Freedom Group, also toured Europe to stir interest in the (largely ignored) ICDU.[15] Neither effort resulted in any tangible agreement or organization. At roughly the same time, however, Moral Re-Armament, led by a magnetic American evangelical Christian named Frank Buchman, bought the Caux Palace Hotel on Lake Geneva in Switzerland as a meeting place for French and German notables brought together for extended visits to encourage reconciliation. The meetings began in 1946, when wartime hatreds had not yet cooled, material shortages made life harsh across Europe, and the occupation prevented Germans from traveling. Buchman succeeded (from 1946 to 1950) in getting permission for more than three thousand German politicians, trade unionists, industrialists, clergy, reporters, and educators (not all Christian Democrats) to attend his majestic retreat center, where they mingled with nearly two thousand French counterparts. The meetings did not explicitly focus on reconciliation, but the peaceful setting, the subtle spiritual nature of the sessions, and the social bonding that occurred as the war-weary participants worked, relaxed, and conversed had a positive effect. Many prominent Christian Democrats attended these conferences, including Konrad Adenauer, but Robert Schuman's participation and the close ties he developed with Buchman may have been Caux's most significant accomplishment. Buchman encouraged Schuman to cultivate Adenauer in 1949 when the latter was still quite obscure, advice Schuman took seriously.[16]

Perhaps the most crucial informal effort to forge new ties among Christian Democrats was the establishment of the Geneva Circle in 1947. A French diplomat, Victor Koutzine, and the German-Swiss director of a Catholic charity, Johann Jakob Kindt-Kiefer, contacted prominent French and German Christian Democrats while working in Switzerland. Kaiser identifies the French MRP leader and foreign minister Georges Bidault as the true power behind Koutzine and Kindt-Kiefer.[17] In any case, starting in November 1947 Koutzine and Kindt-Kiefer arranged for about a dozen leaders to meet in Geneva at three- to four-month intervals. They kept the meetings secret, in part to evade scrutiny from Allied military authorities, suspicious of all German politicians, but also to avoid the wrath of the French public, not yet ready to consider Germans as worthy partners in the reconstruction of Europe.[18] Secrecy also allowed the French and Germans—and, later, the leaders of the other nations—to get acquainted in a relaxed environment conducive to frank conversation.

The Geneva Circle's early years were the most important because Bidault and Adenauer (before he was chancellor) participated regularly and had the chance to size up one another. The conversations continued until 1956, covering topics important to Europe generally (French–German rapprochement, German rearmament, Soviet intentions) and Christian Democrats specifically (the need to give Europe a "Christian face," the mobilization of transnational Christian Democracy, European federation).[19] The talks resulted in no official agreements, but they opened channels of communication between Christian Democratic leaders—most of whom had government responsibilities—that deepened and widened far beyond the Geneva Circle. Friendships emerged across borders between leaders sharing a Catholic confessional culture and general political perspective. The Geneva conversations also provided Catholic politicians with a forum to discuss policy with like-minded officials, and to discretely coordinate common positions when possible.

Although Catholic politicians pursued back-channel contacts with their counterparts abroad, they also created a public transnational organization of Christian parties. The Swiss Christian Democrats took the lead, hosting meetings in Montreux in 1946 and Lucerne in 1947. Delegates from Belgium, Britain, France, Italy, Luxembourg, the Netherlands, and Switzerland (the Germans were not invited) agreed in 1947 to establish an organization for parties of "Christian inspiration."[20] European unity was a high priority. Josef Escher, the Swiss delegate who was presiding, identified "a united Europe" as the "greatest desire" of Christian politicians.[21] In May 1947 Belgium hosted twelve national delegations for the founding Congress of the Nouvelles Équipes Internationales (NEI; New International Teams). (The Germans were still not present, but they were finally invited to join in 1948.) The NEI was established to provide a meeting place and a forum for individuals, political parties, and other social organizations committed to Christian Democratic principles: the dignity of persons, democratic governance, a new national and international social order, and the promotion of Christian values essential to the preservation of democracy.[22] These rather vague objectives left much room for debate over specific policies. There were few disagreements, however, over the need for Franco-German reconciliation leading to a "European union" built on Christian principles.

Subsequent NEI meetings attracted Christian Democratic politicians for policy talks that in every instance included significant discussions of European integration.[23] For instance, the 1947 Congress formed a working group to develop proposals for the reorganization of Europe in light of Winston Churchill's Zurich call for a United States of Europe. The 1948 Congress proposed calling a "European Assembly" to bring about an "economic and political union." And the 1950 Congress urged Europe to allow the free movement of persons, goods, and capital. Later NEI congresses met under themes such as "Europe and Peace" (1951), "Supranational Authority and the Notion of Sovereignty" (1953), and "Political and Economic Integration of Europe" (1955). The NEI was also a key participant in the International Committee of the Movements for European Unity, which organized the 1948 Hague

Congress. The Hague Congress assembled many Christian Democrats from across the still war-scarred Continent, and it thus opened the door to the creation of the Council of Europe in 1949. In addition to these activities, the NEI established a youth organization and several study centers and foundations that facilitated contact among young Christian Democrats, who later rose to positions of responsibility, including Leo Tindemans (Belgian prime minister, 1974–77) and Giulio Andreotti (who served as Italian prime minister seven times between 1972 and 1992).[24]

The NEI never succeeded in directing the political activities of Christian Democratic parties, but it did facilitate regular contacts between Christian—primarily Catholic—politicians. By the early 1960s Christian Democrats saw a need to transform the NEI into a transnational organization that could better coordinate policy, especially within the institutions of the European Communities. In 1965 the NEI adopted a new charter calling for a "common political program"; and in 1971 it adopted a new name, the European Union of Christian Democrats.[25] This new organization widened the Christian Democratic networks, but it was no more successful than the NEI at coordinating policy among parties.

The early drive to reconnect Christian Democrats demonstrated a sense of community among Catholics that most believed had been unnaturally shattered by unbridled nationalism. Catholic leaders felt a desire to reconnect the community—to become a "we" again. The challenge was daunting. A renewed European community required the survivors of occupation to welcome their captors back to the family; French, Dutch, and Belgian leaders had to sit down as equals with Germans and do the hard work of reconciliation. Though it was sometimes difficult, Christian Democrats reopened lines of communication across national borders and rediscovered common ground. In doing so they established Christian Democracy as a movement that could compete for power in Europe with its postwar rivals—liberalism, socialism, and communism. But in the months following Germany's surrender, no one knew just how powerful Christian Democratic ideas and political parties would become.

The early Christian Democratic contacts not only reestablished a movement and a community but also facilitated a necessary socialization process. New contacts allowed political leaders to build trust; exchange ideas; establish common intellectual, moral, and social norms; develop political strategies; marginalize dissent; and coordinate policies across national borders—especially on matters of European integration.[26] This mostly informal network of European leaders—speaking a common cultural language—pushed European integration in a distinctly Christian Democratic direction.

Postwar Christian Democratic Ideology

The postwar Christian Democrats did the hard work of political organization by reconnecting their movement across Europe in formal and informal ways, but they also did the intellectual work of rethinking their ideology. Postwar Christian Democracy was too large a movement not to develop factions, but nevertheless it crystallized around a few distinct ideas while developing a new openness to social elements that had not been part of the prewar movement. The Christian Democrats knew what they believed, and they harnessed tremendous political energy to achieve their vision of European society.

Christian Democracy and the Good Society

The prewar and postwar versions of Christian Democracy were similar, but not identical. Continuity with the past was clear: Christian Democracy remained very Catholic in tone and substance; continued to emphasize a corporatist alternative to free markets and socialism; and remained committed to international, especially European, cooperation. New developments, however, were also evident: Catholic Christian Democrats welcomed political (if not religious) alliances with non-Catholics; they settled on parliamentary democracy as the only system capable of respecting human dignity; and they embraced a crusade against atheistic, totalitarian communism. The details, however, are important.

Postwar Europe experienced a significant religious revival in the 1940s and 1950s. The churches filled up, and people who had previously participated only sporadically in the rhythms of religious life found themselves seeking the comfort and security of belief, ritual, and community.[27] Yet Catholicism, far from opening up, remained closed—"intransigent, hierarchical, and dismissive of the values of other denominations and political traditions." It saw itself standing for "truth in a corrupt and decadent world," and it offered no compromises with modernity. Postwar Catholics lived in a realm of popular piety characterized more by "banners, parades, and youth movements" than "the philocommunism displayed by certain Catholic intellectuals."[28] Emphasizing the aggressive aspects of postwar Catholicism, however, can obscure subtle shifts that were going on beneath the surface, in both intellectual and popular circles. At all levels the shared sufferings of war had eroded some of the walls between confessional communities and between religious and secular people that had stood for over a century and a half. The result was "a new mood of openness" that encouraged "new forms of debate and mutual discovery."[29] Thus, postwar Catholicism was paradoxical—both aggressively retrenched and subtly open.

This new "retrenched openness" prompted Christian Democrats to forge an ideological consensus around Catholic political and social ideas that resonated most broadly across religious communities and social classes. Once again the personalists—most prominently Jacques Maritain, Emmanuel Mounier, and Luigi Sturzo—led the way, having discarded any hint of authoritarian sympathy. Maritain perhaps best summarized the political philosophy of the postwar Christian Democrats in his December 1949 lectures that became the book *Man and the State* (1951).[30] This work merits attention because it captured both the content and spirit of Christian Democracy immediately after World War II.[31]

Maritain argued for the primacy of natural communities (e.g., families, nations, and social classes) and of the state's responsibility to pursue "the good human life of the multitude."[32] States, he asserted, were to uphold the worth and dignity of the human person and serve the people alone: "The people are above the State, the people are not for the State, the State is for the people."[33] Parliamentary democracy was the only practical form of government capable of protecting the rights of persons and upholding justice. The Church, in his view, must relinquish any claim on the state except the right to freely worship, teach, and preach. Still, he hoped for a "Christianly inspired modern democratic society."[34] In this society the Church would radiate a truth and beauty so attractive that it would awaken "unconscious Christian feelings and moral structures embodied in the history of the nations born out of old Christendom" and persuade people of the truth of the Christian faith. Such a "Christianly inspired" body politic would have "its own social and political morality, its own conception of justice and civic friendship, temporal common good and common task, human progress and civilization, vitally rooted in Christian awareness."[35] Here was the Christian Democratic vision of the good society.

Man and the State offered unqualified support for democracy built on a personalist vision of human rights and social justice. Significantly, Maritain carried this vision into the realm of international politics. For him, the problem with the international system began and ended with the concept of "sovereignty." Although kings, emperors, states, and "the people" claim sovereignty, "God alone is sovereign."[36] State claims of sovereignty are based on a "false pretense to be a person, a superhuman person."[37] And the nations they claim to govern have broken through their "natural limits" and have become earthly divinities whose "absolute selfishness is sacred."[38]

Maritain's solution was to discard state sovereignty as a violation of natural law and as an impractical organizing principle in an age of economic and political interdependence.[39] In its place he proposed a European federation. During the early war years, he had written several pieces favoring federation, including an unpublished manuscript ("L'Europe et l'idée fédérale"), several articles published in France, and a 1940 article in *Commonweal*.[40] At the heart of Europe's problems was an uncontrollable Germany: Only a federal Europe could contain a federal Germany. But for federalism to be an effective check on tyranny, Europe must embrace the truths that shaped its civilization: "A federal Europe will not exist unless the Christian spirit makes it exist."[41] For Maritain, a successful federal Europe would need to be a *Christian* federal Europe.

Maritain—and many others in the personalist school—provided the intellectual basis for a Catholic approach to modernity in the late 1940s.[42] The Christian Democrats, however, had already started—perhaps instinctively—to build a modern Catholic political philosophy into their political programs. In good personalist fashion, they began by affirming the supreme worth of the individual, who was endowed with rights and responsibilities. Take, for instance, the 1945 "Action Program" of the French Confederation of Christian Workers: "[Man] is a free and reasonable being, endowed by God with an eternal destiny, and equipped to that end with a supreme value as a person, with inalienable right[s], and with high responsibilities."[43] Persons, however, found fulfillment as members of "natural social groups," which must be recognized and accorded freedom in a just society. Thus, the founder of the MRP, Etienne Borne, wrote: "There can be no justice unless the rights of individuals and natural social groups are protected and encouraged."[44]

Although Christian Democrats organized and encouraged social groups such as labor unions, their most intense passions were reserved for the defense of families.[45] Defending the family had a moral dimension that led Christian Democrats to reject abortion, contraception, and anything else they believed undermined the traditional family. Defending the family also meant addressing "all those material questions which affect the standard of living in a home."[46] Here was the Christian Democratic rationale for a "social market economy" that used state power to boost and protect standards of living. Unbridled markets put pressure on wage earners and their dependent wives and children. Thus, Sturzo wrote: "Wages are often insufficient for supporting a family, so that families go to pieces, leading to a profound crisis of morality."[47] Christian Democrats believed that it was the state's duty to intervene on behalf of workers and, in rural areas, farmers. In practice this meant encouraging cooperation among the great social interests—business, labor, and agriculture—to create and maintain a comprehensive, universal welfare state. It also meant maintaining the right of private property, but granting the state the duty to manage the market in the interest of breadwinners and their families. This was the postwar version of the Catholic "third" or "middle" way with roots deep in the social encyclicals of Pope Leo XIII and Pope Pius XI, minus the traces of authoritarian corporatism.

Christian Democrats had come to fully embrace the spirit and institutions of democracy, but they rejected the tendency of the democratic state, whether liberal or socialist, to centralize authority in itself. Defending the rights of individuals and the autonomy of natural institutions standing outside the state—families, unions, and churches—required a division of responsibilities among governing institutions. The best guarantee for this decentralization was the principle of "subsidiarity." In *Quadragesimo Anno*, Pope Pius XI had laid out the basic principle: "It is an injustice, a grave evil, and a disturbance of right order for a larger and higher organization to arrogate to itself functions which can be performed efficiently by smaller and lower bodies."[48] Pius left the definition of "lower bodies" vague, but most interpreted him to mean families, churches, and vocational corporations, although others also included political institutions. Maritain had spoken of partial authorities stacked in tiers above one another.[49] Eberhard Welty and Adolph Süsterhenn, both Germans, argued that regional governments also constituted natural bodies.[50] Subsidiarity meant that the higher authorities should make decisions only when the lower ones could not do so effectively, thus preserving the dignity of individuals by protecting the autonomy of families, churches, trade associations, unions, and local and regional governments. Christian Democrats always considered subsidiarity the bedrock of their ideology, but they found it hard to explain or codify. It became more weltanschauung than code of practice.

Like its prewar predecessor, postwar Christian Democracy made the freedom of the Catholic Church an important component of its political program. Still, the movement would not be an arm of the Catholic Church; it rejected clericalism and was open to Protestants, although with little success outside Germany. The Christian Democrats embraced what they called "vertical pluralism," whereby various spiritual families, including humanists, were "permitted and enabled to follow their own way of life."[51] They disagreed, however, over the extent to which the state could privilege Catholicism over other religions.

Christian Democracy's new embrace of a secular state and nonconfessional politics was a break with much of its past. Nevertheless, Christian Democracy had not become a secular movement; these parties remained fundamentally and profoundly Christian—and more specifically—*Catholic*. As Conway puts it, for all their new openness, "the Christian Democratic parties were for the most part emphatically Catholic parties."[52] The leaders and electorates were largely Catholic, who thought and spoke as Catholics. And their goal was to create what Maritain had called a "Christian-inspired" society. They hoped "to create a new form of democracy, in which the natural communities of family, workplace, and region would play as important a role as national parliaments."[53] Every man, woman, and child would find fulfillment in community and would enjoy the just distribution of society's resources. Laws would be just and in accordance with natural law. Moral values would be taught by the Church and upheld by the community. Barriers that kept human beings apart as enemies would be challenged and broken down. Christian civilization would be honored. In short, the Christian Democrats still believed in Christendom, but a new Christendom that was now wholly voluntary and democratic. Political parties of "Christian inspiration," if given the opportunity, would work to realize this Christian vision of modern society.

Christian Democracy and European Federalism

This vision, of course, extended to the international system. The Christian Democrats became the federalists of the West—the crusaders for a united Europe. European integration went from being an interesting, if unrealistic, idea in interwar Catholic circles to a central tenet of Christian Democracy and a vital element of Christian Democratic identity, so much so that Etienne Borne claimed for the French MRP in 1954: "We are the party of Europe."[54]

Christian Democrats were certainly not the only Europeans talking about unity after the horror of World War II. Famously, and quite ironically, the British Conservative Winston Churchill in his 1946 Zurich speech had called for a re-creation of the "European family" by building "a kind of United States of Europe."[55] Liberals and Socialists also had strong advocates for some kind of continental unification. Christian Democrats, however, were quite skeptical of these movements and questioned their sincerity. According to Kaiser, the NEI refused to work with several organizations committed to European cooperation. Richard Coudenhove-Kalergi's European Parliamentary Union was too conservative and too closely tied to the Hapsburgs; the Ligue Européenne de Coopération Économique was too market oriented and liberal; and the United Europe Movement was too British and intergovernmental. In 1947 the NEI did join the European Federalist Movement under the leadership of the Dutch socialist Hendrik Brugmans, and it participated in the Hague Congress of 1948.[56] With this exception, Christian Democratic leaders continued to regard other federalist movements as problematic and as tainted by party politics. Relations with other federalists improved only after Christian Democrats had assumed leadership of the movement (Robert Schuman was elected president of the European Federalist Movement in 1955) and socialized the liberals and socialists into a Christian Democratic vision of an institutionalized core Europe.[57] In truth Christian Democrats, after a short period of flux in the 1940s, became ideologically cohesive in their commitment, and they were in fact the only unified political bloc backing concrete integration efforts throughout the postwar period.[58]

Indeed, Christian Democrats put European unity at the center of their foreign policy. In France, the left-wing Catholic Michel Collinet wrote in *Esprit* in May 1945 that the hatred for "Nazi murders" cut across national lines and offered "a unique historical opportunity . . . to establish a community commensurate with the forces of the modern world, which we shall call the United States of Europe."[59] Likewise, Ernest Pezet, a prominent MRP politician, called Europeans in January 1946 to work "resolutely towards a Europe based essentially on federalism, first on a regional and then on a continental scale."[60] The question of whether Germany should be included in a European union divided the French Christian Democrats in the mid-1940s, but by 1947 the MRP was unified enough to call for "immediate steps towards the establishment of a European federation."[61] Meanwhile, Konrad Adenauer was arguing in his March 1946 Cologne University speech that it would soon "be time for the United Nations to tackle the problem of the United States of Europe, including Germany. A United States of Europe will be the best, surest, and most lasting guarantee for Germany's western neighbors."[62] Italian Christian Democrats were a bit slower to jump on the federalist bandwagon, but Sturzo eventually (1948) concluded that "European federation will perhaps be the last stage of an idea [European unity] that has lived subconsciously in our Christian civilization since the fall of the Roman empire."[63] Two years later Christian Democratic prime minister Alcide De Gasperi argued for a gradual but effective approach to "the economic integration and political unification of Europe."[64]

Transnational conversation among Christian Democrats about unification also started early. The second Geneva session (March 1948), which involved both Georges Bidault and Konrad Adenauer, addressed the "security and integration of Europe."[65] European unity, including the specific form (union, confederation, or federation), also remained a central topic of conversation at later meetings that Bidault and Adenauer attended, the last one in June 1949, eleven months before the Schuman Declaration called for the integration of coal and steel. In public, pan-European Christian Democracy was also staking out a preference for integration. In early 1948 the NEI passed a resolution calling for a "fraternal community" that included Germany. In September the organization gave a much more comprehensive defense of a European Federation but stated very clearly that it would need to be built on a firm spiritual foundation.[66]

Christian Democratic leaders were drawn to European federation because integration presented a solution to key postwar problems: what to do with Germany, how to counter Soviet aggression, and how to spark economic development. But the Christian Democrats came to believe in the five years after the war's end that European unity was more than a pragmatic solution to particular postwar problems; it was also the one policy that most completely embodied the modern Christian Democratic—or more exactly, Catholic—worldview. The creation of a European federation along explicitly Christian Democratic lines would fulfill the modern Catholic vision of the good society.

The centrality of European federalism to the postwar Christian Democratic vision is easily understood in light of the core Christian Democratic tenets we have already explored. First, European federalism, because it was democratic, fulfilled the personalist vision of society. Individuals endowed by God with "freedom, dignity, and the right to fulfillment" form a "brotherhood," a community of persons that share a common divine origin and human nature.[67] Democracy is built on this wholly Christian conception of humanity; separated from Christianity, democracy is simply inconceivable. According to Schuman, "democracy will be Christian or it will not be."[68]

Second, living in dignity required paying additional attention to the social and economic well-being of persons, a goal that Christian Democrats thought most achievable at the European level. From the beginning, Christian Democrats had worried that integrating the Continent would overshadow efforts to orient the economy toward human progress. Thus the NEI warned in September 1948 that the elimination of poverty among individuals and families, and the creation of the material conditions necessary for "the fullest personal and collective development," had to remain central objectives.[69] Democracy that attended to the economic and social needs of citizens *on a continental scale* would advance Europe from mere "political democracy" to "real democracy" fully grounded in Christianity.[70] Only in a unified

Europe could democracy in its fullest sense be realized. As Schuman put it, "The implementation of this vast programme of a general democracy, in the Christian sense of the term, finds expression in the construction of Europe."[71]

Third, federalism provided the Christian Democrats with a practical avenue to reconciliation among former enemies. They viewed reconciliation as a divine mandate and a necessary precursor to human flourishing—but erasing national distinctions, even in the service of divine forgiveness, seemed difficult and unrealistic. Federalism, however, with its accent on separate political units delegating powers to a higher authority, made it easier for former enemies to envision living together in the same polity. Federal power would exist, but the member states would preserve much of their autonomy. Thus reconciliation would not mean national annihilation. On the contrary, as the NEI stated in 1948: "In their relations with one another, states should leave behind their stage of nationalism and agree to an organization on the federative principle, or in a federal or confederal form, which will achieve unity while maintaining diversity."[72] Conceived this way, federalism simply extended the Catholic principle of subsidiarity to regional governance. Adding a layer of authority above the nation made perfect sense to Catholics, who were comfortable with multiple levels of authority. After all, they took part in the worship and work of a supranational church. For Christian Democrats, subsidiarity allowed Europe to have both a supranational government and fully functioning member states without conflict between levels of government.

Finally, the creation of a federal Europe meant the salvation of an endangered Christian civilization.[73] Christian Democrats were enamored of Europe's glorious past, and thus they sought to recover its spiritual and moral character—indeed its soul—through integration. Almost every serious postwar exposition on integration included a recounting, sometimes in great detail, of the history of Europe, with special attention paid to the unity of medieval Christendom. Reference was often made to the Carolingian Empire, which for Christian Democrats was a symbol of what Europe had once been and could be again.[74] The story, of course, also included the spiritual crisis of the nineteenth and twentieth centuries, with its roots in the Reformation, and the inevitable political, economic, and moral disaster that followed.[75] For postwar Christian Democrats, the solution to Europe's spiritual crisis was to reestablish a Christian society directed not by the Church but by a set of values grounded in Christian principles. The NEI underlined this point: "European unity will not be achieved without the restoration of the Christian spirit. That spirit is the synthesis of ancient wisdom with the ideal of liberty and respect for law which alone can be the foundation of true order, recognizing the sovereign domain of God and respect for his moral law."[76]

Europe's survival depended upon the restoration of a Christian spirit in the West, but dangers loomed. Ancient internal rivalries continued to threaten destruction. The greater threat was from Latin Europe's historic rival, Asia, with the Soviet

Union representing the latest manifestation of what Adenauer called "Asian barbarism."[77] Even more revealing was the Christian Democratic tendency to compare the conflict with totalitarian communism to the medieval struggle with Islam. Bidault, for instance, at a 1948 Geneva Circle conversation, spoke of "a new Islam that will never retreat even one step and of which we have to expect everything."[78] In the same vein John Murray wrote, "The genuine European of to-day realizes that Europe is facing the onslaught of a new 'Islam'—an 'Islam' of godlessness and militant materialism."[79] Christian Europe embodied civilization itself; any threat against it threatened all humanity.

Christian Democracy, then, offered postwar Europe a comprehensive vision. Human flourishing would be the new European mission: Human persons would enjoy political and social rights and find fulfillment in natural communities; states would protect the dignity of all persons, preserve the autonomy of their social groups, and serve their fundamental interests; and nation-states would renounce their sovereignty and learn to cooperate in peace for the sake of their citizens. European unity was not an ill-fitting policy tacked on to the end of a long list of more important Christian Democratic priorities. It flowed directly from the theological and philosophical assumptions at the heart of Christian Democratic ideology. European federation became the signature policy of the early postwar Christian Democrats because the vision of a spiritually revived Christian civilization required a new unity—not the forced unity of Napoleon or Hitler, but the organic unity of medieval Christendom. The prospect of building a united Europe in the context of freedom captivated the minds and hearts of the Christian Democrats, especially the young, who longed to be part of something grand.[80] And nothing was grander than recreating the glory of Charlemagne's Europe.

The Vatican and Postwar Support for European Unity

The Christian Democratic movement grounded its ideology and political program in late-nineteenth-century and early-twentieth-century Catholic theology and social teaching. But the Church itself managed to exert only modest influence over the political movement, playing even less of a role than before in directly shaping programs and policies. This is not to say that Church officials had no influence over Christian Democratic policy positions, but Church authorities refrained from trying to dictate policy, instead favoring more general pronouncements that allowed some scope for maneuvering. In turn, Catholic political leaders generally enjoyed ecclesiastical support for policies that derived from Church teachings. Thus, as postwar leaders implemented policies consistent with the thrust of Catholic teaching, they could count on the verbal backing of the Church hierarchy, including the pope, on major issues. With the papacy at the height of its midcentury authority, the pope's voice carried considerable weight with Catholic voters.

Immediately after the war, the Vatican took special interest in international relations, including the possibility of a politically united Europe. Absent, however, was any lingering appeal to Catholic universalism in support of a global papal monarchy; instead, Catholic universalism was invoked in support of a new vision of a united humanity free from violence and idolatrous nationalism. Just months before the war ended, Pius XII called for the "formation of an organ for the maintenance of peace, of an organ invested by common consent with supreme power, to whose office it would also pertain to smother in its germinal state any threat of isolated or collective aggression."[81] The pope consistently called for *international* cooperation that would end the dominance of the nation-state. In 1947 he threw his support behind international congresses that represented "a breaking down of needless barriers and a uniting of nations."[82]

Pius's special concern, however, was for the unity of Europe. In his own words, he was "instinctively drawn" to the "practical realization of European unity,"[83] and from the earliest days of the war he repeatedly backed the goal of a united Europe.[84] Catholic organizations, even those as far away as the United States, followed his lead and called for "some kind of voluntary European union."[85] After the war, in the afterglow of the Hague Conference (1948), Pius again called for a European union, and later that same year he stressed the urgency of the situation in an address to the European Union of Federalists: "That the establishment of a European union presents serious difficulties no one will gainsay. . . . Yet there is no time to lose. If it is intended that this union shall really achieve its purpose, if it is desired to make it serve to advantage the cause of European liberty and concord, the cause of economic and political peace between the continents, it is high time it were established."[86] Although the pope was reticent about commenting on specific proposals, he often seemed to time his addresses to benefit particular efforts.

The pope's interventions sought to remind Europe that Christianity was the source of its ideals and values, encouraging national leaders to reunite Europe around these values—a position, as we have seen, well represented in Christian Democratic circles. In a frank speech to a group from the College of Europe in 1953, the pope expressed his desire to see Europe put spiritual values at the heart of its unifying mission: "Beyond its economic and political goals, a united Europe must make it its mission to affirm and defend the spiritual values which formerly constituted the foundation and support of its existence, values it once had a vocation to transmit to other peoples in other parts of the world, values it must seek out again today in a painful effort to save itself."[87] In 1957 he told the Congress of Europe to construct "an earthly home which bears some resemblance to the Kingdom of God."[88] He also made it absolutely clear to the Catholics that their mission was to support in every way possible the integration of Europe. In his June 1948 address to the European Union of Federalists, he said, "Neither have we any doubt that Our faithful children will realize that their position is always at the side of those generous souls who are preparing the way for mutual understanding and for the re-establishment of a sincere spirit of peace among nations."[89] To Pius XII, Catholic universalism and European unity were of the same cloth, and he was more than willing to use the considerable power of the papacy to influence Catholic opinion.

The postwar Vatican thus supported in general terms the idea of an integrated Europe. This unity was to be grounded in explicitly Christian values, which the Catholics recognized as universal. And the Vatican was willing to back integration efforts rhetorically—no small factor in intensely Catholic communities across Europe. But Rome did not dictate foreign policy to the democratically elected Christian Democrats, and it avoided any appearance of doing so. The Vatican gave Catholics permission to identify with a united Europe and to pursue policies that moved nations toward unity, but there was no Vatican-led conspiracy to create a United States of Europe. Pius XII's vague expressions of hope hardly constituted a Vatican-backed political program. Church officials did not mobilize Catholic lay organizations in support of unity. If the creation of the European Community was a Catholic conspiracy, it was well disguised.

Christian Democratic Power

In the late 1940s the Christian Democratic movement from France to Austria developed strong transnational ties and clarified its ideology. In the first few months after the end of the war—despite the physical difficulties of life in postwar Europe—the Christian Democratic movement established a transnational network of individuals and political organizations, articulated a middle way ideology that drew directly on modern Catholic theology and social teaching, took a strong stand against Soviet communism, and forged a European consensus favoring some form of continental union that included Germany—and all with the tacit approval of the Vatican.[90] Much of the Christian Democratic program was little changed from that of its prewar predecessors (although it was clearly more focused), and many thought that it was destined to remain a minor political movement in post-Hitler Europe. But those many were wrong; the Christian Democratic parties proved enormously successful. Postwar Europe was Christian Democratic Europe.

New Parties

Most of the Christian parties that emerged in the 1940s were new. The prewar German Center party reconstituted itself after the war, but it sank into political insignificance as Catholic voters gravitated to the new Christian Democratic Union (CDU). In France the left-wing Jeune République merged with the centrist Popular Democratic Party, forming the Popular Republican Movement, which carried the banner of Christian Democracy.[91] And this pattern was repeated in other Catholic countries; the old confessional parties failed to appear or quickly faded as new Christian Democratic parties emerged. The Austrian People's Party replaced the discredited and defunct Christian Social Party; the Belgian Catholic Bloc cut its ties to the Church and became a unitary party called the Christian Social Party–Christian People's Party (PSC-CVP);[92] Sturzo's Italian Popular Party, having been destroyed by the fascists in 1926, provided the foundation for the new Christian Democratic Party (DC); the Party of the Right in Luxembourg became the Christian Social People's Party (CSV); and in the Netherlands the Catholic People's Party (KVP) replaced the Roman Catholic State Party (RKSP). Only the Catholic-Conservative Party (now the Christian Democratic People's Party—CVP) of neutral Switzerland and the religious nationalist party, Fine Gael, of neutral Ireland entered the postwar era unchanged. These new parties largely eschewed confessional identities but remained religious; they professed to be merely "Christian"—as opposed to "Catholic"—and to be officially open to other confessions. Most of them, however, remained very Catholic, as only the German CDU drew many Protestants.

Christian Democratic parties emerged in the 1940s as the heirs of interwar Catholic politics, which on the whole had experienced only marginal success in the early twentieth century. Why, then, did this movement come to dominate the immediate postwar years? Four factors stand out: the postwar Catholic revival, Catholic political unity, the rejection of confessional politics, and American support.

Religious Revival

We begin with the religious surge. As we mentioned above, a Catholic revival spread across the devastated European Continent as people sought stability and comfort. The Catholic Church, as Judt put it, "could offer its members something that was very much missing at the time: a sense of continuity, of security and reassurance in a world that had altered violently in the past decades. . . . It was the Catholic Church's association with the old order, indeed its firm stand against modernity and change, which gave it a special appeal in these transitional years."[93]

Church attendance figures in this period are hard to come by, and comparison with prewar decades is even more difficult, but a general picture of religious practice can be drawn. Michael Fogarty, using data for the late 1940s and early 1950s, found that regular churchgoing among Catholics was probably highest in the southern dioceses of the Netherlands (97 percent reported fulfilling "Easter Duties"), with attendance somewhat lower in Amsterdam, Rotterdam, and The Hague. Attendance in Belgian Flanders was probably similar to that in the Netherlands. Judt claims that 70 percent of the population in Italy attended Mass regularly, although Fogarty is less confident that the data from this period are trustworthy.[94] German Catholics were somewhat less observant, with about 60 percent regularly attending church, and French and French-speaking Belgians lagged significantly behind, with church attendance at approximately 35 to 40 percent. Variation existed across European regions and demographic groups, of course, with higher attendance characteristic of women more than men, of white-collar workers more than manual laborers, and of rural more than urban dwellers. Exceptions existed; Fogarty reports that some rural French districts had "in effect reverted to paganism." But on the whole, Catholic worship attendance was robust across postwar Europe, providing the Catholic or Catholic-dominated Christian Democratic parties with a sizable potential electoral base.[95]

Uniting the Catholic Electorate

A second factor contributing to the rise of Christian Democracy was, in fact, the uniting of most of the Catholic base behind the Christian Democratic parties. Despite the corrosive effects of postwar migration (especially in Germany) on confessional boundaries,[96] the old prewar insular structures continued for nearly two more decades in much of Europe, with the Catholic hierarchy making every effort to maintain "an organizational infrastructure to encompass Catholics from the cradle to the grave."[97] Catholic security required unity, as the German Cardinal Frings told a British group in 1946: "Neither democracy in itself nor a state formally based on the rule of law offers Catholics . . . enough guarantees. Therefore the necessity of banding together exists as much today as in the time of our fathers."[98]

"Banding together" politically meant uniting all Catholics behind a single party in a monolithic Catholic bloc. Choosing which party Catholics should support was usually relatively simple. The clear choice for Dutch Catholics in highly pillarized Holland was the Catholic People's Party—the only major confessional Catholic party in Europe—which received 93 percent of the Catholic vote in 1948.[99] Other Christian Democratic parties in Catholic countries avoided an explicit confessional commitment but identified closely with the Church's agenda. Such was the case in Belgium (PSC-CVP), Luxembourg (CSV), and Italy (DC).

In occupied Germany, where Catholics remained a minority,[100] the Church hierarchy made a difficult decision to abandon the reconstituted Catholic Zentrum for a new Christian Democratic Union built on an interconfessional partnership with Protestants.[101] The bishops grasped quickly the need to align with Protestants in the new German state if Catholics were to defend their interests. The success of this alliance from the bishops' perspective, however, required Catholic dominance of the new party through the creation of a "Catholic core" closely linked to Church leaders and lay organizations.[102] For the prelates, "the ideal of Catholic solidarity became indistinguishable from a policy of keeping Catholics in the CDU and the CDU in power."[103]

The task of implementing such a CDU-focused strategy fell to Monsignor Wilhelm Böhler, Cardinal Frings's political adviser and a key player in the founding of the Rhineland CDU and the writing of the Basic Law of West Germany. Böhler set about creating a network of Church leaders, journalists, professors, politicians, and bureaucrats who met in an array of formal and informal groups coordinated through his "Catholic Office." In addition, Böhler created the Kirchenpolitisches Gremium, an ecclesiastical-political group that served as a channel for political advice to the bishops. He also established a number of political "working groups" that brought together Church officials, theologians, representatives of lay organizations, Bundestag members, and ministry officials to discuss government proposals and to coordinate political activities.[104]

Through Böhler's extensive and complicated network, the Church maintained an influential—some would say *dominant*—position in the CDU into the 1960s. The Church used its considerable organizational capacities and personal networks to lobby effectively. Most CDU party leaders and Catholic Church officials shared the same worldview, and almost always agreed on goals, although they sometimes differed on political strategy. In the end, the Catholics shaped the postwar CDU because they were more confident, aggressive, and organized than the Protestants in the party.

A unified Catholic elite shaped the German CDU, but a unified Catholic electorate—also organized by the Church—maintained the party in power. The Church put enormous pressure on German Catholics to support the CDU without question on any issue. Sometimes the messages were less than subtle; a German priest stated in 1949 that "if Christ were alive today, he would certainly be in the CDU."[105] But if German Catholics were subject to Church pressure, they were willing recipients. As Frederick Spotts notes, "Ecclesiastical influence was reinforced by a popular drive toward conformity with the Church's viewpoints."[106]

The strategy proved effective in Germany: In 1961, 82 percent of Catholics who attended church several times a week, 76 percent who attended weekly, and 61 percent who attended monthly preferred the CDU, with, respectively, 7 percent, 13 percent, and 26 percent preferring the Social Democratic Party (SPD). Older Catholic women in small towns were the most likely to vote CDU (65 percent).[107] This Catholic electoral bloc provided the stable foundation upon which the Adenauer era rested.[108] But Catholic influence in the CDU—and West Germany as a whole—did not go unnoticed. The Lutheran pastor and respected Protestant leader Martin Niemöller complained that West Germany had emerged as a "Catholic state . . . begotten in the Vatican and born in Washington."[109]

German Catholics, though shy of a majority in the population, controlled the direction of postwar West Germany by forming a disciplined bloc within the CDU. Italian Catholics, conversely, did not find themselves in a confessional minority but faced strident liberal and leftist forces committed to reducing the role of the Church in domestic affairs. As in Germany, however, devout Catholics in Italy, with the full backing of the Church, united as a bloc behind the DC, establishing the party as the dominant political force.

The Italian Church emerged from twenty years of fascism and war in a relatively strong position. The Lateran Accord of 1929 had protected the Church's privileges and organizational structure from fascist erosion, giving it the only nationwide social network apart from the Communist Party. Initially, the Holy Office favored the creation of a Catholic right-wing party to counter the DC's perceived leftist leanings.[110] Eventually, however, the Vatican, under the direct and vocal leadership of Pius XII, mobilized its considerable resources in support of the DC as the only political force capable of holding off communism. The Church hierarchy saw the struggle against communism as a new Christian crusade for the soul of Italy with the pope, for instance, calling the 1946 election a battle between "the champions and the destroyers of Christian civilization."[111] The entire Italian hierarchy unambiguously and forcefully backed the DC and urged Catholics—from the pulpit—to vote as a bloc. To underline the serious nature of the struggle, the Church excommunicated Communist Party members in July 1949.[112]

In Italy support for the DC came not only from the Church hierarchy but also from other powerful Catholic organizations, which constituted a large Catholic subculture, providing the DC with leaders, organizational expertise, volunteers, financial resources, and access to social networks. Catholic Action, for instance, survived the war as the only nonfascist national association permitted by the fascist regime. As the official organization of Catholic laity, it was completely dependent upon the clergy and closely followed clerical direction. Its fervent mobilization efforts in the 1940s contributed significantly to the DC's electoral gains, and many of its young leaders became major DC political figures in the mid-1950s. Also active in support of the DC were two organizations of Catholic workers, the Italian Association of Christian Workers and the Italian Confederation of Labor Unions, as well as an organization for small landowners, the National Confederation of Direct Cultivators (Coldiretti). Overlapping leadership tied these groups to the DC until the late 1960s, when policy disputes split the party from important sources of support. Only the Coldiretti maintained its backing for the DC.[113]

The strong support of the Church and Catholic social groups delivered Catholic votes to the DC. Not surprisingly, the party did best in the Northeast and South of Italy, where the Catholic subculture was strongest, and did worst in the traditional Red Belt of central Italy, where Catholics were weakest. Everywhere, the best predictor of DC voting was church attendance; 67 percent of regular Mass attenders voted Christian Democrat, and more than half of DC voters claimed to attend church once a week or more. (Among the DC party elites, the percentage of frequent church attenders exceeded two-thirds.) The demographic tendencies that students of postwar Italian politics stressed—the DC's advantages among women, rural residents, and older citizens—were accounted for by these groups' more frequent observance. In short, religion mattered in postwar Italy, and the DC reaped the electoral benefits of solid Catholic support.[114]

Blocs of Catholic voters backed the other Christian Democratic parties on the Continent. The prize for Catholic unity probably belongs to the Netherlands, where only 38 percent of the population identified as Catholic. Perhaps not surprisingly, Bakvis found that in 1956, 90 percent of Dutch Catholics who attended Mass regularly (fully 89 percent of Catholics) voted for the Catholic People's Party—strong evidence that Dutch pillarization still held firm. Similarly in Switzerland, where Catholics made up 40 percent of the population, approximately 50 percent voted for the Catholic-Conservative Party. In Belgium, where Catholics were in the overwhelming majority, approximately 45 percent voted for the PSC-CVP in the postwar period.[115]

The electoral story of Christian Democracy in France differed from that of its counterparts in the rest of Europe. The MRP was less popular than its Christian Democratic partners precisely because it was unable to attract a unified Catholic voting bloc. The MRP identified itself as Catholic, but it alienated some conservative Catholic voters by its left-of-center social policies and greater distance from the Church hierarchy than was characteristic of most of the other postwar Christian Democratic parties. Thus, as Irving points out, the "MRP was caught between two stools. It was too Catholic to attract laïc Republican votes, but insufficiently Catholic . . . to appeal to the Catholic electorate as a whole."[116] Consequently, the MRP became a regional Catholic party with strongholds in Normandy, Alsace, and Brittany.[117] Instead of unifying the Catholic electorate, the party watched Catholic voters bleed off to the Gaullists and other right-wing parties. Nevertheless, the party attracted sufficient support to be an influential political force into the 1960s. The MRP attracted about one-quarter of the vote in the 1940s, but saw its support decline to just over 10 percent of the electorate in the 1950s as many Catholics switched to the Gaullist Rally of the French People. In 1946, 75 percent of practicing Catholics voted for the MRP—a high point.[118] A respectable majority (54 percent) of church-attending Catholics continued to support the MRP in 1952, according to Fogarty, but the rest went to the smaller conservative parties (20 percent) and the Gaullist Rally (18 percent).[119] Catholic support for the MRP continued to decline through the 1950s.

Nonsectarian Political Identity

A third factor contributing to the dramatic success of the Christian Democratic parties was the movement's rejection of confessional politics. The exception here is the Netherlands, where the Catholic and Protestant parties remained tied to particular churches until the creation of the interconfessional Christian Democratic Appeal in 1980. The German CDU, however, united Catholics and Protestants, thus explicitly rejecting prewar confessional parties and their commitments to establishing "Christian States."[120] Christian Democratic parties in wholly Catholic Belgium, France, Italy, and Luxembourg did not need to incorporate Protestants, but nevertheless made clear their organizational independence from the Church.

Promoting Christian values in society and defending the rights of the Catholic Church, however, would require political power in postwar European democracies. Initially, the Christian Democratic parties were willing to play a confessional card when it might help win votes. Thus, elections were sometimes portrayed as struggles over ultimate values; and legislative issues were cast as decisions to accept or reject divine mandates.[121] But with time, Christian Democratic leaders came to understand the need for Christian parties to appeal to a broader range of voters. Thus these parties evolved into classic "catchall" parties by downplaying religion and even political ideology in favor of pragmatic policies.

The trick was to keep the support of core Catholic voters while appealing to the center of the national electorate. In general, the Christian Democratic parties successfully performed this electoral stunt by drifting to the right of their prewar predecessors. Strong right-wing, authoritarian parties in most continental countries had disappeared or hung on the political fringe while left-wing communist and socialist parties gained strength. The Christian Democratic parties filled the gap on the center-right by unambiguously opposing communism and Soviet actions in Eastern Europe while supporting state intervention in the economy and an expanded social welfare system. The strategy worked best in Belgium, Germany, Italy, and Luxembourg; the MRP in France, however, tried too hard to create a left-leaning social movement and ended up losing its conservative core. On the whole, however, the Christian Democratic approach worked brilliantly: The parties acquired and maintained power in the postwar period when Catholic belief and practice were still strong across continental Western Europe.

The final factor contributing to the rise of Christian Democracy in Europe was the strong support of the movement by the United States, especially in Germany and Italy, where the potential for a communist or left-wing takeover posed a threat to the defense of democracy. American policymakers were looking to support "a non-Marxist, moderately oriented anti-fascist party that had a mass base."[122] They found Christian Democratic parties, and they threw the weight of the United States behind them.[123]

In sum, Christian Democratic parties succeeded in the postwar period due to a revival of Catholic practice and sense of community, the ability of politicians and Church leaders to unite Catholics in a voting bloc behind Christian Democratic parties, the willingness of most Catholic parties to appeal to a wider electorate, and the American backing of Christian Democratic parties as reliable alternatives to domestic communists. The rise of Christian Democratic parties represented a reinvigorated postwar Catholic front. True, European political Catholicism was no longer clerical. Church officials—especially in Germany, Italy, France, and Austria—had learned how dangerous it was for bishops and clergy to draw too close to secular regimes and had resolved to stay out of active politics. In practice, this meant prohibiting clergy from holding party positions and government offices, but certainly not that the Church hierarchy had no interest in or influence over the Christian

Democratic parties. Political influence took different forms in different countries. At one extreme, the French hierarchy, mainly out of deference to the anticlerical nature of postwar French politics, played almost no role in the MRP, relying instead on the religious devotion of party officials and government ministers to pursue Church-friendly policies.[124] At the other extreme was the German hierarchy, which exercised enormous influence in the CDU during the 1950s. But the Church's influence had its limits, even in Germany; the pious Konrad Adenauer had little trouble deciding against the Church when his political interests so dictated.[125]

Christian Democratic Political Dominance

Christian Democratic parties came to dominate the politics of the continental democracies. The extent of Christian Democratic ascendancy in the six founding member states of the European Community is illustrated in the series of tables and figures presented below. (From this point on, "the Six" refers to Belgium, West Germany, France, Italy, Luxembourg, and the Netherlands.) From 1945 to 1969 approximately one-third of the electorate in the Six voted for the Christian Democratic parties (tables 5.1 to 5.7), with several parties—in Belgium, West Germany, Italy, and Luxembourg in particular—consistently drawing more than 40 percent. Moreover, the Christian Democratic parties in the Six scored the highest proportion of votes in 31 of the 43 elections (72 percent) held during this period. If France is removed from the equation, the Christian Democratic parties won 31 of 34 elections, finishing second in the rest. In fact, the Christian Democrats did not lose an election during this period in Belgium, West Germany, or Italy, and only one in the Netherlands (a result that would be erased if the Catholic and Protestant parties were added together).

The percentage of parliamentary seats won by Christian Democratic parties demonstrates a similar trend. In every country except France, the Christian Democrats consistently won more than 40 percent of the seats with rare outright majorities in three elections—Belgium (1950), West Germany (1957), and Italy (1948)—and exactly 50 percent won in Luxembourg in 1954. In France the MRP won one-quarter of the parliamentary seats in the 1940s but fell to approximately one-eighth of the seats in the 1950s and less than one-tenth in the 1960s.

The Christian Democrats' electoral strength naturally resulted in its playing a leading role in coalition governments (see figure 5.1). From 1946 through 1969 the Christian Democratic parties led every government in Italy and Luxembourg and all but one in Germany. Dutch Catholics participated in every government during this period, leading all but five. Dutch cabinets simply could not be built without the Catholic KVP, which by one measure was the most influential party in the cabinet.[126] In France the MRP in the Fourth Republic still managed to serve as the "fulcrum within the parliamentary system."[127] From 1944 to 1958 the party participated in twenty-three of twenty-seven governments and supported three more. The MRP's Robert Schuman, Georges Bidault, and Pierre Pflimlin served as prime ministers in

Table 5.1 Christian Democratic Party Strength in National Elections
(average percent by decade)

Country	1940s	1950s	1960s
Belgium (PSC-CVP)	43.0	45.1	35.9
France (MRP)	26.4	11.6	10.6
West Germany (CDU/CSU)	31.0	47.7	46.3
Italy (DC)	41.9	41.3	38.6
Luxembourg (CSV)	40.5	42.4	34.3
Netherlands (KVP)	30.9	30.7	29.2
EC-6 average	35.6	36.5	32.5

Key: PSC-CVP = Christian Social Party–Christian People's Party; MRP = Popular Republican Movement; CDU/CSU = Christian Democratic Union / Christian Social Union; DC = Christian Democracy; CSV = Christian Social People's Party; KVP = Catholic People's Party.
Source: Jan-Erik Lane and Svante O. Ersson, *Politics and Society in Western Europe*, 2nd ed. (London: Sage, 1991), 140.

Table 5.2 Party Strength in Belgium, 1946–68

Party	1946	1949	1950	1954	1958	1961	1965	1968
Percent popular vote								
Catholic	42.5	43.6	47.7	41.2	46.5	41.5	34.5	31.8
Socialist	31.6	29.8	34.5	37.3	35.8	36.7	28.3	28.0
Liberal	8.9	15.3	11.3	12.2	11.1	12.3	21.6	20.9
Communists	12.7	7.5	4.8	3.6	1.9	3.1	4.6	3.2
People's Union (Flemish)	—	—	—	—	2.0	3.5	6.7	9.8
Francophone	—	—	—	—	—	—	1.3	3.0
Percent parliamentary seats								
Catholic	45.5	49.5	50.9	44.8	49.1	45.3	36.3	32.5
Socialist	32.7	31.1	34.4	38.7	37.7	39.6	30.2	27.8
Liberal	7.9	13.7	9.4	11.3	9.4	9.4	22.6	22.2
Communist	11.4	5.7	3.3	1.9	0.9	2.4	2.8	2.4
People's Union (Flemish)	—	—	—	—	0.5	2.4	5.7	9.4
Francophone	—	—	—	—	—	—	1.4	2.8

Source: Wolfram Nordsieck, "Belgium," Parties and Elections in Europe, www.parties-and-elections.de/belgium2.html.

Table 5.3 Party Strength in France, 1945–68

Party	1945	1946	1949	1951	1956	1958	1962	1967	1968
Percent popular vote									
Christian Democrat	23.9	28.2	25.9	12.6	11.1	11.1	9.1	—	—
Socialist	23.4	21.1	17.8	14.6	15.2	15.7	12.6	19.0	16.5
Republican	15.6	12.8	12.9	14.1	15.3	22.9	7.7	—	—
Radical	10.5	11.6	11.1	10.0	15.2	8.3	7.8	—	—
Communist	26.2	25.9	28.2	26.9	25.9	19.2	21.7	22.5	20.0
Gaullist	—	—	3.0	21.6	—	19.5	31.9	37.4	44.7
Percent parliamentary seats									
Christian Democrat	25.6	28.8	27.0	15.3	14.1	12.0	11.4	8.4	6.8
Socialist	25.6	22.0	17.0	17.1	16.6	9.3	13.7	23.8	11.7
Republican	10.9	11.4	11.5	17.2	16.3	28.0	2.7	—	—
Radical	9.7	9.0	11.3	15.2	15.8	6.7	8.1	—	—
Communist	27.5	26.1	29.6	16.1	25.2	2.1	8.5	15.0	7.0
Gaullist	—	—	—	19.1	—	41.9	48.3	50.3	73.9

Source: Wolfram Nordsieck, "France," Parties and Elections in Europe, www.parties-and-elections.de/france2.html.

Table 5.4 Party Strength in West Germany, 1949–69

Party	1949	1953	1957	1961	1965	1969
Percent popular vote						
Christian Democrat	31.0	45.2	50.2	45.4	47.6	46.1
Social Democrat	29.2	28.8	31.8	36.2	39.3	42.7
Liberal	11.9	9.5	7.7	12.8	9.5	5.8
Percent parliamentary seats						
Christian Democrat	34.2	48.9	53.4	48.2	48.5	48.3
Social Democrat	33.3	31.8	34.9	39.0	41.9	45.8
Liberal	13.5	10.4	8.5	12.9	9.7	6.0

Source: Wolfram Nordsieck, "Germany," Parties and Elections in Europe, www.parties-and-elections.de / germany2.html.

Table 5.5 Party Strength in Italy, 1946–68

Party	1946	1948	1953	1958	1963	1968
Percent popular vote						
Christian Democrat	35.2	48.5	40.1	42.4	38.3	39.1
Socialist	20.7	—	12.8	14.2	13.8	14.5
Liberal	6.8	3.8	3.0	3.5	7.0	5.8
Republican	4.4	2.5	1.6	1.4	1.4	2.0
Communist	19.0	31.0	22.6	22.7	25.3	26.9
Italian Social Movement	—	2.0	5.8	4.8	5.1	4.5
Percent parliamentary seats						
Christian Democrat	37.2	53.1	44.6	45.8	41.3	42.2
Socialist	20.7	—	12.7	14.1	13.8	14.4
Liberal	7.4	3.3	2.2	2.9	6.2	4.9
Republican	4.1	1.6	0.8	1.0	1.0	1.4
Communist	18.7	31.9	24.2	23.5	26.3	28.1
Italian Social Movement	—	1.0	4.9	4.0	4.3	3.8

Source: Wolfram Nordsieck, "Italy," Parties and Elections in Europe, www.parties-and-elections.de / italy2.html.

Table 5.6 Party Strength in Luxembourg, 1945–69

Party	1945	1948	1951	1954	1959	1964	1969
Percent popular vote							
Christian Democrat	41.4	41.0	33.3	42.4	36.9	33.3	35.3
Social Democrat	26.0	35.8	41.4	35.1	34.9	37.7	32.3
Liberal	16.7	20.7	8.4	10.8	18.5	10.6	16.6
Communist	13.5	2.5	16.9	8.9	9.1	12.5	15.5
Percent parliamentary seats							
Christian Democrat	49.0	43.1	40.4	50.0	40.4	39.3	37.5
Social Democrat	21.6	29.4	36.5	32.7	32.7	37.5	32.1
Liberal	17.6	17.6	15.4	11.5	21.2	10.7	19.6
Communist	9.8	9.8	7.7	5.8	5.8	8.9	10.7

Source: Wolfram Nordsieck, "Luxembourg," Parties and Elections in Europe, www.parties-and-elections.de / luxem bourg2.html.

Table 5.7 Party Strength in the Netherlands, 1946–67

Party	1946	1948	1952	1956	1959	1963	1967
Percent popular vote							
Catholic (KVP)	30.8	31.0	28.7	31.7	31.6	31.9	26.5
Protestant (ARP)	12.9	13.2	11.3	9.9	9.4	8.7	9.9
KVP+ARP	43.7	44.2	40.0	41.6	41.0	40.6	36.4
Social Democrat	28.3	25.6	29.0	32.7	30.4	28.0	23.6
Liberal	6.4	7.9	8.8	8.8	12.2	10.3	10.7
Reformed (CHU)	7.8	9.2	8.9	8.4	8.1	8.6	8.1
Reformed (SGP)	2.1	2.4	2.4	2.3	2.2	2.3	2.0
Communist	10.6	7.7	6.2	4.8	2.4	2.8	3.6
Pacifist Socialist	—	—	—	—	1.8	3.0	2.9
Democrats 1966	—	—	—	—	—	—	4.5
Percent parliamentary seats							
Catholic (KVP)	32.0	32.0	30.0	33.0	32.7	33.3	28.0
Protestant (ARP)	13.0	13.0	12.0	10.0	9.3	8.7	10.0
KVP+ARP	45.0	45.0	42.0	43.0	42.0	42.0	38.0
Social Democrat	29.0	27.0	30.0	34.0	32.0	28.7	24.7
Liberal	6.0	8.0	9.0	9.0	12.7	10.7	11.3
Reformed (CHU)	8.0	9.0	9.0	8.0	8.0	8.7	8.0
Reformed (SGP)	2.0	2.0	2.0	2.0	2.0	2.0	2.0
Communist	10.0	8.0	6.0	4.0	2.0	2.7	3.3
Pacifist Socialist	—	—	—	—	1.3	2.7	2.7
Democrats 1966	—	—	—	—	—	—	4.7

Key: KVP = Catholic People's Party; ARP = Anti-Revolution Party; CHU = Christian Historic Union; SGP = Reformed Political Party.
Source: Wolfram Nordsieck, "Netherlands," Parties and Elections in Europe, www.parties-and-elections.eu/nether lands.html.

five governments; seven MRP leaders served as deputy prime ministers; Schuman and Bidault controlled the Ministry of Foreign Affairs (1944–54); and the MRP dominated the Ministry of Overseas France (Colonies), and to a lesser extent the Ministry of Defense.[128]

Just how dominant were the Christian Democratic parties from 1946 to 1969? If we consider just the Six and count the years available to popularly elected governments (140 total), the Christian Democrats participated in government in 88 percent (123) of the available years and led in 73 percent (102) of those years. Coalition governments require parties to compromise; thus, Christian Democratic power hardly went unchecked. But the strength of Christian Democracy in the Six during the immediate postwar years was truly remarkable. The Christian Democratic parties were the natural parties of government at the core of Western Europe for twenty-five years.

Thus, it is no surprise that Christian Democrats were the central players in the early phases of postwar integration. As we will see in the next chapter, the movement produced the political leaders most responsible for initiating policy proposals

Figure 5.1 Christian Democrats in Government, 1945–70

Member state	1946	1947	1948	1949	1950	1951	1952	1953	1954	1955	1956	1957	1958	1959	1960	1961	1962	1963	1964	1965	1966	1967	1968
Belgium	///	xxx	xxx	•••	•••	•••	•••	•••	///	///	///	///	•••	•••	•••	•••	•••	•••	•••	•••	•••	•••	•••
France	x	xxx	•••	xxx	•••	xxx	xxx	xxx	xxx	xxx	xxx	xxx	•••	///	///	///	///	///	///	///	///	///	///
FR Germany	x	x	x	•••	•••	•••	•••	•••	•••	•••	•••	•••	•••	•••	•••	•••	•••	•••	•••	•••	•••	•••	•••
Italy	•••	•••	•••	•••	•••	•••	•••	•••	•••	•••	•••	•••	•••	•••	•••	•••	•••	•••	•••	•••	•••	•••	•••
Luxembourg	•••	•••	•••	•••	•••	•••	•••	•••	•••	•••	•••	•••	•••	•••	•••	•••	•••	•••	•••	•••	•••	•••	•••
The Netherlands	•••	•••	xxx	xxx	xxx	xxx	xxx	xxx	xxx	xxx	xxx	xxx	xxx	•••	•••	•••	•••	•••	•••	•••	•••	•••	•••

Source: Wolfgang C. Muller and Kaare Strom, eds., *Coalition Governments in Western Europe* (Oxford: Oxford University Press, 2000).

KEY

•••	=	Catholic Party / Christian Democratic Party is the leading party in government
xxx	=	Catholic Party / Christian Democratic Party participates in government
///	=	Catholic Party / Christian Democratic Party in the opposition
x	=	No democratic government

and negotiating treaties. Christian Democracy also provided the most unified and consistent voting bloc in favor of treaty ratification in the member state parliaments. The empirical evidence is quite impressive. On May 9, 1950, the day Schuman announced his plan to create an integrated coal and steel community in Europe, the Six were all governed by coalitions containing Christian Democrats, five had Christian Democratic prime ministers (only the Netherlands did not), and four had Christian Democratic foreign ministers. Of the eight signers of the April 1951 Treaty of Paris establishing the European Coal and Steel Community, five were Christian Democrats.[129] Six foreign ministers signed the treaty establishing the failed European Defense Community on May 27, 1952—five were Christian Democrats.[130] Seven of twelve signatories of the Treaties of Rome (March 25, 1957) establishing the European Economic Community and Euratom were Christian Democrats.[131]

When the treaties were sent to the national parliaments for ratification, Christian Democrats overwhelmingly voted in favor of passage. And Christian Democratic representatives voted unanimously for the European Coal and Steel Community in West Germany and France (where opposition from the Gaullists, socialists, and communists made the votes relatively close) and in all three Benelux countries (where only the communists and a few socialists voted no). Italy did not record the votes, but Christian Democrats voted overwhelmingly in favor of the treaty. The European Defense Community proved more contentious—especially in France, where it was voted down in August 1954—but Christian Democrats held steady in favor of an integrated defense force, with Christian Democratic "no" votes recorded only in France (2), Germany (1), and Belgium (10).[132] Christian Democratic parliamentarians again voted overwhelmingly for the Treaties of Rome, which helped produce large parliamentary majorities in favor of passage in all six countries.[133] Postwar Christian Democracy used its political dominance of the period to shape the Continent in its own image—peacefully.

Conclusion

Christian Democratic parties understood that political power went to organized groups with a coherent message. Socialists, communists, and liberals also understood the realities of democratic politics. Nevertheless, Christian Democrats were more successful in core Europe precisely because their ethos and message resonated with people steeped in a still-powerful Catholic confessional culture. No doubt Christian Democrats had evolved since the interwar period. They were staunch democrats; they were (mostly) nonsectarian; and they supported a mixed economy that addressed the concerns of the working class. But they defended these "new" positions with theological and philosophical arguments that made sense to committed Catholics. They also articulated a vision for the Continent built on the notion that Europe was a single cultural entity unnaturally divided by nationalism. European union, in their view, was the logical and natural culmination of the Christian Democratic program for society. Their experience seemed to confirm this. Christian Democrats, especially the elites, experienced a transnational sense of community through their political and social networks, which seemed to prove that Europe could be reunited if only the Christian principles of forgiveness and reconciliation were applied. Not everyone in Europe shared the same understanding, but the idea of unity was not foreign to the Continent—and, in fact, it struck a deep chord with many citizens, both Catholics and non-Catholics.

It was one thing, however, to believe deeply in European unity; it was another to implement such a radical policy. More than ideology was needed. For the integration process to begin, entrepreneurial leaders had to take advantage of a strategic crisis. For the postwar Christian Democrats, that opportunity presented itself in May 1950.

Notes

1. See Mark Mazower, *Dark Continent: Europe's Twentieth Century* (New York: Vintage, 2000), 213; and Ian Buruma, *Year Zero: A History of 1945* (New York: Penguin Press, 2013).

2. Michael Gehler and Wolfram Kaiser, "Toward a 'Core Europe' in a Christian Western Bloc: Transnational Cooperation in European Christian Democracy, 1925–1965," in *European Christian Democracy: Historical Legacies and Comparative Perspectives*, ed. Thomas Kselman and Joseph A. Buttigieg (Notre Dame, IN: University of Notre Dame Press, 2003), 240–66.

3. Wolfram Kaiser, *Christian Democracy and the Origins of European Union* (Cambridge: Cambridge University Press, 2007), 4.

4. Roberto Papini, *The Christian Democrat International*, trans. Robert Royal (Lanham, MD: Rowman & Littlefield, 1997), 52.

5. Ronald J. Granieri, *The Ambivalent Alliance: Konrad Adenauer, The CDU/CSU, and the West, 1949–1966* (New York: Berghahn Books, 2004), 16.

6. Ironically, the Cologne Congress adopted a strong resolution in favor of European economic integration (seeking the "broadest collaboration of all European nations, in order to create in this continent a common market"), just as SIPDIC started breaking up. See Papini, *Christian Democrat International*, 43.

7. Kaiser, *Christian Democracy*, 111.

8. Ibid., 113–17.

9. Joan Keating, "Looking to Europe: Roman Catholics and Christian Democracy in 1930s Britain," *European History Quarterly* 26, no. 1 (1996): 66.

10. Ibid., 67, 73.

11. Ibid., 73.

12. Ibid., 74.

13. The ICDU was established in 1940 by Sturzo and the People and Freedom Group; Kaiser, *Christian Democracy*, 142.

14. Papini, *Christian Democrat International*, 49.

15. Kaiser, *Christian Democracy*, 191–92.

16. See Edward Luttwak, "Franco-German Reconciliation: The Overlooked Role of the Moral Re-Armament Movement," in *Religion, The Missing Dimension of Statecraft*, ed. Douglas Johnston and Cynthia Sampson (Oxford: Oxford University Press, 1994), 47–53. Buchman also facilitated

relationships between Schuman and the many trade union and industrial leaders from the coal and steel industries who attended the conferences. When Franco-German negotiations over the Schuman Plan reached a difficult stage in 1950, both sides agreed to bring in mediators from Moral Re-Armament to help facilitate agreement; ibid., 52–53.

17. See Papini, *Christian Democrat International*, 67–73; and Kaiser, *Christian Democracy*, 205–12.

18. Kaiser, *Christian Democracy*, 205; Papini, *Christian Democrat International*, 68.

19. Papini, *Christian Democrat International*, 69–70.

20. Ibid., 50.

21. Ibid., 114n2.

22. Disagreement over whether the NEI would organize individuals or parties led to a compromise that allowed individuals, social groups, and political parties to join.

23. Papini, *Christian Democrat International*, 59–60.

24. Kaiser, *Christian Democracy*, 212. For the non–Christian Democratic organization of young federalists, see François-Xavier Lafféach, "An *Avant-Garde* for Europe: The Young European Federalists and the Emergence of a European Consciousness, 1948–1972," in *The Road to a United Europe: Interpretations of the Process of European Integration*, ed. Morten Rasmussen and Ann-Christina L. Knudsen (Brussels: PIE–Peter Lang, 2009), 39–51.

25. See Papini, *Christian Democrat International*, 86; and Kaiser, *Christian Democracy*, 314.

26. See Kaiser, *Christian Democracy*, 9; and Wolfram Kaiser, "Transnational Networks in European Governance: The Informal Politics of Integration," in *The History of the European Union: Origins of a Trans- and Supranational Polity 1950–72*, ed. Wolfram Kaiser, Brigitte Leucht, and Morten Rasmussen (New York: Routledge, 2009).

27. Martin Conway, *Catholic Politics in Europe, 1918–1945* (New York: Routledge, 1997), 49.

28. These quotations are from ibid., 47–48.

29. Conway, *Catholic Politics in Europe*, 89.

30. The French translation appeared in 1953.

31. We are indebted to Catherine McCauliff for explaining to us the importance of Jacques Maritain's thought on postwar Christian Democrats, particularly Robert Schuman. See C. M. A. McCauliff, "Union in Europe: Constitutional Philosophy and the Schuman Declaration, May 9, 1950," *Columbia Journal of European Law* 18, no. 3 (2012): 441–72.

32. Jacques Maritain, *Man and the State* (Chicago: University of Chicago Press, 1951), 12.

33. Ibid., 26.

34. Ibid., 181.

35. Ibid., 167.

36. Ibid., 24.

37. Ibid., 191.

38. Ibid., 7.

39. Ibid., 194.

40. Alan Paul Fimister, *Robert Schuman: Neo-Scholastic Humanism and the Reunification of Europe* (Brussels: PIE–Peter Lang, 2008), 124.

41. Jacques Maritain, "Europe and the Federal Idea," *Commonweal*, April 19, 1940, reprinted by Fimister, *Robert Schuman*, 283.

42. Emmanuel Mounier, Gilbert Dru, Etienne Gilson, Etienne Borne, and Maurice Byé—all French—would have to be included in the group of influential thinkers, as would the Italian Luigi Sturzo and the German Eberhard Welty. See R. E. M. Irving, *Christian Democracy in France* (London: George Allen & Unwin, 1973), 52–58.

43. Quoted by Michael P. Fogarty, *Christian Democracy in Western Europe, 1820–1953* (Notre Dame, IN: University of Notre Dame Press, 1957), 27.

44. Quoted by Irving, *Christian Democracy*, 60.

45. Fogarty, *Christian Democracy*, 49.

46. French Confederation of Christian Workers, quoted by Fogarty, *Christian Democracy*, 49.

47. Malcolm Moos, "Don Luigi Sturzo—Christian Democrat," *American Political Science Review* 39, no. 2 (1945): 276.

48. Quoted by George Reid, "Popes, Politicians and Political Theory: The Principle of Subsidiarity in 20th-Century European History" (PhD diss., University of Ottawa, 2005), 21–22. Pope Leo XIII—drawing on the work of the bishop of Mainz, Wilhelm Emmanuel von Ketteler—in *Rerum Novarum* outlined a theory of "subsidiarity," but without using the term.

49. Maritain, *Man and the State*, 11.

50. See Reid, "Popes," 49.

51. Fogarty, *Christian Democracy*, 42.

52. Conway, "Age of Christian Democracy," 48.

53. Ibid., 52.

54. Quoted by Kaiser, *Christian Democracy*, 189.

55. Winston S. Churchill, "Winston Churchill's Speech [to the Council of Europe], Zurich, 19 September 1946," Archive of European Integration, http://aei.pitt.edu/14362/.

56. Brugmans was the first rector of the College of Europe, which was founded in 1946.

57. Kaiser, *Christian Democracy*, 182–84.

58. For an analysis of the postwar party positions, see Ernst B. Haas, *The Uniting of Europe: Political, Social, and Economic Forces, 1950–1957* (Stanford, CA: Stanford University Press, 1958), chap. 4.

59. "Europe and Its Future, May 1945," in *The Struggle for European Union by Political Parties and Pressure Groups in Western European Countries, 1945–1950*, vol. 3 of *Documents on the History of European Integration*, ed. Walter Lipgens and Wilfied Loth (Berlin: Walter de Gruyter, 1988), 28.

60. "Ernest Pezet: Federalist Solutions, 15 Jan. 1946," in *Struggle for European Union*, ed. Lipgens and Loth, 40.

61. "MRP: Foreign Policy Motion, 10 May 1948," in *Struggle for European Union*, ed. Lipgens and Loth, 67.

62. "Konrad Adenauer: Speech at Cologne University, 24 March 1946," in *Struggle for European Union*, ed. Lipgens and Loth, 462.

63. "Luigi Sturzo: 'European Federation, 29 April 1948,'" in *Struggle for European Union*, ed. Lipgens and Loth, 199.

64. "Alcide De Gasperi: 'European Union,' 20 Feb. 1950," in *Struggle for European Union*, ed. Lipgens and Loth, 250.

65. Papini, *Christian Democrat International*, 70–75.

66. "The Hague Congress of the NEI, 17–19 September 1948," in *Transnational Organizations of Political Parties and Pressure Groups in the Struggle for European Union, 1945–1950*, vol. 4 of *Documents on the History of European Integration*, ed. Walter Lipgens and Wilfried Loth (Berlin: Walter de Gruyter, 1991), 501.

67. Robert Schuman, *For Europe* (Geneva: Nagel Editions, 2010), 54.

68. Ibid., 51.

69. "Hague Congress," 502.

70. Ibid.

71. Schuman, *For Europe*, 58.

72. "Hague Congress," 500–501.

73. Kaiser, *Christian Democracy*, 181.

74. Ibid., 228. According to Giulia Prati, "De Gasperi's ideal Europe was a Christian Democratically updated version of a Carolingian *res publica Christiana*"; Giulia Prati, *Italian Foreign Policy, 1947–1951: Alcide De Gasperi and Carlo Sforza between Atlanticism and Europeanism* (Bonn: Bonn University Press, 2006), 165.

75. The British Catholic historian Christopher Dawson wrote one of the most thoughtful pieces in this vein: Christopher Dawson, "The Religious Origins of European Disunity," *Dublin Review* 207 (1940): 144. A more pointed statement can be found in a 1946 editorial in *The Tablet*, which laments the consequences of "sovereignty," a concept it labels "the great heresy"; "Beyond Sovereignty," *The Tablet* 188 (October 19, 1946): 195–96. For a wartime version of this perspective, see William Thomas Walsh, "From Luther to Hitler," *The Sign* 19 (February 1940): 395–97; and Joseph Conrad Fehr, "Christian Unity Prerequisite of Lasting Peace," *Catholic World* 155 (April–September 1942): 20–28.

76. "Hague Congress," 501.

77. Konrad Adenauer, *Journey to America: Collected Speeches, Statements, Press, Radio, and TV Interviews* (Washington, DC: Press Office of the German Diplomatic Mission, 1953), 144.

78. Quoted by Kaiser, *Christian Democracy*, 228–29.

79. John Murray, "Reflections on European Unity," *Studies* 39 (September 1950): 263.

80. Kaiser, *Christian Democracy*, 230.

81. Pius XII, "Christmas Allocution of 1944," quoted by Edward J. Berbusse, "The Church and International Society," *America* 75 (June 1, 1946): 173. See also Christopher Dawson, "Foundations of European Order," *The Catholic Mind* 42 (May 1944): 313–16.

82. "Address to the International Postal Congress, 31 May 1947," quoted by Raymond F. Cour, "The Political Teaching of Pope Pius XII," *Review of Politics* 22 (1960): 483.

83. Pius XII, "European Union: An Address of Pope Pius XII to the 'Congress of Europe, June 14, 1957,'" *The Pope Speaks* 4 (Summer 1957): 201.

84. Jacqueline Stuyt, "Pius XII and European Unity," *Catholic International Outlook* 18, no. 212 (1962): 9.

85. Catholic Association for International Peace, *America's Peace Aims* (New York: Paulist Press, 1941), as cited in *Plans for European Union in Great Britain and in Exile, 1939–1945*, vol. 2 of *Documents on the History of European Integration*, ed. Walter Lipgens (Berlin: Walter de Gruyter, 1986), 726–27.

86. Pius XII, "Address to the European Union of Federalists," quoted by Edward A. Conway, "Catholics and World Federation," *America* 80 (December 4, 1948): 233.

87. Pius XII, "European Unity: An Address by His Holiness at an Audience Granted to a Group of Professors and Students from the College of Europe, Bruges, Belgium, March 15, 1953," *The Catholic Mind* 51 (September 1953): 560.

88. Pius XII, "European Union: An Address of Pope Pius XII to the 'Congress of Europe, June 14, 1957,'" *The Pope Speaks* 4 (Summer 1957): 204.

89. Pius XII, "Address to the European Union of Federalists," quoted by Conway, "Catholics and World Federation," 234.

90. Altiero Spinelli once wrote this backhanded complement: "When the Catholic parties assumed control of various European countries, they did not prove themselves to be jealous custodians of national sovereignties, but were open-minded enough to admit the possibility of unification at the supranational level, even though they had no clear ideas how this should be brought about; Altiero Spinelli, "The Growth of the European Movement since World War II," in *European Integration*, ed. C. Grove Haines (Baltimore: Johns Hopkins University Press, 1957), 45.

91. Irving, *Christian Democracy*, 48–49.

92. For the complicated history of the Belgian Catholic political movement of the 1930s, see Kris Deschouwer, *The Politics of Belgium: Governing a Divided Society* (New York: Palgrave Macmillan, 2009), 73–77.

93. Tony Judt, *Postwar: A History of Europe since 1945* (New York: Penguin Press, 2005), 229. See also Conway, "Age of Christian Democracy," 49–50.

94. Judt, *Postwar*, 228.

95. For postwar attendance data, see Fogarty, *Christian Democracy*, 348–55.

96. Frederic Spotts, *The Churches and Politics in Germany* (Middletown, CT: Wesleyan University Press, 1973), 48.

97. Ibid., 151.

98. As quoted in ibid., 151.

99. Fogarty, *Christian Democracy*, 359.

100. Catholics made up 46 percent of West Germany, according to Spotts, *Churches and Politics*, 50.

101. Ibid., 152–57; Carolyn M. Warner, "Strategies of an Interest Group: The Catholic Church and Christian Democracy in Postwar Europe, 1944–1958," in *European Christian Democracy*, ed. Kselman and Buttigieg, 149–55.

102. Spotts, *Churches and Politics*, 307.

103. Ibid., 157.

104. For a detailed description of Bohler's work, see ibid., 167–71.

105. Quoted in ibid., 154.

106. Ibid., 157–58. See also Buruma, *Year Zero*, 282.

107. Ibid., 158–59.

108. Ibid., 164.

109. Quoted by Kaiser, *Christian Democracy*, 173.

110. Andrea Riccardi, "The Vatican of Pius XII and the Catholic Party," in *Concilium: The Church and Christian Democracy*, ed. Gregory Baum and John Coleman (Edinburgh: T. & T. Clark, 1987), 41.

111. As quoted by Robert Leonardi and Douglas A. Wertman, *Italian Christian Democracy: The Politics of Dominance* (New York: St. Martin's Press, 1989), 198.

112. Ibid.

113. Ibid., 211–17.

114. Ibid., chap. 6; Herman Bakvis, *Catholic Power in the Netherlands* (Montreal: McGill–Queen's University Press, 1981), 4.

115. Bakvis, *Catholic Power*, 4–5.

116. Irving, *Christian Democracy*, 14.

117. Walter Laqueur, *Europe since Hitler: The Rebirth of Europe*, 2nd ed. (New York: Penguin Books, 1982), 55.

118. Kaiser, *Christian Democracy*, 173.

119. Fogarty, *Christian Democracy*, 361.

120. For an example of a commitment to a Christian State, see the 1875 program for the Bavarian Christian Social Party given by Fogarty, *Christian Democracy*, 312.

121. Spotts, *Churches and Politics*, 163; for a description of the apocalyptic view toward communism in Italy taken by the Church in the late 1940s, see Carolyn M. Warner, *Confessions of an Interest Group: The Catholic Church and Political Parties in Europe* (Princeton, NJ: Princeton University Press, 2000), 84–85.

122. Leonardi and Wertman, *Italian Christian Democracy*, 25.

123. See Granieri, *Ambivalent Alliance*, 15.

124. Irving, *Christian Democracy*, 82.

125. Spotts, *Churches and Politics*, 173.

126. See Bakvis, *Catholic Power*, 69, 204n96, who draws on the work of Ronald Rogowski, *Rational Legitimacy: A Theory of Political Support* (Princeton, NJ: Princeton University Press, 1974).

127. Irving, *Christian Democracy*, 13.

128. Ibid.

129. The Christian Democrats were Konrad Adenauer, Joseph Bech, Robert Schuman, J. R. M. van den Brink, and Paul van Zeeland; the others were Joseph Meurice, Carlo Sforza (Republican), and Dirk Stikker (Liberal).

130. The Christian Democrats were Konrad Adenauer, Paul Van Zeeland, Robert Schuman, Alcide De Gasperi, and Joseph Bech. Dirk Stikker of the Netherlands was a Liberal.

131. The Christian Democrats included Konrad Adenauer, Joseph Bech, Joseph Luns, Lambert Schaus, Antonio Segni, Jean Charles Snoy et d'Oppuers, and Walter Hallstein; the others included Maurice Faure (Radical), J. Linthorst Homan, Gaetano Martino (Liberal), Christian Pineau (Socialist), and Paul-Henri Spaak (Socialist).

132. Haas, *Uniting of Europe*, 156–57.

133. Papini, *Christian Democrat International*, 60.

6

Catholic Construction

O N MAY 9, 1950, exactly five years after the German High Command surrendered in Berlin, French foreign minister Robert Schuman presented a solution
to the perplexing "German problem" to a tired and hungry cabinet chaired by Prime
Minister Georges Bidault. The plan, developed by Jean Monnet and his team, called
for joint management of the coal and steel industries of France, Germany, and possibly other countries by a supranational High Authority. The cabinet swiftly agreed
to the proposal—although some ministers may not have known quite what they had
done. At a press conference in the ornate Salon de l'Horloge at the Quai d'Orsay,
Schuman read out, somewhat haltingly, his declaration to the world. Six countries—
France, Germany, Italy, Belgium, Luxembourg, and the Netherlands—heeded the
call to unite their coal and steel communities and launch the integration process.

Why did these six countries—core Europe—agree to integrate while others did
not? If we step back to look at the big picture, we can see that Deutsch's "background conditions" for integration were present in the Six. First, these countries,
like most in the West, had established compatible political, economic, and social systems—that is, parliamentary democracies and market-oriented economies. Second,
a growing sense of community and common identity among their Catholic elites
and populations had developed in the late 1940s. Their Catholic populations had experienced a religious revival that reinforced confessional and communal ties. Clergy
actively encouraged Catholic unity through religious processions, youth rallies, and
parades. Marian shrines drew large numbers of visitors. Pope Pius XII enjoyed the
intense loyalty of his European flock. In addition, as we have seen, Catholic elites
had established a web of cross-border interactions that reconciled former enemies
and nurtured personal friendships among notables. Contacts between Catholic politicians, moreover, facilitated the spread of political ideas and electoral strategies—
and furthered cross-border relations. In short, the Western European Catholics had
forged a regional Catholic community through sustained interaction—primarily, although not exclusively, among elites.

Third, while postwar interactions among Catholics encouraged a sense of community, the ideas exchanged also mattered. Committed Catholics were in remarkable agreement on the content of their faith and its political implications. That
agreement had its origins in a common intellectual and spiritual tradition, but it also

developed as a consequence of the interactions themselves, a process of socialization. Personalist theology shaped a worldview that dominated the Catholic world in ways it had never done before. Central to this worldview was a deep commitment to the reconciliation of enemies and the breaking down of barriers, especially between former combatants. Thus, not only did postwar Catholics possess a unifying confessional culture, but they also shared a worldview that led them to press for a united Europe.

Acting on this worldview required political power. Liberals, socialists, and communists may have felt some cultural affinity with the larger Catholic community, but these movements were divided or even opposed to integration, especially as envisioned by the Christian Democrats. Thus, without the rise to power of the Christian Democratic parties in the Catholic countries (or the countries with very large Catholic minorities), the steady development of a "we feeling" among elites and (more slowly) among regional populations might have led to nothing. The political success of the Christian Democratic parties—with the strong backing of the clergy—offered Catholic political leaders the opportunity to enact much of their program, including steps toward a united Europe. In short, background conditions were ripe for the takeoff of integration. Perhaps the most important condition was the electoral success of prointegration parties representing the cultural core of the transnational community.

The emergence of background conditions profoundly affected the scope of the integration process. Integration, at least initially, would be among countries sharing this European Catholic way of life and view of the world. As we shall see later, Protestant countries—Britain, Denmark, Finland, Iceland, Norway, and Sweden—and Protestant communities in the Netherlands and Switzerland (and to some extent in Germany) did not share that Catholic sense of community, or the ideology of the Christian Democratic parties. Their ideas of Europe, rooted in Protestant confessional cultures, differed from the Catholic vision embedded in Christian Democracy. Thus the northern Protestant countries did not join the launch of the European Coal and Steel Community (ECSC) in 1950, nor did Orthodox Greece, which also had the disadvantage of being poor and politically unstable.

Even some Catholic countries remained aloof from the integration process. Several lacked the common social structures of parliamentary democracies and market economies. Spain and Portugal certainly shared a Catholic confessional culture, but both were unreconstructed authoritarian regimes with corporatist economies. Prominent Spanish Catholics did encourage the creation of a Spanish Christian Democratic party and a parliamentary democracy, but encountered severe resistance within the Spanish Church.[1] As for integration, some Spanish clerics and theologians cautiously supported a postwar European union that presumably included Iberia.[2] The Christian Democrats in the Six, however, refused to integrate with nondemocracies, leaving Spain and Portugal isolated. The Catholic countries of Eastern

Europe were, of course, excluded because of their communist political systems and Moscow-oriented foreign policies.

Finally, what of Austria, Ireland, and Switzerland? These three shared with the Six similar social structures, Catholic confessional cultures (although Switzerland remained religiously divided), and strong Christian Democratic parties. All three, however, were also neutral. Switzerland adopted a rigid definition of neutrality that extended to economic relations. As the Swiss Foreign Ministry put it in 1954, "An economic neutrality exists only in so far as the permanently neutral state may not conclude a customs or economic union with another state, since this would mean that the neutral state would more or less renounce its independence in political matters as well."[3] The Swiss rejected even simple forms of economic cooperation, putting supranationality and the ECSC beyond the pale. Austria faced different circumstances, having been occupied by the Allies until 1955 and strictly neutral after that occupation ended. The absence of full sovereignty and Austria's precarious location between superpowers precluded any decision to join an international organization that might be perceived as "Western." Thus Austria took little interest in the Council of Europe or the ECSC, sending only low-level observers to both.[4] Ireland saw neutrality as a mark of independence and a safeguard against British domination. Ironically, its close economic ties to the United Kingdom also restricted its choices; Ireland would need to stay out of any economic organization as long as Britain remained outside. Thus, these three countries found in neutrality the solution to problems emerging from the international system. Integration might be an attractive ideal for Catholic leaders there, but there was no strategic crisis in the 1950s potent enough to initiate a search for policies other than neutrality.

Integration does not start automatically when the background conditions fall into place. Something must trigger the process. As the reader will recall, Kupchan identifies two such "triggers": a strategic crisis, and entrepreneurial leaders willing to press for integration as a solution. In the next sections we examine the crisis of 1949–50 that prompted Christian Democratic leaders to launch a process of integration. We also look at the way they sought to lay the foundations for a new European identity.

The European Crisis

Between 1945 and 1947, Christian Democrats came to power in Austria, Belgium, France, Italy, Luxembourg, and the Netherlands. German Christian Democrats had to await their chance until the founding of West Germany in 1949. Catholic leaders, committed in theory to some form of integration, held the reins of power in much of postwar Europe. Still, there was no immediate call for a constitutional convention to create a United States of Europe. Political dreams and party ideologies often crash on the rocks of political responsibility. If Catholic dreams of uniting Europe were to become reality, the vision would need to intersect with the demands of practical politics. Christian Democratic ideology made European unity a desirable goal, but integration would not begin without a spark. Integration needed a problem for which it constituted a possible solution. Only then—if embraced by political elites and fleshed out by diplomats—would the process commence.

Europe's "crisis" began on the day Germany surrendered unconditionally to the Allies. The question facing the Western powers then became "What do we do with a shattered Germany?" The United States took primary responsibility for the problem, but France had most to lose from miscalculation, as two world wars had tragically confirmed. For the French (but also for the Belgians, Luxembourgers, Dutch, and even the Italians), the German Question amounted to a Catch-22. On one hand, Europe needed Germany as its economic engine and first line of defense against a Soviet invasion. A strong Germany meant a strong Europe. On the other hand, a strong Germany would eventually threaten its neighbors and might drag the whole world into another conflagration. Thus the dilemma: Europe needed a strong Germany, but a strong Germany threatened Europe.

Allied intentions toward Germany were naturally belligerent as the war wound down and reconstruction began. President Franklin Roosevelt resisted thinking about reconstruction while the war continued, but in late 1943 he acquiesced to the development of a plan. In September 1944 he embraced a radical proposal formulated, not by the official planning committee headed by Assistant Secretary of State Dean Acheson, but by Secretary of the Treasury Henry Morgenthau, who believed that reconstruction of Germany would doom the world to another war. The Morgenthau Plan (officially titled "Program to Prevent Germany from Starting a World War III") demanded the total destruction of Ruhr industry. Factories would be dynamited, mines flooded. Nothing would be left standing. Germany would be returned to the agrarian world of 1860, even if that meant two decades of depression in Europe.[5] Roosevelt convinced Churchill to sign the Morgenthau Plan, making it official Allied policy. The plan was, however, never implemented. The war's end was followed by an untidy period of military governance in the four zones of occupied Germany. Reparations began in all four zones, but each of the Allies took a different approach. In an attempt to coordinate their efforts, the Americans, British, French, and Soviets hammered out a "Level of Industry Agreement" in March 1946 to direct the reparations process, but by May the United States had ceased shipments to the USSR, bringing that agreement to an end. The division of Germany and Europe was well under way.[6]

The Allied policy of punishing Germany ran its course in a year. It took another year and a harsh winter to find an alternative policy. The idea of rebuilding Germany was broached in the US State Department and encouraged behind the scenes by Jean Monnet as early as April 1946. American policy, however, remained confused until early 1947, when the threat of mass starvation and potential social chaos prompted a decision to inject billions of dollars into the European economy. On June 5, 1947, Secretary of State George C. Marshall made his famous commencement address at Harvard, and the "Marshall Plan" was born.

Marshall's speech was an offer, not a plan. The United States would provide assistance if the Europeans decided what to do with the money. According to Marshall, "It would be neither fitting nor efficacious for our Government to undertake to draw up unilaterally a program designed to place Europe on its feet economically. This is the business of the Europeans. The initiative, I think, must come from Europe. . . . The program should be a joint one, agreed to by a number, if not all, European nations."[7]

Soon it was clear that the Americans had certain assumptions about the disposition of assistance. First, all European countries would be treated equally, including occupied Germany, which now included Bizonia—the combined British and American zones. Second, most American policymakers anticipated that the new Soviet client states in Europe would not be participating. Finally, nations receiving assistance would need to adopt as their goal the creation of some kind of Western European federation.[8] Toward this last, frustratingly vague objective, the United States gave Britain and France the task of drafting the Constitution for the Organization for European Economic Cooperation (OEEC), which was to administer collectively the distribution of American aid. The British, however, balked at granting the OEEC any real power, treating it as an intergovernmental negotiating forum after its creation in April 1948.[9] The Americans were bitterly disappointed and turned to the French for help in realizing a constructive European policy.

The French knew that reconstructing Europe meant reconstructing Germany— and that idea struck fear in their hearts. The risk was most obviously economic. The revival of the French economy hung on the success of Jean Monnet and his Commissariat Général du Plan in reconstructing and modernizing France. Monnet's plan, however, hinged on steady supplies of coal from the Ruhr—as well as restraints on the manufacture of Ruhr steel that would compete with French production. By late 1947 the plan looked perilously close to failure. Monnet heard that German steel producers would soon absorb all the coke (coal) produced in the Ruhr, preventing France from meeting its own steel production goals, which "were the key to the whole French Plan."[10] Already the German economic powerhouse was stoking up the furnaces. Could German economic domination be far behind? And how long before a resurgent Germany built a military machine that threatened its neighbors?

France scrambled to counter these risks. Partial relief from the perceived German military threat came from the east, as the rising threat from the Soviet Union inspired France and Britain to request a defensive alliance with the United States. The United States insisted that an Atlantic alliance would not be created until Europe demonstrated its willingness to cooperate on security matters. The Brussels

Pact of March 1948 extended the Franco-British Treaty of Dunkirk to the Benelux countries, thus opening the way for the establishment of NATO a year later. According to Craig Parsons, however, during the Brussels negotiations the French suggested the pact be explicitly directed at Germany. The Benelux countries objected, and France had to live with a treaty that did not specify an enemy but could be construed as establishing an anti-German alliance.[11]

Still, a military alliance was of limited value when faced with an armed economic giant. For French leaders, the key to France's long-term security—and Europe's—was control of the Ruhr complex; the Allies had to deprive Germany of its superior industrial potential. Reparations had not permanently crippled German recovery, so France turned to long-term approaches. During the long London Conference of 1948, with the creation of a German republic virtually assured, France had tried—unsuccessfully—to prevent the creation of a directly elected national assembly, preferring that power in a future German state be held predominantly by the *Lander*. The other Allies balked; Germany would have a central government.

France continued its search for a solution to its Ruhr problem by pressing for international control of heavy industry there, especially the production of coal and steel. Negotiations centered on the regulatory powers of an International Authority for the Ruhr (IAR) that would eventually take control when military occupation ended. The Allies bickered at length over exactly who would allocate the Ruhr resources and how they would be controlled. France failed to guarantee French, or at least international, governance of the Ruhr and thus failed to achieve its goal. The IAR began functioning in mid-1949, and the French had no illusions that the organization would prevent German control of Ruhr resources. French policymakers were running out of options.[12]

French policy was in a general state of confusion in 1949 and early 1950. Clearly, France's German policy had failed. West Germany was proclaimed in May 1949; the first Bundestag was elected in August; and in September 1949 Konrad Adenauer became West Germany's first chancellor as the occupation ended. France confronted a reconstituted Germany under no effective means of control. The United States understood France's position, but had done about all it could do. Marshall Plan aid was financing recovery, but Germany could not be occupied indefinitely. Cold War pressures required a rebuilt, if not yet rearmed, Germany. It was high time for democratic Europe to get on with the process of incorporating Germany into a united Europe, although US policymakers had little idea what that entity would look like or what steps were needed to create it. That was for the Europeans to figure out, more specifically the French. US secretary of state Dean Acheson told his European ambassadors that the solution to the crisis lay "in French hands." To Schuman, he wrote on October 30, 1949: "I believe that our policy in Germany . . . depends on the assumption by your country of leadership in Europe on these problems." He then told Schuman he wanted a proposal by the meeting of allied foreign ministers set for May 1950 in London.[13]

France faced a strategic crisis: Its defeated enemy now stood poised once again to dominate the Continent economically and politically, while America pleaded for Europe to reach a collective solution, which it expected to come from France. And all the while Britain stood on the sidelines. France had run out of traditional options.[14] Europe, as Monnet put it, was "in the dark."[15] But this was the crisis that triggered the integration process in Europe—light was on the horizon.

Integration, even European "union," was a policy option in the 1940s, and not only in Christian Democratic or federalist circles. Serious proposals came from a number of quarters. The Americans—in large measure due to Monnet's influence— put steady pressure on the Europeans to create a federal organization capable of reconstructing the Continent and preventing the next war.[16] And the more Cold War tensions mounted, the more demands for collective action came from across the Atlantic.[17] But the Americans were not the only ones considering integration as a solution to the vexing problems in Europe. In the chaos of June 1940, just before the French capitulated to the Germans, British and French diplomats had negotiated a union of the two countries: "The two Governments declare that France and Great Britain shall no longer be two nations, but one Franco-British Union."[18] Monnet was behind this bold and desperate proposal.[19] The failure of the Franco-British Union, however, only seemed to encourage his belief that a new "European entity" could eliminate the dangers of war.[20] As the 1940s wore on and French policies ran aground, more proposals unifying European coal and steel sectors or other areas of the economy began to surface.[21] At least one policy paper calling for broad economic, political, and social cooperation with Germany that would lead to a Western union emerged from the French Foreign Ministry.[22] More audaciously, in March 1950 Adenauer proposed in an interview with an American journalist a "complete union between France and Germany, with a merger of their economies, their Parliaments, and their citizenship."[23] Monnet, by his own account, paid little attention. Without doubt, the idea that the German Question could be answered by European unity was floating around not only in federalist intellectual circles but also in the halls of power.

The Schuman Declaration and the subsequent creation of the ECSC were not inevitable. True, many European leaders, especially Christian Democrats, believed that reconciliation with Germany was essential to answering the German Question. By late 1949 even the French public seemed to be coming to the same conclusion. Moreover, many elites had also recognized that the tug of war over the Ruhr and the broader question of German reconstruction would not be solved without pooling Ruhr resources and jointly administering the region through some cooperative arrangement. A few policy makers were even willing to use words such as "integration," "federalism," and "union" to describe the system of governance that would surely emerge. But just a handful of officials had any notion of what all that might look like in practice.

Several options, in fact, remained viable. France, for instance, could enter a series of bilateral arrangements with Germany and other nations to build a web of interlocking relationships designed to check German ambitions. Recent attempts along these lines, however, were not encouraging: a Franco-Italian customs union and a Franco-Benelux customs union had been negotiated but never ratified, though the signing of the Brussels Pact had been more encouraging.[24] A second option— strongly favored by the British and Scandinavians—was to establish multilateral organizations that would address political and economic issues in an intergovernmental fashion. The British had already reduced the OEEC to an intergovernmental aid distribution agency, and the British-Nordic alliance had scuttled any hope that the Council of Europe, established in May 1949, might become a supranational body with federal powers.[25] These countries favored the creation of a zone of interstate cooperation to develop "realistic" solutions to the crucial postwar questions. A final option, of course, was to do nothing. Paralyzed by indecision and division, Western Europe could wait to see what emerged from the sullen fog hanging over the Continent. This option was terrifying to those who expected resurgent German nationalism or aggressive Soviet communism—or both—to emerge. To many frustrated Europeans and Americans, this seemed as likely an outcome as any.

In the end, at the last hour, Europe—more particularly, France—chose none of these options. Monnet and Schuman joined in a bold proposal that superficially resembled a revamped IAR, but upon reflection looked like a whole new way of thinking. In Diebold's words, "This was a drastic change in the direction of French policy. It caught foreigners and Frenchmen by surprise."[26] The American secretary of state was certainly confused. Acheson, who had so bluntly ordered the French to come up with something big, was the first person Schuman briefed outside the French government.[27] But when Schuman laid out his plan to place coal and steel production under a High Authority, Acheson clearly failed to grasp the enormity of the proposal, thinking it a call for a giant cartel. Slightly offended at the misunderstanding, Schuman explained that the purpose was political: to move toward European unification by economic means. Schuman's theme was "the unity of Europe, the end of national rivalries in a new, spacious, and vastly productive Europe." As Schuman talked, Acheson "caught his enthusiasm and the breadth of his thought, the rebirth of Europe, which, as an entity, had been in eclipse since the Reformation."[28] Chancellor Adenauer's response was equally positive, but the same could not be said for British foreign secretary Ernest Bevin, who flew into a "towering rage" when he heard about the plan *after* its announcement (he was not informed by either Schuman or Acheson). Indeed, he "bristled with hostility to Schuman's whole idea."[29]

The creation of the Federal Republic and the need to safeguard Europe against a resurgent and unbound Germany triggered in Monnet, Schuman, and Adenauer—in Catholic Europe—a response transcending the depressing dilemmas of coal and steel in the Ruhr. Perhaps Europe could reverse its inexorable fragmentation "since the Reformation" and become whole. They met this "deep longing for unity" with slow, practical steps.[30] The British grasped none of this (as we show in the next chapter), but the Catholic Christian Democrats who held power on the Continent certainly did. They embraced the proposal and began to integrate Europe, as socialist Christian Pineau observed, "in a very Christian democratic manner."[31]

Leadership

A strategic crisis may trigger new thinking, but entrepreneurial leaders must articulate a new vision of unity, formulate specific policy proposals, and shepherd those changes through stormy political seas. In the process, politicians must begin to construct a new regional identity out of the cultural materials at hand. They must encourage an existing, nascent "we feeling" that extends beyond elite circles into the regional population and begin to knit many peoples into one.

European integration would not have proceeded without the visionary persistence of several national leaders—Robert Schuman, Konrad Adenauer, and Alcide De Gasperi in particular. Christian Democratic leaders were successful, first, because they convinced European elites and electorates—including many who were not Christian Democrats—that their vision of a united Europe provided a way forward. Schuman, Adenauer, and De Gasperi were the main political actors in the three largest continental countries. They led large movements, but with the possible exception of De Gasperi in Italy, did not represent a majority of their citizens. Christian Democracy was influential but not all-powerful. Most European voters had little interest in the details of integration; elites who cared about unity were divided as to the best course of action.[32]

Schuman, Adenauer, and De Gasperi stepped into this moment in history and set a specific course. They chose to integrate economically sector by sector and to limit the process to "core Europe"—the Carolingian heartland. Behind this successful approach was an ideological and political strategy that was undeniably Christian Democratic, Catholic, and revolutionary in intent. It was informed by specific ideas, but not ideas pulled out of thin air. These concepts had been part of the Christian Democratic conversation for three-quarters of a century and were deeply rooted in Catholic confessional culture. They made sense to Schuman, Adenauer, and De Gasperi because these ideas connected to their deepest beliefs. Not every European felt the same resonance, but those who sympathized with the goal of a united Europe had to follow the Christian Democratic approach because it was the "only game in town." The Christian Democrats founded a united Europe in the 1950s, and they stamped their indelible mark on the integration process.

Christian Democratic politicians were successful precisely because they worked at the intersection of idealism and practical politics. They had to respond to structural political and economic pressures: German recovery, Soviet aggression, and European struggles to rebuild. A strong Germany was necessary as an engine of economic growth and a bulwark against Soviet belligerence, but West Germany had to be tied tightly to the West. As Kaiser argues, Western Europe could have responded "with a policy of German membership of NATO and progressive trade liberalisation in the strictly intergovernmental OEEC Europe."[33] Instead, they pursued a form of integration that pointed ultimately toward the economic and political unification of Europe, but this was not a prearranged plan.

As Alan Milward is quick to point out, the postwar leaders were not paid-up members of the wartime federalist movement; they came to their federalism after the war. But they did not launch a process of sectoral integration based solely on national interest, as Milward would have us believe.[34] And they were not seeking political advantage; interest groups were not clamoring for integration (some opposed it), nor were voters demanding federation.[35] Rather Schuman, Adenauer, and De Gasperi were guided by norms and ideas drawn from their confessional culture. They were pious Catholics and Christian Democrats—Milward, somewhat mockingly, refers to them as "the European saints."[36] They were not starry-eyed idealists, but men of practical responsibilities not prone to advancing futile proposals. At this crucial moment, however, idealism and pragmatism intersected. The ideal—the Christian Democratic ideal—became a practical means of addressing the most perplexing issues facing postwar Europe. The genius of the European founders was their ability to seize the moment when a revolutionary ideal became a practical solution to intractable problems.

The Founders

The postwar rise of the Christian Democrats to power in Europe brought an influential set of Catholic politicians to office. In May 1950, when Schuman announced his plan, only one prime minister and two foreign ministers in the Six were not Christian Democrats (Dutch prime minister Willem Drees, Labor; and foreign ministers Carlo Sforza, Italy, Republican; and Dirk Stikker, the Netherlands, Liberal); the other nine officials were Catholic Christian Democrats.[37] Of these, Schuman, Adenauer, and De Gasperi stand out as a trinity central to the founding of the European Communities. While they differed in temperament, what they shared was particularly striking.

Many have observed that all three were born in disputed borderlands, where countries, cultures, and languages collide. All three were, indeed, born in Lotharingia, the middle lands of Charlemagne's patrimony. Schuman himself thought it was important that he was a "man of the frontiers" and attributed the enthusiasm for European unity he shared with Adenauer and De Gasperi to the fact that they were all from the borders.[38] Schuman was born in 1886 in Luxembourg to a Luxembourgish mother and a Lorrainian father who, because of border changes, began life as a Frenchman and ended it as a German. Robert inherited his father's German citizenship and his mother's language, Luxembourgeois, although he certainly learned German and French as a child. (Unfortunately for a French politician, he spoke French with a slight German accent.) In 1903 he moved to Metz, Lorraine (then in Germany), to study, and from then on considered Lorraine his home. After studying law in Bonn, Munich, and Berlin, and finishing his degree in Strasbourg, he returned to Metz to practice. When World War I erupted, Schuman was declared unfit for military service, but worked in the German bureaucracy (another fact his French political opponents would never let him forget). After the war, with Lorraine returned to France, Schuman began his political career in the French legislature, having lived in three countries and been a citizen of two.

Political geography was also unsettled for the postwar leaders of Italy and Germany. Like Schuman, Alcide De Gasperi changed citizenship without changing homes. De Gasperi was born a citizen of the Austro-Hungarian Empire in Pieve Tesino, Tyrol, in 1881. He was ethnically Italian, but he lived close to German-speaking communities. His German was "inadequate," however, until he began university studies in Vienna.[39] In 1911 he launched his political career as an elected member of the Austrian Reichsrat, but he readily accepted Italian citizenship when Tyrol was transferred to Italy after World War I. Adenauer, conversely, was born (1876) in a city that stayed, more or less, in one country. Cologne, Rhine Province, was not far from Schuman's Luxembourg and Lorraine, but while the borders were not as prone to shift around Cologne, Adenauer did experience wrenching regime changes; he was born in the Second German Reich, hid from the Third Reich, and served two German democracies and an occupation force.

Schuman, Adenauer, and De Gasperi were men of the borderlands, but they also shared a classic closed Catholic heritage. What made them unusual, however, was the genuine devotion exhibited in their private and, often, public lives. Schuman's mother was deeply pious and Robert shared that devotion. They took pilgrimages together to Lourdes (1902) and Rome (for the 1909 beatification of Joan of Arc) and shared spiritual and theological insights in their correspondence. Schuman seems to have seriously considered the priesthood in 1911, but while eventually dissuaded, he pursued his vocation as though he had taken religious vows. When studying in Germany, he joined Unitas, a pious alternative to university fraternities. He devoured religious texts, including nine (of twenty-six) volumes of a history of the popes, and the works of Thomas Aquinas and Saint John of the Cross while in prison, under house arrest, or in hiding in monasteries or private homes during the Vichy period.

He lived simply and never married.[40] His disciplined devotion impressed everyone who knew him; Acheson once referred to his "monkish asceticism."[41]

Like Schuman, Adenauer and De Gasperi were also raised in pious homes. Adenauer's parents insisted that the family pray together daily, attend weekly Mass, and study diligently the teachings of the Church. Adenauer's schooling through his completion of a law degree, while not in Church-controlled schools, was unquestionably Catholic. And he was never shy about the impact of his faith on his politics. When asked for a definition of his policies, he responded: "Do you know the Shorter Catechism? It contains what I believe and hence all my political objectives can be found there."[42] De Gasperi, too, grew up in a thoroughly Catholic environment and continued his devotion into adulthood. He went to Mass, read the Bible, and recited the rosary—daily. He was known to carry a copy of the Scriptures in his jacket pocket.[43] His Catholicism was not merely formal or separated from other aspects of his life. He did not, as Carrillo notes, "consider his obligations to God discharged by mere attendance at services or by mechanical acts of piety, for his was an integral Catholicism, the 'spirit and heart of all things.' Catholicism was something to be applied first to one's own life, then to society and all public activities."[44] De Gasperi's fourteen-year sojourn as a political exile in the Vatican Library (1929–43) weighed on him heavily, but it gave him much time to read, reflect, and write, literally in the shadow of Saint Peter's. The journal he kept there reflects the thought processes of a privately spiritual man with very public interests.[45]

Thus, devout Catholics who instinctively made their politics an extension of their religious commitments led postwar Europe at midcentury. All three were deeply influenced in their thinking on politics, economics, and modern society by their reading of the social encyclicals of Pope Leo XIII and Pope Pius XI.[46] They sought a viable third way between communism and radical individualism and joined Catholic movements dedicated to this end before World War II. Schuman and De Gasperi were also deeply influenced by Thomas Aquinas and the twentieth-century personalists he inspired. Schuman, in fact, was well acquainted with Maritain and shared private meals with him even while in office.[47] Moreover, all three were deeply committed to democracy as the only system of government capable of treating human beings with proper dignity. They were not only committed to Christian Democratic ideology but also to Christian Democracy as a movement. De Gasperi founded the Italian People's Party with Sturzo in 1919; Adenauer was the driving force behind the creation of the Christian Democratic Union; and Schuman helped establish the French Popular Republican Movement (Mouvement Républicain Populaire, MRP).

Catholic Christian Democrats were the most visible shapers of early integration efforts, but they were not alone. Non-Catholics, even those from Catholic countries, avoided religious language, and emphasized Enlightenment principles and the pragmatic benefits of unity. On the Socialist left, for instance, Paul-Henri Spaak, Belgium's most prominent postwar leader, often spoke of peace and economic competitiveness when defending integration, but when he did refer to European civilization, used the language of the Enlightenment:[48] "I am . . . a believer and a supporter of [European unity] because, in the end, it is the sole way to maintain and to radiate the principles of liberty, of democracy and of human dignity which are foundations of our way of life."[49] Some tried to avoid ideology altogether, like Jean Monnet, the pragmatic genius behind the integration of Europe.

Monnet was born in Cognac, a Calvinist bastion after the French Reformation, to a Catholic mother and laïc father. In 1934 he married Silvia Giannini, an Italian painter almost two decades his junior, but only after Silvia (with much diplomatic assistance) secured a complicated divorce from a former employee of Monnet's. Silvia was a devout Catholic, but Monnet never practiced himself—until calling for a priest on his deathbed.[50] He was not a Christian Democrat—indeed, he never identified with a party[51]—but sympathized with the movement, believing that European unity was essential to prevent the "destruction of civilized life."[52] His contribution to the federalist movement was not primarily ideological, although he clearly understood the role ideology played. Instead he provided organizational leadership, a keen eye for political spectacle, and a concrete plan for achieving union based on common rules enforced by supranational institutions.

Monnet, like Spaak, was raised in a Catholic culture but did not explicitly connect political integration to a sense of Europe's spiritual or religious unity. Although he did not share religion or political identity with the Christian Democrats, he did reflect the same Catholic culture that was woven into the fabric of continental societies, so much so that Buruma detected "a whiff of Holy Roman incense wafting over his European dreams."[53] That culture powerfully influenced those socialized by it, whether or not they practiced the religion. It was in the Catholic countries (Belgium, France, Italy, and Luxembourg) and countries with large, politically powerful Catholic minorities (West Germany and the Netherlands) where ideas of European unity resonated most deeply with leaders and citizens—strongly Catholic or not.

Monnet, Spaak, and others played important but secondary roles in the launch of European institutions. Monnet was the technocratic genius who devised the plan. Ultimately, however, Schuman carried the political weight—and risk—of the proposal to integrate, soon sharing that burden with Adenauer and De Gasperi. These three men knew each other, spoke a common language (German), shared a faith and confessional culture, and viewed the world through similar lenses. They ably capitalized on the strategic crisis to turn their region in a different direction. They knew they were creating a new European union, and they intended to shape not only the institutions of the fledgling organization but also, more important, the very nature of the emerging European society. In short, they were creating a new European identity to support a new European union.

The Foundations of a European Identity

The ideology of "European union"—which was articulated in bits and pieces by Schuman, Adenauer, and De Gasperi—naturally drew on Christian Democratic thinking. Each accepted the main lines of that ideology, although they sometimes emphasized different elements: Adenauer, the strong stand against communism; Schuman, reconciliation of enemies; De Gasperi, the unity of Christian civilization. Together they articulated a rationale for their pragmatic steps toward integration and a coherent (if vague) vision of the future. Their Christian Democratic justification of integration, coupled with Monnet's pragmatic "community method" (the step-by-step assignment of common tasks to supranational institutions), carried the day in the 1950s. The strength of the Christian Democratic parties and the lack of a practical alternative to the Schuman Plan made possible the victory of a Christian Democratic approach to uniting Europe.

Traditional narratives usually neglect the revolutionary intent of the Christian Democrats. Governments committed to applying Christian principles to every aspect of life were in theory ready to transform politics, economics, and social relations in Europe. It was the Schuman Declaration that brought this vision to life; European unity was the truly revolutionary side of the Christian Democratic project. Without the Schuman Declaration, the Christian Democrats were locked in dreary wrestling matches with the traditional left and right. But with the declaration they were (quite suddenly) at the center of an enormous project backed by a grand vision that made the other parties look parochial. The Christian Democratic vision reached out across the Continent and back to an idealized sacred past, appealing to both mind and heart. It offered suffering people concrete hope that decades of war and deprivation were at last over. And it was constructed by leaders who were framing, however tenuously, the sacred foundations for a new European polity. As Schuman proudly claimed, "We are laying the foundations of a spiritual and political co-operation from which there will arise the European spirit, the promise of a broad and lasting supranational union."[54]

The first challenge for union-building elites was to define the scope of their project. Monnet's early presentation of his idea for a coal and steel community stressed his view that achieving peace on the Continent required conscious efforts to create a single entity called "Europe." For Monnet this entity was new: "Europe has never existed. The sum of sovereignties meeting in Councils does not make up an entity. We must genuinely create Europe."[55] Schuman agreed that "for peace to have a real chance, there must first be a Europe," but for him and his fellow Christian Democrats, Europe had existed and did exist as a single *cultural* entity.[56] Christianity, particularly Catholic Christianity, bound the peoples of Europe together in a broad but clearly defined community. Monnet was wrong: Europe existed. But Monnet was also right: Political leaders must wake Europe up to its essential unity.

For most people in 1950, "European unity" was a hard sell; national divisions and resulting wars had brought the world to the brink of disaster. Christian Democrats, moreover, insisted that the Continent's fragmentation was unnatural, producing what De Gasperi called "a fateful heritage of *civil* wars" (emphasis added).[57] Europe's continued commitment to the nation-state remained an existential threat and a barrier to the emerging European union. The doctrine of national sovereignty—which Christian Democrats questioned on principle—must be replaced by institutionalized cooperation. In 1950 Schuman indicated that he accepted "the principle of a renunciation of sovereign rights not for its own sake alone . . . but as a necessity, as the sole means at our disposal for overcoming the national selfishness, the antagonism and narrow-mindedness which are destroying us."[58] A year later he appraised the state system in theological terms, calling it a "heresy"—an implicit critique of the Reformation and the division of Europe into sovereign nations.[59]

De Gasperi, too, saw the value of "self-imposed limitations on national sovereignty in favor of confederated or federated structures."[60] He came to this conclusion only reluctantly; for him *European* union was the second-best option. A commitment to Christian universalism and global solidarity led him to prefer strong *international* institutions governed by Christian principles, a "universal *res publica Christiania*."[61] The Cold War ended such dreams, but De Gasperi soon embraced a European integration process that revived Carolingian unity. In a thoroughly Christian Democratic manner, he saw human governance as a hierarchy of layers stretching from the individual through the national, European, and Western layers, and culminating in a universal unity. National authority, so long the problem on the Continent, had to be subjected to the authority of a united Europe.[62]

Christian Democratic leaders thus envisioned a peaceful revolution that would awaken a latent sense of European oneness, renounce national sovereignty on the Continent, and build a new union strong enough to command popular loyalty. They had no master plan to accomplish these goals, but employed a number of tools to encourage what amounted to a new national identity. They very early recognized that concerted effort was needed to transform relationships between the peoples of Europe. For half a century Europeans had allowed language, law, and violence to divide them into ethnic groups. World War II unleashed unspeakable evil as elites and masses employed forced migration, ethnic cleansing, mass murder, genocide, and total war to create purified racial or ethnic factions.[63] The convulsive violence had ended, but the relationships remained broken. Schuman and Adenauer knew that Europe could not be built until its peoples were reconciled. Thus for both strategic and symbolic reasons, they were determined to heal the ancient Franco/German rift, instinctively drawing on religious language and imagery to encourage reconciliation. Schuman, for instance, invoked Christian themes of forgiveness and love of enemies: "We are now holding out our hand to our former enemies, not only to forgive them, but to build tomorrow's Europe together."[64] Sustained effort, however, was needed to effect lasting change. Much of this effort, as we have seen, went on behind the scenes as European leaders met in Geneva, Caux, and elsewhere. But private meetings would eventually have to yield a public effect: Human relationships across Europe would need to be fundamentally transformed. Speaking at Caux with the activities of Moral Re-Armament in mind, Schuman argued for a Christian-inspired transformation:

> What we need, and what is quite new, is a school where, by a process of mutual teaching, we can work out our practical behaviour towards others; a school where Christian principles are not only applied and proven in the relationships of man to man, but succeed in overcoming the prejudices and enmities which separate classes, races and nations. To begin by creating a moral climate in which true brotherly unity can flourish, over-arching all that today tears the world apart—that is the immediate goal. The acquisition of wisdom about men and their affairs by bringing people together in public assemblies and personal encounters—that is the means employed. To provide a team of trained men, ready for the service of the state, apostles of reconciliation and builders of a new world, that is the beginning of a far-reaching transformation of society in which, during fifteen war-ravaged years, the first steps have already been taken. It is not a question of a change of policy; it is a question of changing men.[65]

Schuman was optimistic that the Christian principles he so often invoked—and which, he believed, Europe intimately knew—could transform human beings and generate a new society. Schuman was a revolutionary creating "new men"—not with the violence of the French or Bolshevik radicals, but with appeals for Europeans to live up to the values they held in common: brotherhood, equality, love, forgiveness. These were values that he knew would resonate through Catholic confessional culture.

Schuman spoke of a cadre of men—"apostles of reconciliation"—who would build this new world. Assembled groups and personal encounters were useful in raising such a cadre, but Christian Democrats naturally saw their own parties as central to the transformation. These parties promoted the Christian values common to Europe, built institutional bridges between nations, and nurtured transformed leaders. Christian Democratic parties, in their view, could be the teachers of the new Europe. As Adenauer put it in 1951, "The Christian Democratic parties have a special vocation to do this work [bridge differences among European countries], since the traditions of Western Europe are Christian, and since the parties which hold those traditions in high esteem and which strive to make them again fruitful for the requirements of our time hold the assurance of an interior renaissance of Western Europe from its finest elements."[66]

The transformation of Europe, however, could not rely on socialization and political activity alone. Europe would need new institutions that would both govern and teach. And here, again, Monnet's contribution is key. Schuman needed an organizational vehicle for his reconciliation agenda, which the institutions of the European Communities provided. Former enemies would need to sit together in supranational institutions and forge common policies. No wonder the Christian Democrats agreed on a representative assembly as part of the supranational institutional arrangements. Not only would a European Parliament add an important democratic element to Monnet's supranational structure, but it also would play a transformative role by shaping leaders of a new Europe. Common institutions would be Europe's teachers.

Christian Democrats took pains to create a "positive" identity for the new Europe. They pressed for a transformation of persons and relationships by promoting Christian principles (especially forgiveness), encouraging cross-border contacts, developing a network of Christian Democratic parties, and creating supranational institutions to socialize national leaders into thinking and acting as "Europeans." References to Christianity as a unifying element were present in Christian Democratic rhetoric, but were generally muted and nonsectarian. More emphasis was placed on democracy, liberty, and human dignity. The religious element, however, was unmistakably present. The founders were bestowing upon the new Europe a denatured civil religion, albeit with Catholic roots.

The Christian Democratic founders wanted to create a positive identity for the new Europe, but they were also willing to limit the boundaries of Europe. They could not create "Europe" unless they also identified "non-Europe." The obvious first exclusion was Soviet communism—only the latest threat from the East. But Christian Democratic leaders also drew a line at the English Channel. Schuman's decision not to consult his British counterpart before announcing plans for the coal and steel community underscores his view that Britain was apart from Europe— a notion that, as we will see in the next chapter, the British did little to counter. Writing in his memoirs, before Britain joined the European Communities, Schuman stated: "I do not wish to quote England as a particularly representative model of the European spirit. Insular and cosmopolitan, traditional and instinctively distrustful of any ideological innovation. . . . England does not, in my opinion, appear to be a good example of the European spirit. . . . It is hostile, on principle and in all circumstances, to any form of integration or federal structure."[67]

Schuman believed that Britain would eventually join Europe, but out of necessity, not principle—and on European terms. Adenauer was also hesitant to include Britain, not least because of his difficult relations with the British occupation. Not all continental federalists, however, were quite so skeptical. Monnet had worked for French federation with Britain during the war and hoped for British involvement in the construction of a united Europe. But Christian Democrats had no problem defining "Europe" as the six continental countries willing to sacrifice sovereignty for peace, the countries with the "European spirit." Other countries were either unable or unwilling to overcome the chains of national sovereignty. They remained outside "Europe."

Europe for Christian Democrats was more than a region where governments were learning to cooperate. Europe had a world-historical role to play, as the source of civilization and humanity's natural leader. Its wars were tragedies that had threatened to undermine the pinnacle of social and cultural development. The threat to Europe was a threat to civilization. Christian Democratic rhetoric was sprinkled with the kind of not-so-subtle assertions of Western Christian superiority that irritate twenty-first-century sensibilities. But it was just this sense of uniqueness that marked the Christian Democratic vision of Europe. Schuman, Adenauer, and De Gasperi were, in fact, constructing a new European identity by subtly, but forcefully, asserting Europe's sacred vocation—in a sense, its *chosen-ness*. De Gasperi saw an integrated Europe as a step toward a revived universal Christendom, but Adenauer most powerfully expressed the belief that Christian civilization was under threat and that only European unity could save the region and the world: "We not only agree with the creation of a United Europe; we even regard it as imperative, and we are striving to bring it about as speedily and as completely as possible, because . . . Christian civilization is in danger, and because that danger can only be overcome by joint effort."[68] Later, he wrote: "The world cannot exist without a Christian and Occidental Europe. . . . We want to save this Europe of ours. For Europe is in truth the mother of the world, and we are her children."[69]

Christian Democrats consciously sought a new Europe with a common mission and sense of identity. They understood that the peoples of Europe needed something grand to believe in and work for: "From now on let this idea of a reconciled, united, strong Europe be the motto for the young generations anxious to serve humanity, free of hatred and fear and which after so many rifts is learning what Christian brotherhood means once more."[70] Building a united Europe was a splendid project, but the Christian Democrats, with their constant references to Europe's Christian heritage, wanted people to see the project as a sacred quest. They felt a sense of urgency in shaping an identity essential to Europe's survival. Schuman's memoir ends with an illustrative plea: "Europe is searching for an identity; it is aware that it has its own future in hand. It has never been so close to the goal. May God not let Europe miss the hour of its destiny, its final chance of salvation."[71]

Symbols of Unity

The "construction of Europe"—a phrase postwar leaders embraced—required a new European identity and vocation, which the Christian Democrats were eager to ground in Christian culture and a particularly Catholic notion of Latin Christendom.[72] Their attempts to create a new collective identity, however, went beyond religious references and were implemented by many European leaders who were not themselves Christian Democrats. In the 1950s and early 1960s, the founders of Europe created symbols and engaged in symbolic actions to represent to Europeans and others the reality of a new unified Europe and to elicit emotional responses of pride and loyalty. Many of these were secular; some were religious or semi-sacred. All were attempts to transcend national boundaries and tie Europeans together as one people.

The symbolic acts began early. Monnet appreciated grand gestures and orchestrated the Schuman Declaration with an eye to public reaction. Instead of quietly issuing a press release, he assembled more than two hundred reporters in the splendid Salon de l'Horloge at the Quai d'Orsay. Characteristically, Schuman fumbled his speech, even skipping a page of text. More alarming, however, was the absence of photographers and radio reporters. In his haste to prepare the press conference, Monnet had overlooked that crucial detail. Rather than let such a symbolic moment escape him, Monnet recreated the event "some months later," with Schuman reading his speech again and the photographers (now) present taking the pictures and film clips that we have of the Schuman Declaration announcement.[73] Monnet understood the symbolism of "the founding" as a national myth.

Following the Schuman Declaration and the adoption of Monnet's "community method" for the supranational organization of the coal and steel industries, policymakers in the Six began suggesting additional economic sectors for similar treatment. The French proposed a community for agriculture (the so-called Green Pool) in 1950 and a European Health Community (the so-called White Pool) in 1952. Far more important were the Korean War–inspired October 1950 Pleven Plan for a European Defense Community to oversee the formation of a European army and the rearmament of Germany and the 1952 proposal to unite the ECSC and the European Defense Community into a single European Political Community. Neither was ratified. In fact, the most stunning blow to European integration in the 1950s came on August 30, 1954, when the French National Assembly defeated the European Defense Community treaty on a procedural vote, 319 to 263.[74] Except for the ECSC, the early 1950s were piled high with the wreckage of supranational proposals. In hindsight, the damage to integration was not as significant as it looked. These efforts, successful or not, were symbolically important. The Christian Democratic leaders had effectively shifted the creative energies of Europe away from national competition to community construction. Each new proposal added to the conviction, at least among elites, that creating Europe was the mission of the Continent. Too many defeats, of course, would undermine confidence that Europe could reconcile its differences and govern jointly, but the decade was saved by the negotiation and implementation of treaties establishing the European Economic Community (the Common Market) and Euratom (cooperation in nuclear energy).

The signing of the Treaties of Rome establishing the Common Market and Euratom on March 25, 1957, soon became an iconic moment for the new Europe, on par with the Schuman Declaration. These treaties were again Monnet's handiwork, but they were also the crowning achievement of Christian Democratic politicians. This is not an obvious conclusion. Of the founding trinity, only Adenauer remained in office, Schuman and De Gasperi having stepped down in 1953 (De Gasperi died in 1954). The MRP had slipped in France, and Catholics were junior partners in the Dutch government. Still, Christian Democrats led three governments and participated in two more (Catholics were in the opposition only in Belgium). Furthermore, seven of the twelve signatories of the Treaties of Rome were Christian Democrats.

The significance for Christian Democracy, however, was not in its control of the Continent's governments in the mid-1950s—as important as that was—but in the triumph of its method of constructing Europe. Other political groups were also backing the community method of integration, if not the Christian Democratic ideology undergirding it. Prominent socialists in particular were leading efforts to integrate Europe through supranational institutions: the Belgian Paul-Henri Spaak and French foreign ministers Antoine Pinay and Christian Pineau, for instance, played pivotal roles in the negotiations.[75] The result was a Common Market limited to core Europe and governed by (with some nuances) the extended supranational institutions of the ECSC. The Treaties of Rome were thus symbols of Christian Democratic success. Europe was learning to cooperate through the establishment of common institutions; it was developing a community spirit. And the member states of the European Economic Community were pledged "to lay the foundations of an ever-closer union among the peoples of Europe."[76]

The treaties represented a growing consensus on how integration was to proceed. They were to play more than a policy role, designed to tie the new Europe to the glorious past. For appropriate symbolism, the Six's leaders could have chosen democratic Paris, disputed Strasbourg, or even Charlemagne's Aachen as venues to sign these historic documents. Instead, they picked Rome, in particular the Capitoline Hill, the most famous of the Seven Hills, in a palace designed by Michelangelo and commissioned by Pope Paul III for the expected visit of Emperor Charles V in 1538. This was the Rome of Julius Caesar, Caesar Augustus, and Charlemagne—the Rome of the popes, the Rome where Europe's greatest cultural achievements were displayed at every turn. Signing at Rome evoked more than two millennia of European history, putting the emerging European Communities in the line of the great unities in the Latin West. Rome symbolized a united Europe now on its way to reclaiming global leadership.

Another symbol of identity drew on medieval unity but stood outside the treaties. Kurt Pfeiffer, a leading businessman in Charlemagne's medieval capital of Aachen, proposed an annual prize for "deserving personalities who have fostered the idea of Western unification in political, economic, and intellectual-spiritual endeavors."[77] His idea quickly drew support from city leaders, including Mayor Albert Maas, Bishop Johannes Joseph van der Velden, and University Rector Wilhelm

Müller. On Christmas Day 1949 (chosen to coincide with the start of the Holy Year announced by Pius XII), the leading citizens of Aachen announced an international prize, named the "Charlemagne Prize of the City of Aachen" in honor of "the great founder of Western culture."[78] Pfeiffer and his associates were clear that the prize tied integration (which was then still struggling for traction) to the unity of "Occidental" culture.[79] To underline the religious and civic elements in Western unity, the founders would hold the annual ceremony on Ascension Day, a holy day on the Church calendar, in the grand Coronation Hall in Aachen's Town Hall, the site of medieval imperial ceremonies. The first prize in May 1950 went to Count Richard Coudenhove-Kalergi of the Pan-European Movement in a hall still marked by war damage. The prize gained international recognition when it went to Prime Minister Alcide De Gasperi in 1952. From that point on, the winners constituted a *Who's Who* of postwar integration: Monnet (1953), Adenauer (1954), Churchill (1956), Spaak (1957), Schuman (1958), and Bech (1960). The Charlemagne Prize Society made no secret of its desire to create a symbol that bridged the past and present and would promote integration: "The award was and is a symbol of the European will to unification and at the same time a means of conveying political messages."[80]

The Charlemagne Prize symbolically linked the European integration process of the Schuman Declaration and Treaties of Rome to medieval Christendom. The name of the prize, the imperial image on the medallion, the use of the Coronation Hall, and the choice of a holy day to bestow the award wrapped the postwar European Communities in ancient symbols of Christian unity and sacral kingship. These images connected with the confessional culture of Catholic Europe, sowing among disparate Europeans a "we feeling" and the seeds of a common identity. Other early symbolic acts representing the reconciliation of former enemies had similar effects.

Reuniting the divided European family preoccupied the Christian Democratic founders. Schuman and Adenauer in particular spoke in the 1950s of the deep transformation needed to make former enemies recognize their common heritage and essential brotherhood and reconcile their differences. But forgiveness and reconciliation were hard enough for individuals. Schuman and Adenauer represented whole societies with ancient grievances against one another. Symbolic acts over time were necessary to help divided societies accept reconciliation. Given the postwar climate, only Schuman, speaking for the French (and all the occupied nations), could talk of holding out the hand of forgiveness to the enemy. Although the Germans and Italians had also suffered during and after the war, as victims of fascist aggression the French possessed the moral right—even the Christian obligation—to forgive. Germany's responsibility was to repent of its crimes; though the nation did not fully come to terms with its past until much later, Adenauer did admit soon after taking office that Germany was guilty of aggression and unspeakable crimes in occupied territories, especially against Jews.[81] But words mean little unless backed by actions. Thus, it was the public meetings between Schuman and Adenauer, and later

Adenauer and De Gaulle—not to mention the treaty signings—that symbolized for all Europeans the new spirit of reconciliation and friendship between France and Germany.

The most important such meeting occurred on July 8, 1962, in a ceremony that bathed the new Europe in the rich religious and political symbolism of its medieval past. French president Charles De Gaulle, no advocate of political integration but a strong believer in Franco-German friendship, invited Adenauer to conclude his state visit to France with a thanksgiving Mass and Te Deum at Reims Cathedral. The site could not have been more symbolic; there, Bishop Remigius had baptized King of the Franks Clovis I into the Catholic Church; there, Pope Stephen IV had crowned Charlemagne's son, Emperor Louis I (the Pious); there, the French had crowned their kings; and there, the army of the Third Reich had capitulated on May 7, 1945. De Gaulle poignantly reminded the audience that the place was "the symbol of our age-old traditions," but also "the scene of many an encounter between the hereditary enemies, from the ancient Germanic invasions to the battles of the Marne."[82] There two Catholic statesmen went to High Mass and reconciled their two nations using a cultural language the whole Continent understood. De Gaulle, by worshipping with Adenauer, affirmed their essential oneness in the Church and in Europe. Under the gaze of God, they engaged in a public act of forgiving and forgetting— what Churchill once called that "blessed act of oblivion."[83]

European elites, most of them Christian Democrats, consciously laid the foundations—the *sacred* foundations—for a new European identity. The heart of this identity was an ideology of "Europe." Adenauer once told his cabinet, "One has to give the people an ideology and that can only be a European one."[84] The ideology, although most forcefully articulated by the Christian Democrats, was not sectarian; but like any civil religion, it evoked religious ideas and symbols without being theologically explicit. Europe existed as a cultural formation based on Latin Christendom. Its postwar leaders did not claim that God had chosen the Europeans as a special people with a unique mission, as their seventeenth-century counterparts had once done for their nations, but these leaders clearly expected the Europeans to apply Christian values to public policy and to project these values to the world. Union was part of Christian Europe's mission.

How Successful?

Christian Democratic attempts to construct a European identity are difficult to assess. Their invocations of Europe's common cultural (mainly Christian) and historical heritage resonated most strongly with committed Catholics, the electoral backbone of the Christian Democratic parties in the Six. When poll evidence finally appears in 1970, devout Catholics prove to be the strongest supporters of integration.[85] They were the true believers in a unified Europe. For them, Europe had sacred foundations that rested on the unity and authority of the Roman Church and the mystical memories of Charlemagne. As Schuman said in 1949, "The European spirit signifies being conscious of belonging to a cultural family"—and this cultural family had Charlemagne as its father and the Catholic Church as its mother.[86] Less devout Catholics and nonbelievers were less supportive of integration, but only marginally so. As we will see in the next chapter, however, the Christian Democrats' attempts to create a European civil religion with Catholic roots were not as well received among Protestants.

So how successful were the Christian Democrats? Catholic Christian Democrats created postwar Europe. Acting on a Catholic moral vision and leading predominantly Catholic political parties, Catholic elites created a Europe in their own image: democratic, personalist, capitalist, and integrated. Integration, both economic and political, helped solve the problems facing European politicians, including economic stagnation and the German Question. But political integration through supranational institutions went beyond the needs of the moment. Political integration was not inevitable; it was a choice among several options. It became a viable option, and then the preferred choice, of postwar leaders because those with power in the core countries of Western Europe belonged to a cultural community that nourished ideas of unity and dreamed of ways of implementing a common vision for European society.

The shared worldview of Catholic politicians, of course, does not *fully* explain efforts to unify Europe. A politically and economically integrated Europe offered solutions to many problems: what to do with Germany, how to counter American dominance, how to ensure prosperity and prevent social conflict. Cold War pressures and commercial interests surely help explain why European politicians chose to create supranational institutions with real authority. But this was not the only option available: Britain, Ireland, Austria, Switzerland, and the Nordics avoided deliberate political integration and found economic development strategies that did not require deep sacrifices in sovereignty. France, Germany, Italy, and the Benelux countries chose to go beyond economic cooperation and launch an explicitly *political* community because Christian Democratic politicians thought the option risky but deeply appealing; they had what Lincoln Gordon called a "mystic faith" in the prospect of European union.[87] Political integration, far from sounding bizarre, seemed the best of all possible worlds. The obstacles to implementation, in their view, were practical and not ideological. Unlike Protestant leaders in Britain and Scandinavia, the leaders of the Six shared a Catholic ideology that privileged unity; unlike their Protestant counterparts, they possessed a sense of community that was grounded in their shared religious culture and animated by their prewar and postwar contacts in Christian Democratic circles. Thus, Catholic confessional culture made credible the "crazy" option of uniting France and Germany in a new supranational community—a credibility that was not perceived in non-Catholic Europe.

Catholic political dominance in the Six made it possible to choose the supranational option that was so ideologically attractive to Christian Democrats. Other political and economic factors also helped shape the integration process, but the political power of Catholics in the founding member states must be considered decisive in launching the European Communities. In no small way, the European Union owes its existence to the postwar power of Catholic Christian Democrats.

Notes

1. See Manuel Gimenez Fernandez, "Christian Democracy in Spain: An Advocate of a Christian Social Party Expresses His Fears and Defines the Problem," *Commonweal* 44, no. 26 (1946): 615–18.

2. See the long, if politically careful, discussion by John Murray of the proceedings of the Congress on European Unity convened by Spanish Catholics and held at San Sebastian in September 1950: John Murray, "Unity in Europe: Further Reflections," *Studies* (March 1951): 1–10.

3. Quoted by Sieglinde Gstöhl, *Reluctant European: Norway, Sweden, and Switzerland in the Process of Integration* (Boulder, CO: Lynne Rienner, 2002), 51.

4. Oliver Rathkolb, *The Paradoxical Republic: Austria, 1945–2005*, trans. Otmar Binder, Eleanor Breuning, Ian Fraser, and David Sinclair-Jones (New York: Berghahn Books, 2010), 177–78.

5. John Gillingham, *Coal, Steel, and the Rebirth of Europe, 1945–1955: The Germans and French from Ruhr Conflict to Economic Community* (Cambridge: Cambridge University Press, 1991), 101.

6. Gillingham, *Rebirth*, 105–7.

7. George C. Marshall, "Harvard Commencement Speech, 5 June 1947," Wikisource, http://en.wikisource.org/wiki/The_Marshall_Plan_Speech.

8. Gillingham, *Rebirth*, 118–19.

9. For a full discussion of the negotiations leading to the establishment of the OEEC, see Alan S. Milward, *The Reconstruction of Western Europe, 1945–51* (London: Routledge, 1984), chap. 5.

10. Jean Monnet, *Memoirs*, trans. Richard Mayne (New York: Doubleday, 1978), 274.

11. Craig Parsons, *A Certain Idea of Europe* (Ithaca, NY: Cornell University Press, 2003), 47.

12. Milward, *Reconstruction*, 141–67; Gillingham, *Rebirth*, 161–63.

13. The quotations here are from Desmond Dinan, *Europe Recast: A History of European Union* (Boulder, CO: Lynne Rienner, 2004), 35.

14. Parsons, *Certain Idea*, 45–48.

15. The title of chap. 11 in Monnet's *Memoirs* is "Europe in the Dark (1947–1949)."

16. Derek W. Urwin, *The Community of Europe: A History of European Integration since 1945* (London: Longman, 1991), 25.

17. In February 1949 George Kennan wrote a policy review for Dean Acheson making clear the American perspective. According to Gillingham (*Rebirth*, 166), "The message was clear enough: No solution of the German problem without some form of European federation; no federation incompatible with basic American values; and US support for a federating power but no direct intervention, least of all in delaying German recovery."

18. Monnet, *Memoirs*, 28.

19. François Duchêne, *Jean Monnet: The First Statesman of Interdependence* (New York: W. W. Norton, 1994), 76–83.

20. Gillingham, *Rebirth*, 152; Duchêne, *Jean Monnet*, 126.

21. William Diebold, *The Schuman Plan: A Study in Economic Cooperation, 1950–1959* (New York: Praeger, 1959), 42–43; Gillingham, *Rebirth*, 170.

22. Ibid., 169–70.

23. Ibid., 231; Monnet, *Memoirs*, 285.

24. Diebold, *Schuman Plan*, 14.

25. Urwin, *Community of Europe*, 30–35.

26. Diebold, *Schuman Plan*, 11.

27. Acheson was in Paris for informal get-togethers before proceeding to the London ministerial meeting.

28. Dean Acheson, *Sketches from Life of Men I have Known* (New York: Harper & Row, 1961), 37.

29. Ibid., 39.

30. This phrase is from Gillingham, *Rebirth*, 371.

31. Wolfram Kaiser, *Christian Democracy and the Origins of European Union* (Cambridge: Cambridge University Press, 2007), 251. Pineau was a signer of the Treaties of Rome.

32. Leon N. Lindberg and Stuart A. Scheingold, *Europe's Would-Be Polity: Patterns of Change in the European Community* (Englewood Cliffs, NJ: Prentice Hall, 1970).

33. Kaiser, *Christian Democracy*, 251.

34. Milward, *Reconstruction*, 465.

35. Kaiser, *Christian Democracy*, 250.

36. Alan S. Milward, *The European Rescue of the Nation-State*, 2nd ed. (London: Routledge, 2000), 318.

37. The prime ministers were Konrad Adenauer, Germany; Georges Bidault, France; Alcide De Gasperi, Italy; Pierre Dupong, Luxembourg; and Gaston Eyskens, Belgium. The foreign ministers were Adenauer, Germany; Joseph Bech, Luxembourg; Robert Schuman, France; and Paul Van Zeeland, Belgium.

38. Alan Paul Fimister, *Robert Schuman: Neo-Scholastic Humanism and the Reunification of Europe* (Brussels: PIE–Peter Lang, 2008), 141. See also Jeff Fountain, *Deeply Rooted: The Forgotten Vision of Robert Schuman* (Heerde, the Netherlands: Schuman Centre for European Studies, 2010).

39. See Elisa A. Carrillo, *Alcide De Gasperi: The Long Apprenticeship* (Notre Dame, IN: University of Notre Dame Press, 1965), 1–13.

40. Fimister, *Robert Schuman*, 164.

41. Acheson, *Sketches*, 32.

42. Robert Wendelin Keyserlingk, *Fathers of Europe: Patriots of Peace* (Montreal: Palm, 1972), 143. It is not known exactly to which catechism Adenauer was referring. It could have been Luther's *Shorter Catechism*, but more likely it was the *Catechism of Saint Pius X*.

43. Giulia Prati, *Italian Foreign Policy: 1947–1951* (Göttingen: V&R Unipress, 2006), 135–36.

44. Carrillo, *Alcide De Gasperi*, 7.

45. Ibid., 99–114.

46. See Keyserlingk, *Fathers*, 24, 55; and Charles Williams, *Adenauer: The Father of the New Germany* (New York: John Wiley and Sons, 2000), 221.

47. Fimister, *Robert Schuman*, 197.

48. Spaak was a self-described agnostic; Paul-Henri Spaak, *The Continuing Battle: Memoirs of a European, 1936–1966*, trans. Henry Fox (Boston: Little, Brown, 1971), 17.

49. Paul-Henri Spaak, *Face to Face with Europe* (London: Conservative Political Centre, 1967), 11.

50. See Duchêne, *Jean Monnet*, 9, 27; and Frederic Fransen, *The Supranational Politics of Jean Monnet: Ideas and Origins of the European Community* (Westport, CT: Greenwood Press, 2001), 10. See also Monnet, *Memoirs*, 37–38.

51. Duchêne, *Jean Monnet*, 346.

52. Jean Monnet, "A Ferment of Change," *Journal of Common Market Studies* 1, no. 1 (1962): 203.

53. Ian Buruma, *Year Zero: A History of 1945* (New York: Penguin Press, 2013), 255.

54. Schuman said these words at the May 1949 signing ceremony establishing the Council of Europe, which soon proved unable to fulfill the federalist vision. But he could have very well repeated the words one year later, when he announced the Schuman Plan. "Statement by Robert Schuman (London, 5 May 1949)," Historical Archives of the Council of Europe, www.cvce.eu /content/publication/2003/1/22/97217713-8cb6-4679-a6ce-8bd77660bd17/publishable_en.pdf.

55. Jean Monnet, "'Memorandum to Robert Schuman and Georges Bidault,' May 1950," in *Building European Union: A Documentary History and Analysis*, ed. Trevor Salmon and Sir William Nicoll (Manchester: Manchester University Press, 1997), 43–44.

56. Schuman made these remarks to the press before his reading of the Declaration on May 9, 1950; Pascal Fontaine, "The Schuman Declaration, 9 May 1950," www.ius.bg.ac.rs/prof/Materi jali/lukmaj/schuman-en.pdf.

57. "Address Given by Alcide De Gasperi (Strasbourg, 10 December 1951)," Council of Europe, www.cvce.eu/obj/address_given_by_alcide_de_gasperi_strasbourg_10_december_1951-en -7dbeb557-c313- 4703-a237-d909f35a2c25.html.

58. "Address Given by Robert Schuman to the Council of Europe (Strasbourg, 10 August 1950)," Council of Europe, www.cvce.eu/obj/address_given_by_robert_schuman_to_the_coun cil_of_europe_strasbourg_10_august_1950-en- 2e84835a-5a3f-4490-b676-b9cbc1471e90.html.

59. Quoted by R. Poidevin, *Robert Schuman: Homme d'état* (Paris, 1986) as cited by Milward, *European Rescue*, 326.

60. Prati, *Italian Foreign Policy*, 134.

61. Ibid., 134, 139.

62. Ibid., 151.

63. See Mark Mazower, *Dark Continent: Europe's Twentieth Century* (New York: Vintage, 2000).

64. Robert Schuman, *For Europe* (Geneva: Nagel Editions, 2010), 32–33.

65. Quoted by R. C. Mowat, *Creating the European Community* (New York: Barnes & Noble, 1973), 52.

66. "The Future of Christian Democracy: An Exclusive Interview with Dr. Konrad Adenauer, Chancellor of the West German Federal Republic," *The Tablet* 198 (September 22, 1951): 185.

67. Schuman, *For Europe*, 85–86.

68. "Future of Christian Democracy," 186.

69. Konrad Adenauer, *World Indivisible: With Liberty and Justice for All* (New York: Harper & Brothers, 1955), 12.

70. Schuman, *For Europe*, 34.

71. Ibid., 143–44.

72. Ibid., 54.

73. Monnet, *Memoirs*, 303–4.

74. For an excellent discussion of the European Defense Community debate, see Parsons, *Certain Idea*, 68–83.

75. Ibid., 102–15.

76. "Preamble to the Treaty Establishing the European Economic Community, 25 March 1957," Publishing Services of the European Communities, www.cvce.eu/obj/treaty_establish ing_the_european_economic_community_rome_25_march_1957-en-cca6ba28-0bf3-4ce6-8a76 -6b0b3252696e.html.

77. "Proclamation 1949," Stadt Aachen, www.aachen.de/en/sb/pr_az/karls_pr/proclama tion/index.html.

78. "Proclamation 1949"; Walter Eversheim, "Charlemagne Prize," Stadt Aachen, www.aachen .de/en/sb/pr_az/karls_pr/charlemagne_prize/index.html.

79. According to Walter Eversheim, "this 'Occidental idea' was a dominant feature of the Proclamation of 1949 by the founders of the Charlemagne Prize, and it was repeatedly used thereafter as a theme with variations—initially in symbolic retrospect, looking back at the Carolingian empire as emblematic of a European empire and of unity in rules, values, language, currency, administration, religion, and culture—but also looking forward as a model and programme for the task at hand: the economic and political unification of Europe." Walter Eversheim, "A Citizens' Prize for Distinguished Service on Behalf of European Unification," www.karlspreis.de/englische_texte /the_prize.html.

80. Ibid. The society has used the award to convey legitimacy on integration efforts, or to encourage certain developments in the European Communities. Edward Heath, for instance, received a prize in 1963 for his support of British membership in the Communities. In 1981 the first

president of the European Parliament Simone Veil became the first female laureate, which indicated support for a directly elected parliament and for the participation of women in leadership. King Juan Carlos I received the prize in 1982 to recognize the birth of Spanish democracy. And in 2004, the year ten new member states joined the EU, the society honored Pope John Paul II for his efforts to reunite Western and Eastern Europe with a "Charlemagne Prize Extraordinary" in a ceremony held in Rome on March 24.

81. Adenauer's carefully worded apology made to the Bundestag in September 1951 in some people's minds fell short of an unequivocal admission of guilt: "In the name of the German people, unspeakable crimes were committed which create a duty of moral and material restitution." See Stefan Engert, "A Case Study in 'Atonement': Adenauer's Holocaust Apology," *Israel Journal of Foreign Affairs* 4, no. 3 (2010): 116.

82. Charles de Gaulle, *Memoirs of Hope: Renewal and Endeavor*, trans. Terence Kilmartin (New York: Simon & Schuster, 1971), 180.

83. Winston S. Churchill, "Winston Churchill's Speech [on a Council of Europe], Zurich, 19 September 1946," Archive of European Integration, http://aei.pitt.edu/14362/.

84. Quoted by Milward, *European Rescue*, 330.

85. Brent F. Nelsen, James L. Guth, and Cleveland R. Fraser, "Does Religion Matter? Christianity and Public Support for the European Union," *European Union Politics* 2, no. 2 (2001): 191–217.

86. Robert Schuman, "The Coming Century of Supranational Communities," Strasbourg, May 16, 1949, Schuman Project, www.schuman.info/Strasbourg549.htm.

87. Michael Charlton, *The Price of Victory* (London: British Broadcasting Corporation, 1983), 97.

7

Protestant Resistance

G REAT BRITAIN AND the Nordic countries did not join integration efforts on the Continent in the 1950s. When some majority Protestant states did join the European Community in the 1970s, they did so tentatively and with reservations. Protestant elites were wary of economic integration with the Six for fear of hardships. But these fears were no greater than the fears of the Catholic political leaders who had earlier signed the Treaties of Paris and Rome. What distinguished Protestant political elites from their continental counterparts was their rejection of *political* integration and the idea of a federal United States of Europe. This attitude did not change when the Protestant countries later joined the Community, as they always pushed back against attempts to transfer powers to supranational authorities. The resulting split over the vision for Europe made Community decision making more difficult and ended any early hope for a United States of Europe.

The division of Europe in the 1950s reflected a cultural and ideological divide rooted in the Reformation. The community spirit displayed so prominently among continental Christian Democrats and shared by many other politicians in the Six did not extend to Britain and Scandinavia—or to many Protestant leaders in the confessionally mixed countries of West Germany and the Netherlands. The absence of a shared confessional culture helps explain why Britain and the Nordics could not overcome the very real (but manageable) economic and political obstacles to integration with the Catholic-led countries of the Continent in the 1950s. It also helps explain why Charles de Gaulle blocked enlargement in the 1960s. Without a shared culture, there could be no agreement on the nature of an integrated Europe; there could also be no new common European identity. That is the story of this chapter.

Protestant Ambivalence

Protestant countries initially watched the European integration process largely from the outside, but by 1961 some had decided to join, only to find the door closed. More than a decade later, Britain and Denmark had finally become members of the Community; but Finland, Iceland, Norway, and Sweden stayed out. Clearly, relations between the Community and the Protestant north were complicated.

Why was that relationship so difficult? Economic interests differed, as did geopolitical strategies, but negotiations produced pragmatic solutions to all the obvious problems. The less obvious but very real barrier was that the Protestant nations were struggling with a deeper question: Did they *want* to integrate? Were they part of "Europe"? What was meant by "European unity"? Protestants, both outside and inside the Six, were skeptical about integration in principle, perceived Catholic Europe as "other," and envisioned a very different "united Europe." At bottom, the question was "Who are we?"

A deep ambivalence ran through the Protestant North's approach to integration. Commercial interests and Cold War insecurity drew both mighty (but diminished) Britain and the peripheral Nordics toward Western European cooperation, even "integration," but the Protestant countries instinctively demurred when the Six insisted on adding a political dimension to that project. Britain and the Nordics did not boldly denounce and publicly work to undermine integration efforts in the 1950s. Rather, they hesitated, tried to become enthusiastic about integration, and, in Britain's case, even halfheartedly joined in negotiations, only to quietly slip away at the last minute. When Britain and two of the Nordics applied for membership in the European Economic Community (EEC) in the early 1960s, they entered the talks warily and defensively—reluctant to give up any more than necessary. All negotiating parties proclaimed their desire to conclude accession talks, yet all felt awkward. The Six worried that the new members would change everything once they were in; the applicants worried that the Six wanted to limit their freedoms. In truth, each side more or less accurately perceived the intentions of the other. In the end, the courtship of the Six with their northern neighbors felt like negotiations for an arranged marriage—all rules and no passion.

Britain

The ambivalence of Britain toward the integration of its continental neighbors emerged early. Winston Churchill, assuming the role of the "archetypal Brit," reflected this uncertainty both during and after the war. He had shown enthusiasm for European federation in the interwar years and had embraced Monnet's desperate 1940 plan for an Anglo-French union. As the war began to turn in the Allies' favor, the prime minister took to musing about a postwar "Council of Europe in which the barriers between nations will be greatly minimized"—to the general horror of the Foreign Office.[1] As for the nature of Britain's involvement in any new "instrument of European government," he remained vague. To his confidants, it was clear that he thought of Britain as a builder of Europe, but one that stood slightly aloof from the Continent. According to Gladwyn Jebb, a wartime Foreign Office official, Churchill "never really came to a conclusion, never said that we ourselves would be part of this new Europe."[2]

After the war, and now in opposition, Churchill took the lead in calling for a united Europe—but without British participation. In his famous Zurich speech (1946) he spoke first of resolving the tragic conflicts in Europe by recreating "the European Family" through the building of "a kind of United States of Europe." Regional organization was desirable and not at all in conflict with efforts to create a world organization, which in his view would only survive if founded upon "coherent natural groupings," such as the "Western Hemisphere," Britain's "Commonwealth of Nations," and a "Europe" built on "a partnership between France and Germany." But for Europe to take its rightful place as one of the world's regional organizations, it would need assistance from the United States, the Soviet Union, and Britain, acting as outside benefactors: "In all this urgent work, France and Germany must take the lead together. Great Britain, the British Commonwealth of Nations, mighty America, and I trust Soviet Russia—for then indeed all would be well—must be the friends and sponsors of the new Europe and must champion its right to live and shine."[3]

Thus, Churchill in Zurich embodied the British sense of identity: Britain was the Island Nation, the war victor and rescuer of the "Continent," the center of a world Empire, and the first friend of "mighty America." To accept equality with the suspect and struggling continental states seemed a step down in status. Britain had a global role to play and would not limit its influence by accepting a diminished role in a united Europe. As the journalist and diplomat Sir Con O'Neill observed: "I don't think Churchill thought for a moment that this country, that Britain would be part of his United Europe."[4] Yet in opposition, Churchill publicly pressured the Labour government to take the lead in Europe, while holding back on articulating specific policies. He preferred instead to play the role of great statesman and romantic visionary—especially at the Hague Congress (1948) and in the new parliamentary assembly of the Council of Europe.[5] When he returned to government as prime minister in October 1951, he made no serious effort to join the European project of the Six. In fact, in a November 1951 Cabinet memorandum, he stated emphatically, "I am not opposed to a European Federation. . . . But I never thought that Britain or the British Commonwealth should either individually or collectively become an integral part of a European federation and have never given the slightest support to the idea."[6] Thus, in the end, Churchill embodied British ambiguity toward Europe, articulated best in 1930: "We are *with* Europe, but not *of* it."[7]

Churchill only reflected the contradictions and tensions that from the beginning characterized British attitudes toward integration. The tensions cut in several different directions across the two main parties, with both Conservatives and Labour harboring both Europe enthusiasts and skeptics. The tensions also cut through individual decision makers—politicians and civil servants alike—with several high-profile "conversions" taking place in the 1950s and 1960s. For instance, Labour leader Hugh Gaitskell and Conservative member of Parliament Enoch Powell both became hard-line Euroskeptics, but Harold Wilson adopted a pro-European line when prime minister. Such disagreements over joining with the Six in constructing a new regional organization actually masked a broad consensus that continental Europe was not to be fully trusted, that federalism was anathema to British interests, and that free markets rather than economies managed by supranational institutions should undergird a new European economy. What was remarkable about the British attitudes toward integration between 1950 and Britain's eventual accession in 1973 was not the conflict but the consensus.

Britain never *wanted* to join an integrating *anything*.[8] Unlike its small-state Nordic partners, it had been large and isolated enough to avoid hard choices that might erode its freedom of action. Although Britain's status had changed in the late 1940s and 1950s, it failed to notice until 1960. In the early postwar years British politicians and publics still believed that the country could remain a great power. When Europe began to integrate and invited Britain to participate, the British declined the invitations, pointing to its Commonwealth commitments as the reason it could not pursue a European strategy. But what the British *wanted* to do and what they were discovering they *had* to do were different things. In the end, Britain joined the Common Market (1973), but reluctantly and without the enthusiasm of a true believer.

The Nordics

The Nordic countries, too, approached the Europe to the South with great ambivalence. They understood that their civilization was solidly Western, with the greatest cultural divide on the eastern Finnish border (splitting Eastern and Western Christianity), not on the southern Danish boundary. At the same time, the Nordic peoples felt a strong mutual affinity, recognizing the common cultural community they often called simply "Norden" (the North). The exclusion of the region from continental power politics after the early nineteenth century made it politically and culturally peripheral to the Franco-German core of Europe. The continental Europeans largely ignored the Nordics, and the Nordics themselves focused inward. World War II reminded them, however, that they were not so far from Europe that they could avoid a continental conflict. They did not, however, think of themselves as central actors on the European stage. If anything, they wanted nothing more than to stay out of continental entanglements. But Norden was not monolithic; each nation had its unique identity and sense of mission. Each related to the Six in its own way, keeping one eye on developments in their own region. Each country, in short, demonstrated its own ambivalence toward an integrating Europe.

Iceland was least likely to be conflicted. Its physical isolation from the Continent, its wealth of resources (particularly fish), and its recent achievement of independence from Denmark made it fiercely nationalistic and independent. Any suggestion that the country join others to promote security or prosperity ran into a wall of both elite and public opposition. But Iceland was very small, and was dependent on other nations for security and trade. Thus, Iceland joined the Organization for European Economic Cooperation (OEEC) and NATO as charter members, and it participated in free trade talks in the late 1950s. Serious consideration was given to joining the EEC during negotiations over the first British–Danish–Irish–Norwegian applications, but after discussions with EEC officials, Iceland applied for associate membership. De Gaulle's veto ended discussions with the EEC, but fishing disputes with Britain prevented the country from participating in the founding of the European Free Trade Association (EFTA). Thus, Iceland stayed out of any trade association until finally joining EFTA in 1970. Icelandic rhetoric remained staunchly nationalistic, even as the nation cooperated with Europe in ways that significantly limited its independence. This disconnect prompted one scholar to note that "while Icelandic politicians have pledged their unyielding belief in the sanctity of national sovereignty, they have not hesitated to limit the legislative power of the Icelandic Parliament through international treaties, but it has been very difficult for them to *admit* that the treaties have had these effects."[9]

On the other side of Norden, Finland struggled to find a new role. It was steadfastly Western in culture, but Russia's presence just over the border made accommodation to the east necessary if uncomfortable. The achievement of independence from Bolshevik Russia had given Finland a new unity of purpose as the eastern protector of the West.[10] When the West left Finland to stand alone against the Soviet Union's aggression in the fall of 1939, however, the nation felt abandoned. Its alliance with the Nazis against the Soviets until late 1944 did not endear the Finns to the victorious Allies; after the war they treated the Finns like Germany's other wartime allies, making no allowance for Finland's defensive war in 1939 and its preservation of democracy under immense totalitarian pressure. This Allied treatment deeply disillusioned the Finnish public. According to the Finnish diplomat Max Jakobson, "The Finnish people knew they were on their own. Making a virtue of necessity, they concluded they were better off on their own."[11] The result was the Finnish-Soviet Treaty of 1948, which guaranteed Finnish independence but required that it defend the USSR in case of attack. During the Cold War, Finland recognized the limits on its freedom and adopted a policy of neutrality.[12]

Finland was not absorbed completely into the Soviet sphere of influence; it remained a distinctly Nordic democracy with deep political and economic ties to the West. Finland expressed some desire to join in European economic cooperation, but its relations with the Soviet Union acted as a constraint. In the 1950s Finland depended on Western products (54 percent of imports) and markets (57 percent of exports), but politics limited its ability to participate in intergovernmental discussions.[13] The Finns abstained from early talks on a Common Nordic Labor Market (until joining in 1954). Nor did it join the Nordic Council until 1955, the Council of Europe until 1989, the OEEC until joining the Organization for Economic

Cooperation and Development in 1969, or the European Payments Union until a creative arrangement was worked out in 1957. As for the European Coal and Steel Community (ECSC), the European Economic Community (EEC), and EFTA, these more intrusive organizations were simply off limits.[14] Finland eventually negotiated special association agreements with EFTA (1961) and the EEC (1973), but only after getting the green light from Moscow. In sum, Finland came late to most of the Western European economic and, to a limited extent, political organizations. Culture and economics tied the country to the West, but some national resentment of the Allies and, more important, geopolitical considerations made Finland the slightly suspect ugly duckling of the postwar Nordic region.

The three Scandinavian countries were more "normal" in their relations with their neighbors to the South, but they still exuded ambivalence. Sweden maintained its policy of armed neutrality and, thus, stayed out of Western organizations such as NATO that took sides in the Cold War. It maintained, however, an active role as self-appointed bridge builder between the Cold War superpowers in broader organizations, especially the United Nations, and found nothing particularly difficult about joining the intergovernmental Council of Europe or OEEC. But joining a continental organization intent on limiting the sovereignty of members was an entirely different matter. Sweden favored a Nordic economic community or Europe-wide free trade area as an intergovernmental alternative to continental integration.

The Swedish political elite rejected participation in talks leading to political integration as being inconsistent with Sweden's neutrality and undesirable on principle. Sweden wanted to protect its trade relations with its most important partners—Britain and the Continent—but it would not sacrifice sovereignty.[15] A sense of superiority also pervaded its attitudes about the Continent: Europe was unstable and the source of mortal threats to democracy and the peaceful Nordic way of life. Political integration was out of the question, putting the ECSC and the EEC beyond the pale, but economic realities demanded that Sweden respond to British choices. Thus, Sweden played a key role in the creation of EFTA (the Stockholm Convention of 1959), and it agreed to negotiate an association agreement with the EEC when Britain applied for membership. That effort failed with de Gaulle's veto. No decision on membership was made after the second British application, but the Swedish government left an "open" application with the Commission that was discussed formally in 1970–71. The EEC was wary of Sweden's insistence on neutrality, and Sweden became more concerned with political developments in the EEC after de Gaulle's departure. Thus, in March 1971, the Swedish government broke off talks, "much to the relief of the Commission."[16]

Denmark and Norway approached the Continent much as Sweden did. Both maintained deep economic ties to Europe, but neither was attracted to Schuman-style integration. They readily joined Western economic organizations, such as the OEEC, and, like Sweden, participated in Nordic cooperation efforts. Denmark often led Nordic regional efforts; but Norway, with a weaker and less developed economy, proved a constant drag on Nordic cooperation. Unlike Sweden, however, Denmark and Norway rejected Cold War neutrality and embraced the Western Alliance by joining NATO, albeit with significant internal resistance. Without the constraint of neutrality, Denmark and Norway were able to follow Britain more closely in relations with the Continent. When Britain proposed a free trade area as a counter to the talks leading to the Treaties of Rome (the so-called Messina process), Denmark and Norway participated in negotiations. When the free trade talks failed, both joined Britain in forming EFTA. When Britain applied for EEC membership, Denmark and Norway applied for full membership as well—twice.

Here we must draw some distinction between Denmark and the other Scandinavian countries. Denmark shared a border with Germany and was, consequently, physically and emotionally more attached to the Continent. Though culturally more attached to the Nordic region, Denmark was more willing than its Scandinavian partners to consider closer economic ties to the South. Hans Branner, for instance, points out that in early meetings of Uniscan (1950–51), a loose organization of Britain and the three Scandinavian countries, Denmark was less willing than the others to reject out of hand the Six's approach to integration.[17] Denmark adopted a wait-and-see policy, but it eventually followed Britain in staying out of the ECSC. Later it followed Britain in applying for EEC membership, and it entered after the French lifted their veto. Norway, conversely, also followed Britain in negotiating an accession treaty but tore itself apart debating whether to join the EEC. When the dust cleared, the Norwegians had rejected membership in a 1972 referendum (53 to 47 percent). With Britain and Denmark securely behind the EEC tariff wall, however, Norway was desperate to maintain access to two of its main trading partners. In April 1973 it secured a free trade agreement with the newly enlarged EEC.[18]

The common thread running through all six of these Protestant countries is a deep ambivalence about the Continent. Britain and the Nordics felt both part of and not part of the "Europe" to their South. They were broadly connected to the Continent by Western culture and even more connected by economic ties. They needed Europe but were wary of getting too close; all wished to be associated with Europe, but on terms consistent with their national interests. Britain and Denmark were willing to go further than the other Protestant countries in integrating with the Six, but without great gusto. In reality, the Protestant countries did not see the Continent as part of their cultural community. They did not experience the "we feeling" common to the continental Christian Democrats.

A Missing Sense of Community

The ambivalence of the Protestant countries toward integration reflected an underlying sense that Europe, defined culturally, was somewhere else. Britain understood its loyalties to be to the Commonwealth, to the Atlantic region, and to the European continent, in that order. The British Empire and the Atlantic community of English-speaking peoples felt much more comfortable to the British than the lands across the Channel. The Nordics—bound by language, Lutheranism, and historical unions (and rivalries)—also felt more at home with each other than with the peoples of the Continent. This was more than just a sense of diverse loyalties. The British and the Nordics actually distrusted the Europeans. "Europe" carried negative connotations for many, thus making any integration with the Six vaguely repulsive. Such was the legacy of the Reformation.

Britain

British distrust of the "Continent" (a sometime pejorative term for the land across the Channel[19]) spanned the political spectrum while taking several different forms. Religious prejudice was one. Both the socialist left and the traditional right could at times emit a strong scent of historic British anti-Catholicism.[20] Talk in Europe of recreating Charlemagne's empire, the public Catholic piety of the major European leaders, and the perceived centrality of the Roman Church to the European project set many British citizens on edge. For the postwar British, "the Catholic nature of 'Europe' was a generous source of prejudice against it. . . . Britain in 1950 was still an emphatically Protestant country, in which Catholicism was something foreign and therefore suspect. . . . Anti-Catholic prejudice was instinctive."[21] Examples abound. Foreign Office officials, for instance, were well aware of Foreign Secretary Ernest Bevin's superstitious discomfort around Catholic priests, whom he believed brought bad luck.[22] More seriously, Bevin's deputy, Kenneth Younger, became quite disturbed by aspects of the Schuman Declaration. Schuman, he noted in his diary, was "a bachelor and a very devout Catholic who is said to be very much under the influence of the priests." As for the Schuman Plan, Younger confided that it "may be just a step in the consolidation of the Catholic 'black international,' which I have always thought to be a big driving force behind the Council of Europe."[23] After the signing of the Treaty of Rome in 1957, the Conservative Party published a "helpful" explanation that reassured skeptical readers that the document had "nothing to do with the Vatican, the Pope, or religion."[24]

The Labour Party's left wing, which opposed any move toward the Six, was deeply suspicious of an integrating Europe dominated by Christian Democrats resistant to international planning for full employment.[25] The Christian Democrats were thought to be the political arm of the Roman Church. And of course there was some evidence to support that view. Labour's Denis Healey, for instance, was deeply troubled by the *Mandement* (letter of admonition) issued by the Dutch bishops in 1954 that listed penalties, including excommunication, for those participating in socialist organizations or political activities.[26] Christian socialists were also suspicious of the "'Roman' flavor of European integration" and often expressed their distrust in anti-Catholic terms.[27] More moderate Labour forces were less likely to write off Europe as hopelessly clerical, but they were aware of the pressure from the left. Labour leader Hugh Gaitskell favored a move toward Europe (i.e., until October 1962), but even he had to acknowledge the conspiracy theorists in his party, if only to take them to task: "You hear people speaking as though if we go into the Common Market . . . [t]his is the end as far as an independent Britain is concerned. That we're finished, we are going to be sucked up in a tunnel of giant capitalist, Catholic conspiracy, our lives dominated by Adenauer and de Gaulle, unable to conduct any independent foreign policy at all. Now frankly, this is rubbish."[28]

Anti-Catholic views were not confined to the socialist left. Similar, if more theologically extreme, perspectives could be found on the evangelical and nationalist right. The National Union of Protestants, for instance, warned that "Romanism is trying to knock out, not only Protestantism, but any suspected revival [sic] to world domination."[29] Not all anti-Catholic rhetoric was quite so direct; but as Philip Coupland reminds us, "Suspicion of Catholicism remained, and it continued to be seen as a definite threat—'the Roman menace.'"[30] Many British Protestants had come to see some good in the Catholic Church, but they continued to find much of its ecclesiology, doctrine, theology, and worship repellant. They also objected to its reactionary politics, corruption, and worldly intrigue, which made it a "terrible menace to freedom and even in many places to true religion itself."[31]

For some Protestants the distrust extended to battles against a common foe. The Protestants and Catholics, for instance, could agree that communism must be resisted, but some evangelicals rejected co-belligerency with Catholics as a cure worse than the disease. As one writer in *The English Churchman and St. James Chronicle* put it, "The choice is not between Communism and Vaticanism, both are from a common source and are characterized by the same spirit and practices." This anti-Catholic view was applied effortlessly to the Common Market when the *English Churchman* warned that "Rome is endeavouring to create a Rome-sponsored bloc of nations," and later opined, "By all means co-operate, but not amalgamate. For England to surrender her sovereign power to a super-state would be yet another step towards our downfall."[32]

Mainstream British Protestantism remained suspicious of Catholicism, and by extension of a European Community that popular perception closely associated with the Vatican. But anti-Catholicism had begun to mellow in the British mainstream, making it less central to the debate over British accession to the EEC. That mellowing, however, did not extend to Northern Ireland. The hard-line Ulster Protestants, led by the Reverend Ian Paisley, still brought seventeenth-century Protestant passion to bear on the question of British membership. Paisley, for whom the world had entered "the final unfolding of the great drama of world empires of history," saw the Common Market as the "final manifestation" of the evil Roman Empire, the kingdom of the Antichrist. As Paisley read and interpreted the books of Daniel and

Revelation, he saw that as history drew to a close there would be "ten kingdoms in Europe and at the head of those kingdoms there will be the beast and in association with the beast there will be a church, and that church will be the Church of Rome in her final manifestation." The Common Market, established by the Treaty of *Rome* (not an insignificant detail), was in Paisley's view dominated and controlled by the Roman Catholic Church, which Revelation 17 depicts as a woman representing the city of Rome ("Mystery, Babylon the Great, the Mother of Harlots"). Paisley was convinced that the EEC was the seat of evil, and the last thing he wanted was to see Britain voluntarily join the forces of darkness.[33]

Paisley also feared that joining Europe would weaken Protestantism and undermine the liberty of Protestant peoples. Speaking during the 1975 national referendum debate on UK membership, Paisley lamented the fact that "when we [Britain] joined the Common Market we became a Protestant minority in an overwhelmingly Roman Catholic federation of nations"—a federation he dubbed "the greatest Catholic super State the world has ever known." Moreover, he was convinced that the "Roman Catholic States of Europe" would ignore Protestant Ulster ("Do you think they will have any time for this part of the United Kingdom which is the last bastion of Protestantism?") and would institutionalize a soft prejudice that would reduce Protestant freedoms:

> I have found in this Common Market struggle the intense hatred of pro-Marketeers for the true Protestantism of God's Word. . . . If you stand up and say, for religious reasons, you are against the Common Market, then you are branded as a bigot. You are branded as a traitor. You are branded as an extremist. . . . And I want to tell you that we are moving into a time of religious persecution, when these nations of Europe are going to insist on one church; one church for Europe and that church will be the Roman Catholic Church.

Not surprisingly, Paisley urged his followers to vote "no" in the 1975 referendum: "I trust that every man and woman . . . across our Province will take their stand against what is nothing less than the kingdom of the Anti-christ."[34]

The British distrust of Europe, of course, was not expressed solely in religious terms. As one British official put it in a 1982 radio interview, "We were [in the 1940s] highly skeptical about Europe. Europe was a collection of aliens and foreigners . . . who were erratic. They were unreliable."[35] In British eyes, Europeans were less than democratic and prone to violence on a horrific scale. As the postwar period wore on, however, British policymakers became less concerned about the erratic nature of Europeans and more worried about their formation of an independent political and economic bloc that struck some as faintly conspiratorial. Prime Minister Harold Macmillan, who had a reputation as being quite friendly to the European project, confided to his colleagues in June 1958 that "there were three elements who wanted supra-nationalism and who were playing no small part on the Commission: . . . the Jews, the Planners, and the old cosmopolitan élite."[36] Certainly these were private musings, but in public he also, if less colorfully, questioned the formation of a European "continental bloc."[37] In July 1960, as the Macmillan government considered joining the EEC, Whitehall officials warned ministers that any such move would confront the public's "innate dislike and suspicion of 'Europeans.'"[38] In September 1962 a Conservative Party analysis of public opinion found that only 40 percent of the British favored EEC membership, with an increasing number of citizens worried about being forced "to surrender our independence to 'Frogs' and 'Wogs.'"[39]

The issue of trust did not disappear after the British application in 1961. Negotiations involving the first application (1961–63), the second application (1967), accession (1970–72), and Labour's rethink in late 1974 and early 1975 were all difficult. Difficult negotiations were nothing new to the Six; the talks leading to the Treaties of Paris and Rome had been far from painless. But the British redefined "difficult." The Six were accustomed to treaty talks with partners who agreed on fundamental principles—particularly the need for supranational institutions with powers to enforce common decisions—thus creating an atmosphere of trust that facilitated agreement. Negotiators argued over details, but often they would agree on vague legal language, which they understood would be worked out later through practice.

The negotiations on the ECSC, for instance, were opened to any country willing to accept the supranationalism central to the Schuman Plan. The British, however, were unwilling to agree to "the principle of supranationalism—the pooling of sovereignty in common institutions" before the talks began.[40] They wanted the supranational institutions to be the *subject* of the talks.[41] When they did enter talks for membership in the 1960s, little had changed. The British continued to distrust the very supranational institutions and the community decision-making system they were now hoping to join.[42]

The Six reciprocated Britain's distrust. A close associate of Monnet's noted that the United Kingdom's negotiating style contributed to the wariness: "I remember very well in the summer of 1962 and later on until the end, the horror of Monnet and all around him, about all the technical problems that were brought up again and again, and there was never the feeling 'they really are willing to make the jump.'"[43] The British were looking for detailed, legal solutions to problems; Monnet was looking for true believers willing to subordinate individual interests to the good of the community. The British wanted business partners; Monnet wanted family.

The British, following Churchill, did not consider themselves part of the "coherent natural grouping" that existed on the Continent. Their natural grouping, for both the Conservatives and Labour, was the Commonwealth, bound together by language, law, Crown, and custom. Britain's "special relationship" with the United States also constituted a natural grouping. Continental Europe, conversely, usually spelled trouble; it was too often the source of British suffering. The British did recognize a common bond with the nations on the Continent as Western-style democracies with market-based economies facing a common Cold War enemy, but the sense of community, at least among elites, did not reach the depths found among the Christian Democrats. For the British, their relations with the Six would always be more utilitarian than emotional.

The Nordics

From both the outside and the inside, the Nordic region seemed to encompass a single cultural unit. The deep similarities were striking: similar languages (except for the Finns); a common religion and "view of life"; similar laws, customs, social, and political views; almost identical political systems and political party families; and very similar welfare states.[44] According to Gylfi Gíslason, the postwar Nordic cultures had, "in fact, merged—they formed a single identity."[45] Norden became for its peoples the region in which they felt most comfortable. Europe, however, was a foreign place that could be feared or pitied, but not considered "us."

"Nordism," in the hands of national elites, became a vision for human flourishing both at home and abroad. The values were rooted in a Lutheran sense of personal and corporate responsibility and were practiced by government leaders with missionary zeal.[46] At home each person was to work hard and care for his or her family and neighbors. Society, however, was solidaristic: Leave no one behind. The state used its power to ensure equality and spread the benefits of managed capitalism across classes and generations. The predictable hardships of life were anticipated, and needs were met. In the international arena these small countries became "moral superpowers" as they worked tirelessly through international organizations, most particularly the United Nations, to establish international standards of human rights and democratic governance, and to call on the global powers to enforce universal moral norms.[47] These were the countries most willing to dispatch their diplomats and peacekeeping troops to the most violent spots on Earth as they played the role of "social conscience for the world."[48] By becoming global models and respected voices for justice—collectively a "moral community"[49]—the Nordic countries distinguished themselves from the rest of the world as "a specific egalitarian social democratic community of destiny"[50]—to use a somewhat overwrought phrase.

However, as much as the Nordics saw themselves as part of a single cultural community, they also—paradoxically—clung to their specific national identities. The Danes and Swedes, both peoples from former imperial powers, remembered their unhappy fifteenth-century union and their centuries of armed rivalry; Finns, Icelanders, and Norwegians recalled their Danish and Swedish overlords and their recent achievement of national independence. Thus, though a common culture encouraged greater Nordic unity, historical memory kept the region's individual countries stubbornly distinct. Borders still mattered within the Nordic community.

Hence, like the British, the postwar Nordics maintained strong national identities and a sense of mission to bring the just, peaceful society to the world.[51] They also shared with Britain an insular sense that "Europe" was elsewhere—somewhere you went when traveling, a place where people lived differently. To the Nordics the distance that separated them from Europe seemed greater than the distance separating Europe from Britain. As one Norwegian scholar put it, "The Skagerak is even wider than the English Channel."[52] Both national identities and Nordic identity were based on a strong perception of Europe as "other" and were "historically represented in terms of opposition to Europe."[53]

The distance was certainly made greater by the postwar political differences that developed between the Nordics and the continental governments. Although the Christian Democrats dominated the Six after 1945, the Social Democrats governed the Nordic region, although more clearly in the Scandinavian countries than in Finland or Iceland (see tables 7.1–7.7 and figure 7.1). Social Democracy shared with Christian Democracy a desire to carve a "third way" between capitalism and communism by using state power to create a comprehensive, coherent, and universal welfare state. The two ideological camps differed, however, on the exact division between public and private ownership, with the Social Democrats being more distrustful of private enterprise. The two groups also differed over the appropriateness of using the state to create the socialist dream of an egalitarian and just society, with the Christian Democrats being more distrustful of the state's coercive power as a threat to persons and to the natural institutions of society (e.g., the family).

But the major divide between the two camps was cultural, and often religious. The Catholicism of the Christian Democrats stirred the embers of Nordic antipapism and Catholic stereotypes and grated on the mostly secular or at best nominally religious Social Democrats. The Christian Democrats' tendency to ground political thinking in Christian concepts and religious rhetoric struck the Social Democrats as archaic and coercive. The Nordic Social Democrats, like the left wing of the British Labour Party, saw continental Europe as a bastion of capitalism and Catholic traditionalism. In Sweden, the Social Democrats, indeed most Swedes, could summarize the threat of Europe using four Cs (or Ks in Swedish): "capitalism, Catholicism, conservatism, and colonialism."[54] The socialists of the North found the European continental bloc insufficiently progressive. According to Tony Judt, Swedish prime minister Tage Erlander (in office 1948–68) "ascribed his own ambivalence about joining [the EEC] to the overwhelming Catholic majority in the new Community."[55] Niels Matthiasen, the internal secretary of the Danish Social Democrats in the late 1950s, articulated the party line: "As a member of the Common Market, we would become the seventh country in a union dominated by the Catholic Church and right-wing movements."[56] Even Gunnar Myrdal described the European Community as consisting of states "with a more primitive form of social organization than ours," arguing that "it is above all the securely Protestant countries that have progressed

Table 7.1 Social Democratic Party Strength in National Elections
(average percent by decade)

Country	1940s	1950s	1960s
Britain (Labour)	47.7	46.3	45.0
Denmark	39.1	40.2	38.7
Finland	25.7	25.3	23.4
Iceland	16.0	15.4	15.0
Norway	43.4	47.5	45.5
Sweden	48.9	45.6	51.7

Source: Jan-Erik Lane and Svante O. Ersson, *Politics and Society in Western Europe*, 2nd ed. (London: Sage, 1991), 140.

Table 7.2 Party Strength in the United Kingdom, 1945–70

Party	1945	1950	1951	1955	1959	1964	1966	1970
Percent popular vote								
Labour	47.8	46.1	48.8	46.4	43.8	44.1	47.9	43.0
Conservative	39.8	43.5	48.0	49.7	49.4	43.3	41.9	46.4
Liberal	9.0	9.1	2.5	2.7	5.9	11.2	8.5	7.5
Percent parliamentary seats								
Labour	61.4	50.4	47.2	44.0	41.0	50.3	57.6	45.7
Conservative	33.3	47.8	51.4	54.8	57.9	48.3	40.2	52.4
Liberal	1.9	1.4	1.0	1.0	1.0	1.4	1.9	1.0

Source: Wolfram Nordsieck, "United Kingdom," Parties and Elections in Europe, www.parties-and-elections.eu /unitedkingdom2.html.

Table 7.3 Party Strength in Denmark, 1945–71

Party	1945	1947	1950	1953a	1953b	1957	1960	1964	1966	1968	1971
Percent popular vote											
Social Democrat	32.8	40.0	39.6	40.4	41.3	39.4	42.1	41.9	38.2	34.2	37.3
Agrarian Liberal (Venstre)	23.4	27.6	21.3	22.1	23.1	25.1	21.1	20.8	19.3	18.6	15.6
Conservative	18.2	12.4	17.8	17.3	16.8	16.6	17.9	20.1	18.7	20.4	16.7
Liberals (Radical Left)	8.1	6.9	8.2	8.6	7.8	7.8	5.8	5.3	7.3	15.0	14.4
Communist	12.5	6.8	4.6	4.8	4.3	3.1	1.1	1.2	0.8	1.0	1.4
Libertarian (Justice Party)	1.9	4.5	8.2	5.6	3.5	5.3	2.2	1.3	0.7	0.7	1.7
Socialist People's	—	—	—	—	—	—	6.1	5.8	10.9	6.1	9.1
Percent parliamentary seats											
Social Democrat	32.2	38.0	39.1	40.4	41.3	39.1	42.5	42.5	38.5	34.6	39.1
Agrarian Liberal (Venstre)	25.5	32.7	21.2	21.9	23.5	25.1	21.2	21.2	19.6	19.0	16.8
Conservative	17.4	11.3	17.9	17.2	16.8	16.8	17.9	20.1	19.0	20.7	17.3
Liberals (Radical Left)	7.4	6.7	7.9	8.6	7.8	7.8	6.1	5.6	7.3	15.1	15.1
Communist	12.1	6.0	4.6	4.6	4.5	3.4	0.0	0.0	0.0	0.0	0.0
Libertarian (Justice Party)	2.0	4.0	7.9	6.0	3.4	5.0	0.0	0.0	0.0	0.0	0.0
Socialist People's	—	—	—	—	—	—	6.1	5.6	11.2	6.1	9.5

Source: Wolfram Nordsieck, "Denmark," Parties and Elections in Europe," www.parties-and-elections.eu /denmark2 a.html.

Table 7.4 Party Strength in Finland, 1945–70

Party	1945	1948	1951	1954	1958	1962	1966	1970
Percent popular vote								
Social Democrat	25.1	26.3	26.5	26.2	23.2	19.5	27.2	23.4
Centre (Agrarian)	21.3	24.2	23.2	24.1	23.1	23.0	21.2	17.1
Socialist Left	23.5	20.0	21.6	21.6	23.2	22.0	21.1	16.6
Conservatives								
(National Coalition)	15.0	17.1	14.6	12.8	15.3	15.0	13.8	18.0
Swedish People's	7.9	7.3	7.2	6.8	6.5	6.1	5.7	5.3
Liberals (National								
Progressive)	5.2	3.9	5.7	7.9	5.9	6.3	6.5	6.0
Percent parliamentary seats								
Social Democrat	25.0	27.0	26.5	27.0	24.0	19.0	27.5	26.0
Centre (Agrarian)	24.5	28.0	25.5	26.5	24.0	26.5	24.5	18.0
Socialist Left	24.5	19.0	21.5	21.5	25.0	23.5	20.5	18.0
Conservatives (National								
Coalition)	14.0	16.5	14.0	12.0	14.5	16.0	13.0	18.5
Swedish People's	7.0	6.5	7.0	6.0	6.5	6.5	5.5	5.5
Liberals (National								
Progressive)	4.5	2.5	5.0	6.5	4.0	6.5	4.5	4.0

Source: Wolfram Nordsieck, "Finland," Parties and Elections in Europe, www.parties-and-elections.eu/finland.html.

Table 7.5 Party Strength in Iceland, 1946–71

Party	1946	1949	1953	1956	1959	1959	1963	1967	1971
Percent popular vote									
Social Democrat	17.8	16.5	15.6	18.3	12.5	15.2	14.2	15.7	10.5
Independence	39.4	39.5	37.1	42.4	42.5	39.7	41.4	37.5	36.2
Progressive	23.1	24.5	21.9	15.6	27.2	25.7	28.2	28.1	25.3
Communist	19.5	19.5	16.1	19.2	15.3	16.0	16.0	17.6	17.1
Percent parliamentary seats									
Social Democrat	17.3	13.5	11.5	15.4	11.5	15.0	13.3	15.0	10.0
Independence	38.5	36.5	40.4	36.5	38.5	40.0	40.0	38.3	36.7
Progressive	25.0	32.7	30.8	32.7	36.5	28.3	31.7	30.0	28.3
Communist	19.2	17.3	13.5	15.4	13.5	16.7	15.0	16.7	16.7

Source: Wolfram Nordsieck, "Iceland," Parties and Elections in Europe, www.parties-and-elections.eu/iceland2.html.

economically and in all other ways."[57] Another leading Social Democrat, Enn Kokk, put it even more starkly. His description of a Europe ruled by capitalism and papism ended with a dismal assessment: "Today's Franco-German combination, an alliance between General de Gaulle and Dr. Adenauer at the forefront of a Catholic, conservative, and capitalist Western Europe, is a disquieting creation, . . . a politically dead landscape."[58]

The animosity that Social Democrats felt for continental Christian Democrats sat atop an iceberg of popular cultural distrust. Rural populations in all the Nordic

Table 7.6 Party Strength in Norway, 1945–69

Party	1945	1949	1953	1957	1961	1965	1969
Percent popular vote							
Social Democrat (Labor)	41.0	45.7	46.7	48.3	46.8	43.1	46.6
Conservative	17.0	18.3	18.6	18.9	20.0	21.1	19.7
Liberal	13.8	13.1	10.0	9.7	8.8	10.4	9.4
Christian People's	7.9	8.5	10.5	10.2	9.6	8.1	9.4
Center (Agrarian)	8.0	7.9	9.1	9.3	9.4	9.9	10.3
Communist	11.9	5.8	5.1	3.4	2.9	1.4	1.0
Percent parliamentary seats							
Social Democrat (Labor)	50.1	56.7	51.3	52.0	49.3	45.3	49.3
Conservative	16.7	15.3	18.0	19.3	19.3	20.7	19.3
Liberal	13.3	14.0	10.0	10.0	9.3	12.0	8.7
Christian People's	5.3	6.0	9.3	8.0	10.0	8.7	9.3
Center (Agrarian)	6.7	8.0	9.3	10.0	10.7	12.0	13.3
Communist	7.3	0.0	2.0	0.7	0.0	0.0	0.0

Source: Wolfram Nordsieck, "Norway, Parties and Elections in Europe, www.parties-and-elections.eu/norway2.html.

Table 7.7 Party Strength in Sweden, 1948–70

Party	1948	1952	1956	1958	1960	1964	1968	1970
Percent popular vote								
Social Democrats	46.1	46.1	44.6	46.2	47.8	47.3	50.1	45.3
Liberal	22.8	24.4	23.8	18.2	17.5	17.0	14.3	16.2
Center (Agrarian)	12.4	10.7	9.4	12.7	13.6	13.2	15.7	19.9
Conservative	12.3	14.4	17.1	19.5	16.5	13.7	12.9	11.5
Communist	6.3	4.3	5.0	3.4	4.5	5.2	3.0	4.8
Percent parliamentary seats								
Social Democrats	48.7	47.8	45.9	48.1	49.1	48.5	53.6	46.6
Liberal	24.8	25.2	25.1	16.5	17.2	18.5	14.6	16.6
Center (Agrarian)	13.0	11.3	8.2	13.9	14.7	15.5	16.7	20.3
Conservative	10.0	13.5	18.2	19.5	16.8	14.2	13.7	11.7
Communist	3.5	2.2	2.6	2.2	2.2	3.4	1.3	4.9

Source: Wolfram Nordsieck, "Sweden," Parties and Elections in Europe, www.parties-and-elections.eu/sweden2.html.

countries feared the cultural changes that integration with the Continent might bring. Religiously conservative Scandinavians, heirs of the nineteenth-century revivals, were quite willing to express religious concerns. Free Church partisans in the Swedish Riksdag in 1951 "saw the threat of Catholic monasteries as being almost as dangerous as secularization and de-Christianization." For them, "Europe" was "synonymous with Catholicism."[59] During the 1962 Norwegian Storting debate on whether Norway should apply for Common Market membership, religious conservatives from the Liberal and Christian People's parties, with some help from Labor, argued against membership "on the basis that the Protestant religion in Norway

Figure 7.1 Social Democrats in Government, 1945–71

Member state	1945	1946	1947	1948	1949	1950	1951	1952	1953	1954	1955	1956	1957	1958	1959	1960	1961	1962	1963	1964	1965	1966	1967	1968	1969	1970	1971
Britain	•••	•••	•••	•••	•••	•••	///	///	///	///	///	///	///	///	///	///	///	///	///	•••	•••	•••	•••	•••	•••	///	///
Denmark	•••	///	///	•••	•••	•••	///	///	•••	•••	•••	•••	•••	•••	•••	•••	•••	•••	•••	•••	•••	•••	•••	///	///	///	•••
Finland	xxx	xxx	xxx	•••	xxx	xxx	xxx	xxx	xxx	•••	•••	///	///	x	///	///	///	///	x	///	///	///	xxx	xxx	xxx	xxx	x
Iceland	xxx	xxx	•••	•••	•••	///	///	///	///	///	///	xxx	xxx	xxx	•••	xxx	xxx	xxx	xxx	xxx	xxx	xxx	xxx	xxx	///	xxx	xxx
Norway	•••	•••	•••	•••	•••	•••	•••	•••	•••	•••	•••	•••	•••	•••	•••	•••	•••	•••	•••	•••	•••	///	///	///	///	///	•••
Sweden	•••	•••	•••	•••	•••	•••	•••	•••	•••	•••	•••	•••	•••	•••	•••	•••	•••	•••	•••	•••	•••	•••	•••	•••	•••	•••	•••

Source: Wolfgang C. Muller and Kaare Strøm, eds., Coalition Governments in Western Europe (Oxford: Oxford University Press, 2000).

KEY

•••	=	Socialist Party / Social Democratic Party is the leading party in government
xxx	=	Socialist Party/Social Democratic Party participates in Government
///	=	Socialist Party / Social Democratic Party in the opposition
x	=	Caretaker government

would be weakened"; that the EEC countries would exert a "conservative influence, as a result of the strong position of the Catholic church in these countries"; and that, in general, "full membership would constitute a threat to Norwegian culture."[60] Such arguments disappeared from the Storting debates in the 1970s, but not from political campaigns. During the 1972 referendum campaign "a number of people were worried about the EEC closing down the Protestant Norwegian state church, and also feared . . . a 'Catholic invasion.'"[61] More generally, the opponents of EEC membership claimed that "the country would be invaded by foreign workers, Catholic ideas, continental drinking habits, and foreigners buying up their mountain huts, lakes, and forests."[62] The state alcohol monopoly was possibly in danger, which greatly bothered teetotalers, among others.[63] As late as the early 1990s, conservative Christians in Norway were denouncing the European Community as the kingdom of the Antichrist.[64]

The Social Democrats, unlike their Christian Democratic counterparts, also believed in national borders. Keynesian demand management—the foundation of the Nordic economies—required control of the key levers of the national economy. Trade liberalization was desirable, but not at the expense of full employment or generous welfare benefits. All the Nordic political elites accepted this commitment to national economic autonomy, which made them skeptical about any arrangement that limited economic sovereignty, a view they shared with Britain, especially under Labour.[65] This was not a simple ideological divide between the socialists and nonsocialists. The Nordic countries were committed to national economic and political development behind meaningful borders. Their vision of European integration, therefore, would need to begin with national sovereignty—as would Britain's.

The Protestant Vision

The Protestants lived and traveled in different circles than did Catholics in the Six. British elites experienced community when moving among the leaders of the Commonwealth (albeit a feeling that was not always reciprocated), or when they sat with Canadians and Americans. The Nordics, too, found their own warm community in Norden. But neither group thought of the Continent in the same way as they thought of their own "natural" communities. They were never part of the transnational web of personal relationships built on a common "sense of community" spun by the Christian Democrats. Europe was seemingly far away and very different.

Britain and the Nordics also lived in a world where national borders felt comfortable and right. With the exception of a few world federalists and pan-Scandinavian cranks, it had not dawned on most of the British or Nordics to seriously question the principle of national sovereignty, or to advocate for a new federation of which they would be willing participants. Though not understanding the motivation behind Schuman and Monnet, they were willing to allow the Six to pursue their federalist dream more or less unimpeded. The Anglo-Nordics were surprised, however, that the Six expected them to sign on to such a utopian project when they joined the EEC. What they were looking for was a trustworthy free trade organization, not a new federal state.

This disconnect between the Protestant North and the Catholic Continent proved crucial. Protestants saw their borders as safeguards against tyranny. Their borders guaranteed their identities and freedom to create their own societies. The struggle in the postwar period was over identity and autonomy, and for the Anglo-Nordics these concepts were grounded in their experience of the Reformation. It is no accident that these Protestant nations consistently raised the threat of Catholicism when speaking of relations with Europe. Europe was safe when it was divided; but a united Europe, a new Holy Roman Empire, whether Schuman's version or de Gaulle's, looked entirely too familiar.

Nevertheless, the Europe of the Six was too dynamic for the British and the Nordics to ignore. A rejuvenated heart of Europe began drawing the periphery into its orbit. In this section we explore the clash of visions as the Six and the Anglo-Nordics worked out their new relationship.

Britain

Psychologically and sociologically, the English Channel proved a wide divide for the postwar British elites and the general population.[66] But the wariness with which the British approached European integration was not merely emotional—it was also substantive. The intellectual objection to British membership in an integrated Europe had a negative side—it rejected federalism and supranational institutions—and a positive element—it preferred free market (liberal) solutions to centralized (regulatory) ones. We take the negative element first.

British elites and their publics rejected notions of European federalism and supranational institutions from the very start of the postwar era. There were federalists in Britain (as we have seen); but compared with the Continent, there were very few, as was evident to British decision makers. According to Gladwyn Jebb, "There were some English who were Federalists and some who pretended to be, but they were many fewer than on the Continent."[67] The British vision for Europe could not include a deliberate sovereignty giveaway. Federalism became the first—and in some ways the only—insurmountable sticking point in Britain's relations with Europe. But that, of course, was the crux of the matter.

British politicians, even those considered "pro-European," always feared that any British "concession" on supranational institutions would inexorably lead to a loss of sovereignty—which nearly all assumed would be disastrous, on principle and in practice.[68] Foreign Minister Anthony Eden made this abundantly clear in 1952, when he told an American audience that Britain would not join "a federation on the Continent of Europe" because "this is something we know in our bones we cannot do."[69] When Britain did join the Brussels negotiations leading to the Treaties of Rome in 1955, significant parts of the Whitehall bureaucracy resisted. For instance, Sir Edward Bridges, the permanent secretary to the Treasury, wrote the chancellor in September, saying: "I remain firmly convinced that Britain's interest certainly does not lie in this direction and we must not let ourselves be misled by the kind of mysticism which appeals to European Catholic federalists and occasionally—I fear—to our Foreign Secretary [Harold Macmillan]."[70] Britain broke off talks in November 1955, based in part on a Whitehall study (the Trend Report) that identified four "decisive considerations" against membership, one being that "participation would in practice lead gradually to further integration, and ultimately perhaps to political federation, which was not acceptable to public opinion in Britain."[71]

What exactly was acceptable to British public (and elite) opinion? Successive governments were not opposed to European cooperation, just to any cooperation that might lead to a purposeful or accidental loss of sovereignty. Thus, British proposals for cooperation were consistently intergovernmental and focused on opening rather than managing markets. The British and Scandinavians prevented the Council of Europe from becoming a federal body by insisting on a Council of Ministers, with each minister possessing a vote and a veto.[72] The 1948 Brussels Pact—which was primarily a defense accord between the United Kingdom, France, and the Benelux—also included provisions encouraging economic and cultural cooperation—all through intergovernmental means. After the breakdown of the European Defense Community (EDC) process in 1954, the British took the lead in proposing an expanded Brussels Pact that added Italy and West Germany as members and transformed the organization into the Western European Union.[73] This agreement paved the way for German membership in NATO, but did not erode the sovereignty of member states. The postwar British approach to the organization of Europe, especially with respect to national defense, was to promote integration without federation.

This same principle held for economic matters. When faced with a continental proposal that included a supranational element, the British developed an alternative plan that tried to preserve the spirit of cooperation without undermining national sovereignty. The Schuman Declaration and the speed with which the Six came to a coal and steel agreement caught them off guard. Whitehall drafted an alternative proposal, which Bevin planned to offer when the Schuman Plan failed.[74] Bevin never got his opportunity. Conservatives Harold Macmillan and David Eccles, then in the opposition, also suggested an alternative coal and steel community that put the High Authority in industry hands, subject to a ministerial committee with the right of veto.[75] There was no hint of supranationalism. This proposal, which Macmillan made to the Council of Europe on August 8, 1950, so angered Monnet that he told Schuman "the British are waging a skilful campaign to sabotage our plan."[76] But if saboteurs, the British were incompetent ones.

A better case for attempted sabotage can be made for Plan G. In November 1955 the Conservative Eden government effectively withdrew from the Messina process while Whitehall officials began drafting plans for a European free trade area—known to most as the Wide Free Trade Area (WFTA), but to the British as "Plan G"—that would effectively replace the customs union being discussed by the Six. While developing the plan, the British attempted to impede the customs union negotiations by appealing to Washington, Bonn, and the OEEC to consider the implications of dividing Western Europe economically. The Messina Six did not appreciate Britain's actions, which they interpreted as hostile meddling—the sabotage of "perfidious Albion."[77] By the time the British announced their plan in July 1956, the Six were well on the way to agreeing to a treaty text.[78] Thus, instead of acting as an alternative to a failed Messina initiative (the secret hope of British decision makers), the British plan became a proposal to form an OEEC free trade area with the new EEC operating as a single unit within the broader organization.[79] Free trade in industrial goods (excluding agriculture) would be achieved in stages without the oversight of strong central institutions or any suggestion that Europe would be integrated economically or politically.

The talks began in October 1957 (just three months before the EEC came into existence), but they were plagued by mistrust and general ideological disagreement over the benefits of free trade (French foreign minister Maurice Couve de Murville: "France has never been a free trade country, and it believes more in organisation"[80]). By this time the Macmillan government was serious about associating with the Six,[81] but many on the Continent agreed with Couve de Murville, who assessed Plan G "as a desperate move in order to prevent the entry into force of the Rome Treaty. . . . It was the last . . . effort to avoid what they considered and which was in fact—at least temporarily—the break between Britain and the Continent."[82] The talks bogged down and were eventually ended by Charles de Gaulle in December 1958, almost a year after the EEC's inauguration. The nations left standing in the cold by de Gaulle shuffled off to form the decidedly nonsupranational EFTA.

The resistance to federalism that characterized most of the political class and electorate in Britain stemmed directly from the nation's commitment to national sovereignty as the organizing principle of the international system. Unlike the Christian Democrats, who scorned sovereignty as the bane of the twentieth century, the British saw no reason to yield on a principle that protected them from the diktats of kaisers, fuhrers, and Soviet general secretaries. To compromise sovereignty was to compromise national identity.[83] To compromise sovereignty was to fall back into the pool of lesser nations. So strong was this sense of sovereignty that all future efforts to move Britain closer to Europe required proponents to highlight the practical benefits of "more Europe" and to downplay or deny any possible loss of sovereignty.

As a corollary, all the Euroskeptics appealed to British national identity to derail integration. And in Britain, as opposed to almost anywhere else in Europe, this sentiment played well with voters.

Macmillan set the pattern for the pro-Europe pragmatists. With the debacle of Plan G behind him, he began the process of "taking the plunge" into Europe in 1960. Pragmatic reasons dominated his thinking. Britain was too small to dominate the world stage and too large to be inconspicuous. It was relying less on Commonwealth markets and more on European ones. The Americans wanted Britain to join Europe, and most EEC members did too. Nevertheless, the best Macmillan and most of his cabinet could work up was a grudging acceptance of the inevitable: Britain would join Europe because it had to, not because it wanted to.

Acceding to the Treaty of Rome, Macmillan knew, would require Britain to accept a loss of sovereignty. In a brutally honest report in November 1960, the lord chancellor, Viscount Kilmuir, outlined three ways that accession would erode British sovereignty: Parliament would surrender some legislative power to the Council of Ministers; some treaty-making powers would go to an international organization; and the British courts would become subordinate to the European Court of Justice.[84] Macmillan understood these implications, but he saw no other way forward. He convinced his cabinet in the summer of 1961 to endorse negotiations with the EEC with a view toward membership. In July he told Parliament of his intention "to make formal application to join the Community," assuring his colleagues that "the ultimate decision whether to join or not must depend on the result of the negotiations."[85] This was not a decision to join, but to negotiate.

Parliament debated the announcement on August 2 and 3. Without a detailed agreement to discuss, the House of Commons focused on the fundamental principles underlying any move to join the EEC. Macmillan opened with a list of problems that membership in the EEC might help to alleviate: political instability in Europe, the changing nature of the Commonwealth, and problems in British agriculture and industry. But eventually he got around to the central issue, sovereignty and national identity:

> This problem of sovereignty, to which we must, of course, attach the highest importance is, in the end, perhaps a matter of degree. . . . Although the federalist movement exists in Europe it is not one favoured by the leading figures and certainly not by the leading Governments of Europe today. Certainly not by the French Government.
>
> The alternative concept, the only practical concept, would be a confederation, a commonwealth if hon. Members would like to call it that—what I think General de Gaulle has called Europe des patries—which would retain the great traditions and the pride of individual nations while working together in clearly defined spheres for their common interest. This seems to me a concept more in tune with the national

traditions of European countries and, in particular, of our own. It is one with which we could associate willingly and wholeheartedly. At any rate, there is nothing in the Treaty of Rome which commits the members of EEC to any kind of federalist solution, nor could such a system be imposed on member countries.[86]

Macmillan was minimizing the issue by essentially claiming that the Six had already recognized the impracticality of European federation and had moved on to a Gallic "Europe of nations," a more comfortable domicile for Britain. No group of countries would force Britain to cede its independence to a federation. In the heat of debate, the secretary of state for the colonies, Duncan Sandys, stated emphatically through several interruptions that "we shall not . . . in the course of the negotiations give any undertaking, . . . implied or otherwise, which would commit Britain to join a European political federation, and, I must add, nor, I am sure, shall we be asked to do so."[87] Other members of Parliament, however, Labour and Tory, were not so sure.

Ironically, the most eloquent response to the government came from the Tory backbench. Following Macmillan's remarks, Derek Walker-Smith, a onetime minister of health, asked if EEC membership would have "wider implications of the long-term effect in relation to our sovereignty and our constitutional machinery":

If we adhere to the Economic Community now and the Six proceed, as they are entitled to proceed, to the next stage of political union, what then is our position? If we do not want to go along with them on the political side, could we stay in on the economic side, or could we get out at that stage even if we wanted to? Or is the real position this, that if the decision is taken now we forfeit the power of political decision? And what is the intention of the Government in this regard? Do they want to take a step forward into political union or not? So far we have not had an answer to that question. If we tried to come out of the Community in those circumstances, would not the Six be justified in saying to us, "But you knew all along of our enthusiasm for the next political step. If you did not share it, why did you join us in the first place?" Then the last state of our relations with Europe would be worse than the first.[88]

Similar arguments came from the left. Some socialists still groused that the EEC was a capitalist conspiracy, but it was Hugh Gaitskell, the usually right-leaning Labour leader, who sounded the loudest alarm. At a party conference in October 1962 he argued that Common Market membership would "mean the end of Britain as an independent European state"—indeed, "the end of a thousand years of history." Achieving a European federation, he insisted, was the point of the EEC—making Britain "a province of Europe, which is what federation means."[89]

Macmillan's response was to ignore, dismiss, deflect, and minimize the sovereignty issue as much as possible—a strategy every subsequent British leader has also adopted. In a telling passage from his autobiography, Macmillan ran through several of the arguments that he deployed against those who worried about losing Britain to Europe. He sought first to redefine the terms: "Accession to the Treaty of Rome would not involve a one-sided surrender of 'sovereignty' on our part, but a pooling of sovereignty by all concerned." Next, he minimized the effects of accession, contradicting his own Kilmuir Report: "Our obligations would not alter the position of the Crown, nor rob our Parliament of its essential powers, nor deprive our Law Courts of their authority in our domestic life." Then he dismissed the issue as essentially moot: "The talk about loss of sovereignty becomes all the more meaningless when one remembers that practically every nation, including our own, has already been forced by the pressure of the modern world to abandon large areas of sovereignty and to realise that we are now all interdependent."[90] When these arguments failed, he asserted that Britain would change the essence of the European project from within—or, as he once put it more creatively, we will "embrace them *destructively.*"[91] This argument was offensive to the Europeans, and it struck others as quite naive. When he heard such arguments coming from the socialist left, Michael Foot, a Labour Euroskeptic, quipped: "One of my hon. Friends said that he wanted to see our country playing in the European first league. My right hon. Friend . . . seem[s] to be saying, 'Yes, we wish to enter the West European football league as long as . . . the rules of the game are so altered that it resembles cricket.'"[92]

Labour prime minister Harold Wilson and Conservative prime minister Edward Heath employed similar smokescreens when defending the second British application and the accession treaty, respectively. Wilson, for instance, argued in his 1967 parliamentary defense of Britain's second application that the vision of a federal Europe had died and that Britain need not worry about future integration: "I still believe—and here I am echoing words of the late Hugh Gaitskell, five years ago—that, for the immediately foreseeable future, British public opinion would not contemplate any rapid move to a federal Europe. . . . That does not imply any difference in approach by Britain from that of the Six."[93] Wilson seemed to believe that the EEC was a static organization without a vision, however dim, of the way forward. In his thought and rhetoric he conveniently ignored the Treaty of Rome's commitment to an "ever-closer union."

Prime Minister Edward Heath, the only world-class British leader to back the European project with both head and heart, had a more nuanced view of national sovereignty that offered the possibility of sacrificing some of it in the larger national interest.[94] In his public campaign for accession, however, he often played down the loss of sovereignty and emphasized the economic and political benefits of membership—so much so that critics accused him of outright deception.[95] In the white paper he put before Parliament in 1971, for instance, the issue was blurred: "There is no question of any erosion of essential national sovereignty. . . . What is proposed is a sharing and enlargement of individual national sovereignties in the general interest."[96] In summing up the debate on accession, Heath told Parliament, "In joining we are making a commitment which involves our sovereignty, but we are also gaining an opportunity."[97] Young rightly sees in these obfuscations a clear strategy: "Only by sweetening the truth about national sovereignty, apparently, could popular support be kept in line."[98]

British nationalists, of course, would have none of it. The most effective opposition to the line established by Macmillan and Heath came from the leaders of the "new right," especially Enoch Powell. A brilliant but quirky Conservative, Powell turned against EEC membership in 1968 after Heath, angered by Powell's racially charged "Rivers of Blood" speech, sacked him from the Shadow Cabinet. For the first time, Powell brought together traditional nationalist arguments against membership with new critiques from a free market perspective.[99] In his view Britain would not benefit economically from joining the EEC because it had become a statist, overregulated, and politically managed entity reflecting the character of its member states. In no way did it encourage the freer markets needed to deliver true prosperity. More important, joining the Community would undermine Britain's Parliament, and therefore its independence, national identity, and common purpose.

Powell was an unabashed nationalist who believed that "Britain was a united and homogeneous nation with a tradition and temperament which was ill suited to membership of a united Europe."[100] Britain had lost its national myths to postwar reality, but it needed to rebuild its sense of national self, not by meekly joining a second-rate foreign bloc but by focusing again on parliamentary supremacy as the common expression of a great people. Britain, he believed, was fully capable of going it alone in the world.[101] He never spoke for more than a handful in Parliament, but his arguments struck a deep chord in the Conservative Party.

Unlike the Six, Britain entered the European Community without accepting the fundamental principles upon which it was built. Britain never rejected the principle of national sovereignty or embraced supranationalism. It never saw its national identity connected in any significant way to its continental partners. And it brought a utilitarian approach to an organization that still lived on a European dream. In short, Britain was different—different and awkward.

Charles de Gaulle and Britain

Britain's European partners, of course, were well aware of its awkwardness. They were quite willing, however, to bring the United Kingdom into the club—but on European terms. What they could not understand was why Britain's leaders insisted on joining an organization about which they were at best ambivalent and at worst in fundamental disagreement. The leaders of the Six were willing to negotiate a detailed accession treaty with Britain because they believed it made sense politically and economically to bring in the largest Western European nation-state—all, that is, except Charles de Gaulle.

To say that de Gaulle was a complex figure may be an understatement. A nationalist whose interest in restoring French glory cannot be overstated, de Gaulle was both a geostrategist with an eye on global power politics and a canny domestic politician with an eye on French industrialists, unions, and farmers. Moreover, he was also a thinker with a deep desire to understand the present so he could see the future, and shape it—to his own ends, certainly, but also for humanity's sake.

De Gaulle believed in a united Europe, one independent of but equal to the United States and the Soviet Union, a kind of "third force" that, under French leadership, would break the stalemate between the superpowers. He supported European unity, but his differences with Monnet, Schuman, and Adenauer over what that meant were real. He did not believe in supranational institutions that could bind France economically and politically; he preferred intergovernmental cooperation that would preserve national sovereignty and the identities of the European peoples.[102] Writing in his memoirs, he stated: "It is my belief that a united Europe could not today, any more than in previous times, be a fusion of its peoples, but that it could and should result from a systematic rapprochement. . . . My policy therefore aimed at the setting up of a concert of European states which in developing all sorts of ties between them would increase their interdependence and solidarity."[103]

De Gaulle spoke approvingly of achieving deep economic interdependence among the European nations that shared a common Christian civilization and could become, literally, "an extension of each other."[104] Moreover, the increasing integration of the European states—over some length of time—gave him "every reason to believe that the process of evolution might lead to their confederation."[105] But he did not believe in a functional approach to integration that allowed supranational bureaucrats to integrate by stealth. Rather, he preferred an explicitly political process that gave control to state leaders who, under the guidance of France, would develop Europe into a global superpower. Thus, he was no federalist; but his vision of an interdependent confederation in Europe went far beyond mere international cooperation. The close, constant interaction between the nations of Europe would allow a type of "general will" to emerge (mostly along French lines), implemented by small European institutions with minimal independent powers. His vision of a French-led Europe that would gradually and quite naturally grow together was every bit the reunited Carolingian Christendom envisioned by most of the founders, but achieved by more organic means.[106]

Was Britain part of de Gaulle's Europe? De Gaulle allowed accession talks with Britain; but did he want them to succeed? The negotiations were conducted in good faith, significant progress was made in difficult areas, and the participants had no reason to suspect the French of sabotage.[107] But several pieces of evidence suggest that de Gaulle never intended to let Britain join the EEC. First, he was unwilling to entertain British entry into his proposed European political union—the so-called Fouchet Plan of 1961.[108] His new union would have been intergovernmental in character—a "Europe of states"—with few institutions and a mandate to bring political direction to foreign, defense, cultural, and economic policies. The British were happy to stay out of these negotiations, but the Dutch and the Belgians insisted that they be included as a counter to the Franco-German bloc. The Belgian Paul-Henri Spaak told the French: "Since you do not wish to have supranationality as a guarantee for the small states and since you wish to construct a Europe à l'Anglaise, at least grant us the English who will be there to restore balance."[109] The talks failed in mid-1962, when de Gaulle refused to allow the Low Countries to make a political union conditional on British membership in the EEC.[110] A second piece of evidence for de Gaulle's doubts about Britain was a leaked memorandum known as the "Peyrefitte Note" of August 29, 1960 (quoted publicly in September 1962). The note seemed to indicate a Gaullist strategy to exclude Britain from the EEC without appearing anti-British.[111]

Then, finally, there were the utterances of the general himself. De Gaulle was unwilling to rule out British membership directly, but he was hardly enthusiastic. In his first public appearance after the British application, he was asked directly if he approved. His answer was typically vague: "We know very well how complex the problem is, but it seems that it is now the time to tackle it, and for my part I am quite happy that this is so."[112] In private the general said "he feared that it would take a long time for the many difficulties to be settled."[113] One cause for his concern was the change that Britain (and the Scandinavians) would bring. Would an enlarged EEC be altered beyond recognition? At one point, he quite openly acknowledged to Macmillan that France's voice would be muted in an expanded Common Market, which he clearly regretted. He was also sure the larger organization would be more susceptible to demands from the "rest of the world" (presumably meaning the Commonwealth and, perhaps, the United States). "The result," he said, "would be a sort of world free trade area which might be desirable in itself, but would not be European."[114] In short, de Gaulle was not sure that the Six were ready for Britain.[115]

In the end, however, the most troubling question for de Gaulle was whether Britain was ready for the Six. After rounds of difficult negotiations, it was, indeed, a question that all six EEC member states were asking, even those that disagreed with de Gaulle's vision of Europe. Were the British "really prepared to become European, in either the 'European' or the Gaullist sense?"[116] De Gaulle had his doubts, which he was willing to express directly.

In June 1962 de Gaulle hosted Macmillan at a summit that many of the negotiators hoped would provide the political will for an agreement. Technical issues were touched on, but the focus was on "Britain's readiness to become fully European."[117] Macmillan made his best case for Britain's new approach to Europe. De

Gaulle seemed impressed by the lengths to which Macmillan now seemed willing to go to secure membership, but he still had questions.[118] Thus, de Gaulle enumerated Britain's distinctions: an island psychology, an open perspective on the world, a natural connection to the United States, and Anglo-Saxon habits. Britain was reorienting toward Europe, but it was not yet ready to break its ties with "the world beyond Europe." "Great Britain," he later told George Pompidou and Maurice Couve de Murville, "is coming towards Europe, but it has not yet arrived."[119]

De Gaulle continued his questioning of Britain's fitness for becoming integrated with Europe at a second summit with Macmillan at Rambouillet in December 1962. Freed from reliance on the Mouvement Républicain Populaire and centrist support in the National Assembly, he was now able to take a harder line. He was not surprised by the difficulty of the negotiations, given the great changes that both sides would need to make before Britain could be accepted in the EEC. According to notes from the meeting, de Gaulle announced that "it was not possible for Britain to enter [the EEC] tomorrow and . . . felt that the arrangements inside the Six might be too rigid for the United Kingdom." Britain and the Six, however, had launched on a certain course and "in the end agreement would be reached."[120] Macmillan was crushed; he knew that no agreement would appear soon.[121]

The denouement came on January 14, 1963, at one of de Gaulle's famous Élysée Palace press conferences. De Gaulle answered a direct question about Britain's entry into the Common Market with a long speech touching on all the great themes he had raised since the British application. Emphasizing the compatibility of the six member states of the EEC, he highlighted their economic, commercial, and geopolitical similarities, but he also underlined the common way of life that the continentals shared.[122] Britain, de Gaulle argued, had not participated in the Common Market's formation, and it had, in fact, tried to undermine it. When it did apply for membership, it had demanded entry on its own terms. This led to only one conclusion: Britain was not ready for EEC membership; it was not "one of us," it was not European. As de Gaulle put it, "England in effect is insular, she is maritime, she is linked through her exchanges, her markets, her supply lines to the most diverse and often the most distant countries; she pursues essentially industrial and commercial activities, and only slight agricultural ones. She has in all her doings very marked and very original habits and traditions. In short, the nature, the structure, the very situation (conjuncture) that are England's differ profoundly from those of the continentals."[123]

De Gaulle thus made it clear that geography, history, and economic development had made Britain different in many ways, but the ways that mattered most were cultural—England's "original habits and traditions," its very "nature." Furthermore, Britain in de Gaulle's view would bring with it the United States, which would one day come to dominate the EEC. Britain would be America's "Trojan Horse":[124] "This community, increasing in such fashion, would see itself faced with problems of economic relations with all kinds of other States, and first with the United States. It is to be foreseen that the cohesion of its members, who would be very numerous and diverse, would not endure for long, and that ultimately it would appear as a colossal Atlantic community under American dependence and direction, and which would quickly have absorbed the community of Europe."[125]

De Gaulle would not let Britain in; Europe did not span the English Channel. De Gaulle thought of "Europe in continental or, rather, in Carolingian terms, and . . . [regarded] the United Kingdom not as a natural part of Europe but as a part of a rival Anglo-Saxon power group."[126] Britain could change, but that would take a long time. Meanwhile, de Gaulle would exercise his veto.

De Gaulle's press conference did not immediately end negotiations, however. France's EEC partners believed that an agreement was imminent, and they expressed anger at de Gaulle's unilateral decision. A flurry of activity achieved some progress toward an agreement, but on January 29 the French brought the negotiations to a screeching halt. In a defiant tone, Couve de Murville stated, "We are trying to be sure that the Europe we are building is a European Europe."[127] There was some talk of the Five (minus France) creating a grouping that included Britain, but the British were ambivalent and the Five were unwilling to stand up to the French.[128] Any effort to overturn de Gaulle's decision, moreover, would need to be led by Adenauer, but the German leader had already made clear his first priority: rapprochement with France. A week after de Gaulle's fateful press conference, Adenauer cemented Franco-German friendship by signing the Élysée Treaty alongside de Gaulle in Paris. For the chancellor, integration was first and foremost a Franco-German affair: "Without reconciliation with France, Europe is unthinkable."[129] The British would have to wait.

The British, of course, did enter the EEC, but only after both Adenauer and de Gaulle had left the scene. The applications, the negotiations, and the debates in Britain and in the EEC looked very familiar in the late 1960s and early 1970s. The only difference was the outcome. Britain entered only after Edward Heath had convinced the British people that national sovereignty would be guarded with utmost care, and the Six accepted the fact that Britain would always be an awkward partner, but thought it better in than out. The historic divisions remained after accession; the two visions of Europe had not grown together, but were planted next to each other in the same garden.

Nordic Cooperation

No major postwar political force in Norden advocated joining a federal Europe, although a few exceptions proved the rule. For example, in 1949 the Conservative Danish politician Ole Bjørn Kraft advocated a gradual relinquishment of sovereignty to a United States of Europe, but he toned down his federalist rhetoric when he became foreign minister in 1950.[130] Later, Trygve Bratteli, Norway's prime minister during the 1972 accession debate, argued almost alone for the supranational pooling of sovereignty (using the principle of subsidiarity, without labeling it as such).[131] But most Nordic elites, even those considered "pro-European," ignored continental notions of political Europe.[132] Why should the Nordic countries exchange their tested institutions for new inventions? As Lee Miles described Sweden, "The Swedish elite . . . spurned a federal Europe on political grounds. The Erlander government saw little attraction in replacing the country's successful and mature national institutions with untried and rather nebulous European ones. . . . This essentially chauvinistic pride in the superiority of 'Swedish democracy' was a substantial buffer to the economic attractions of European integration."[133]

Suspicion of supranational institutions discouraged the Nordics from joining a Community that offered obvious economic benefits. Their reluctance to seek full membership did not signal a lack of interest in other forms of cooperation. Various groups of the Nordic countries had joined the OEEC (Denmark, Iceland, Norway, and Sweden), the Council of Europe (Denmark, Norway, and Sweden), NATO (Denmark, Iceland, and Norway), and soon EFTA (Denmark, Iceland, Norway, Sweden—and eventually Finland). And all but Finland participated in the failed WFTA talks. All these organizations, however, were intergovernmental; none required a substantial sacrifice of sovereignty. The Nordics' vision of European "unity" lined up much more with Britain's than with the Six's: They favored free trade, rather than an all-encompassing common market, or much worse, an economic and political "union" (a word that still reminded the Norwegians of their uncomfortable century under Swedish rule[134]).

Nordic cooperation was the other alternative to Europe-wide political and economic organization. For the Nordic countries, cooperation among themselves was favored on cultural grounds. Immediately after the war, the Nordic elites had begun considering new efforts to cooperate based on their shared way of life. As the Danish Social Democratic chair, Hans Hedtoft, told the Swedes in 1945, "Such a striving towards greater unity in Norden finds its natural justification in the solidarity which is rooted in the Nordic peoples' mutual descent, common linguistic heritage and the rest of the cultural affinity binding the area together for more than a thousand years."[135] Frederik Dalgaard, a Danish labor leader, put it more colorfully: "Within the context of international cooperation, the old saying, birds of a feather flock together [lige børn leger bedst], seems relevant."[136]

Although a common culture drew the Nordics together, differing interests made reaching agreements difficult. The first initiative came, ironically, from neutral Sweden, which proposed the creation of a Scandinavian Defense Alliance in May 1948.[137] After the experience of the war, the Nordic countries sought collective agreements for defense, as none of them wanted ever again to face a more powerful foe alone. The Swedes, however, demanded that the alliance remain neutral in the Cold War, while Denmark and Norway wanted to link the Nordic alliance to the emerging Atlantic Alliance to ensure American protection. The talks ended when Denmark and Norway joined NATO and Sweden reconfirmed its policy of neutrality.

A second attempt at Nordic cooperation involved economic policy and spanned a decade. In 1947 Norway called for closer economic coordination among the Scandinavian countries, in part to counter a perceived US threat to their economic sovereignty.[138] Sweden and Denmark responded positively, and a committee was established to explore options, including a Nordic customs union. By 1950 that option had been ruled out—largely due to Norway's high tariffs and domestic opposition to "domination" by its former imperial masters.[139] The Norwegians then suggested the possibility of a free trade area. More studies were conducted, and again, in March 1954, a customs union (which crept back into discussions) and other types of cooperation were discussed, but without result. The Scandinavians, however, launched a new effort for a customs union in late 1954, which achieved a consensus on common tariffs over most intra-Scandinavian trade in late 1958. A formal agreement was ready a few months later, but no action was ever taken; the customs union was "stillborn."[140] As Danish prime minister Per Haekkerup put it, "No stone was left unturned, no question unanswered. . . . But while we were discussing and elaborating these problems from every conceivable angle, developments in Europe passed us by."[141] While these trade talks wore on, the Nordics joined the WFTA negotiations, which ultimately led to the creation of EFTA in 1960.

The final effort to create a Nordic organization came after the second de Gaulle veto in 1967. All five Nordic countries agreed in February 1970 to establish the Nordic Economic Union (NORDEK), which established a customs union, a common agricultural policy, and a schedule for deeper cooperation in "taxation, budgetary policy, credit policy, and regional policy."[142] The agreement envisioned a significant organizational structure for NORDEK, but decision making would remain intergovernmental. Finland soon made it clear, however, that it would not join NORDEK if any members joined the EEC. And because Denmark, Norway, and possibly Sweden intended to do just that, NORDEK died a swift death.

Not all efforts to achieve Nordic unity ended in failure. The region's national aviation companies established the Scandinavian Airlines System in 1951. The Nordic governments created a passport union in 1952 and a common labor market in 1954. More important, in 1952 the Nordic parliaments established the Nordic Council (Finland joined in 1955) to facilitate the discussion of issues of mutual interest in an informal, nonbureaucratic environment. The council promoted Nordic cooperation on education, culture, and the environment, but it left high politics to other organizations. All these ventures led to a running conversation that produced joint action when national interests converged. Nils Andrén called it "cobweb integration," an apt metaphor for the sort of integration desired by the Nordics: informal, noncoercive, without any odor of supranationality.

The Scandinavian Debates

Mitigating their visceral rejection of federal ideas and supranational institutions, the Nordic countries recognized that they were small players in an economically and politically competitive environment. They valued their independence, but they found themselves dependent on bigger players for security and markets. They could not sit on the sidelines while their neighbors entered cooperative arrangements. Thus they were constantly searching for membership in economic organizations that would bring them commercial benefits without political costs.

This searching created domestic tensions and divisions in the region's three Scandinavian countries as they grappled with their relations with an integrating Europe. The debates over integration in Denmark and Norway—countries that held referenda on the question—roughly pitted a prointegration cosmopolitan center against an alliance of left-wing socialists and nationalists of various stripes. Sweden escaped a full-fledged national debate because it chose not to apply for membership alongside Britain, Ireland, Denmark, and Norway, and consequently it did not hold a popular referendum. A lively debate among political and economic elites from July 1961 until the de Gaulle veto in January 1963, however, did establish Sweden's EEC policy for a generation. Sweden, like Denmark and Norway, faced the possibility that its major trading partners would all join the Common Market, leaving the country to fend for itself. But would membership be compatible with Swedish neutrality and social democracy? Swedish politicians struggled with this question as Britain, Denmark, and Norway moved toward EEC membership.

Sweden's decision to reaffirm its international neutrality forced national leaders to draw a dark line between economic and political policy. Its leaders assumed that any political cooperation restricting its freedom of association could be construed as "taking sides" in global political struggles, thus undermining its credibility as a neutral power. And its officials also assumed that it needed to deepen economic cooperation with its major trading partners or risk undermining its hard-won prosperity. The trick for Sweden would be to join the EEC's efforts to integrate economically while opting out of the neutrality-busting political bits. The Social Democratic government led by Tage Erlander decided very early to bypass accession in favor of official "association" (Article 238 of the Rome Treaty). Erlander outlined the policy in a famous August 1961 speech to the Metal Workers' Union in which he rejected full EEC membership as unnecessary to protect the economy, and as threatening to Sweden's national identity. But the key reason for rejecting accession was its incompatibility with the policy of neutrality. Membership, in Erlander's view, would prevent Sweden from pursuing an independent trade policy with third parties, preclude Sweden's withdrawal from obligations during wartime, and force it to take part in a process that the Six took for granted as "a step on the way to a real federation."[143] The alternative for the Social Democrats was an association agreement that allowed

Sweden to negotiate away unacceptable elements of EEC membership. Erlander's "Metal Speech" sparked a discussion among the political parties and sectoral interests that culminated in a Riksdag debate in October 1961. The Communist Party rejected any association with the EEC, but most Swedish interests lined up behind the government's approach. Differences were over means, not ends. Sweden applied for associate membership in December 1961, with Erlander claiming "the support of practically unanimous Swedish public opinion."[144] The Six, however, were not entirely enthusiastic about Sweden's condition-laden application. And the French veto made the point moot.

By the time of the second British application, the Swedish government had modified—if ever so slightly—its position on Europe. After the Empty Chair Crisis of the mid-1960s, some Nordic leaders were convinced that the EEC had moved significantly in their direction. In a 1969 speech in Malmö, the Swedish ambassador to France, Gunnar Hägglöf, argued that the era of supranational integration was over: "Against the background of the past twelve years' experience of applying the Rome Treaties, and considering the changing world political climate, it is difficult to believe that the original political aims of the Rome Treaties will be achieved and that Western Europe will become a supranational unity. . . . The ideas that dominated in Western Europe at the time of the foundation of the Rome Treaties appear today as fairly outdated."[145]

If, in fact, the Community had rejected its supranational method, the way might be open for full EEC membership. Once again Sweden applied to the Commission, but this time left open the "form" of membership. Once again the French aborted the application process; but in 1970, with de Gaulle gone, the Swedes faced a real possibility for membership. New developments in the EEC, however, gave Swedish elites cause for concern. The Werner Plan (1969), calling for economic and monetary union, and the Davignon Report (1970) on political cooperation, calling for a single foreign policy, convinced the Swedes that the Six were again serious about supranational cooperation. Swedish attempts to engage the Six about association without membership were rebuffed, leaving no option but complete withdrawal from the membership process. Sweden settled for signing a free trade agreement with the Community in July 1972, and with that the discussion of Sweden's relations with the EEC went quiet.[146]

Of the other two Scandinavian countries, Denmark experienced the least contentious debate. The country was still very much under the influence of the nineteenth-century Grundtvigian people's democracy, which had created a homogeneous society, even by Scandinavian standards. Typical rural/urban, left/right, and elite/mass cleavages were less important in Denmark than in the other Nordic countries, especially on the question of Europe. To most Danes, the facts were clear. The country depended heavily on two trading partners, Germany (which they did not much care for) and Britain (which they quite liked). It could live with Germany being inside the EEC; but if Britain joined, Denmark could not afford to remain on the outside.[147] The Danes agreed, however, that they were not interested in joining a federal Europe and that the country should continue to pursue a Nordic solution.[148]

Debates occurred over Denmark's first two applications for EEC membership in the 1960s, but the key public discussion took place during the referendum campaign for membership in 1972. For the "yes side"—including most of the political establishment—EEC membership was the only practical choice; the economic benefits of full membership far outweighed any minimal costs to national autonomy. These "pragmatists"—found mostly among right-wing Conservatives and Liberals, but also in the Radical Liberal and Social Democratic parties—argued that the continental federal dream was no longer realistic and would not challenge Danish sovereignty. Moreover, the accession of Britain, Ireland, and a new Nordic bloc (Denmark and Norway) would surely push the Continent in a more democratic and intergovernmental direction.[149]

The "no side," of course, disagreed. Drawn more heavily from the political left (in particular, the Socialist People's Party), these Danes stressed the threats to national identity posed by membership. "The People's Movement Against the EC" and other antimembership groups tried to move the debate away from economics, where a pragmatic cost/benefit analysis would prevail, to politics, where new commitments (as entailed in the Davignon Report) would abridge Danish sovereignty. As Gert Petersen of the Socialist People's Party complained to the Folketing: "The continuing tendency to view the Common Market as a matter of cattle and how much butter we can sell is amazing. The Common Market is a lot more than that. It is also narrow political cooperation, including foreign policy cooperation, and one can blame the Common Market for a lot of things, but not that it is trying to hide its political nature, because it isn't."[150]

That "political nature," argued the antimembership groups, would force the country into a capitalist liberal order that would soon threaten the Danish welfare state. Furthermore, the Germans would soon buy up all the Danish summer cottages. Membership in the EEC, according to the no side, was not the only alternative. Norden, they argued, was the right choice for Denmark; EEC membership was a Nordic sellout.

The first referendum campaign in Denmark, unlike the ones that followed, remained relatively calm. The no side was ultimately unable to strike a nationalist nerve in the electorate, and the referendum passed easily. But proponents had downplayed the European political project, thus risking voter ire if the EEC took a federalist turn—as it most certainly did.

Finally, it was in Norway where the membership debate was most contentious. Norway found itself in a situation much like Denmark's: bound economically and politically to Britain and unhindered by a commitment to neutrality. Like Denmark, a pragmatic elite found in EEC membership the answer to the threat of economic isolation. But unlike the situation in Denmark, the classic European social cleav-ages did divide Norway: center versus periphery, urban versus rural, owner versus worker.[151] Norway had forged its independence from Denmark and Sweden in social revolts involving a nationalist periphery—the "people"—against a statist center with ties to Copenhagen or Stockholm. For many Norwegians, the fight against EEC membership looked much like the battles that had forged the Norwegian nation.[152]

Before the referendum campaign, the political elites, led by both Labor and non-socialist governments, won Storting approval of necessary constitutional changes for membership (March 1962) and for Norway's first and second applications. The popular debate in Norway in the 1960s developed in anticipation of the consultative referendum the parties had promised the electorate before applying for membership in 1962. The debate was, of course, cut short twice by de Gaulle in the 1960s, but it bloomed in full in 1971 after a scandal brought down the center-right government of Per Borten and freed former coalition partners (particularly the Center Party) to argue against membership. A minority Labor government led by Trygve Bratteli picked up the promembership mantle.

The Norwegian yes side, like its counterparts in the other Protestant applicant countries, was forced to minimize the political agenda of the Six. With the excep-tion of Bratteli, who accepted the need to pool sovereignty, Norwegian promarket elites denied that the Community would evolve toward a federal model.[153] They, like their Danish counterparts, focused on economic benefits of membership. More frequently, the yes campaign took a negative approach, stressing the perils facing a small country and the dire commercial and security consequences if Norway were to reject an offer to join. To the yes side, Norway was a European nation like other European nations, and it was imperative to join wider efforts to improve the Con-tinent—perhaps by introducing to the rest of Europe the more democratic and solidaristic ways of Scandinavia. Norway, for many cosmopolitan urban voters, was small and a bit stifling; membership in the Common Market promised a bigger world and greater freedom.

As in the other Protestant countries, the pro-EEC side in Norway was an uneasy alliance between left and right, socialist and nonsocialist. The Labor Party estab-lishment supported membership, despite misgivings about the conservative nature of the Continent and threats to the Scandinavian welfare state. Norway, in their minds, could not risk isolation. The probusiness Conservative Party staunchly fa-vored membership, as did the more cosmopolitan and urban parts of the Liberal and Christian People's parties. Business associations and labor unions fell in behind their respective pro-EEC parties. The left-wing and right-wing establishments worked to-gether—uneasily to be sure—but their power and money could not overcome the resistance of their ragtag opponents.

Membership opponents coalesced around an extraparty social organization, "The People's Movement against Norwegian Membership in the Common Market," which was founded in late 1970. The political left figured prominently in this organization. The Communists, the new Socialist People's Party, and left-wing members of the Liberal Party played important roles, as did the leftist elements of the ruling Labor Party, openly defying their leaders. Many of these activists were young and had been deeply influenced by the democratic, grassroots, counterculture movement sweeping North America and Western Europe. But these activists were joined by nonsocialists from the agrarian Center Party, and mostly rural and conservative elements of the Liberal and Christian People's parties. Financial backing came largely from agricultural groups. These were "the people," the "true Norwegians," once again fighting the international establishment to save the nation.

The arguments on the no side were designed to touch Norwegian hearts. Anti-marketers, rejecting assertions that EEC membership would entail no loss of sovereignty, pointed out that the Treaty of Rome clearly envisioned "an ever-closer union." This wording proved difficult to explain away. As Neumann points out, "in Norwegian debate, formulations in treaties tend to be taken at face value . . . There exists an ideal that people do and should 'mean what they say,' and variations on this theme are not treated simply as a matter of cultural variation, but as a moral flaw."[154] An ever-closer union with the Continent was not attractive to the left, because Europe was not a worthy partner. As the anti-EEC activists in the Labor Party put it: "Yet there is also a Europe which has been responsible for wars of conquest, colonialism, as well as economic and social oppression. The danger is great that . . . [this European tendency will] envelop us if we join the Common Market."[155] Rather than stand for equality and justice, Norway in the EEC would become one of the oppressors.

The country's rural nationalists took a different approach. Joining the EEC, in their eyes, would hasten the process of modernization in Norway. Centralization, urbanization, and secularization all threatened the Norwegian way of life. EEC policies would undermine farmers and fishers, forcing them out of business, depopulating the countryside, and ending these traditional vocations that embodied the very essence of Norwegianness. Norwegian control of Norwegian land would become more and more tenuous, making any claim to territorial sovereignty a complete sham.[156] Community, sovereignty, self-government, nation—these were the values of "the people."[157] And the no side played on these effectively.

The campaign in 1972 devolved into shrill slogans shouted across a widening social gap. Friends fell out, families divided, and—after the votes were counted and the referendum had been soundly defeated—the Labor government fell and the political parties split. Labor lost members to the Socialist People's Party; the Liberals went into severe decline; and a new right-wing movement appeared. An exhausted nation went silent and tried to forget.

By the end of the postwar period, two of Europe's Protestant countries had joined the EEC, and the rest had become formally associated economically. But

Britain and Denmark had entered on what amounted to false pretenses. The British and Danish elites had promised their electorates that joining the EEC would cost little in sovereignty and that federation was no longer the goal of integration. Britain and Denmark busied themselves inside the EEC trying to make sure they could keep their promises. Meanwhile, Protestants within the Six also found themselves at odds with Catholics over the nature of integration.

Protestants in the Catholic Six

Britain and the Nordics were Protestant countries standing outside the Community until 1973, but two of the original Schuman Six were countries with large Protestant populations: West Germany and the Netherlands. West Germany was closely divided between Catholics and Protestants, with Protestants by 1950 holding a small (51 percent) advantage over the very large Catholic minority (46 percent). Protestants had marginally increased their relative size in the new West Germany (up from 49 percent in 1939), but the biggest change was not in the sizes of the confessional communities but in their homogeneity. Due to the massive migration of peoples in Central Europe just after the war, most boroughs in the new West Germany became more confessionally mixed, with more Protestants and Catholics living side by side than in 1939.[158] In the Netherlands, World War II had proved less disruptive to the confessional pillarization of society and the general religious trends evident before the war. Catholics continued to increase their strength, mainly through higher birthrates, to approximately 40 percent of the population, with Protestants falling and citizens with "no religious identification" rising to claim equal shares of about one-quarter of the public.[159]

The relative sizes of the confessional communities in West Germany and the Netherlands, however, mask the political strength of the Catholics (see chapter 5). This was particularly true in West Germany, where the Catholics dominated the Christian Democratic Union of Germany (Christlich Demokratische Union Deutschlands, CDU) until at least the mid-1960s. But this was also true of the Netherlands, where the Catholics participated in every postwar coalition, taking the lead in six of ten governments from 1946 to 1970. That being said, the Protestants in both countries were not without a political voice. The question is, How did they view European integration? Did they adopt views consistent with their Protestant confessional cultures and those of the Anglo-Nordics? Or did they embrace the Christian Democratic perspective?

Taken as a whole, German and Dutch Protestants demonstrated a commitment to European economic and political cooperation, but they resisted—at least initially—the drive to federalism. These Protestants pressed for free trade alternatives to common markets, and they longed for Britain's accession to champion the free

trade (and Protestant) cause. In general, the Protestants here advocated strong Atlantic ties and resisted de Gaulle's attempt to create a European "third force" strong
enough to stand between the superpowers. They, like their Anglo-Nordic counterparts, distrusted (at least to some degree) their Catholic colleagues, who belonged
to an extraordinarily tight community. Tensions between the communities characterized intraparty politics in the CDU and intracoalition politics in the Netherlands.
But in both settings the friction seldom led to bouts of anti-Catholic rhetoric. Restraint, of course, was less necessary among the Dutch antiestablishment Protestant parties, which resulted in occasional eruptions of a type that Ian Paisley would
recognize and embrace.

West Germany

The Christian Democratic Union in West Germany was a large "catchall" party that
captured several political tendencies. It was also, as we have noted, biconfessional,
with approximately 30 percent of its members identifying as Lutherans.[160] In foreign
policy, including European policy, CDU leaders tended to diverge along confessional
lines. The Catholics—led by Konrad Adenauer and assisted by Walter Hallstein,
Heinrich von Brentano, and Franz Josef Strauß—pressed the Catholic Christian
Democratic vision of a united Christian Continent and a new European identity as
a defense against Anglo-Saxon materialism and the totalitarianism and barbarism
of the East. This new "bias toward continental cooperation" was not the product
of pragmatic policy debates but was, in fact, "part of the very nature of the [Chris-
tian Democratic] Union."[161] Although the Catholics defined the party's ideological
core, they were sometimes opposed by a small, more pragmatic party faction led
primarily by Protestants—most prominently the minister of economic affairs, Ludwig Erhard, who was joined in the 1960s by the minister of foreign affairs, Gerhard
Schröder.[162]

Erhard was the man most responsible for the postwar lifting of German price
controls, the introduction of a new currency (the deutschmark) and the design of
West Germany's "social market economy." As the man in charge of the country's
economy for nearly two decades, he was the architect of the nation's famed economic miracle. Unlike most of his Catholic Christian Democratic colleagues, he was
an unabashed economic liberal. He thought highly of the Austrian School's Ludwig
von Mises and Fredrick von Hayek, but he considered the German/Swiss economist
Wilhelm Röpke his greatest influence.[163] Röpke, a Protestant from a long line of
Lutheran pastors, was an advocate of free markets in an age of state-led planned
economies. This support, however, was tempered by a belief that unchecked freedom could "weaken the social order and undermine the civic foundation of the market system."[164] Markets would succeed only if they rested on solid communities:
"Only a solid social structure predicated upon individual virtue, cohesive families,

and local communities could counterbalance the frequently disruptive side effects of the dynamic, highly efficient market system. A decay in those fundamental building blocks of social order must lead to atomization, alienation, and ever-increasing demands for state control over the economy."[165] Röpke vehemently opposed bureaucratic state planning, but he spoke just as strongly against the centralizing, atomizing, mechanizing, and ultimately dehumanizing tendencies of modern capitalism. In his view, families, local communities, civic organizations, and churches, as well as democratic governments at every level, had a role to play in checking the dark side of capitalism. Small was beautiful; local was best.

Röpke's economic vision was Erhard's social market economy. It had much in common with Catholic social teaching, especially in its emphasis on subsidiarity and support for the family. But his version differed in two important ways. First, Röpke eschewed protectionism as bureaucratic and market distorting, and he promoted the freeing of trade on as wide a scale as possible. Second, he opposed supranational institutions that would centralize decision making and proliferate bureaucracies that would simply spew regulations. He did not, however, reject integration out of hand. He believed in the spiritual unity of Europe and supported efforts to increase cooperation, but he also believed it absurd to think that simply creating institutions would somehow produce a united Europe. "Europe, rightly understood," he argued in 1964,

> cannot be primarily defined as a vast machine designed for maximum production, and the goal of integration cannot be determined by the output of automobiles or cement. What holds Europe together in the widest sense is something of a spiritual nature: the common patrimony of Humanism and Christianity. Nothing can be more ludicrous than the belief that this bond can be replaced by the bureaucracy of the European Commission and high authorities, by planners, economocrats, and technical visionaries. The danger, however, is very real that the true order of values and aims may be reversed and that economic integration may be carried through in such a way that it endangers the real meaning of Europe.[166]

Europe would not be built through technical efforts. If Europe were to unite politically, it would do so organically after many years and much peaceful exchange. For Röpke integration was a bottom-up, not top-down, process.

Erhard approached European integration in the same vein. A strong proponent of free trade, like Röpke he had severe reservations about the integration process and the top-down Monnet method. At one point he even called the EEC "macroeconomic nonsense" and "European incest" (*europäische Inzucht*).[167] Erhard resisted the creation of the Common Market among the Six "because of its protectionist and *dirigiste* elements," pressing hard for a wider free trade agreement when the British offered their proposal.[168] His objective was to create a liberal trading system by "functional integration." In his view, "the abolition of trade barriers and discrimination, currency convertibility, and other liberalizing policies would lead (almost automatically, he thought) to political union." He rejected the federalist approach of

Foreign Minister Heinrich von Brentano and his deputy Walter Hallstein and even a milder form of institutionalism in his own ministry that called for trade liberalization within the institutional structure of the Common Market. Erhard saw these efforts as too narrow and too tied to the French. He feared the division of the West if a wider agreement could not be reached, and he quite frankly favored an arrangement that would bring Germany into closer contact with the "Anglo-Saxons." He commented to Adenauer in 1956: "[It] is becoming ever clearer that we can achieve our most important objectives only through the closest cooperation with the United States and Great Britain."[169] Moving toward the Europe of the Six was moving away from the Atlantic Alliance. Adenauer rejected that assumption and backed the Treaty of Rome and the Community of the Six. He then prevented Erhard from leading the German delegation to Paris for the last round of free trade talks in November 1958.

The conflict between the German Protestants and their free trade approach to integration and the Catholics and their continental approach spilled into the 1960s as a battle between the Protestant "Atlanticists" and Catholic "Gaullists."[170] The Protestants in the CDU were on the rise in the early 1960s, as Adenauer's long tenure as chancellor came to a close. Erhard became chancellor (1963), and fellow Protestants Gerhard Schröder (foreign affairs) and Kai-Uwe von Hassel (defense) took key cabinet posts. These Atlanticists argued for the closest possible ties with the United States and Britain, and they vehemently protested the French veto of British EEC membership. The French—and probably most of the Gaullists in his own party— considered Erhard "no friend of European integration."[171] The Gaullists, led by Adenauer, still party chair, and Christian Social Union leaders Franz Josef Strauß and Baron Karl Theodor zu Guttenberg, supported de Gaulle's push for an integrated Europe as a third force in international relations, perhaps with its own nuclear force. A reconciled France and Germany were at the core of this vision of Europe—all other relationships were secondary. In truth, the real dispute between the Atlanticists and Gaullists was about the international community in which the two sets of elites felt most at home. Protestants looked north to Britain, and Catholics looked west to France.

The Netherlands

The Dutch approach to integration was complex and paradoxical. Their governments often resisted continental integration, yet championed supranationalism. They promoted supranational institutions, but insisted on final authority resting with a Council of Ministers. They favored free trade agreements, yet proposed a common agriculture policy and insisted on a customs union. They pressed for British membership, but ignored Britain's obvious distaste for supranationalism.

Dutch European policy cannot be explained using a simple Catholic/Protestant dichotomy. The presence of secular and Socialist influences in almost every postwar government and the mostly minor nuances that distinguished Protestants from

Catholics in the Dutch consensual system doom to failure any attempt to apply a strict rule based on confessional community. Dutch integration policy is better understood as a peculiar synthesis of several competing tendencies. Nevertheless, Dutch leaders still tended to favor the visions of integration characteristic of their confessional cultures. Catholic political elites (often with the backing of Labor Party leaders) were more likely than Protestants to support European federalism on principle and favored integration with the Six over broader cooperative schemes. Protestants, conversely, supported supranationalism on pragmatic grounds—as protection for small countries—and looked to Britain, rightly or wrongly, as a welcome, like-minded partner in the integration process.

The synthesis of these two dynamics played out in Dutch policy throughout the postwar period. In the late 1940s Dutch governments, whether led by Catholics or Labor, approached integration cautiously, much to the consternation of the principled federalists sitting in Parliament.[172] The Netherlands was far more interested in economic integration than in political union. Liberal foreign minister Dirk Stikker, following an earlier British proposal in the OEEC, drew up a plan in 1949–50 to dramatically reduce import tariffs on a sector-by-sector basis. The Stikker Plan, however, ran into opposition from several quarters (although not from the Scandinavians) and was soon lost in the excitement over the Schuman Declaration.[173] The Dutch were, again, initially skeptical about the supranational elements of the coal and steel community. In Stikker's view, Monnet's High Authority represented an unacceptable erosion of national sovereignty. The Dutch agreed to participate in the Schuman discussions only on the condition that a workable institutional arrangement for the new community be found (a condition that, incidentally, the Six did not extend to the British). During negotiations the Dutch proposed a Council of Ministers to oversee the High Authority, a plan the other five countries accepted. Meanwhile, the Dutch government directed socialist Agriculture Minister Sicco Mansholt, a committed federalist, to develop a plan (the "Green Pool") for integrating agriculture. Mansholt took a very different approach to sectoral integration than Stikker and proposed a community based on the institutional structure being developed for coal and steel. By now the Six were bogged down in negotiations over the EDC and the European Political Community, in which the Dutch had only reluctantly agreed to participate. Dutch negotiators pushed hard to make the EDC as intergovernmental as possible and insisted on an association agreement with the British.[174] All, of course, came to naught in 1954.

Already in 1953, however, the Dutch were pressing for more comprehensive economic integration. Foreign Minister Wim Beyen launched his Beyen Plan for a "common market" method of economic integration to little effect in 1953, but after the failure of the EDC, the Six returned to the core of Beyen's plan at Messina in 1955. The Dutch, like the British, preferred to negotiate a detailed treaty; but the French refused. The alternative for the Dutch, short of abandoning the talks altogether, was to support the creation of supranational institutions as the best defense against big state bullies. Thus the Netherlands, led by Catholic foreign minister Joseph Luns, converted and became a champion of Monnet-style European integration—just as the French under de Gaulle took a dramatic intergovernmental turn.[175] The Dutch opposed de Gaulle's efforts to gut the Commission, squeeze the Community's budget, and delay the implementation of weighted voting in the Council of Ministers. De Gaulle's attempt to build an intergovernmental umbrella over the entire Community structure (the Fouchet Plan) also ran into the Dutch supranational agenda, not to speak of their Atlanticist instincts.[176] From the Dutch point of view, de Gaulle's actions showed why the Community needed supranational institutions. As for reconciling their new commitment to supranationalism with continued advocacy of British membership, the Dutch placed their faith in the process of socialization. According to Bernard Bouwman, "[Foreign Minister] Luns hoped that the British government would undergo a process of 'socialisation' and realise that in the era of interdependence decision making should move beyond the nation-state."[177]

By the end of the 1970s, then, the Netherlands was a staunch defender of supranational integration while maintaining an Atlanticist and free trade orientation. Dutch policy was a compromise. There were committed federalists in the Netherlands, many of them Catholics with deep ties to the Christian Democrats of the Continent. Minister of Social Welfare Marga Klompé, Union leader Jos Serrarens, and longtime Catholic People's Party (Katholieke Volkspartij, KVP) leader Carl Romme were prominent Catholic federalists in the 1950s. But the Catholics were not uniformly committed to the Continent. Luns himself, though a supporter of integration among the Six, questioned the idea of a continental bloc when he noted, "For the Netherlands this conception of continental Europe is strange. It is contrary to its history, its traditions and secular interests."[178] The Protestants, for their part, wondered if the Catholics were up to something devious. Andeweg and Irwin note that all the political parties save the KVP feared a "papist Europe."[179] That fear spilled over most spectacularly into the 1952 government negotiations, when the parties balked at giving the Catholic Luns and the KVP the Foreign Ministry when every other member of the Six had a Catholic foreign minister. To avoid a Catholic monopoly among the European partners, the Dutch parties agreed to appoint two foreign ministers, Luns and the nonaffiliated banker Wim Beyen, with Beyen given responsibility for European negotiations. Ironically, Beyen proved to be somewhat more "European" than Luns, although when Luns took sole control of foreign affairs in 1956, he moved the Netherlands to embrace supranationalism.[180]

Protestants in the Netherlands were still inclined to see their nation as free, sovereign, and specially chosen by God. Early Protestant opinion was against a European federation, which threatened to envelope the special nature of Dutch identity in a "monistic superstate." European ideology to some smacked of "pseudo religion."

By the end of the 1940s, however, Protestant opinion had softened toward European integration as a credible alternative. Anti-Revolutionary Party (ARP) foreign policy spokesman Sieuwert Bruins Slot conceded that there were traces of Christianity left in the old Carolingian Empire, but he stated, "as a Calvinist I cannot be wholly pleased when I take note of the strong Roman Catholic and socialist influences upon this [European] venture."[181] The ARP and Christian Historical Union (CHU), however, strongly favored free trade areas and recognized the need to participate in European integration to achieve this goal; they resisted perceived Catholic and socialist efforts to create an interventionist European state. Gradually, the main Protestant parties accepted integration, but a strong elite/mass divide remained as grassroots resistance to European federalism continued.[182]

The fiercest opposition to integration remained, without a doubt, in the two small Protestant fringe parties, the older Reformed Political Party (Staatkundig Gereformeerde Partij, SGP) and the newer Reformed Political Union (Gereformeerd Politiek Verbond, GPV), created in 1948. Both were anti–Roman Catholic, anti–French Revolution, pro-Dutch sovereignty parties and both took strong stands against the continental community and Dutch participation. The SGP, for instance, favored a decentralized society focused on family and community, but saw the evolving European Community as a concentration of evil power that represented a major step toward world government and the final judgment of God.[183] The fiery GPV, conversely, saw as its mission the defense of the Dutch nation against external and internal foes. For the GPV, the threat was so great that Dutch independence hung in the balance. Evoking the symbols of Dutch nationalism, GVP party leader Piet Jongeling railed against his old party and a federal Europe in 1956:

> The continuance of our people as a free, independent nation under its own lawful government is directly at stake here. . . . But what makes us afraid, yes, what oppresses us to the point of suffocation, is that the children of the reformation today want to go along with the revolution on this matter. . . . These people today march enthusiastically behind the federalist banner with the Catholics and the socialists, on their way to the servants' house of the single European state. Therein lies nigh incomprehensible tragedy. . . .
>
> But when [the ARP and CHU] start cutting the national dikes with their own hands, so that the tides of European secularism, European nihilism, are allowed free reign here, what will remain of this base line of our people's character? . . . If ever a party denied its best and noblest traditions, no, worse, denied the Scripture itself, it is the ARP when it went along with federalism.[184]

As in Northern Ireland and Scandinavia, the deepest opposition to a united Europe came from the vestiges of Protestant nationalism.

The lesson from the mixed confessional member states is that confessional culture matters. The presence of Protestants in West Germany and the Netherlands allows us to test the impact of confessional culture on national leaders operating under the same domestic and international conditions—in effect, controlling for context. What we see in both Germany and the Netherlands are clear tendencies for the Catholics to favor continental integration and for the Protestants to enlarge, liberalize, and Atlanticize the process.

Conclusion

Postwar Protestants understood that security and prosperity depended on cooperation in Europe. Their idea of European cooperation was big and expansive. Throw open the doors; get everyone in; tear down protectionist walls; unleash energy. Protestants wanted to establish some basic rules and then let markets do the work. There was no need to abandon national identities, national ways of life, or distinctive domestic policies. Just as every individual is free, so are nation-states. Anything undermining the autonomy of a free society is unnecessarily coercive and ultimately harmful. Protestants from Britain to Norway to the Netherlands and West Germany all pursued essentially the same vision for Europe: intergovernmental cooperation on a wide scale, free trade, and reliance on the United States for security. Protestant theology that emphasized invisible unity and individual freedom, coupled with the experience of national identity formation and nation building, led Protestants to feel most comfortable with this kind of intergovernmental integration.

To Protestants the European continent felt alien, foreign, stifling, conspiratorial, and aggressive. Some of this was cultural animosity left over from the sixteenth century, but some of it carried a kernel of truth. The continental Catholics were not involved in any Vatican-inspired conspiracy, but approached European cooperation in a far more closed and clubbish way. Catholic leaders favored the culturally comfortable confines of the Continent. They spoke different languages, but despite linguistic differences felt deeper connections that reminded them of village, family and altar. Integration to them was more about trust than rules and institutions. They shared an understanding that a united, federal Europe was the ultimate (if somewhat distant) goal. They trusted the use of state power to manage the economic, political, and social relationships of traditional societies. Continental Europe was the center of their world and the Christian culture that held that world together had to be nurtured and protected from its enemies (the totalitarian Soviet Union) and its friends (the materialistic United States). As Adenauer illustrated so vividly after de Gaulle's veto of Britain's membership, leaders can disagree over policies, but in the end you stick with family. For Catholics of Europe, the Community was warm—like home. New members with disruptive ideas about everything from God to markets were not necessarily welcome. They all knew that Protestants, if they got their way, would change everything—but only de Gaulle faced up to it publicly.

When Protestant majority countries finally entered the EEC they did not abandon their vision of Europe, nor modify it. Instead they fought their corner against the centralizing tendencies of continental Catholics. They entered awkwardly and remained awkward. Most significantly, the presence of Britain and Denmark in the Common Market put the necessary community spirit or "we feeling" out of reach for the European Community as a whole. The entrance of Protestant-majority member states divided a uniting Europe. For many in the Six, de Gaulle was proved right: Britain ruined it.

Notes

1. Michael Charlton, *The Price of Victory* (London: British Broadcasting Corporation, 1983), 13.

2. Ibid., 21.

3. All these quotations are from Winston S. Churchill, "Winston Churchill's Speech [on a Council of Europe]. Zurich, 19 September 1946," Archive of European Integration, available at http://aei.pitt.edu/14362/.

4. Charlton, *Price of Victory*, 40.

5. For a similar interpretation, see Hugo Young, *This Blessed Plot: Britain and Europe from Churchill to Blair* (Woodstock, NY: Overlook Press, 1998), 5–25.

6. Alan Bullock, *Ernest Bevin: Foreign Secretary, 1945–1951* (New York: W. W. Norton, 1983), 787. See also John W. Young, *Britain and European Unity, 1945–1999*, 2nd ed. (Basingstoke, UK: Macmillan, 2000), 37–38.

7. Quoted by Young, *This Blessed Plot*, 13—originally in the *Saturday Evening Post*; also quoted by Wolfram Kaiser, *Using Europe, Abusing the Europeans: Britain and European Integration, 1945–63* (Basingstoke, UK: Macmillan, 1996), 10; and Andrew Moravcsik, *The Choice for Europe: Social Purpose and State Power from Messina to Maastricht* (Ithaca, NY: Cornell University Press, 1998), 124.

8. Charlton, *Price of Victory*, 32.

9. Gumundur Hálfdanarson, "Discussing Europe: Icelandic Nationalism and European Integration," in *Iceland and European Integration: On the Edge*, ed. Baldur Thorhallsson (London: Routledge, 2004), 138.

10. See Henrik Meinander, "On the Brink or In Between? The Conception of Europe in Finnish Identity," in *The Meaning of Europe: Variety and Contention within and among Nations*, ed. Mikael af Malmborg and Bo Stråth (Oxford: Berg, 2002), 156–57.

11. Max Jakobson, *Finland in the New Europe* (Westport, CT: Praeger, 1998), 63.

12. For a discussion of the role of President Urho Kekkonen as protector of Finnish freedom or Soviet collaborator, see Martti Häikiö, "Finland's Neutrality 1944–1994," in *Die Neutralen und die Europäische Integration 1945–1995 / The Neutrals and the European Integration 1945–1995*, ed. Michael Gehler and Rolf Steininger (Vienna: Böhlau Verlag, 2000), 206–8.

13. Tapani Paavonen, "Finland's Relationship to West European Economic Integration 1947–1958," in *Die Neutralen*, ed. Gehler and Steininger, 226.

14. Ibid., 218–25.

15. Lee Miles, *Sweden and European Integration* (Aldershot, UK: Ashgate, 1997), 54–64.

16. Ibid., 97.

17. Hans Branner, "Denmark and the European Coal and Steel Community, 1950–1953," in *Interdependence versus Integration: Denmark, Scandinavia, and Western Europe, 1945–1960*, ed. Thorsten Olesen (Odense: Odense University Press, 1995), 116–19.

18. There are many interesting accounts of the Norwegian referendum debate. Two of the best are given by Hilary Allen, *Norway and Europe in the 1970s* (Oslo: Universitetsforlaget, 1979);

and Clive Archer and Ingrid Sogner, *Norway, European Integration and Atlantic Security* (Oslo: Peace Research Institute Oslo, 1998).

19. For an excellent discussion of the use of the terms "Europe" and "Continent" in postwar British discourse, see Piers Ludlow, "Us or Them? The Meaning of Europe in British Political Discourse," in *Meaning of Europe*, ed. Malmborg and Stråth, 101–4.

20. George Wilkes, "The First Failure to Steer Britain into the European Communities: An Introduction," in *Britain's Failure to Enter the European Community, 1961–63: The Enlargement Negotiations and Crises in European, Atlantic and Commonwealth Relations*, ed. George Wilkes (London: Frank Cass, 1997), 15.

21. Young, *This Blessed Plot*, 50.

22. Charlton, *Price of Victory*, 46; Young, *This Blessed Plot*, 50.

23. Both quotations are from Young, *This Blessed Plot*, 50–51.

24. David Gowland, Arthur Turner, and Alex Wright, *Britain and European Integration since 1945: On the Sidelines* (New York: Routledge, 2009), 50.

25. Bullock, *Ernest Bevin*, 781, 786. See also the May 1950 pamphlet titled "European Unity: A Statement by the National Executive Committee of the British Labour Party." For a thorough analysis of Labour's position on integration, see Andrew Mullen, *The British Left's "Great Debate" on Europe* (New York: Continuum, 2007).

26. Young, *This Blessed Plot*, 51. On the *Mandement*, see Herman Bakvis, *Catholic Power in the Netherlands* (Montreal: McGill–Queen's University Press, 1981), 33–34.

27. Philip M. Coupland, "Western Union, 'Spiritual Union,' and European Integration, 1948–1951," *Journal of British Studies* 43 (July 2004): 389.

28. Young, *This Blessed Plot*, 150.

29. Coupland, "Western Union," 390. The word "revival" is obviously a misprint and should read "rival."

30. Nathaniel Micklem, quoted by Coupland, "Western Union," 390.

31. Ibid., 391.

32. Ibid., 390 (all quotations).

33. All quotations are from Ian Paisley, "The Common Market, the Kingdom of the Anti-Christ, Why It Must Be Resisted," *The Revivalist*, June 1975, www.ianpaisley.org/revivalist/1975/Rev75jun.htm. See also Steve Bruce, *God Save Ulster! The Religion and Politics of Paisleyism* (Oxford: Oxford University Press, 1986), 221–31.

34. All quotations are from Paisley, "Common Market."

35. Charlton, *Price of Victory*, 62.

36. Young, *This Blessed Plot*, 118.

37. Maurice Vaïsse, "De Gaulle and the British 'Application' to Join the Common Market," in *Britain's Failure*, ed. Wilkes, 51.

38. Gowland, Turner, and Wright, *Britain and European Integration*, 59.

39. Ibid., 59–60.

40. Young, *Britain and European Unity*, 29.

41. In its letter to Monnet declining an invitation to the negotiations, the government stated, "It should . . . be realized that if the French Government intend to insist on a commitment to pool resources and set up an authority with certain sovereign powers as a prior condition to joining in the talks, His Majesty's Government would reluctantly be unable to accept such a condition." Jean Monnet, *Memoirs*, trans. Richard Mayne (Garden City, NY: Doubleday, 1978), 312.

42. N. Piers Ludlow, "British Agriculture and the Brussels Negotiations: A Problem of Trust," in *Britain's Failure*, ed. Wilkes, 117.

43. George Wilkes, "Eye-witness Views of the Brussels Breakdown," in *Britain's Failure*, ed. Wilkes, 219.

44. On Nordic welfare states, see Gøsta Esping-Andersen, *The Three Worlds of Welfare Capitalism* (Cambridge: Polity Press, 1990).

45. Gylfi Gíslason, "In Defense of Small Nations," *Dædalus* 113, no. 1 (special issue, "The Nordic Enigma") (1984): 199.

46. See Nina Witoszek, "Fugitives from Utopia: The Scandinavian Enlightenment Reconsidered," in *The Cultural Construction of Norden*, ed. Øystein Sørensen and Bo Stråth (Oslo: Scandinavian University Press, 1997), 72–90.

47. Christine Ingebritsen, *Scandinavia in World Politcs* (Lanham, MD: Rowman & Littlefield, 2006), 2.

48. Patricia Bliss McFate, "To See Everything in Another Light," *Dædalus* 113, no. 1 (special issue, "The Nordic Enigma") (1984): 48.

49. Tore M. Bredal, "Norway and the European Union: An Overview of Public Opinion in Norway," in *The Fourth Enlargement: Public Opinion on Membership in the Nordic Candidate Countries*, CEPS Paper 56, ed. Peter Ludlow and Jan O. Berg (Brussels: Centre for European Policy Studies, 1994), 78.

50. Mary Hilson, *The Nordic Model: Scandinavia since 1945* (London: Reaktion Books, 2008), 143.

51. A global purpose was a characteristic that they also seemed to share in the postwar period with the United States, the Soviet Union, and Gaullist France.

52. Nils Örvik, "Fears and Expectations," in *Fears and Expectations: Norwegian Attitudes toward European Integration*, ed. Nils Örvik (Oslo: Universitetsforlaget, 1972), 12.

53. Hilson, *Nordic Model*, 142.

54. Charles Silva, "An Introduction to Sweden and European Integration 1947–1957," in *Die Neutralen*, ed. Gehler and Steininger, 286. See also Lars Trägårdh, "Welfare State Nationalism: Sweden and the Specter of the European Union," *Scandinavian Review* 87, no. 1 (1999): 18–23. In Denmark it was similar; see Johnny N. Laursen and Thorsten Borring Olesen, "A Nordic Alternative to Europe? The Interdependence of Denmark's Nordic and European Policies," in *Denmark's Policy towards Europe after 1945: History, Theory and Options*, ed. Hans Branner and Morten Kelstrup (Odense: Odense University Press, 2000), 229.

55. Tony Judt, *Postwar: A History of Europe since 1945* (New York: Penguin Press, 2005), 158.

56. Laursen and Olesen, "Nordic Alternative," 229.

57. Quoted by Lars Trägårdh, "Sweden and the EU: Welfare State Nationalism and the Spectre of 'Europe,'" in *European Integration and National Identity: The Challenge of the Nordic States*, ed. Lene Hansen and Ole Wæver (London: Routledge, 2002), 154.

58. Trägårdh, "Sweden and the EU," 156.

59. Both quotations are from Bo Stråth, "The Swedish Demarcation from Europe," in *Meaning of Europe*, ed. Malmborg and Stråth, 137.

60. Daniel Heradstveit, "The Norwegian EEC Debate," in *Fears and Expectations*, ed. Örvik, 189. Haradstveit's assessment is based on a content analysis of the Storting debates. Cultural issues did not rank high in the number of times they were discussed in Parliament, but Haradstveit makes the point that the issues were considered very important by members of the Christian People's Party in southwestern Norway.

61. Iver B. Neumann, "This Little Piggy Stayed at Home: Why Norway Is Not a Member of the EU," in *European Integration*, ed. Hansen and Wæver, 114.

62. Allen, *Norway and Europe,* 107. See also David L. Larson, "Selected Foreign Policy Elites," in *Norway's No to Europe, International Studies*, Occasional Paper 5, ed. Nils Örvik (Pittsburgh: International Studies Association, 1975), 53.

63. For an excellent study of alcohol norms and public policy in the Nordic region, see Paulette Kurzer, *Markets and Moral Regulation: Cultural Change in the European Union* (Cambridge: Cambridge University Press, 2001).

64. Brent F. Nelsen, "The European Community Debate in Norway: The Periphery Revolts, Again," in *Norway and the European Community: The Political Economy of Integration*, ed. Brent F. Nelsen (Westport, CT: Praeger, 1993), 56.

65. Hilson, *Nordic Model*, 142. For more on British and Scandinavian social democracy, see Robert Geyer, *The Uncertain Union: British and Norwegian Social Democrats in an Integrated Europe* (Aldershot, UK: Avebury, 1997).

66. Kaiser states: "Whatever its economic merits, the mental barriers against closer British association with Western Europe, which were prevalent in the political class and the public at large,

should not be underestimated in their importance for European policy-making." Kaiser, *Using Europe*, 8.

67. Charlton, *Price of Victory*, 57.

68. Ibid., 92; Young, *Britain and European Unity*, 49–50.

69. Charlton, *Price of Victory*, 159; Young, *Britain and European Unity*, 36.

70. Simon Burgess and Geoffrey Edwards, "The Six plus One: British Policy-Making and the Question of European Economic Integration, 1955," *International Affairs* 64, no. 3 (1988): 404.

71. Ibid., 407.

72. Protestant countries confirmed their approach to federalism when the Council Assembly in May 1950 bypassed the Committee of Ministers and sent to the member state parliaments a series of federalist recommendations. The six parliaments from eventual ECSC members received the recommendations positively, but the British House of Commons rejected their federalist intent in favor of the Council of Ministers as a forum for expressing ideas. The Scandinavian parliaments refused to even debate the recommendations. See Derek W. Urwin, *The Community of Europe: A History of European Integration since 1945* (London: Longman, 1991), 37–38. Paul-Henri Spaak, the first president of the Council Assembly, was so disgusted by the stubbornly intergovernmental Committee of Ministers that he said of the institution, "Of all the international bodies I have known, I have never found any more timorous or more ineffectual"; cited by Mark Gilbert, *European Integration: A Concise History* (Lanham, MD: Rowman & Littlefield, 2012), 22.

73. Kaiser, *Using Europe*, 14–17.

74. Ibid., 21.

75. Monnet, *Memoirs*, 315.

76. Quoted by Young, *Britain and European Unity*, 32. Monnet was also put off in 1952 by the new Conservative government's "Eden Plan," which proposed intergovernmental links between the Six and the Council of Europe (p. 37).

77. James Ellison, "Perfidious Albion? Britain, Plan G and European Integration, 1955–1957," *Contemporary Political Studies* 1 (1996): 21–32.

78. The Eden Cabinet did not formally adopt the plan until November 1956.

79. See Kaiser, *Using Europe*, 62.

80. Charlton, *Price of Victory*, 226.

81. For a strong argument supporting the sincerity of British diplomacy, see Ellison, "Perfidious Albion?"

82. Charlton, *Price of Victory*, 227; Ellison, "Perfidious Albion?" 21.

83. See Ben Wellings, "Losing the Peace: Euroscepticism and the Foundations of Contemporary English Nationalism," *Nations and Nationalism* 16, no. 3 (2010): 488–505.

84. Young, *This Blessed Plot*, 126.

85. European Economic Community (Government Policy), Hansard, HC Deb 31, July 1961, vol. 645, cc928-42, http://hansard.millbanksystems.com/commons/1961/jul/31/european-economic-community-government#S5CV0645P0_19610731_HOC_266.

86. European Economic Community, Hansard, HC Deb 02, August 1961, vol. 645, cc1480-606, http://hansard.millbanksystems.com/commons/1961/aug/02/european-economic-community#S5CV0645P0_19610802_HOC_242.

87. European Economic Community, Hansard, HC Deb 03, August 1961, vol. 645, cc1715-86, http://hansard.millbanksystems.com/commons/1961/aug/03/european-economic-community-1.

88. European Economic Community, Hansard, HC Deb 02, August 1961, vol. 645, cc1480-606, http://hansard.millbanksystems.com/commons/1961/aug/02/european-economic-community#S5CV0645P0_19610802_HOC_242.

89. Quoted by Young, *This Blessed Plot*, 163.

90. All quotations are from Phillip Lynch, *The Politics of Nationhood: Sovereignty, Britishness and Conservative Politics* (London: Macmillan, 1999), 26.

91. Young, *This Blessed Plot*, 127.

92. European Economic Community, Hansard, HC Deb 03, August 1961, vol. 645, cc1715-86, http://hansard.millbanksystems.com/commons/1961/aug/03/european-economic-community-1.

93. European Communities (Membership), Hansard, HC Deb 08, May 1967, vol. 746, cc1061-184, http://hansard.millbanksystems.com/commons/1967/may/08/european-communities-membership.

94. Lynch, *Politics of Nationhood*, 30.

95. John Turner, *The Tories and Europe* (Manchester: Manchester University Press, 2000), 67–68; John Campbell, *Edward Heath: A Biography* (London: Jonathan Cape, 1993), 401.

96. Young, *This Blessed Plot*, 246.

97. Ibid., 247.

98. Ibid., 248.

99. Turner, *Tories and Europe*, 61–63.

100. Ibid., 62–63.

101. Lynch, *Politics of Nationhood*, 38–40.

102. Oliver Bange, "Grand Designs and the Diplomatic Breakdown," in *Britain's Failure*, ed. Wilkes, 207.

103. Charles de Gaulle, *Memoirs of Hope: Renewal and Endeavor*, trans. Terence Kilmartin (New York: Simon & Schuster, 1970), 171.

104. Quoted by Urwin, *Community of Europe*, 123–24.

105. De Gaulle, *Memoirs*, 171.

106. Edward Heath said as much when he looked back on what in his view was a missed opportunity by de Gaulle: "Internationally, he could have gone down as the man who created the real unity of Europe which has been the endeavor of so many throughout the ages, which has existed since Charlemagne, and now was going to be the most potent power in the world to come. But that he denied himself [by vetoing British membership]." Charlton, *Price of Victory*, 301.

107. See Edward Heath's remarks quoted by Charlton, *Price of Victory*, 269. Heath led Britain's negotiating team during the first application talks.

108. See Pierre Gerbet, "The Fouchet Negotiations for Political Union and the British Application," in *Britain's Failure*, ed. Wilkes, 135–43.

109. Ibid., 141.

110. Ibid., 140.

111. Bange, "Grand Designs," 195–96.

112. Quoted by Vaïsse, "De Gaulle," 53.

113. This is as reported by a British diplomat who delivered the message regarding the British application to de Gaulle: N. Piers Ludlow, *Dealing with Britain: The Six and the First UK Application to the EEC* (Cambridge: Cambridge University Press, 1997), 43.

114. Ibid., 198.

115. Wilkes, "First Failure," 15.

116. Miriam Camps, *Britain and the European Community 1955–1963* (Oxford: Oxford University Press, 1964), 428.

117. Ludlow, *Dealing with Britain*, 120. Ludlow's description of the Champs talks, which is based on British and French government records, calls into question Moravcsik's argument that de Gaulle's primary concerns were commercial, with agriculture primary. For Moravcsik's account of the de Gaulle–Macmillan summits, see Moravcsik, *Choice for Europe*, 192.

118. Ludlow, *Dealing with Britain*, 120.

119. Ibid., 121.

120. Both quotations are from Ludlow, *Dealing with Britain*, 197.

121. For a gripping account of the talks at Rambouillet, see John Newhouse, *De Gaulle and the Anglo-Saxons* (New York: Viking Press, 1970), 184–212.

122. Charles de Gaulle, "Press Conference, 14 January 1963," General Affairs Committee, Political Union of Europe, Archive of European Integration, University of Pittsburgh, http://aei.pitt.edu/id/eprint/5777.

123. Ibid.

124. Nora Beloff, *The General Says No: Britain's Exclusion from Europe* (Harmondsworth, UK: Penguin Books, 1963), 161–62.

125. De Gaulle, "Press Conference, 14 January 1963."

126. Camps, *Britain and the European Community*, 499.

127. Ludlow, *Dealing with Britain*, 225.

128. Ibid., 226–27.

129. Konrad Adenauer, "Without French–German Reconciliation, 'Europe Is Unthinkable,' July 2, 1963," in *Pioneers of European Integration and Peace, 1945–1963: A Brief History with Documents*, ed. Sherrill Brown Wells (Boston: Bedford / St. Martin's, 2007), 153.

130. Branner, "Denmark," 119.

131. Neumann, "This Little Piggy," 112.

132. Mikael af Malmborg, "Gaullism in the North? Sweden, Finland, and the EEC in the 1960s," in *Crises and Compromises: The European Project 1963–1969*, ed. Wilfried Loth (Baden-Baden: Nomos Verlag, 2001), 500.

133. Miles, *Sweden and European Integration*, 55.

134. Allen, *Norway and Europe*, 107.

135. Quoted by Laursen and Olesen, "Nordic Alternative?" 227.

136. Ibid., 229.

137. See Miles, *Sweden and European Integration*, 145–49.

138. Archer and Sogner, *Norway*, 15.

139. Ibid., 16.

140. Miles, *Sweden and European Integration*, 153.

141. Quoted by Urwin, *Community of Europe*, 90.

142. Miles, *Sweden and European Integration*, 156.

143. Ibid., 74–75.

144. Quoted by Miles, *Sweden and European Integration*, 78.

145. Quoted by Malmborg, "Gaullism in the North?" 502.

146. See Miles, *Sweden and European Integration*, 80.

147. Ulf Hedetoft, "The Interplay between Mass and Elite Attitudes to European Integration in Denmark," in *Denmark's Policy*, ed. Branner and Kelstrup, 292.

148. Lene Hansen, "Sustaining Sovereignty: The Danish Approach to Europe," in *European Integration*, ed. Hansen and Wæver, 62.

149. Ibid., 64.

150. Quoted by Hansen, "Sustaining Sovereignty," 62.

151. See the classic works—e.g., Stein Rokkan, "Geography, Religion, and Social Class: Cross-cutting Cleavages in Norwegian Politics," in *Party Systems and Voter Alignments: Cross-National Perspectives*, ed. Seymour M. Lipset and Stein Rokkan (New York: Free Press, 1967), 367–444; Henry Valen, "Norway: 'No' to EEC," *Scandinavian Political Studies* 8 (1973): 214–26; Henry Valen and Daniel Katz, *Political Parties in Norway: A Community Study* (Oslo: Universitetsforlaget, 1964); Stein Rokkan and Henry Valen, "Regional Contrasts in Norwegian Politics: A Review of Data from Official Statistics and from Sample Surveys," in *Mass Politics: Studies in Political Sociology*, ed. Erik Allardt and Stein Rokkan (New York: Free Press, 1970), 190–247; Philip E. Converse, "Dimensions of Cleavage and Perceived Party Distances in Norwegian Voting," *Scandinavian Political Studies* 6 (1971): 107–52; Henry Valen and Stein Rokkan, "Norway: Conflict Structure and Mass Politics in a European Periphery," in *Electoral Behavior: A Comparative Handbook*, ed. Richard Rose (New York: Free Press, 1974), 315–70; and Sten Sparre Nilson, "Norway and Denmark," in *Western European Party Systems*, ed. Peter Mair (Oxford: Oxford University Press, 1990), 205–33.

152. For a superb examination of the creation of a Norwegian identity, see Neumann, "This Little Piggy."

153. Ibid., 112.

154. Ibid., 113.

155. Quoted in ibid., 109.

156. Ibid., 115.

157. Quoted in ibid., 110.

158. See Frederic Spotts, *The Churches and Politics in Germany* (Middletown, CT: Wesleyan University Press, 1973), 48–50.

159. Rudy B. Andeweg and Galen A. Irwin, *Governance and Politics of the Netherlands* (Houndmills, UK: Palgrave, 2002), 18–19.

160. Anthony Trawick Bouscaren, "Survey of Christian Democracy in Europe," *Thought* 26, no. 3 (1951): 398–99.

161. Ronald J. Granieri, *The Ambivalent Alliance: Konrad Adenauer, the CDU/CSU, and the West, 1949–1966* (New York: Berghahn Books, 2003), 16.

162. Schröder was also the minister of defense (1966–69) under Kurt Georg Kiesinger.

163. John Zmirak, *Wilhem Röpke: Swiss Localist, Global Economist* (Wilmington, DE: ISI Books, 2001), 5.

164. Ibid., 14.

165. Ibid., 13–14.

166. Quoted in ibid., 190.

167. Quoted by Sabine Lee, "German Decision-Making Elites and European Integration: German 'Europolitik' during the Years of the EEC and Free Trade Area Negotiations," in *Building Postwar Europe: National Decision-Makers and European Institutions, 1948–63*, ed. Anne Deighton (New York: St. Martin's Press, 1995), 43.

168. Ibid., 43–44.

169. Quoted by Granieri, *Ambivalent Alliance*, 90.

170. Ibid., 193; Torsten Oppelland, "'Entangling Alliances with None': Neither de Gaulle nor Hallstein—The European Politics of Gerhard Schröder in the 1965/66 Crisis," in *Crises and Compromises*, ed. Loth, 236.

171. Granieri, *Ambivalent Alliance*, 123.

172. Susanne Jonas Bodenheimer, "The Denial of Grandeur: The Dutch Context," in *The Foreign Policy of the Netherlands*, ed. J. H. Leurdijk (Alphen aan den Rijn: Sijthoff & Noordoff, 1978), 249. See also J. J. C. Voorhoeve, *Peace, Profits and Principles: A Study of Dutch Foreign Policy* (The Hague: Martinus Nijhoff, 1979), 161.

173. Wendy Asbeek Brusse, "The Stikker Plan," in *The Netherlands and the Integration of Europe 1945–1957*, ed. Richard T. Griffiths (Amsterdam: Nederlandsch Economisch-Historisch Archief, 1990), 80.

174. See Jan van der Harst, "The Pleven Plan," in *The Economy and Politics of the Netherlands since 1945*, ed. Richard T. Griffiths (The Hague: Martinus Nijhoff, 1980).

175. Although Luns was a Catholic and committed to integration, his views were complex. He tended to favor a broader EEC than a "little Europe" of the Six. See R. T. Griffiths, "The Netherlands and the EEC," in *Economy and Politics of the Netherlands*, ed. Griffiths, 280.

176. See Griffiths, "Netherlands and the EEC," 280; and Anjo G. Harryvan and Jan van der Harst, "For Once a United Front. The Netherlands and the 'Empty Chair' Crisis of the Mid-1960s," in *Crises and Compromises*, ed. Loth.

177. Bernard Bouwman, "'Longing for London': The Netherlands and the Political Cooperation Initiative, 1959–62," in *Building Postwar Europe*, ed. Deighton, 155.

178. Quoted by Bodenheimer, "Denial of Grandeur," 291.

179. Andeweg and Irwin, *Governance and Politics of the Netherlands*, 199.

180. Richard T. Griffiths, "The Common Market," in *Economy and Politics of the Netherlands*, ed. Griffiths, 194.

181. Quoted by Hans Vollaard, "Protestantism and Euro-Scepticism in the Netherlands," *Perspectives on European Politics and Society* 7, no. 3 (2006): 282.

182. Ibid., 282–83.

183. Ibid., 283–85.

184. Quoted in ibid., 285.

PART IV

Divided Europe

8

Member States and Elites

THE ENLARGED European Community (EC) of the late 1970s may have been divided in its approach to integration, but it was a remarkably successful organization. The Protestant EU member states did not share their Catholic partners' passion for "ever-closer union," but they still had enough community spirit to desire stronger economic and security ties. Did these deep interactions diminish the confessional divide in Europe? To what extent did Karl Deutsch's learning process contribute to a thicker community spirit and a growing sense of European identity? In the remaining chapters, we explore the persistence of the confessional cultural divide in the contemporary EU.

Despite rapid secularization in Europe, the confessional divide remains. In this chapter, we examine the impact of Protestant confessional culture on the EU member states' behavior, particularly on controversial proposals for deeper integration. We also empirically assess whether both Protestant and Catholic confessional cultures have exerted an independent influence on states' behavior. Then we explore how the confessional cultures have shaped contemporary elites' attitudes and behavior, examining two archetypal figures, the Catholic Jacques Delors and the Protestant Margaret Thatcher. In the final two chapters, we examine the religious influences on the Continents' political parties and on the EU's interest groups (chapter 9), and the continued attempts by the elites to construct a new European identity (chapter 10). European culture is certainly evolving, but change has not yet erased the legacy of the Reformation.

Confessional Culture and Member States' Behavior

The cultural divide between the Protestant newcomers and the Six was evident from the start. To say, however, that Britain and Denmark were at odds with their partners in every EC venue and on every issue would dramatically overstate the case. For the most part, those British and Danish officials who joined the European policy process in the early 1970s worked well with their Catholic counterparts and gained reputations for being bright and conscientious team players. That being said, Britain and Denmark consistently resisted any move to give supranational institutions more authority or independence, often blocking efforts to increase supranational policy coordination unless granted national safeguards.

Difficulties emerged early. In the 1970s both Britain and Denmark dragged their feet on two vital issues: direct elections to the European Parliament (EP), and the creation of a European currency system to replace the collapsed Bretton Woods fixed exchange rate regime. In the first case, the Euro-federalists were keen to bolster the EP's powers; direct elections would help give the body true democratic legitimacy. Although Germany, Italy, the Netherlands, and, eventually, France favored expanded EP influence, Britain and Denmark resisted. In principle, EC members had agreed to direct elections at the 1974 Paris Summit, but the British Labour government delayed implementation as it dealt with division within its ranks. The British House of Commons eventually approved direct elections, but only after asserting that "no treaty providing for any increase whatever in the powers of the Assembly will be ratified by the United Kingdom unless it has been approved by an Act of Parliament."[1] And the British Parliament also rejected proportional representation in favor of familiar first-past-the-post rules with single-member constituencies. Denmark also resisted direct elections as a federalist bid to strengthen supranational institutions, but it eventually acquiesced. The government refused, however, to drop its support for dual mandates allowing members of the EP (MEPs) to serve in national parliaments.[2] Some Danes saw the dual mandate system as a valuable link between national and supranational governments (which they wanted to maintain), but other Danes with more sinister intents hoped that the dual mandates would turn the EP into a second-rate legislative body with third-rate powers.

The European Monetary System (EMS) also became a source of controversy. In 1977 the new Commission president, Roy Jenkins (a former British Labour minister), proposed a European system of managed exchange rates. This idea languished until German chancellor Helmut Schmidt and French president Valéry Giscard d'Estaing championed the cause. This time only Britain balked, showing little interest in the talks creating the EMS and opting out of its key element, the Exchange Rate Mechanism. All the remaining EC members joined the mechanism, including Ireland, which thereby ended its decades-long currency union with Britain.[3]

The 1980s were packed with drama compared to the soporific 1970s. Greece joined the EC in 1981, but Portugal and Spain were held up by France's objection to further expansion (especially one including economic rival Spain) and Britain's concern about the resulting drain on rich members' budgets, primarily its own. Nevertheless, after difficult talks the EC accepted the Iberian expansion, set for January 1, 1986. Although enlargement was controversial, the major struggle of the early 1980s was over the so-called British Budgetary Question, which involved the EC's Common Agriculture Policy (CAP). Given its smaller farm sector, Britain paid considerably more into the CAP than it received from it. Rather than seeing the net payment as a contribution to European solidarity, the British insisted on breaking even.

When Conservative prime minister Margaret Thatcher assumed office in 1979, she demanded a CAP rebate from her partners. British intransigence occupied European leaders and precluded other important business, until they finally reached a deal in 1984 at the Fontainebleau Summit.

Settling the British Budgetary Question broke a logjam that opened the EC to new initiatives. Most EC members were eager to push integration forward. The EP had even presented a draft "Treaty on European Union" to the Fontainebleau Summit. Italy, West Germany, and the Benelux nations were eager to implement at least some of the EP's proposals to increase supranational decision making. Britain, Denmark, and Greece, however, showed little enthusiasm. The British were inclined to focus on completing the promised single European market and on coordinating foreign policy more closely, but the Six were determined to tie completion of the single market to institutional reforms. The British and the Danes supported the new policy initiatives but insisted that they could be achieved without sacrificing sovereignty. Thus they opposed increasing qualified majority voting (QMV) in the Council of Ministers, increasing the powers of the EP, or eliminating the national veto (which had been enshrined in the Luxembourg Compromise).[4] The conflict boiled over at the Milan Summit in June 1985, resulting in deadlock. Not willing to go down in defeat, the Italian EC presidency employed a little-known procedural rule and called for a vote on an Intergovernmental Conference (IGC). The IGC proposal passed 7–3, with the "no" votes cast by the usual resisters, Britain, Denmark, and Greece.

The result of the IGC negotiations was the Single European Act (SEA), which envisioned completing the single market by the end of 1992. The SEA called for modest increases in the EP's power and for the extension of QMV to most single market issues, but retained the national veto. The Thatcher government saw the new powers of supranational institutions as a small price to pay for the freer movement of goods, services, and capital; Britain ratified the treaty without difficulty (an outcome Thatcher herself came to regret[5]). The Danish Folketing, conversely, refused to approve the document, fearing the erosion of national sovereignty. This forced the Danish government to refer the treaty to a popular referendum, which passed with 56 percent of the vote. In Ireland the treaty ran into constitutional trouble, and the high court forced the government to call a referendum. But like the Danes, the Irish electorate viewed the treaty favorably, approving it with 70 percent of the vote. Meanwhile, the leaders of the Six were criticizing the SEA as a very weak compromise. For instance, when signing the treaty, Italian foreign minister Giulio Andreotti lamented that "the SEA was merely a partial and unsatisfactory response to the need for substantial progress."[6]

The divergence of attitudes and actions continued in 1985 when five EC members signed the Schengen Agreement establishing a borderless region between them. Here, the confessional divide made little difference. The Benelux states had enjoyed passport-free travel since 1948, so Schengen merely extended this freedom to France and West Germany (Italy joined five years later). Schengen remained outside the EC structure due to objections by Britain, Denmark, and Ireland until 1999, when it was finally assimilated to the European Union, but only after Britain and Ireland secured opt-outs. Members of the Nordic Passport Union—including the EU nonmembers Iceland and Norway—joined Schengen in 1996, bringing in all the Nordics. The island nations of Britain and Ireland remained outside the Schengen fold.

The success of the single market project and the end of the Cold War inspired new proposals to meet new challenges in the early 1990s. France backed the Commission's designs for a single currency for the single market; and now-reunified Germany sought a political union to make Europe safe for its reunified country. Thatcher and the British wanted neither. Thatcher, however, lost her job in November 1990; and her successor, John Major, committed Britain to negotiate a new treaty. The Maastricht Treaty (the Treaty on European Union) of December 1991 created a watered-down version of European union (thanks largely to British and French resistance) and set out a rigid plan for Economic and Monetary Union (EMU) with a signature new currency, the euro. Britain secured exemptions for two central elements of the treaty, the single currency and the "social chapter" (which was not actually part of the treaty) governing labor and employment.[7]

Despite these "opt-outs" the Conservative government in Britain strained to secure approval from the House of Commons. Denmark, for its part, secured no opt-outs during negotiations, but the Danes defeated the Maastricht Treaty in a referendum (51 to 49 percent), sending the entire EC into a tailspin. The European Council eventually devised a way forward; and at the Edinburgh Summit (December 1992), it officially clarified the concept of "subsidiarity" and gave Denmark opt-outs on the euro, the Common Security and Defence Policy, Justice and Home Affairs, and EU citizenship—in short, most of the treaty's key provisions. The Danes approved the revised treaty in a second referendum in 1993, 57 to 43 percent. In the end, the only two Protestant-majority states chose to opt out of key parts of the most important agreement since the Treaties of Rome.

Despite early difficulties, the Maastricht Treaty generated economic and political momentum across this Continent that had been newly opened by the fall of the Berlin Wall. Like the center of a large spiral galaxy, the European Union of twelve states became the political, economic, and social vortex of this reorganized and reenergized region. EU membership soon became the goal of both the Continent's former Soviet Bloc states and smaller Western countries, including Cyprus and Malta. The Nordics left in the European Free Trade Association (EFTA) also reevaluated their options, as did the neutral states of Austria and Switzerland. Efforts by the EU to delay the applications of EFTA members resulted in a European Economic Area (EEA) agreement in May 1992; but by November Austria, Finland, Norway, Sweden, and Switzerland had found the EEA unsatisfactory and had applied for EU membership.

Austria, Finland, and Sweden joined in 1995, after their voters approved their respective accession treaties. But the Swiss and Norwegian voters rejected membership in referenda held, respectively, in December 1992 and November 1994.[8] The Eastern European and Mediterranean countries—which were mostly Catholic (the Czech Republic, Hungary, Lithuania, Malta, Poland, Slovenia, Slovakia) or Orthodox (Cyprus)—had all applied for membership by 1996.[9] The ten-state Eastern enlargement occurred in 2004, with two more countries, Bulgaria and Romania, joining in 2007, and Croatia in 2013. Of the latter three, only Romania had a small pocket of Protestants.

Beginning in 1995, the EU struggled to digest this massive influx of new members. Two revisions of its treaties—the Amsterdam (1997) and Nice (2000) treaties—fell short of the significant institutional reforms many practitioners and scholars thought necessary. Member states continued efforts to modify the antiquated institutional structure by launching the Convention on the Future of Europe in 2002, ahead of the Eastern enlargement. Under the guidance of former French president Valéry Giscard d'Estaing, the convention drafted what all would call a "Constitution," although it was officially titled the "Treaty Establishing a Constitution for Europe." The convention released a text in July 2003, and the Intergovernmental Conference concluded with a treaty signing in Rome in October 2004.

Several new EU members' parliaments ratified this treaty almost immediately, but nevertheless it soon ran aground. The British tabloids had screamed for months that the treaty was a sellout to the federalists and marked the end of British sovereignty.[10] Backed into a corner by the Tory opposition, the press, and the members of his own party, in April 2004 Prime Minister Tony Blair promised to hold a referendum. France followed suit; and in the end, ten member states pledged to schedule popular votes. Spain and Luxembourg passed the treaties, but France and the Netherlands voted "no." This ended the ratification process, saving Britain, the Czech Republic, Denmark, Ireland, Poland, Portugal, and Sweden from divisive campaigns over the merits of deeper integration. A few months later, European leaders picked up the pieces of the wrecked Constitution, jettisoned a few of the most controversial bits (e.g., the symbols of statehood), and reassembled the rest into a new Lisbon Treaty, which was signed in December 2007 and implemented in December 2009. This time the EU's leaders refused to put the treaty before their electorates for a vote—except in Ireland, where events confirmed elite fears; the electorate rejected the treaty in 2008. Ireland held a second—this time, successful—vote in 2009.

The Protestant EU member states maintained their reputations as difficult and stubborn partners during the first decade of the new century. In Denmark (2000) and Sweden (2003), popular referenda rejected adoption of the euro. Later, member states took to squabbling over the 2007–13 EU budget framework. As Gilbert put it, "The first European Council after the referendum defeats . . . was a flashback to the early 1980s, with an 'awkward squad' of Britain, the Netherlands, and Sweden flatly refusing to accept a significant increase in the EU budget."[11] But this budget battle was a good-humored tussle compared with the sullen struggle for survival that soon consumed Europe after the financial tsunami in the fall of 2008.

The 2008 global banking crisis exacerbated an existing European sovereign debt crisis, which revealed an economic growth crisis that pointed to a competitiveness crisis. No European state (with the arguable exception of Poland) escaped the effects of the 2008 disaster. Those outside the euro zone felt the full force of bank collapses (e.g., Britain and Iceland) and deep depression (e.g., Latvia, Hungary), but these states had monetary and fiscal instruments available to address the crisis.[12] Tackling the crisis was painful, but policymakers and electorates were generally satisfied with the flexibility provided by independent currencies.

The focus of the crisis, however, was the euro zone, where design flaws in the EMU were evident. A single monetary policy without the budget discipline of a unitary fiscal policy had encouraged the poorer EU members to finance their deficits by borrowing in the financial markets, where low interest rates made for easy money. When the global banking crisis revealed the extent of indebtedness in Ireland, Greece, Portugal, Spain, Italy, Slovenia, and Cyprus, borrowing costs soared, making it impossible to service national debts. Closing the money spigot halted economic growth and revealed just how economically uncompetitive these high-debt states had become compared with their EU partners, especially Germany. An unsettled period of austerity at home, bailouts from richer EU members, and expanded bond purchases by the European Central Bank ensued as the euro zone's elites fought to save the euro—and even, perhaps, the viability of the EU.

For our purposes, two developments stand out. First, the euro zone nonmembers were almost completely sidelined during the campaign to save the currency. But how could it have been otherwise? Those states had deliberately excluded themselves from the euro zone—or had failed to qualify for membership. They had little interest in bailing out profligate states or in creating new supranational rules or institutions to solve the crisis.[13] As we know, these non-euro member states—Britain, Denmark, and Sweden—were overwhelmingly Protestant, as were the nonmember states Iceland, Norway, and (less Protestant) Switzerland. EU members still hoping to join the euro zone but not yet qualified were Catholic or Orthodox Eastern states.[14] The second important development was that inside the euro zone, the great fault line now ran between fiscally sound states and dangerously indebted states—the "bailers out" and "bailees." Again, those euro zone countries with large Protestant populations—Germany, the Netherlands, and Finland—stood for fiscal rectitude, austerity, and limited assistance to debt-ridden members, whereas the supplicants were Catholic (Ireland, Spain, Portugal, and possibly Italy) and Orthodox (Greece and Cyprus). France under President Nicolas Sarkozy tried to side with the Protestants, but in the 2012 elections the French voters chose a new president, the Socialist François Hollande, who then joined the South's call for easing austerity.

The critical question was whether the euro zone could survive the cultural division that limited the northern countries' willingness to pay for its survival and the southern states' ability to endure the pain of adjustment. The Protestants in the North could not quite hide their disdain for the profligate ways of their Catholic partners in the South. In their view, bloated bureaucracies, official corruption, and tax avoidance were symptoms of an undisciplined approach to governance—indeed, to life. To those in the South, however, the northern Protestants looked smug and judgmental, without any appreciation for their own culpability in the fiasco. Austerity economics looked like a Protestant attempt to end easygoing Mediterranean ways—to turn Catholics into Protestants—and to do so in an authoritarian manner, dredging up images of diktats and jackboots. Pragmatism has so far kept the euro zone (and the EU) together; but cultural differences, primarily defined along confessional lines, and a new nationalism manifest in the rise of Euroskeptic parties (see chapter 10) are straining the bonds of utilitarian interest.

This brief narrative of the years since 1975 reveals a clear division between the majority-Protestant countries and the EU's other members. The Protestant states have resisted advances toward a federal union, either by remaining outside the EU (Iceland and Norway) or by acting as a drag on supranationalism inside it. The mixed Catholic/Protestant countries of Germany and the Netherlands have also, on occasion, resisted integration efforts. Thus, those member states with large Protestant populations do seem to constitute the EU's "awkward squad." Can we test this assertion empirically?

The EU's practice of allowing opt-outs during treaty negotiations and its more recent policy of "enhanced cooperation"—known informally as "flexibility"—offers an opportunity to explore the relationship between confessional culture and state behavior.[15] Enhanced cooperation, first incorporated into the Amsterdam Treaty, allows any group of EU states to pursue deeper integration (usually in a specific policy area) beyond that acceptable to other members. This policy, combined with the many opt-outs allowed by the treaty, has created a "multispeed" Europe, with members participating in a varying number of "integration formations." Thus, the number of formations in which a country participates is a reasonable measure of its enthusiasm for integration. Counting the number of integration formations in the EU is difficult, but we include the following:[16]

- European Union
- Schengen Area
- euro zone
- Euro Plus[17]
- Fiscal Compact (technically outside the EU's legal structure)
- Common Security and Defence Policy (CSDP)
- Area of Freedom, Security, and Justice (AFSJ)

- Charter of Fundamental Rights (CFR)
- Prüm Convention (which enhances the Schengen Agreement)
- Symbols[18]
- European Divorce Law.

In our analysis, we include all the European states eligible for membership in these various integration formations. Based on their wealth and democratic systems, we consider Iceland, Norway, and Switzerland eligible for EU membership and include them in the study. The Balkan applicant states and Turkey are excluded.[19] Table 8.1 displays the European states and the formations each has joined.

On the basis of our narrative of intra-EU relations, we expect states with a Protestant confessional culture to be reluctant to join those EU formations that might

Table 8.1 Integration Formations

Country	EU	Schengen	Euro Zone	Euro Plus	Fiscal Compact	CSDP	AFSJ	CFR	Prüm	Symbols	Divorce	Total
Austria	x	x	x	x	x	x	x	x	x	x	x	11
Belgium	x	x	x	x	x	x	x	x	x	x	x	11
Bulgaria	x			x	x	x		x	x	x	x	8
Cyprus	x		x	x	x	x	x	x		x		8
Czech Republic	x	x			x	x						4
Denmark	x	x		x	x			x				5
Estonia	x	x	x	x	x	x	x	x	x			9
Finland	x	x	x	x	x	x	x	x	x			9
France	x	x	x	x	x	x	x	x	x		x	10
Germany	x	x	x	x	x	x	x	x	x	x	x	11
Greece	x	x	x	x	x	x	x	x		x		9
Hungary	x	x			x	x	x	x	x	x	x	9
Iceland								x				1
Ireland	x		x	x	x	x						5
Italy	x	x	x	x	x	x	x	x		x	x	10
Latvia	x	x	x	x	x	x	x	x			x	9
Lithuania	x	x		x	x	x	x	x		x	x	9
Luxembourg	x	x	x	x	x	x	x	x	x	x	x	11
Malta	x	x	x	x	x	x	x	x		x	x	10
Netherlands	x	x	x	x	x	x	x	x	x			9
Norway		x										1
Poland	x	x		x	x	x	x					6
Portugal	x	x	x	x	x	x	x	x		x	x	10
Romania	x			x	x	x		x	x	x	x	8
Slovakia	x		x	x	x	x	x	x	x	x		10
Slovenia	x	x	x	x	x	x	x	x	x	x	x	11
Spain	x	x	x	x	x	x	x	x	x	x	x	11
Sweden	x	x			x	x	x	x				6
Switzerland		x										1
United Kingdom	x					x						2

Sources: "Multi-Speed Europe," Wikipedia, http://en.wikipedia.org/w/index.php?title=Multi-speed_Europe&oldid =562298030; "Enhanced Cooperation," Wikipedia, http://en.wikipedia.org/w/index.php?title=Enhanced_coopera tion&oldid=566104725.

further limit their sovereignty. As a test, we ran a simple bivariate correlation between the proportion of Protestants in each state (a measure of "confessional culture") and the number of formations each country has joined (see table 8.2). The
results demonstrate a strong, inverse relationship between percent Protestant and
formation joining (see table 8.3): The more Protestant a country, the less often it
joins efforts to integrate more deeply. Of course, there may be other explanations.
The timing of a country's accession (measured by year of entry into the EU) might
have an effect, given that new members have had less time to consider their options
and less exposure to Euro-enthusiastic core Europe, thus joining fewer formations.
In addition, a country's wealth (measured by gross domestic product per capita)
may have an impact, with the wealthier countries *less likely* to join formations as
they seek to protect their economic positions. In fact, later entrants are less likely

Table 8.2 Integration Formations: Percent Protestant, and Year of Accession to EU

Country	Number of Formations	Percent Protestant	Year of Accession
Slovenia	11	1	2004
Luxembourg	11	1	1952
Germany	11	34	1952
Belgium	11	1	1952
Austria	11	5	1995
Spain	11	1	1986
Italy	10	1	1952
Slovakia	10	17	2004
Portugal	10	1	1986
Malta	10	0	2004
France	10	2	1952
Netherlands	9	21	1952
Lithuania	9	1	2004
Hungary	9	24	2004
Greece	9	0	1981
Finland	9	85	1995
Estonia	9	52	2004
Latvia	8	50	2004
Romania	8	6	2007
Cyprus	8	2	2004
Bulgaria	8	1	2007
Sweden	6	86	1995
Poland	6	0	2004
Ireland	5	5	1973
Denmark	5	91	1973
Czech Republic	4	5	2004
United Kingdom	2	60	1973
Norway	1	90	[a]
Iceland	1	91	[a]
Switzerland	1	35	[a]

[a]Missing values replaced with the year 2020 for multivariate analysis.

Table 8.3 Confessional Culture and
Involvement in Enhanced Cooperation
(OLS, standardized coefficients)

Measure	Pearson's r	Beta
Percent Protestant	−.573***	−.386*
Late accession	−.427*	−.444**
GDP per capita	−.232	−.286
Adjusted $R^2 =$		.416
$N =$	30	30

*$p < .05$; ** $p < .01$; *** $p < .001$.

to have joined formations as the first column of table 8.3 shows, but wealth is unrelated to the number of memberships.[20]

Confessional culture and timing, thus, are viable explanations for the number of formations a state has joined. What happens when we pit these explanations head to head? As table 8.3 also shows in an ordinary-least-squares regression analysis, both Protestant population and the timing of accession are significant predictors of formations joined, even when holding the other variables constant (wealth is still not a statistically significant factor). In other words, for two countries that joined the EU at the same time, the one with the highest proportion of Protestants will have joined the fewest formations. Confessional culture thus remains a strong, independent explanation for why some countries join many formations and other countries pick and choose.

Political Elites

Confessional culture affects the behavior of the EU's member states. But does confessional culture affect elites' behavior? We would expect elites in EU institutions to generally support the integration project but would also expect Catholic and Protestant politicians and officials to demonstrate some differences in attitudes and behaviors. In this section we explore the influence of confessional culture on elites in EU institutions, but we also examine in more intimate detail the role of religion in shaping the European visions of two representative elites, Margaret Thatcher and Jacques Delors.

Confessional Culture in the European Institutions

Little research has been done on the impact of religion on the attitudes and behaviors of those working in the EU institutions. Data, of course, are difficult to obtain. But from the few studies that do look at religious variables, we have learned several things. First, EU politicians and officials reflect to a large degree the secularism of European society—but more so. François Foret's study of the EP, for instance, revealed that MEPs were somewhat more willing to identify themselves as convinced atheists (18.4 percent) than the population at large, but found no difference in the proportion calling themselves "religious."[21] "There is no 'faith gap' between elites and masses in the EU but differences in degrees of secularization"—with Brussels politicians a bit more secular than their constituents.[22] This does not mean, however, that religion is inconsequential in Brussels; religion does matter to the elites, primarily as an "identity marker," although it is nearly always subordinated to nationality and political party. Religion helps shape a decision maker's "world vision." It may be only one influence among many—and a relatively weak one—but it remains resilient and normatively significant.[23]

Religion is certainly not central to most European elites, and for most it may not even make the list of conscious priorities. Nevertheless, Foret observes the curious phenomenon that at the College of Europe in Bruges, the premier training ground for young Eurocrats, many attend weekly Mass. He explains:

> Attendance at the Catholic Mass every Sunday in Bruges is for a significant part of the students, including non-believers, a way to calm down, to take a deep breath, to turn one's attention back to the past and to project oneself into the future. . . . Meanwhile, it is also a way to commemorate the religious heritage of the College of Europe and the memory of the numerous devout Christians who were among its Founding Fathers. This function of religion as both an escape and a restoration of tradition should not be underestimated, and may work in the same way for MEPs, civil servants, and other professionals in European affairs working in Brussels.[24]

Foret also finds that confessional culture shapes elite attitudes and behavior. European elites are generally more supportive of integration and are more willing to surrender policy to supranational authorities. The gap between elite support for integration and mass Euroskepticism, however, is greater in the Protestant and mixed confessional countries of Britain, Denmark, and Germany than in the other twelve member states surveyed.[25] Even more to the point, the larger the proportion of Protestants, the more likely a country's Commission officials will believe that EU leadership belongs with member states rather than the Commission or the EP—an "intergovernmentalist" stance.[26]

Cultural differences clearly seem to characterize the EP, with non-Catholics feeling less at home than their Catholic colleagues. Non-Catholics, for instance, think religion plays a more important role in the EP than in his or her national institutions, and that it is, in fact, *too* important there. Non-Catholics are also more likely to perceive that denominational identities create differences in the EP.[27] The Catholic/

Protestant confessional cleavage, however, has little or no independent impact on policy decisions in the EP, except for a limited number of religious and cultural questions. Catholics there, for instance, have supported including a reference to Christianity in the preambles to the European Constitution and the Lisbon Treaty and have expressed doubts about the accession of Turkey. Even here it is hard to disentangle the effects of religious affiliation, national identities, and party loyalties.

A more evident division between Catholics and other MEPs occurred in October 2004, when Italian prime minister Silvio Berlusconi put forward political science professor and European Affairs minister Rocco Buttiglione as a candidate for José Manuel Barroso's first Commission. Buttiglione was a "fervent Catholic" and one of Pope John Paul II's "closest friends and counselors."[28] During his confirmation hearing before the EP Committee on Civil Liberties, Justice, and Home Affairs, he expressed a traditional Catholic perspective on homosexuality, but stated clearly that his job would be to uphold the law, not his personal beliefs: "Many things may be considered immoral which should not be prohibited. . . . I may think that homosexuality is a sin, and this has no effect on politics, unless I say that homosexuality is a crime. The state has no right to stick its nose into these things and nobody can be discriminated against on the basis of sexual orientation; . . . this stands in the Charter of Human Rights, this stands in the Constitution, and I have pledged to defend this Constitution."[29]

Such assurances did not mollify a Liberal and left-wing coalition, which moved to block Buttiglione's confirmation. A chorus of MEPs asserted that a Catholic with conservative views on sexuality, even if held in private, was unfit to hold the Justice, Freedom, and Security portfolio. Members of the European People's Party, particularly Catholics, strenuously defended Buttiglione, as did the Vatican, which lamented a "new inquisition." Despite this defense, Barroso withdrew Buttiglione's candidacy to avoid parliamentary rejection. Clearly, interparty rivalries and ideological tensions contributed to the controversy, but confessional loyalties played a significant role in heightening parliamentary passions.[30]

These findings on Brussels parliamentarians are generally consistent with our argument. Conversely, a study of national parliamentary elites in eighteen European countries carried out in 2007 argued that religion was not generally a significant predictor of ideas about integration. If anything, Catholic identity seemed to work against attitudes favoring European "unification."[31] Unfortunately, the study has significant methodological shortcomings, at least for our purposes.[32]

Nevertheless, the time frame of the study and the inclusion of new member states suggest the possibility that the finding may well be real. As we have discovered in research on the mass public, the influence of confessional culture on attitudes toward European integration has been waning over time, especially in younger age cohorts, while Catholic identity and practice both decline. And the impact of confessional culture is much less in new member states, such as Poland, where devout Catholics often resent the failure of the EU to embody Christian values. Thus, it is very possible that these elites are simply reflecting recent tendencies found in the mass public.

Ironically, another analysis in the same project discovered that the religious composition of national societies still influences these parliamentary elites' attitudes toward integration. Contrary to the authors' expectations (but consistent with ours), elites in Catholic countries (regardless of their own affiliation) showed the strongest support for integration, with those in Orthodox countries next, followed by those in "mixed" nations, with elites in Protestant nations bringing up the rear. The authors explain this pattern by ad hoc reliance on several other factors, such as economic wealth, regional location, and historical experiences. Tellingly, however, in a multivariate analysis including these factors, Protestant countries' elites are still significantly less likely to support integration; indeed, the coefficient for "majority Protestant" obtains a higher level of statistical significance than any other variable.[33]

The impact of confessional culture may sometimes be difficult to detect in the attitudes of contemporary European elites, but this culture continues to shape the functioning of important national institutions. Ivy Hamerly found that Protestant confessional culture encourages stronger national oversight of decisions taken in Brussels. If Protestant political parties are members of coalition governments when their national parliaments create European oversight committees, these committees are much more likely to scrutinize Brussels closely than are oversight bodies established by governments that include Catholic or mixed confessional Christian Democratic parties. In other words, the presence of skeptical Protestants produces more scrutiny by parliamentary committees protecting the national interest.[34]

There is much we do not know about the way confessional culture works in the European institutions or how its impact has changed over time. Enlargement to include the Protestant and Eastern European member states and rapid secularization have expanded the religious diversity of the European elites. We are just beginning to explore how the increase in religious diversity has altered outcomes.[35]

European Archetypes: Delors and Thatcher

Confessional culture does not—usually—have an obvious visible impact on the behavior of the European elites. Rather, it works quietly over a longer time to shape a politician's worldview. We explore this notion by examining two European archetypes: British prime minister Margaret Thatcher, and Commission president Jacques Delors. No two politicians exemplified the confessional divide better than Thatcher and Delors, who were both at the height of their powers in the late 1980s and were legendary combatants in the struggle for control of European integration as the Cold War ended.

For all their disagreements, Thatcher and Delors had much in common. The two leaders were both born just three months apart in 1925 to middle-class families. Thatcher grew up in the small East Midlands town of Grantham, where her father ran the grocery store and post office just below the family apartment.[36] Delors was born in Paris, but his father was a peasant boy who had moved there after the war, married the daughter of a dance hall owner, and settled in the working-class neighborhood of La Petite–Roquette after securing a job as a bank messenger.[37] Thatcher and Delors both attended local public schools (although Thatcher eventually made her way to a private school) and won praise for diligence and academic performance. And both grew up in intensely religious families—Thatcher's shaped by her father's austere and rigid Methodism, and Delors's by his mother's pious Catholicism. Not surprisingly, both found their early years filled with religious instruction and the rhythms of religious practice. Thatcher's father, Alfred Roberts, was a Methodist lay preacher who delivered Bible-based sermons stressing individual responsibility before God and personal salvation. He applied his Christian ethical principles to his business life and to his work as a local politician. He believed in godly discipline and hard work, and taught his daughter never to waste time or money. He also centered the family's life on church activities, which meant spending weeknights at various functions and Sunday mornings, afternoons, and evenings at worship and Sunday School. Roberts was a relatively broad-minded man who had friendly relations with the Catholic priest at the church across the street; but he remained a man of his times, and of Protestant conviction, and refused to step inside his friend's church when invited.[38] If not exactly bigoted, the Thatchers were certainly anti-Catholic, like many other English households of the time.

Jacques Delors's mother nurtured the sense of religion he always claimed he was born with by taking him to church, where he sang in the choir and joined the *patronage* (church boys club), which became the center of his social and athletic life. His upbringing was not quite as rigid as Thatcher's (his father was not very religious), but his household was known in the neighborhood for being strict. He considered briefly becoming a priest, but decided against it and instead, at the age of twelve years, became the only boy from his class to move on to the *lycée*. War forced him to transfer schools several times. While in school, he joined both the Christian workers and Christian student organizations and was active in them until the Vichy regime banned them both.

Delors and Thatcher began their university studies in 1943, Delors to study law at Strasbourg University (at its Clermont-Ferrand campus), and Thatcher, after winning a coveted scholarship, to study chemistry at Oxford. Thatcher finished her degree without incident; but the war forced Delors onto a more difficult path. When the Nazis shut down Strasbourg, Delors attended night school to earn a banking degree. Both politicians always felt like outsiders—Thatcher because of her sex and shopkeeper background, and Delors because of his working-class roots and hardscrabble education. They were self-made people, thanks to their assiduous work and native intelligence, and they were both hard on their subordinates.

Despite similar circumstances and temperaments, Thatcher and Delors developed very different political commitments. Thatcher was a moralist, free marketeer, and Atlanticist; Delors was a personalist, social democratic unionist, and European-ist. It is thus not surprising that Thatcher and Delors—for all the years they had to work together—did not like each other much.[39] Each represented for the other the "worst of"—the worst of English nationalism and liberalism, the worst of French smugness and dirigisme. However, for the generation at the end of the Cold War, they defined the alternative visions of Europe rooted in their distinct confessional cultures. These visions were on display in two classic speeches given in Bruges in 1988–89, as history raced toward the climatic fall of the Berlin Wall. Both visions were rooted in the past but looked very much to the future.

Thatcher very consciously set out to explain her vision for Europe in a speech delivered on September 20, 1988, at the College of Europe, the intellectual high command of European federalism. Charles Powell, Thatcher's closest adviser, wrote the first draft, which then went through several revisions.[40] Although the Foreign Office and others may have softened the original rhetoric, the speech was clearly Thatcher's.[41] She began by firmly tying Britain culturally and historically to Europe, which she asserted was not, in fact, the "creation of the Treaty of Rome." Sound-ing almost like a continental Christian Democrat, she went on to assert that Britain had borrowed from European thought the "concept of the rule of law" and from "the idea of Christendom, . . . with its recognition of the unique and spiritual nature of the individual," Britain's "belief in personal liberty and other human rights."[42] Britain, she said, had "fought to prevent Europe from falling under the dominance of a single power" and had spilled its blood to preserve Europe's freedom. Thus, contrary to some assumptions, the country "does not dream of some cozy isolated existence on the fringes of the European Community. Our destiny is in Europe, as part of the Community."

But what did she mean by "Community"? Certainly not a constantly evolving set of institutions or an ever-expanding list of regulations. Rather, the EC was "the practical means by which Europe can ensure the future prosperity and security of its people in a world in which there are many other powerful nations and groups of nations." The best way to build a successful EC was through "willing and active co-operation between independent sovereign states." The suppression of nationhood and the centralization of power in Brussels would lead to disaster. "Europe will be stronger precisely because it has France as France, Spain as Spain, and Britain as Britain, each with its own customs, traditions, and identity. It would be folly to try to fit them into some sort of identikit European personality." Recognizing national diversity, however, did not preclude attempts by European partners "to speak with a single voice." Thatcher asserted that coordinated efforts in trade and defense would make Europe stronger, but coordination did not require centralization:

> Working more closely together does not require power to be centralised in Brussels or decisions to be taken by an appointed bureaucracy. Indeed, it is ironic that just when those countries such as the Soviet Union, which have tried to run everything

from the centre, are learning that success depends on dispersing power and decisions away from the centre, there are some in the Community who seem to want to move in the opposite direction. We have not successfully rolled back the frontiers of the state in Britain, only to see them re-imposed at a European level with a European super-state exercising a new dominance from Brussels. Certainly we want to see Europe more united and with a greater sense of common purpose. But it must be in a way which preserves the different traditions, parliamentary powers and sense of national pride in one's own country; for these have been the source of Europe's vitality through the centuries.

For Thatcher, integration did not mean the end of the nation-state and national identity. Such notions were not only idealistic but also dangerous; achievement of such ends would require the curtailing of liberty. The nation-state preserved individual freedom and a human sense of destiny, belonging, and home—summarized in her phrase "one's own country"—that was necessary for a nation to flourish. "Let Europe," she said, "be a family of nations, understanding each other better, appreciating each other more, doing more together but relishing our national identity no less than our common European endeavour."

Thus Thatcher, in one short speech, had outlined in stark relief the vision of Europe that had guided Britain's approach since the war. Although her pointed rhetoric and obvious passion were not to everyone's liking, her central ideas were in the mainstream of British thinking on Europe. She was declaring her opposition to giving more powers to supranational institutions, to introducing into the system more elements of European corporatism, to setting up a European Central Bank, to loosening border controls, and to weakening NATO.[43] These were clearly contentious issues, but Thatcher was not being a fringe radical; she was being Conservative, British, and thoroughly Protestant.

Delors did not attend Thatcher's speech, having been warned away by the British Foreign Office.[44] Nevertheless, according to Grant, "the speech's virulence wounded Delors, who lay low for several months."[45] But he got an opportunity to respond to Thatcher on the same College of Europe stage on October 17, 1989, just three weeks before the fall of the Berlin Wall. His rather convoluted "counterblast" was as much a personal statement of philosophy as a rejoinder to Thatcher, whom at times Delors seemed to be addressing as though she were in the room.[46] In the speech's lengthy but significant preamble, Delors identified himself as a federalist and personalist ("a disciple of Emmanuel Mounier"). Both identities coursed through his text.

Delors began by praising the College of Europe for being a place where "faith in the European ideal has never wavered" despite the ups and downs of the integration process.[47] He then joined the college in paying tribute to Denis de Rougemont by stating: "As a European militant [*militant europeen*], I, like many others, am carrying on the work he began in his time. He was an ardent federalist." Federalism, he argued, was the only "method" capable of reconciling the demands of continental governance with the diversity of the member states. He embraced the label:

I often find myself invoking federalism as a method, with the addition of the principle of subsidiarity. I see it as a way of reconciling what for many appears to be irreconcilable: the emergence of a United Europe and loyalty to one's homeland; the need for a European power capable of tackling the problems of our age and the absolute necessity to preserve our roots in the shape of our nations and regions; and decentralization of responsibilities, so that we never entrust to a bigger unit anything that is best done by a smaller one. This is precisely what subsidiarity is about.

For Delors, dividing responsibilities among levels of government was important. But federalism still required the exercise of top-down authority. On this point he diverged from de Rougemont; whereas de Rougemont abhorred power, Delors welcomed it. "I would," he said, "link power with the necessity I have so often invoked to promote the revitalization of European integration. Today I would like to get power working for the ideal." "History does not wait," he pleaded.

Most of Delors's speech was a passionate, almost stream-of-consciousness response to Thatcher's objections to the continental vision of integration. To her charge that integration threatened national identities, Delors countered with a rather vague assurance that the principles of pluralism and subsidiarity would prevent elimination of national differences. But he also warned that the failure to construct a new European identity would doom Europe to a return to the bad old days:

There is no conspiracy against the nation-state. Nobody is being asked to renounce legitimate patriotism. . . . As the Community develops, as our governments emphasize the need for a people's Europe, is it heresy to hope that all Europeans could feel that they belong to a Community which they see as a second homeland? If this view is rejected, European integration will founder and the specter of nationalism will return to haunt us, because the Community will have failed to win the hearts and minds of the people, the first requirement for the success of any human adventure.[48]

To Thatcher's dismissal of European idealism in favor of pragmatic problem solving, Delors countered that conflicts of interest could not be overcome without appealing to "a family feeling, a sense of shared values" that constituted a transcendent ideal. For Delors, idealism was exactly what Europe needed: "The time has come, my friends, to revive the ideal." To Thatcher's fear of bureaucratic centralization and her frustration with the constant tinkering with European institutions, Delors insisted that the "Institutions" (which in some printed copies always appear capitalized[49]) embody the rule of law and allow for the "transparent exercise of sovereignty." Strengthening supranational institutions was exactly what the EC must do to seize the historical moment. To Thatcher's emphasis on free markets and rejection of European social policy, Delors offered the standard social democratic position: "Think what a boost it would be for democracy and social justice if we could demonstrate that we are capable of working together to create a better-integrated society open to all." To Thatcher's rejection of EMU, Delors trumpeted the proposed federal structure of the new central bank and called EMU "the political crowning of economic convergence." And as if to turn the knife, he doubled down on the pace of change: "I have always favored the step-by-step approach—as the experiment we are embarked upon shows. But today I am moving away from it precisely because time is short. We need a radical change."

Delors was in a hurry; his speech was an almost breathless plea for the immediate realization of a European federal union. Whether the speech influenced the course of history is questionable, but it did reflect the spirit of the times, as the EC hurtled toward the end of the Cold War and the signing of the Maastricht Treaty. Delors did not get all he wanted; but Thatcher got almost none of what she wanted—at least not immediately. Thatcher's speech did not prevent Maastricht or Schengen, but it did give voice to the frustrated British minority that soon came to plague the Conservative Party and make an impact on the politics of integration throughout the EU.

After leaving office, Thatcher repeated her concerns in public. She came to see integration as not only objectionable as a threat to freedom but also troublesome from a practical standpoint. Her last major work, *Statecraft* (2002), stressed the fact that Britain was essentially "different" from other European countries. With just a hint of traditional British anti-Catholicism, she stated her belief "that if they were willing to investigate the matter honestly and intelligently the politicians of Europe would discover that the interests of their nations were 'different' and conflicting in important ways too; but, of course, in euro-land that would be heresy, and the Euro-Inquisition would soon set the political funeral pyres a-smoking."[50]

Thatcher was, by that time, convinced that the entire European experiment was "unnecessary and irrational" and that leaders on the Continent would realize one day that building a "European superstate" was "perhaps the greatest folly of the modern era." That Britain "should ever have been part of it will appear a political error of historical magnitude." The British should "fundamentally reassess our relationship with the rest of the EU and renegotiate it in order to secure our national interests and sovereignty." Furthermore, they should refuse to rule out any particular framework for cooperation, consider joining the North American Free Trade Agreement (NAFTA), and think globally rather than regionally.[51] This advice, which essentially meant withdrawing from the EU, sounded radical at the time. But it was not her ideas concerning national identities, state sovereignty, and Britain's role in the world that set Thatcher apart after her 1988 Bruges speech. What made her different was her willingness to articulate these ideas in plain language, without any concessions to claims that sovereignty was outmoded and that globalization and the decline of European power made deep cooperation necessary. She was also willing to suggest actions consistent with her vision and not care whom she angered. With her exit from public office, young Tory firebrands such as MEP Daniel Hannan and politicians further to the right—including MEP Nigel Farage, leader of the United Kingdom Independence Party—assumed her Euroskeptical mantle.[52] Indeed, in 2013 the pressure of the Tory Euroskeptics on the party forced Prime Minister David Cameron to call for a renegotiation of Britain's relationship with the EU and a referendum on the results. Thus, what sounded almost loony in 2002 became government policy in 2013.

In the late 1980s Thatcher and Delors articulated archetypal visions of Europe rooted in their respective confessional cultures. These visions were not exactly the ones offered by Bevin or Schuman in 1950, but nevertheless they were remarkably little changed after forty years. The Catholic Delors described a European ideal that Schuman would recognize; the Protestant Thatcher expressed reservations that Bevin would—aside from the emphasis on markets—understand. Not all the European elites, of course, lined up perfectly with one of these options; but these were the nuclei around which politicians, officials, and civil society leaders orbited—some closer to and some farther away from the center, with some orbits intersecting. Echoes of Delors can be heard in the calls by former German foreign minister Joschka Fischer to "leap into full integration,"[53] and by former Belgian prime minister and MEP Guy Verhofstadt to create a United States of Europe "capable of acting decisively."[54] His voice can also be heard in the chorus of leaders and commentators calling for a fiscal union followed by a political union to solve the European economic crisis.[55] Thatcher can be heard as well—in the tones of Tony Blair: "Europe can, in its economic and political strength, be a superpower; a superpower, but not a superstate";[56] of David Cameron: "For us, the European Union is a means to an end . . . not an end in itself. . . . This vision of flexibility and co-operation is not the same as those who want to build an ever-closer political union—but it is just as valid";[57] and in the parliaments of Denmark, Finland, Iceland, Northern Ireland, Norway, Sweden, and certainly Great Britain. A hint of Thatcher can even sometimes be heard in the utterances of the Protestant leaders on the Continent. Angela Merkel, the austere daughter of a Protestant pastor, has not been an instinctive and enthusiastic federalist like her mentor, the gregarious Catholic Helmut Kohl, nor has she shied away from applying Protestant values to policy questions, as she did when famously suggesting that southern debtor countries must "atone for past sins."[58] The fit between confessional culture and European perspective is not always perfect; but European leaders tend to conform to the general pattern, reflecting the confessional cultures from which they have emerged.

European Elites and the nations they govern still fit the mold set in the EU's formative period. Protestant states have resisted deeper integration and have often resented the sacrifice of sovereignty when forced to cut a deal. Religion is not always an important issue in the halls of the EU institutions, but the atmosphere in Brussels is still heavily saturated by Christian Democratic culture. Catholic Christian Democrats and the continental socialists and liberals they co-opted in the 1950s and 1960s are at home in the sheltered world of the institutions. They believe they are building something important. Protestants, conversely, still feel a bit like usurpers—like the foreign guest at the dinner table who cannot keep up with the colloquial conversation.

The division among Europe's elites is not, of course, just about comfort levels. They are divided over what Europe should be. Leaders from Catholic confessional cultures tend to follow Delors in pressing for a federation that can act decisively at home and abroad; those from Protestant cultures blanch at the thought of a federal union and tut-tut about the European dreamers. This disagreement is not merely over tactics; it is also a dispute over ends. And it threatens integration.

Notes

1. Quoted by Mark Gilbert, *European Integration: A Concise History* (Lanham, MD: Rowman & Littlefield, 2012), 114.

2. Desmond Dinan, *Europe Recast: A History of European Union* (Boulder, CO: Lynne Rienner, 2004), 171–73.

3. Gilbert, *European Integration*, 110.

4. A weighted voting system that gives larger member states more votes than smaller states. Supermajorities are required to approve legislative proposals.

5. Margaret Thatcher wrote in *Statecraft*: "Already, towards the end of my time as Prime Minister, I was becoming increasingly concerned at the way Single Market measures were being used to impose socialist-style regulation by the back door." Margaret Thatcher, *Statecraft: Strategies for a Changing World* (New York: HarperCollins, 2002), 376.

6. Quoted by Gilbert, *European Integration*, 138.

7. Britain formally subscribed to the Agreement on Social Policy in 1997.

8. Switzerland rejected European Economic Area membership, and therefore any thought of EU membership.

9. Several of these countries—the Czech Republic, Estonia, Hungary, Latvia, and Slovakia—have significant Protestant communities.

10. Gilbert, *European Integration*, 197–98.

11. Ibid., 207.

12. Latvia joined the euro zone in 2014.

13. Two non–euro zone member states, Britain and the Czech Republic, refused to sign the 2013 Fiscal Compact (formally, the Treaty on Stability, Coordination, and Governance in the Economic and Monetary Union), forcing European leaders to create the new treaty outside the official EU legal framework.

14. The exceptions to this statement are the confessionally complex and economically tiny Baltic states of Estonia and Latvia.

15. For a discussion of the policy of flexibility, see Alexander C.-G. Stubb, *Negotiating Flexibility in the European Union: Amsterdam, Nice, and Beyond* (Houndmills, UK: Palgrave, 2002).

16. We chose only agreements that have been signed and implemented. The Prüm Convention and the Fiscal Compact exist outside the EU treaty structure due to member state objections, making them issues in the integration debate and therefore valid indicators of enthusiasm for

integration. The European Stability Mechanism is omitted because it precisely duplicates the euro zone. Although these agreements do not carry the same significance, we chose not to weight the various formations to reduce the risk of bias.

17. The Euro-Plus Pact commits members to broad strategic goals and specific strategies in the areas of competitiveness, employment, public finances, and financial stability.

18. Sixteen countries assented to an attachment to the Lisbon Treaty, stating that the EU flag, anthem, motto, currency, and Europe Day "will for them continue as symbols to express the sense of community of the people in the European Union and their allegiance to it." "Final Act (2007/C 306/02)," *Official Journal of the European Union*, 267, http://eur-lex.europa.eu/LexUriServ/Lex UriServ.do?uri=oj:c:2007:306:0231:0271:en:pdf.

19. As a new member state still in transition, Croatia was not included in this study.

20. The coefficient of $r = -.232$, had the predicted sign but did not achieve statistical significance.

21. François Foret, *Religion and Politics in the European Union: The Secular Canopy* (Cambridge: Cambridge University Press, 2014), 50.

22. Ibid., 61.

23. We thank François Foret for this insight.

24. Foret, *Religion*, 79.

25. Wolfgang C. Müller, Marcelo Jenny, and Alejandro Ecker, "The Elites/Masses Gap in European Integration," in *The Europe of Elites: A Study into the Europeanness of Europe's Political and Economic Elites*, ed. Heinrich Best, György Lengyel, and Luca Verzichelli (Oxford: Oxford University Press, 2012), 167–91. Finland, the Netherlands, and Sweden were not included in the sample.

26. Renaud Dehousse and Andrew Thompson, "Intergovernmentalists in the Commission: Foxes in the Henhouse?" in *Euroscepticism within the EU Institutions: Diverging Views of Europe*, ed. Nathalie Brack and Olivier Costa (London: Routledge, 2012), 23.

27. Foret, *Religion*, 113–15.

28. Pascal Fontaine, *Voyage to the Heart of Europe, 1953–2009: A History of the Christian-Democratic Group and the Group of the European People's Party in the European Parliament* (Brussels: Éditions Racine, 2009), 418; Stephanie Holmes, "Profile: Rocco Buttiglione," BBC News, October 21, 2004, http://news.bbc.co.uk/2/hi/europe/3718210.stm.

29. Holmes, "Profile."

30. See Foret, *Religion*, 143–54.

31. This finding, according to Best, "suggests that Catholic politicians consider an integrated Europe as a threat to their religious values rather than as an institutional frame for the Christian occident." Heinrich Best, "Elite Foundations of European Integration: A Causal Analysis," in *Europe of Elites*, ed. Best, Lengyel, and Verzichelli, 225–26.

32. The study has no measure of Catholic or Protestant religious commitment, which has always been a stronger predictor of attitudes toward integration than simple affiliation and did not report the bivariate findings for affiliation. The multivariate analysis includes ideology, assessment of EU institutions, the perceived benefits of the EU, and other variables that are themselves correlated with religion (at least in the mass public) and does not consider possible indirect effects. The residual negative effect of Catholic affiliation on national parliamentarians may also be an artifact of nonrandom sampling procedures, the absence of weighting or, perhaps, other methodological choices.

33. In the multivariate analysis, parliamentarians in Orthodox and mixed religion states are not significantly less supportive of unification than those in Catholic countries, although the mixed religion category comes fairly close to statistical significance. Mladen Lazi , Miguel Jerez-Mir, Vladimir Vuleti , and Rafae Vázquez-Garcia, "Patterns of Regional Diversity in Political Elites' Attitudes," in *Europe of Elites*, 147–66, esp. 160–163. Finland, the Netherlands, and Sweden were not included in the sample.

34. See Ivy Hamerly, "Christian Democratic Parties and the Domestic Parliamentary Response to European Integration," *Journal of Church & State* 54, no. 2 (2012): 214–39.

35. The reverse is also true; we are just beginning to explore how Europeanization has affected religious diversity.

36. For Thatcher's early life, see John Campbell, *The Iron Lady: Margaret Thatcher, from Grocer's Daughter to Prime Minister* (New York: Penguin Books, 2009), 1–16.

37. For Delors's early life, see Charles Grant, *Delors: Inside the House that Jacques Built* (London: Nicholas Brealey, 1994), 5–9.

38. Charles Moore, *Margaret Thatcher: The Authorized Biography, from Grantham to the Falklands* (New York: Alfred A. Knopf, 2013), 8.

39. Hugo Young recounts a particularly difficult early press conference where Thatcher gave Delors no time to speak and then proceeded to address the Commission president: "Would you very kindly confirm that what I said was absolutely strictly accurate and that you are looking forward to this, and rising to the challenge it represents." Hugo Young, *This Blessed Plot: Britain and Europe from Churchill to Blair* (Woodstock, NY: Overlook Press, 1998), 327. This illustrated, in Young's opinion, Thatcher's treatment of Delors as nothing more than a "bureaucratic flunky." Grant, paraphrasing one of Thatcher's advisors, says, "since Thatcher had an instinctive dislike of both Frenchmen and commissioners, Delors did not stand much of a chance." For Delors's part, Grant quotes one British diplomat who said, "Delors made the mistake of being visibly frightened of her. . . . But he found her fascinating and hated her much less than she hated him." According to Delors, the relationship between the two leaders did not deteriorate dramatically until after Geoffrey Howe left the Foreign Office in 1989; Grant, *Delors*, 90. Thatcher states in her memoirs that "by the summer of 1988 he [Delors] had altogether slipped his leash as a *fonctionnaire* and become a fully fledged political spokesman for federalism." Margaret Thatcher, *The Downing Street Years* (New York: HarperCollins, 1993), 742.

40. Young, *Blessed Plot*, 348–49.

41. The speech, which differs somewhat from the official text, can be watched in its entirety at Margaret Thatcher, "Speech to the College of Europe ('The Bruges Speech')," September 20, 1988, www.youtube.com/watch?v=wkRwMFy0CVM.

42. All the quotations here are from Margaret Thatcher, "Speech to the College of Europe ('The Bruges Speech'), 20 September 1988," Margaret Thatcher Foundation, www.margaretthatcher .org/document/107332.

43. For the speech's policy elements, see Gilbert, *European Integration*, 149–50.

44. Young, *Blessed Plot*, 350.

45. Ibid., 89.

46. Ibid., 129.

47. All quotations here are from Jacques Delors, *Address by Mr. Jacques Delors, President of the Commission of the European Communities, Bruges, 17 October 1989* (Brussels: European Communities, 1989).

48. Jacques Delors, "Address Given by Jacques Delors (Bruges, 17 October 1989)," Agence Europe SA, www.cvce.eu/obj/address_given_by_jacques_delors_bruges_17_october_1989-en -5bbb1452-92c7-474b- a7cf-a2d281898295.html.

49. Ibid.

50. Thatcher, *Statecraft*, 394.

51. All the quotations here are from ibid., 410–11.

52. See Daniel Hannan, blog, http://blogs.telegraph.co.uk/news/author/danielhannan/; and European Parliament / MEPs, "Nigel Farage," European Parliament, www.europarl.europa.eu /meps/en/4525/nigel_farage_home.html.

53. Joschka Fischer, "From Confederacy to Federation: Thoughts on the Finality of European Integration," speech given at Humbolt University, Berlin, May 12, 2000, Jean Monnet Program, www.google.com/url?sa=t&rct=j&q=&esrc=s&source=web&cd=1&ved=0CCEQFjAA&url=h ttp%3A%2F%2Fwww.jeanmonnetprogram.org%2Farchive%2Fpapers%2F00%2Fjoschka_fischer _en.rtf&ei=abmuU9mHGMSnyAS2ooCQCA&usg=AFQjCNHSVzpbE4vE93LSRTtnmgQADOK Lzg&bvm=bv.69837884,d.aWw.

54. Guy Verhofstadt, *The United States of Europe: Manifesto for a New Europe* (London: Federal Trust, 2006), 16.

55. See Nicolas Berggruen and Nathan Gardels, "The Next Europe: Toward a Federal Union," *Foreign Affairs* 92, no. 4 (2013): 134–42.

56. Tony Blair, "Address Given by Tony Blair to the Polish Stock Exchange (Warsaw, 6 October 2000)," European Union, www.cvce.eu/obj/address_given_by_tony_blair_to_the_polish_stock _exchange_warsaw_6_october_2000- en-f8c765d9-ad33-4ce3-bfbe-7dd6d01141d7.html.

57. David Cameron, "David Cameron's EU Speech—Full Text," *The Guardian*, January 23, 2013, www.guardian.co.uk/politics/2013/jan/23/david-cameron-eu-speech-referendum.

58. Quoted by Timothy Garton Ash, "The New German Question," *New York Review of Books*, August 15, 2013, 54. See also Steven Ozment, "German Austerity's Lutheran Core," *New York Times*, August 11, 2012, www.nytimes.com/2012/08/12/opinion/sunday/in-euro-crisis-germany -looks-to-martin-luther.html.

9

Political Groups

THE EUROPEAN UNION's member state behavior and elite attitudes, as we saw in the last chapter, demonstrate the continued influence of confessional culture in contemporary Europe. Other social and economic factors also exert pressure on national decision makers, resulting in a sometimes-less-than-perfect match between confessional culture and member state behavior. But the general postwar pattern still holds: Elites in Catholic countries support deeper integration, while those in Protestant countries resist yielding sovereignty, preferring intergovernmental cooperation over supranationalism.

In this chapter we extend our exploration of European integration since 1975 to political groups, in particular churches and political parties. If confessional culture continues to divide the European Union, the Catholic Church and its associated political organizations should remain staunch supporters of integration and Protestant churches should show relatively less enthusiasm—or even outright hostility. Likewise, political parties with a strong Catholic influence should support integration, while parties based in Protestant-majority countries or sectarian parties should be Euroskeptics. As we will see, the general pattern holds—but with a new wrinkle or two.

The Catholic Church

The religious revival after World War II delayed but did not reverse the waning of the Catholic Church's influence over government leaders and decline in religious observance among ordinary Europeans. Indeed, starting in the mid-1960s, these developments accelerated. The Church had lost its official status throughout much of Europe in the nineteenth and twentieth centuries (Germany and Malta excepted), but it remained privileged in several Catholic-majority countries, including Ireland and Poland. In the Age of Democracy, the Church found the focus of its European dialogue shifting from "church–state" to "church–society"; it no longer attempted to shape a confessional state, but rather a confessing society.[1] As John Paul II put it in *Ecclesia in Europe*: "In her relations with public authorities the Church is not calling for a return to the confessional state" but instead offers "the engagement of believing communities committed to bring about the humanization of society on the basis of the Gospel, lived under the sign of hope."[2] Thus, as the twentieth century wore on, the Church put less emphasis on mobilizing Catholics behind favored political parties and more on persuading leaders and citizens to back its policy positions. In short, the Catholic Church transformed itself into a transnational interest group that could operate on both the international and domestic levels.[3]

Vatican II

The foundation for this new role of the Church was laid, of course, during the deliberations of the Second Ecumenical Council of the Vatican (commonly known as Vatican II). Pope John XXIII initiated the process of reform and set the tone by telling the council's first session in October 1962 that the church must "[bring] herself up to date."[4] The council responded with decisions that left the core doctrines of Catholicism unchanged but effectively revolutionized the Church's approach to the modern world. First, the council aimed for greater cultural relevance by opening the liturgy to the laity through the use of vernacular languages, increased lay participation, and the incorporation of indigenous cultural expressions into the Mass. Second, the council effectively ended the Church's monopoly on earthly salvation by welcoming dialogue with other Christian traditions—or, as Pope John called them, "the brethren who are separated"[5]—and with other Abrahamic faiths, namely Judaism and Islam.[6] The Church made explicit its intention to work for the unity of Christian people everywhere, ending whatever remained of the Counter-Reformation. Third, the council acknowledged the benefit of bishops working together in national or regional councils and allowed such gatherings as long as they were conducted in cooperation with the pope. In effect this action recognized the importance of national contexts to the life and governance of the Church—a development bound to erode the authority of the pope if carried through. Finally, the council acknowledged the impact of "personalism" by placing new emphasis on the dignity of the human person and by committing the church to defend the rights and freedoms of human beings of every faith or no faith.[7] In sum, Vatican II constituted a peace treaty between the Catholic Church and modernity. Gone was the closed, angry Catholicism of the nineteenth and early twentieth centuries; in its place was an open, more accommodating Catholicism, determined—as far as God would allow—to shape the modern world in its own image.

For the Church, coming to terms with modernity meant a withdrawal from direct political responsibility. Vatican II ratified the modern separation of church and state when it declared: "Christ, to be sure, gave His Church no proper mission in the political, economic, or social order. The purpose which He set before her is a religious one."[8] To underline this position, the European bishops explicitly rejected any notion of a "confessional Christian state."[9] Thus, after Vatican II, "the Church no longer claimed to have a privileged place in politics or in state authority."[10]

The Church's withdrawal from a direct political role, however, did not mean its withdrawal from politics entirely. Public policy pronouncements and organized efforts to influence decision makers were still consistent with the Church's evangelistic, prophetic, and moral mission. But such activities would take place through normal methods of participatory politics rather than through backdoor diplomatic channels. Because the Church still carried significant weight with many Europeans, it remained fairly effective, although its political clout diminished as the twentieth century wore on. The Church's mobilization efforts, of course, still varied across Catholic Europe. In southern Europe—including Portugal, Spain, and particularly Italy—the Church remained a key mobilizer of support for Catholic-oriented political parties. But with John XXIII's election to the papacy in 1958, the tone changed. John (and his five successors) refrained from personal involvement in Italian politics. That was less true for the Italian bishops, who remained active supporters of the Christian Democratic Party until the party's demise in the early 1990s. Throughout the 1980s they continued to call for the "unity of Catholics," signaling "Church support for the [Christian Democratic Party]."[11] Nevertheless, they changed their tone after Vatican II, relying less on authoritative pronouncements and more on "rational persuasion." In the more secular northern and mixed countries of Germany and the Netherlands—but also in Belgium, Luxembourg, and France—the Church's role was even more muted, as the bishops stepped back from supporting the Christian Democratic parties, preferring to speak more directly about specific public policy issues.[12]

Vatican II changed the political role of the Catholic Church, but it did not reduce the Church's support for a more peaceful international community through cooperation and integration. Although the council did not endorse Pope John's explicit call for world government in his 1963 encyclical, *Pacem in Terris*, the bishops threw their weight behind regional organizations as the precursors to "a community of all men": "Already existing international and regional organizations are certainly well-deserving of the human race.[13] These are the first efforts at laying the foundations on an international level for a community of all men to work for the solution to the serious problems of our times, to encourage progress everywhere, and to obviate wars of whatever kind."[14]

The council's official words, however, were only the tip of the iceberg. Behind the scenes, the Vatican was developing a long-term approach to the European Community as it was evolving in the early 1960s. Rome's position was outlined in a public letter written by the papal secretary of state, Amleto Cardinal Cicognani, and sent on behalf of Pope John to the Forty-Ninth Annual French Social Week in July 1962.[15] The letter developed four great themes that were entirely consistent with past Catholic approaches to Europe, but were also suited to the Church's new role as a moral voice in the modern world. First, the Vatican affirmed the existence of a common European "interest"—which would perhaps be better termed a common European culture or sense of community—that served as the foundation for European unity:[16] "Beyond any doubt, this European common interest exists; it must be affirmed and an effort must be made to bring about its realization." This "common interest" runs deeper than economic, social, and political interests. Its essence "expresses itself in common ways of thinking, feeling, and living," which "draw their unifying force" from "the European spirit," a set of "common spiritual values."

The second major theme is that Catholic Christianity, with its emphasis on the "human person," is the most important source of this "European spirit": "Above all, what has shaped the European soul for 2,000 years is Christianity, which has outlined the traits of the human person, a free being, independent and responsible." For the Vatican, a commitment to the freedom and dignity of the human person stood at the heart of European culture. Christianity taught Europe to value human beings and defend their rights before the state; thus, to ignore or minimize the role of Christianity in the creation of the European Community would be to cut the regional organization off from its cultural roots and deprive it of nourishment—without Christianity, a united Europe would never survive.

The letter's third theme is the importance of families for the success of the European Community. Europe, the letter argues, will not be built by governments alone; "intermediate bodies"—organizations that stand between the state and the individual—will need to assist with the creation of a common European community by bonding with each other in joint areas of responsibility. The trade unions must be involved, but the letter places special emphasis on the "primary and irreplaceable role of the family" in the building of Europe. European officials must implement policies designed to meet the needs of families, for "it is quite clear that they form the vital center of the Europe of persons and peoples and that they cannot be sacrificed for the organization of the European countries." Finally, the letter calls Catholics to participate actively in the building of Europe: "Catholics must be in the first rank in this eminently pacific undertaking."

Thus the Vatican of Pope John XXIII renewed its support for the fledgling European Community, but it also staked out a clear approach to contemporary European integration. For the sake of humanity, Europe must be built. The basis for European unity would be its common culture, not the Continent's material self-interest. Furthermore, Europeans would need to recognize that their culture, especially their extraordinary emphasis on the importance of the human person, was deeply indebted to Christianity as the main fountain of their common values. European public policy would focus on strengthening families as the building blocks of the new Europe. And the European Catholics would work with their hearts and hands to build a united Continent.

These themes, all with their roots in earlier Catholic teaching, constituted a general Catholic strategy toward the European Community, but not a blueprint for integration. As under Pius XII, the Church gave its general approval to federalist efforts, but it studiously avoided pronouncing on specific integration proposals. It would speak directly to public policies emerging from Brussels in areas such as human cloning and stem cell research, as it would to policies coming from member state governments, but it would not advise European leaders on how to integrate the Continent beyond continued reminders on the value of greater unity.[17]

The Roman Church would have plenty of opportunities to articulate its vision for Europe, beginning in the 1980s, as the European Community relaunched its integration efforts and incorporated new members. The bishops would play a key role in voicing the views of the Church, but the primary responsibility fell to a charismatic Pole who took a deep interest in European politics—Pope John Paul II.

The Papacy of John Paul II

John Paul II, elected in October 1978, understood very well his role as missionary, prophet, and pastor to Europe.[18] He grasped quickly the constraints on the modern Church, but he also understood the tremendous impact it could have with wise deployment of its "soft power" resources. The pope brought the Church to the world by traveling personally to its far corners. He skillfully used his charismatic personality, youthful vigor, and rhetorical skill in many languages to attract global media attention. Very soon he had achieved "rock star" status (augmented by his close scrape with death at the hands of a would-be assassin in May 1981) and a platform for his often-pointed messages to the peoples of the world and their leaders.

The pope's message to Europe differed little from that of his predecessors. Coming from this pope, however, it carried more weight because of the historical circumstances of late-twentieth-century Europe, his perspicacity, and his particular history. The Church in his care would not waver in its commitment to European unity, and he would personally promote integration with the tools of his office. His support for integration efforts was unmistakable. For example, in October 1988 in Strasbourg, he responded to President François Mitterrand's welcome by saying that the Catholic Church "can but greet with satisfaction the efforts made by the European countries to tighten still more their bonds and forge a common future."[19] And in his address to the European Parliament a few days later, he emphatically stated, "Since the end of World War II, the Holy See has not ceased to encourage the construction of Europe."[20] He did not confine himself to general statements of support for unity, however. Without entering into detailed policy discussions, he nevertheless spoke approvingly of the Single European Act by name, predicting that it would "hasten the process of European integration."[21] Thus he fearlessly supported a uniting Europe. For him, European integration was a passion, not a mere duty.

The pope's passion for integration was a natural extension of his belief in the deep spiritual unity of Europe, which transcended the Continent's divisions, and even its secularism. His 1979 trip to his native Poland offered clear, early evidence that he would emphasize European unity in both word and deed. This unity, however, would not be that of the Six or the Nine (the Six, plus Britain, Denmark, and Ireland); it would be unity of the entire divided Continent. "East" and "West," as Cold War concepts, had to disappear. Europe must, as he put it, "breathe with both lungs."[22] And Christianity was the only force that could bring both parts of Europe together. The pope told the Polish bishops gathered at Częstochowa that "despite the different traditions that exist in the territory of Europe between its Eastern part and its Western part, there lies in each of them the same Christianity, which takes its origins from the same Christ, which accepts the same Word of God, which is linked with the same twelve apostles."[23] Christianity was what made Europe "Europe." And the Church's role, especially in communist Europe, was to "commit itself anew to the formation of the spiritual unity of Europe."[24] The challenge to communism was obvious: The Iron Curtain was illegitimate and immoral; Europe was whole from "the Atlantic to the Urals." But once the Berlin Wall came down, the challenge to the whole of Europe was also obvious: Europe's unity was found not in its search for peace or material wealth, but in its common culture—in Christianity, as the source of its values and historical mission.

Throughout his pontificate, but more urgently after the fall of the Berlin Wall, Pope John Paul II labored to reteach Europe its vocation, reminding the Continent that its roots were in Christianity. Like so many Catholic leaders before him, he identified Christianity as the creator of Europe. Christianity gave Europe its form; and only in Christianity could Europe find its essential unity. In his June 28, 2003, encyclical, *Ecclesia in Europa*, the pope powerfully articulated his case:

> The history of the European continent has been distinctively marked by the life-giving influence of the Gospel. . . . There can be no doubt that the Christian faith belongs, in a radical and decisive way, to the foundations of European culture. Christianity in fact has shaped Europe, impressing upon it certain basic values. Modern Europe itself, which has given the democratic ideal and human rights to the world, draws its values from its Christian heritage. More than a geographical area, Europe can be described as "a *primarily cultural and historical concept*, which denotes a reality born as a continent thanks also to the unifying force of Christianity, which has been capable of integrating peoples and cultures among themselves, and which is intimately linked to the whole of European culture."[25]

John Paul insisted that Christianity—as a matter of historical record and moral necessity—was the key source of what defined Europe. He was more than willing to acknowledge other contributions, "from the spirit of Greece to that of Roman law and virtue; from the contributions of the Latin, Celtic, Germanic, Slav, and Finno-Ugric peoples, to those of the Jewish culture and the Islamic world."[26] But no one could doubt that in his view there would be no Europe without Christianity.

Christianity was Europe's life-giving fountain, but a united Europe's "true identity" was in its values. These were the values of the Christian Democratic personalists: "the transcendent dignity of the human person, the value of reason, freedom, democracy, the constitutional state and the distinction between political life and religion."[27] All the peoples who shared Europe's heritage and affirmed its values should, he claimed, be welcome in a united Europe, where their "historical and cultural distinctions" and "national identities" would be valued, especially if the principles of subsidiarity and solidarity were properly developed and implemented.[28]

Finally, the pope urged Europe's leaders to draw on the assistance of the "one and universal" Church as they built a new "European home." The Church was first of all a model of unity, the visible embodiment of "unity in a diversity of cultural expressions" and an institution to be emulated.[29] Second, the Church and other religious bodies that stand apart from the state should be consulted as privileged voices on "authentic ethical and civil values."[30] Third, individual Christians should fill "the various European agencies and institutions, in order to contribute . . . to the shaping of a European social order which is increasingly respectful of every man and woman, and thus in accordance with the common good."[31]

Pope John Paul II longed for Europe to recognize its spiritual unity and recommit to its Christian roots. *"Europe,"* he pleaded, "as you stand at the beginning of the third millennium, *'Open the doors to Christ! Be yourself. Rediscover your origins. Relive your roots'"* (emphasis in the original).[32] But was Europe listening? The writing of a Constitution for Europe was the perfect opportunity to accept the pope's argument and acknowledge the contribution of Christianity to the values and culture of Europe. An early draft of the Constitution's preamble mentioned the inspiration of the "cultural, religious, and humanist inheritance of Europe" but identified its sources as "the civilisations of Greece and Rome," the "spiritual impulse always present in its heritage," and the "philosophical currents of the Enlightenment."[33] With Christianity left out of the preamble, Pope John Paul II began a campaign to convince the European Convention to revise the draft. He made public pronouncements, called for a "reference to the religious and in particular the Christian heritage of Europe," and spent an hour in private conversation making his case to Convention chairman Valéry Giscard d'Estaing.[34] The European bishops followed his lead, as did several European governments—but all to no avail. The Convention redrafted the preamble, but it remained religiously generic, referring only to "the cultural, religious, and humanist inheritance of Europe, from which have developed the universal values of the inviolable and inalienable rights of the human person, freedom, democracy, equality, and the rule of law."[35] The pope lived long enough to see the new draft, but he died before the treaty embodying the Constitution ran up against the intransigent French and Dutch electorates.

The failure to modify the proposed European Constitution's preamble only underlined the growing frustration that John Paul felt as the new millennium dawned.[36] The flush of excitement at the fall of communism and the reintegration of East and West faded quickly. The East seemed far more enamored with the secular, materialistic West than the West was with the spiritual, long-suffering East. The pope never doubted the necessity of a united Europe, but he began to realize that Europe could unite, and metaphorically thus gain the whole world, but still lose its soul. As the pope once exclaimed in anger, the European project looked more and more like an "ultra-liberal, consumerist system that is devoid of values."[37] Catholicism, for the first time, felt ambivalent. On one hand the Church, with a single voice, had supported postwar efforts to build a united Europe on principle. Beneath the divisions, Mother Church united Europe spiritually and morally. On the other hand, Europe had increasingly pursued unity for its material benefits alone, rejecting the spiritual unity of all European peoples and the gentle moral guidance of the Church in favor of a soulless consumerism and a decadent individualistic ethos. The Church had always sought to define the idea of "Europe" and the values that it would espouse.[38] But now those values were under attack, as was demonstrated by the constitutional debate and—just as shocking—the European Parliament's 2002 passage of a nonbinding resolution calling on current and prospective EU members (including Ireland and Poland) to guarantee legal abortions, sex education in public schools, and the universal availability of contraceptives. Such actions showing obvious disregard for Catholic contributions and moral sensibilities encouraged some Catholics to begin questioning not the principle of European unity but the character of the uniting Europe. And nowhere was this growing division within the Church more evident than in Pope John Paul II's native Poland.

Euroskeptical Catholicism in Poland and Ireland

Poland is a Catholic country with a Reformed sense of "chosen-ness." From the time of King Mieszko I's conversion to Christianity in 966, Poland has viewed itself as the easternmost bastion of Western Christian civilization. Pagan barbarians, Orthodox Slavs, and Muslim Turks lurked beyond its eastern borders, eager to conquer the nation and invade the West. Poland, however, had successfully held the line for Latin Christendom, fighting off the Protestant Swedes and the Muslim Turks in the seventeenth century to save Catholic Europe. The Poles took their mission to guard the eastern gate seriously, and consequently they saturated their public life with symbols of their sacred nation. By the early nineteenth century Poles saw their politically partitioned but spiritually united nation in messianic terms: Suffering Poland was Christ to the world—and thus a crucified Poland would become an instrument of divine renewal. As the romantic poet Count Zygmunt Krasinski wrote in 1847: "The real reason for the existence of Poland is to realize on Earth the Kingdom of Heaven."[39]

In the eyes of the Catholic Poles, God had chosen the Polish nation to perform special tasks in support of the universal mission of the Church. In the late twentieth century Pope John Paul II defined this "great apostolic assignment" as the "new evangelization" of an integrating Europe.[40] Speaking to the Polish bishops in Krakow in 1997, John Paul outlined this mission: "Today we cannot refrain from following the path we have been shown. The Church in Poland can offer Europe, as it grows in unity, her attachment to the faith, her tradition inspired by religious devotion, the pastoral efforts of her Bishops and priests, and certainly many other values on the basis of which Europe can become a reality endowed not only with high economic standards but also with a profound spiritual life."[41]

Poland's return to its home in the West was an opportunity for the Church to reawaken Europe's sleepy spirit and reinvigorate its common Christian values. John Paul II's Poland had the potential to transform the European Union with its example of an authentic Christian society. For this reason, the pope never wavered in his support for Polish accession to the EU; he was "perfectly happy to have Poland rejoin Europe, so long as that meant that Europe would in time become more like Poland, rather than the other way around."[42]

Many Polish Catholics, however, doubted that Poland could transform the EU before the EU—or more appropriately, the West—transformed Poland. In the early postcommunist era, several prominent Polish bishops—including Primate Josef Cardinal Glemp and Tadeusz Cardinal Pieronek—expressed reservations about joining what Glemp called "the rich proprietors' club."[43] They were clearly concerned—with good reason—about cultural imperialism. As Pieronek put it in 1998: "I most fear that which is habitually called the Western culture and which is quite often a distortion of that culture. The popular name for this is *McDonaldization*" (emphasis in the original).[44] The bishops, however, had no real choice but to line up behind the pope and to support Poland's accession to the EU. Polls indicated that more than 80 percent of Polish Catholic priests accepted the hierarchy's position, but a small number vociferously opposed accession, and their resistance took on political significance.[45]

Catholic opposition to the EU centered early on Father Tadeusz Rydzyk, a Redemptorist, and Radio Maryja, the radio station he founded in 1991.[46] The station's religious programming attracted a traditional Catholic audience of elderly, less educated, and poor listeners from rural areas.[47] But Rydzyk's right-wing, nationalistic politics and his penchant for anti-Semitic conspiracy theories gained him broader attention and a political following. His diatribes against the secular West, with its decadent values and liberal economics, touched that deep, conflicted current in the Polish Catholic soul, which the pope and bishops worked out in favor of the West and EU membership, but which the less cosmopolitan clergy and laity resolved in favor of a defense of traditional Polish identity. For Radio Maryja's listeners the EU threatened to undermine the religious unity of Poland, the moral foundations of the family, and the economic supports of rural Polish life.[48] Joining this "Europe" did not sound like the fulfillment of a heavenly vision but the realization of a satanic nightmare. It would be better to hang on to what was left of Catholic Poland than to see it swallowed by a soulless empire.

Similar but less extreme currents could also be found in the Republic of Ireland, where Catholicism and national identity are closely intertwined. At first the Irish Catholics found little to object to in a unifying Europe.[49] They had sought converts or employment across Europe for centuries, and were eager for greater economic opportunities. Their Euro-enthusiasm was genuine, with none of the Protestant hand-wringing so prevalent across the Irish Sea. And they were willing to tie their faith to the European project. For Fine Gael prime minister John Bruton (1994–97), "the building of a united Europe is God's work in politics."[50]

Signs of trouble emerged, however, when the Irish electorate considered the constitutional changes that would be needed to implement the Nice Treaty in June 2001. The referendum had the support of the political establishment and the Catholic Church's hierarchy, but voters rejected the treaty 54 to 46 percent. Several factors accounted for the treaty's defeat, but conservative Catholics made up one group voicing discontent.[51] David Quinn of the Irish Catholic, for instance, asserted that growing numbers of Irish Catholics were "concerned the EU is moving in an increasingly anti-Christian—indeed, antireligious—direction.[52] Quinn cited European parliamentary pressures on religious organizations to accept women clergy as one reason for concern, but it was perceived European demands that Ireland change its restrictive abortion laws that greatly exercised Quinn and an increasingly skeptical Catholic minority. Two bishops, Philip Boyce and Thomas Finnegan, argued during the campaign that the EU's Charter of Fundamental Rights might be used to undermine Ireland's constitutional ban on abortion. But it was the pop singer and pro-life Catholic member of the European Parliament Dana Rosemary Scallon, a Fine Gael member, who became the public face of opposition to a secularizing EU. Her strong anti-Nice stand during the referendum campaign caused her expulsion from the European People's Party in the European Parliament.[53] But despite the efforts of antitreaty activists, the Nice Treaty was approved in a second vote in October 2002.

The abortion issue emerged again in 2008 and 2009, when the Irish (again) rejected, then (again) approved a treaty—the Lisbon Treaty—in two referenda. The Catholic hierarchy now exhibited a more conflicted approach to Europe. Sean Cardinal Brady, the primate of all Ireland, spoke directly to the struggle of conscience among Catholics when he pointed out that the EU's decisions on the role of the family, abortion, and faith issues "have made it more difficult for committed Christians to maintain their *instinctive commitment to the European project*" (emphasis added).[54] In 2009 the Irish bishops stated that Catholics could vote either way in the second referendum on the Lisbon Treaty with a clear conscience. They warned, however, that "it remains our responsibility, as citizens of Ireland and as citizens of the European

Union, to promote vigorously the 'Gospel of life' as described by Pope John Paul II."[55] Thus, on one hand, the bishops declared their neutrality on Lisbon ratification; but on the other hand, they tied the issue of abortion to the EU.

This connection between the EU and a liberal position on abortion again pushed some Irish Catholics into the "no" camp. Catholic prolife opponents of the treaty believed that changes in the EU institutions made it more likely that Ireland's "constitutional defense of an unborn child's right to life could be overridden by a European court."[56] Irish sovereignty, in their view, protected Ireland's strict stand on abortion; additional treaty revisions were bound to erode national autonomy in social and cultural affairs. Prolife Catholics believed that subsequent events proved these fears well founded. Following the approval of the Lisbon Treaty by Irish voters, three women challenged Ireland's constitutional ban on abortion by filing suit against the Irish state, a case known as *A, B et C v. Ireland* (2010).[57] The case, however, was brought not to the European Court of Justice but to the European Court of Human Rights and was, thus, not technically a European Union issue. In the event, the Court decided in favor of Ireland, finding no right to abortion in Article 8 of the European Convention on Human Rights.[58]

Poland and Ireland are outliers in Europe. Their broad mix of religion and politics is uncharacteristic in the EU. But the Polish and Irish Catholic churches are losing political and social influence as secular European culture takes deeper root. In addition, clergy sex scandals and ecclesiastical cover-ups have further undermined the credibility of the Church. This is a bad omen for Catholics. If Roman Catholics cannot hold the center in Poland and Ireland, where can they prevail?

The Contemporary Church

Pope Emeritus Benedict XVI requires only a brief discussion because he did not take a discernibly different approach to Europe than his predecessor, supporting European unity while pointedly critiquing the moral character of European society.[59] As Joseph Cardinal Ratzinger (before April 2005), he had a close relationship with Pope John Paul II, and the two shared a critical but hopeful perspective on Europe. Cardinal Ratzinger articulated his views in a book published in Italian just before he was elected pope. The book, which came out in an English edition in 2007 under the title *Europe: Today and Tomorrow*, echoes the themes outlined by John Paul II. Europe is a single "cultural and historical concept" shaped profoundly by the Roman Empire and Christianity. Christianity is the key to understanding Europe's distinctly Western concept of human rights, the dignity of all human persons, and the separation of spiritual and temporal powers. Without Christianity, Europe could not be Europe.

Cardinal Ratzinger locates the source of Europe's crisis in Reformation schisms and the revolutionary era, when "God and his will ceased to be relevant in public life."[60] The loss of God and the deification of the state led to the disastrous wars of the twentieth century. But soon after the dust cleared, Europeans, according to

Ratzinger, "quickly realized that only a united Europe could have a say in history and in its own future."[61] A remarkable group of men, in his view, put aside thoughts of revenge or humiliation and built a peaceful Continent. He located the source of their success in the application of their Christian values. He stated: "These politicians drew their moral concept of the State, of peace and responsibility, from their Christian faith, a faith that had overcome the challenges of the Enlightenment and to a great extent had been purified in its confrontation with the distortion of the law and of morality caused by the [Nazi] Party."[62] But Europe did not follow their lead. Instead, secular Europe "is denying its religious and moral foundations. . . . Europe, precisely in this hour of its greatest success, seems to have become hollowed out, paralyzed in a certain sense by a crisis of its circulatory system, a crisis that endangers its life."[63] This hollowing out was leading to demographic decline, as Europeans turned away from traditional marriage and the family.[64] Yet despite his disappointment, Cardinal Ratzinger—now become Benedict XVI—remained supportive of unifying Europe and called on Christians to contribute to its construction. "The destiny of society," he said, "always depends on creative minorities. Believing Christians should think of themselves as one such creative minority and contribute to Europe's recovery of the best of its heritage and thus to the service of all mankind."[65]

What will Pope Francis do with regard to European integration? He is not likely to deviate from the position taken by John Paul II and Benedict XVI. Indeed, his early pronouncements support the European project, but he is unlikely to make European unity a priority. As a representative of the Global South, he is less Europe-centered in perspective and more ready to highlight the universality of the Church over the unity of Europe.

To summarize: The Catholic Church remains supportive of a European project that—if constructed on the proper (dare we say *sacred*) foundations of Christian inspiration, brotherly reconciliation, just law, human rights, and moral norms—will bring peace and justice to Europe and beyond. But is Europe being properly constructed? For many Church leaders and lay communicants alike, this question is becoming more and more disturbing. They believe in the idea of Europe—it permeates every fiber of their beings—but they are less certain they believe in *this* Europe. The new Europe has broken free of its moral moorings. And the Church is increasingly hard-pressed to support a Europe unwilling to acknowledge the sustainer of its soul. For the EU, this may be bad news. The loss of its core Catholic supporters could leave the EU without passionate, ideologically driven *militants* (in the French sense) willing to endure economic hardship for the hope of a united Europe.

The Protestant Churches

The Protestant churches of the North did not emerge as strong political actors in the postwar period. The official churches, which historically were more instruments of the state than independent actors, drifted toward political and cultural irrelevance. The established Church of England remained vocal on many issues, such as wars in the Middle East, but its internal divisions over the role of women clergy and homosexual ordination and the collapse of Church attendance undercut its credibility as a political actor. The Nordic and German Lutheran churches—a variegated mix of state, national, and "people's" churches—all still enjoyed some form of state support for their personnel and for public service activities, but they had gained autonomy from the state in matters of theology and church leadership. The Nordic churches played an important social function, but they were no longer "threatening" enough for the state to demand organizational control. Thus the Protestant churches of Europe were indecisive political actors—too national to become an effective transnational force, and too bound up in state structures to become effective domestic pressure groups. Much of this weakness, of course, is explained by the secularization of European society that struck all Europe, especially after 1970, but hit the Protestant churches most severely.

The Protestant churches, like the Catholic Church, have begun to demonstrate some variations in their approach to European integration. Although Catholics' doubts about the EU still represent nuances rather than major divisions in an otherwise unified approach to European integration, the same cannot be said for the fragmented Protestant churches. A few important Protestant churches have welcomed integration efforts with some enthusiasm, thus seeming to call into question the importance of confessional culture in shaping church attitudes and actions. Yet conversely, other Protestant churches have taken an approach more consistent with the expectations posited in this volume and have vociferously opposed European integration. Why have they taken these divergent paths?

The answer can be found in two important divisions that opened in postwar Protestant churches: a liberal/conservative divide, and a leadership/lay divide. The first division had its roots in the struggle over theological liberalism in the late nineteenth and early twentieth centuries, which opened a doctrinal and cultural chasm within Protestantism. On one side stood those churches—most often the mainline, or established, Protestant bodies—that embraced new critical approaches to interpreting the Bible and more open theologies. On the other side were the conservative (often "free" or nonconformist) churches that rejected biblical criticism and consequent changes to traditional beliefs and practices. The second division, which had a clearer impact on the liberal, established churches, opened between the more educated and theologically liberal church leadership and the diminishing numbers of people in the pews, who were often more traditional in perspective. These divisions had implications for European integration: The liberal churches—represented by their clergy—tended to support integration, but with some resistance from lay members; but the conservative Protestant churches remained staunch in their opposition to integration. There were, of course, national variations.

Liberal Protestantism and the Ecumenical Turn

Some educated nineteenth- and early-twentieth-century European Protestants questioned the theological certainties of the past. For them, Enlightenment rationality, advances in science, and modern biblical scholarship raised questions about the core truths of Christianity. However, other Protestant leaders believed that the European churches were venturing too far from their theological roots and moved to counter the trend either by creating evangelical factions within state churches (as within the Church of England and the state Lutheran churches of Sweden and Norway) or by leading schisms that gave rise to new denominations (as occurred in the late nineteenth century in Scandinavia and the Netherlands). Other Protestant leaders took a more moderate approach and accepted many of the new religious ideas, but without embracing the most radical implications of historical criticism or modern theology.

What emerged in the early twentieth century was an establishment Protestantism less willing to employ biblical and theological arguments to reinforce narrow sectarian differences over beliefs and practices. In addition, as establishment or "mainline" (here we consciously use the North American term) Protestantism became less sure of the objective content of its faith, it became more willing to embrace the social implications of the Gospel teachings of Jesus of Nazareth, particularly those pertaining to world peace and relief for the poor. The result was an ecumenical turn from the traditional Protestant tendency to divide over theological and national differences in favor of unity in spirit and mission. These Protestants no longer attempted to set themselves apart as especially pure or chosen, but sought to make visible the unity in Christ they had once believed was invisible. The Swedish bishop Jonas Jonsson dramatically underlined this position in 1993 on the occasion of the four-hundredth anniversary of the consolidation of the Swedish Reformation when he said that "the Church of Sweden is an Evangelical church indissolubly united to the One, Holy, Catholic, and Apostolic Church. The continuity that we represent and cherish determines our ecumenical work, it gives openness and direction to it. That hidden unity in Christ which the Church possesses will be made visible. With the whole of God's congregation on Earth we should, in reconciled diversity, be tokens of that peace and unity which God has prepared for humankind."[66] For this mainline wing of the Protestant movement, the Reformation was over.

The Protestant ecumenical turn also developed an institutional dimension. Although joint Protestant efforts on several fronts began in the nineteenth century, the 1910 World Missionary Conference at Edinburgh marks the start of the institutionalized ecumenical movement. Several international conferences were held in the 1920s, and by the 1930s Protestant church leaders were ready to establish the World Council of Churches (WCC). World War II, however, delayed the WCC's creation until 1948, when Protestant leaders from around the world finally met in

Amsterdam.[67] Most of the established and mainline European Protestant churches joined the WCC, as did the Eastern Orthodox churches. Conspicuous by their absence were the conservative Protestant churches, which refused to join the WCC because it was too theologically liberal—or worse, a harbinger of the end times and a herald of the Antichrist—and the Catholic Church, which still preferred to think of itself as the one true Church.

The WCC was committed to *worldwide* reconciliation in religion and politics, but Cold War divisions soon threatened its global strategy. The WCC's leadership decided in the late 1940s not to endorse European unity for fear of alienating the churches in the Soviet Bloc. Neither Eastern nor Western church leaders wanted any part of a revived Christendom that was perceived by the world as concomitant with "Europe" or "the West." Ecumenical Protestants thus looked past Europe to the world; European unity was only desirable if united Europe was a step toward world peace.[68] But the Protestants also hesitated for another reason: They remained suspicious of the Catholics. To many Protestants, especially the Germans, European unity meant a "Europe of the Vatican, ruled by Christian Democrats and political leaders who took their orders from the Roman Catholic Church."[69]

The WCC's early resistance to endorsing European unity inspired some Protestant politicians and businessmen involved in early integration efforts to form a separate regional group in September 1950 called the Ecumenical Commission on European Cooperation (ECEC). This network of Protestant elites from continental Europe—but also prominently from Britain, Scandinavia, and the United States—linked together pro-Europe political leaders.[70] It did not, however, attempt to mobilize churches. As Leustean points out, "These leaders regarded churches as playing a prime role in the process of reconciliation and cooperation rather than as actors directly involved in the political mechanism of European integration."[71] The ECEC continued until 1974, but a second regional ecumenical group that emerged from the WCC proved more durable. In the 1950s Protestant church leaders from both West and East began talks aimed at achieving peaceful cooperation on a deeper level than that offered by the WCC. In 1964 these talks resulted in the formation of the Conference of European Churches (CEC), which developed into a large network of national ecumenical councils and member churches that eventually stretched from Iceland to Russia. Most of its member churches were also affiliated with the WCC, but several of the national councils included the Catholic Church as well.

The ecumenical turn within the mainline churches marked a new era in European Protestantism. The Protestants were now open to cooperation across denominational and national lines in areas of common interest, the most important being East–West relations and development assistance. The new ecumenism, however, did not unify Protestantism; many cross-denominational organizations emerged, often on a regional level. For most of these organizations, European unity was not an issue of fundamental importance. Many ecumenical groups were now quite in favor of any political development that promised cooperation among nations, but that is about as far as things went. Some major figures in the movement—such as Willem Visser 't Hooft, the Dutch Protestant theologian and first secretary general of the WCC—were known European unity enthusiasts, but the Protestant churches, both individually and as a transnational movement, did not generally share that enthusiasm.

This ambiguous attitude toward European integration can be seen in the mainline churches of Britain. British Christians seemed to give the idea of unity early support. In 1944, for instance, the Peace Aims Group, chaired by Archbishop of Canterbury William Temple under the auspices of the WCC (which was then in formation), called for common social, political, and economic institutions for the Continent.[72] After the war British foreign secretary Ernest Bevin tried to recruit the British churches to promote a "spiritual union" of Western countries to resist Soviet communism. The result was an ecumenical conference held at Albert Hall in London in April 1948 that brought together Protestants and Catholics—along with politicians from both major parties—to call for a united Europe built on spiritual foundations. Subsequently, several British organizations with both Protestant and Catholic representation emerged to advance the European idea in the late 1940s and early 1950s. As Philip Coupland points out, however, "the pro-European lobby among Christians was as shallowly rooted as the European movement in British society generally."[73] Most of the groups wobbled and collapsed in the early 1950s, due to several factors. First, the British Catholics were overrepresented in most of the pro-Europe Christian organizations and provided much of the initial enthusiasm. Some of the groups, such as the British Group of the Union of Christian Democrats, focused on forging ties with Christian Democratic groups on the Continent—not a particularly popular alliance in Britain. Second, the groups failed to achieve political balance and largely tilted toward the political right. Christian socialists remained conspicuously aloof from the European movement, the exceptions being several prominent Catholic Labour leaders. Finally, the coup de grace was the government's perceived loss of interest in European integration in the 1950s. The result was that "just as the state turned its back on European integration until the late 1950s, so the churches ignored it until the 1960s."[74]

In the 1960s the British Protestant churches somewhat reluctantly entered the public discussion concerning British membership in the European Community. The archbishop of Canterbury, Michael Ramsey, strongly supported Britain's first application during debate in the House of Lords. But it was not until 1967 that the British Council of Churches (BCC)—which at that time did not include the Roman Catholic Church—offered a full statement on European integration generally and British membership specifically, titled "Christians and the Common Market," in which the BCC somewhat tepidly declared that "on balance" it favored entry into the European Community but declined "to pronounce a verdict for or against such entry."[75]

Hardly a ringing endorsement of British membership, the report nevertheless made a strong case for Christian involvement in the process of European integration. Decrying the "almost complete silence of the British Churches during the past twenty years concerning European unity"—a charge it also leveled at the WCC—the report argued that the churches should have a deep interest in European integration because they were partly responsible for the division of the Continent and the rise of idolatrous nationalism.[76] The churches should therefore embrace the opportunity to help reconcile the nations in Europe. As for the kind of community for which the churches should be looking, the report urged Europe to embrace peace, human rights, openness to the world, and democracy. Achieving these values, however, did not require political union. Europe was working quite well without creating a unitary or federal state: "Europe is not to be seen as a unitary State, or even as a federal State in the making," but rather a system of "sovereignty shared between the European institutions in Brussels and the national institutions of Member States."[77] As if to underline this point, the report seemed to assert that any movement toward increased federalism—such as direct election of the members of the European Parliament—was undesirable, even if it increased democratic accountability.[78] And though the authors argued that Europeans should break down barriers to cooperation, they strongly opposed the notion of a homogenized European identity: "However close relations between the partners in the Community may come to be, it is neither desirable nor intended that their identities should become entirely merged in an undifferentiated whole."[79]

The BCC's report, like the British government of the day, and the British electorate in general, viewed the European Community as a worthy project to which Britain could contribute and from which it could benefit, but there was little enthusiasm for joining the European endeavor. There was certainly no shining vision of a future united Europe. In light of the report, the BCC passed a rather weak endorsement of British membership: "The Council considers that British membership of a Community which . . . counts among its aims the reconciliation of European enmities, the responsible stewardship of European resources and the enrichment of Europe's contribution to the rest of mankind, is to be welcomed as an opportunity for Christians to work for the achievement of these ends."[80] Once Britain had joined the Community, the churches again went silent, preferring to let the CEC, their regional organization, speak on European issues.

A postwar ecumenical spirit permeated the network of European Protestant leaders, which led most mainline ecclesiastical elites in Britain (including the leaders of the Church of England, the Methodist Church, and the Church of Scotland[81]) to take a positive if lukewarm approach to integration. This spirit did not necessarily trickle down to the people in the pews. Many lay members of the mainline churches no longer attended regularly as the process of secularization picked up speed in Britain. Observant members often remained more traditionally Protestant than their liberal leaders, and thus they took a more skeptical approach to Europe. The result was a definite, though muted, division between the cosmopolitan British church elites and their more traditional parishioners. And this same phenomenon appeared in the Scandinavian countries during their own membership debates.

Scandinavians have played a prominent role in the postwar ecumenical movement. One of the nine WCC assemblies held since 1948 convened in Uppsala (1968), and the Norwegian Olav Fykse Tveit served as secretary-general of the WCC beginning in 2009. On a regional level, six of the fourteen CEC assemblies have been held in Scandinavian countries. These activities have put Scandinavians in contact with Protestants elsewhere; but just as important have been the intense contacts between Lutherans and Catholics since Vatican II. According to Susan Sundback, the "improved relations between the Lutheran churches and Roman Catholicism on the national and local levels" proved crucial in developing pro-EU positions among Lutheran leaders in the run-up to the 1994 membership referenda in Finland, Norway, and Sweden.[82] Although the Nordic churches, speaking as institutions, did not "authoritatively, publicly, or unanimously declare themselves as being for or against the EU in 1994," many church leaders supported membership as consistent with the universality of Christianity.[83] Several prominent theologians, for instance, recommended "yes" votes, as did the Finnish archbishop and several Swedish bishops.[84] The churches as a whole, however, remained ambivalent. Antti Raunio observed that the Finnish Church's position on Europe was "critical, yet positive,"[85] whereas Hørgaard-Højen noted that Danish church leaders, more than the state or the people, were "terrified of losing [Danish] sovereignty and autonomy."[86] But though the top clergy almost unanimously, although in some cases reluctantly, endorsed Nordic membership in the EU, the people in the pews, few as they were, expressed far less support, especially in Norway. Moreover, the churches' support for EU membership seems to have had only a marginal impact on the referenda.

Not all the established churches' opinions were quite so positive toward integration in Europe. Ironically, many liberal Protestants inside the European Community, though supportive of integration, still harbored long-standing doubts about Catholic power. Liberal Protestants sharply criticized Pope John Paul II, for example, for his vocal plea to integrate Eastern with Western Europe and for his frequent calls to "reevangelize" the Continent. Several Reformed and Lutheran churches deliberately bypassed the CEC and met in Budapest in March 1992 to discuss ten "theses" that together constituted an alternative to the pope's call to reevangelize newly united Europe. The theses emphasized the pluralistic and secular nature of the Continent and the separation of the spiritual and political—all attributes of Europe that many Protestants attributed to the rise of Protestantism. Implicit in these theses was the assumption that the Catholic Church was seeking to reverse the secular wave crashing over Europe by reimposing its monopoly over European religion, politics, and society. To these Protestants, reevangelization looked like re-Vaticanization.[87]

The Protestant leaders explicitly rejected "the idea that Christianity should reconquer Europe."[88] But they did not completely reject European integration. As Pastor Michel Hoeffel, president of the Church of the Augsburg Confession in Alsace-Lorraine, put it in 1990: "There can be no question of reverting to a 'Christian Europe' where churches would wield some kind of power. The Church must place itself in the service of European society *as it gropes towards unity*" (emphasis added).[89] The Evangelical Church in Germany (Evangelische Kirche in Deutschland)—which brought together Lutheran, Reformed, and United churches in a single organization—seemed particularly ready to support the German state's European strategy. It had not always done so; in the early postwar period, the church had held "views on the Europe idea [that] bordered on the skeptical."[90] But in the mid-1990s the Evangelical Church took a decisive European turn and declared that the European peoples and nations "must be prepared to surrender part of their sovereignty and also their monopoly of power to supra-state bodies."[91] This unequivocally federalist position made the Germans the most pro-European of the Protestant churches.

Continental liberal Protestantism was too divided to speak with any weight in the European debate, and more important, as one German theologian noted, Protestantism did "not yet know what it should say to Europe."[92] Most of what Protestants did say was expressed through the CEC, which occasionally offered its views on developments in the EU. In May 2001, for instance, the CEC's Church and Society Commission issued a report of its Working Group on the European Integration Process—the first that included input from the whole of Europe, both East and West.[93] The report took a generally positive stance toward European integration but criticized its overemphasis on economics: "The churches support an integration of Europe which must not be confined to its political and economic aspects. Without common values, unity cannot endure." It called for a decision on the "ultimate goal of the current process of integration," but it declined to put forth its own vision of a "final aim." A new identity for the Continent was desirable but nevertheless must be "shaped as a mutual interplay between unity and diversity."[94]

The increased openness to integration demonstrated by this CEC report reflected a degree of harmonization of church positions across confessional cultures. In the 1990s and the early twenty-first century, the ecumenical Protestants and Vatican II Catholics found many occasions to cooperate. In 1990 the British Roman Catholics joined the BCC, and in 1999 the organization renamed itself Churches Together in Britain and Ireland. The Catholic Church still remained outside the WCC, but the CEC and the Catholic Church's Council of European Bishops' Conferences agreed in April 2001 to a set of guidelines for the deepening relationship between them, the Charta Oecumenica. The Charta included a statement favoring the integration process—which was directly echoed by the CEC report of the following month—but also mentioned several social issues that show the influence of Catholic thinking: "The churches support an integration of the European continent. Without common values, unity cannot endure. We are convinced that the spiritual heritage of Christianity constitutes an empowering source of inspiration and enrichment for Europe. On the basis of our Christian faith, we work towards a humane, socially conscious Europe, in which human rights and the basic values of peace, justice, freedom, tolerance, participation, and solidarity prevail. We likewise insist on the reverence for life, the value of marriage and the family, the preferential option for the poor, the readiness to forgive, and in all things compassion."[95]

In sum, the Protestant establishment churches had softened their theological anti-Catholicism but continued to fear the centralizing and monopolizing tendencies of the Roman Church as it pursued its vision of a united Europe. Postwar theological reflections on Christian unity and new ecumenical efforts freed the Protestant leaders to think more positively about integration, but they were far from fervent European federalists. The British and Nordic Protestant leaders were generally positive toward integration, but they often found the issue peripheral to their interests, which were often more global than regional. Moreover, in Britain and the Nordic countries, the religious leaders were more pro-Europe than the people in the pews—and were certainly more supportive of integration than the vocal sectarian Protestants, who staunchly opposed the erosion of Protestant and national identities. "EU negativism," observed Sundback, "increased the further one went from the centre of the national churches."[96]

The Sectarian Protestants

Some Protestants in the Netherlands, Britain, and the Nordic countries never made the ecumenical turn. These conservative and evangelical denominations perceived the WCC as a club for theological liberals who had abandoned their commitment to the authority of the Scriptures and the fundamental tenets of the Christian faith. Some churches were not opposed to cooperation among Christians, but they were rather choosy about their partners. In addition to being theologically conservative, these churches often defended a religion-based national identity; for them, the Norwegians were Lutherans, the Dutch were Reformed, and the British were Anglicans. For these Protestants, eroding the beliefs and practices of the faith meant eroding the markers of national identity. Thus, for some churchgoing Protestants, the Reformation was not over; Catholicism was still the enemy of the true church.

The conservative Protestant churches in Europe after 1970 were small and politically inconsequential in increasingly secular societies. But their members were staunch believers and frequent church attenders. They were often not interested in commenting on public issues; nor were they frequently asked for their opinions by the political establishment or the press. In multiparty systems they usually made their voices heard through the small conservative Christian parties, such as the Christian Democratic parties of the Nordic countries; the Reformed Party, the Reformed

Political Alliance, and the Reformatory Political Federation (later combined in the Christian Union) in the Netherlands; and the Democratic Unionist Party in Northern Ireland. Their positions on European integration never carried much political weight.[97]

These old-style Protestants, however, continued in the tradition of Protestant skepticism toward continental integration.[98] Different churches highlighted different dangers; but taken together, conservative Protestants were concerned that integration would bring increased secularization, a loss of national identity, and greater Vatican influence. Some churches preached their anti-EU message with fire and brimstone. The Free Presbyterian Church of Northern Ireland railed against the Common Market as a scheme of the Antichrist during the British referendum debate in 1975, and it continued to accuse the EU of being a papal puppet well into the twenty-first century. In June 2000 Ian Paisley—then a member of the European Parliament, and former first minister of Northern Ireland—posted a summary of his perspective on the website of the European Institute of Protestant Studies. Speaking of the EU, he declared: "Knowing the Bible should make us realise that it is pure folly to want to join (via ecumenism) this final apostasy of Babylon which is Biblically and historically wrong. Rome is unchanging, unrepentant and arrogant without change. People are striving for unity with this beast as though it was something required as a necessity in this life and for the next. Such folly when our gracious Lord brought us out of such bondage in the sixteenth century. . . . What folly to return."[99]

Those associated with Paisley's brand of hard-line British Protestantism spoke of a Vatican conspiracy to create a "Roman Catholic European Superstate" as a first step to world domination. The fingerprints of the Vatican were all over the EU. They pointed to the twelve stars in the EU flag and saw a symbol of the Madonna; they note the repeated references to Charlemagne and saw a plan to recreate the Carolingian Empire; they observed a depiction of Europa riding on a bull (Zeus) on a postage stamp and saw the whore of the Book of Revelation; they saw an EU Common Foreign and Security Policy and expected a military takeover by the Vatican.[100] For these British Protestants, however, the central issue was identity. They saw themselves as a chosen people called by God to resist the forces of the coming Antichrist. For them, to join with the Catholics in building Europe would mean the end of their sacred mission and the loss of their identity as a separate people. And they refused to give in.

Other Protestant churches were less vivid in their anti-EU rhetoric, but they were just as opposed to integration. In the Netherlands conservative Reformed churches were concerned about the loss of national identity and the undue influence of Brussels. In the Nordic countries the conservative free churches and evangelical congregations were very skeptical about the nature of the EU. Some Nordic churches, like the Free Presbyterians in Northern Ireland, identified integrating Europe with the evil forces of the end times.[101] During the Maastricht Treaty debate in Denmark, for instance, conservative Christians debated in the pages of *Idé Politik* whether or not the EU was the resurrected Roman Empire of biblical prophecy.[102] One Norwegian bishop grew so concerned by such rhetoric in the early 1990s that he warned "believers against indulging too much in demonising the EEC."[103] Conservative Nordic Protestants joined the anti-EU movements as nationalists defending their "non-Catholic and/or tribal type of collective religious identit[ies]."[104]

The conservative Protestants in Europe in the late twentieth and early twenty-first centuries remained uncompromising Euroskeptics. They saw the establishment Protestant leaders as sellouts to worldly religion and traitors to the nation. They remained the true believers in the sacred foundations of national identity. They continued to carry the flame of the Reformation, refusing to give up their distinctive religious or national beliefs. And all that put them at odds with the European Union, which still smelled of conspiracy and control.

Religious Groups and the European Union

If the general pattern has been for the Catholics and Catholic groups to favor European integration and for the Protestants to hesitate, we would expect religious representation in Brussels to favor the Catholic Church. That is in fact very much the case. Several Catholic organizations established offices in Brussels soon after the launch of the European Coal and Steel Community. A further jump in Catholic representation occurred after 1965 in response to the Merger Treaty (signed in 1965) and—more important—Vatican II and the Roman Church's new engagement with the broader world. Other Christian representations (including Protestants), conversely, got a very slow start in Brussels with few organizations appearing before the mid-1970s. Non-Catholic Christian organizations, though still lagging behind the Catholics, established offices at a more rapid clip after the Single European Act in the mid-1980s and caught up to the Catholics in the pace of new establishments in the early 2000s. The Catholic Church, however, "remains the dominant confession in terms of the number of religious representations" in Brussels.[105]

The Roman Church also seems to be more effective in its lobbying. Popes have special access to Europe's top leaders; since 1970 Brussels has hosted a permanent papal nuncio in charge of diplomatic relations between the Holy See and the EU; and the Commission of Bishops' Conferences of the European Community is one of the most important voices of civil society in Brussels. Furthermore, nearly forty major Catholic organizations carry on the day-to-day job of representing Catholic interests in the EU.[106] Protestants are represented by the CEC and the agents of individual churches, but that representation is uneven. Some Protestant churches, such as the Quakers and the Evangelical Church in Germany, have fairly visible representations. But the Church of England sent a representative to the European institutions only in May 2008. Such a paltry presence prompted Mark Hill to ask, "Why does the Church of England seem to lack visibility in Europe?"[107] This same question could be asked of many Protestant churches.

The overall trend is for more religious representation in Brussels—of Christian faiths, non-Christian faiths, and "convictional" organizations. The European Union itself has encouraged this dramatic expansion. Commission president Jacques Delors had called on Europeans in early 1992 to "give a soul to Europe, to give it spirituality and meaning."[108] This led to a "structured" dialogue between the religious organizations then represented in Brussels (and many more that soon opened offices) and the Commission and other European institutions. Much of this dialogue took place through an office established by Delors called the Forward Studies Unit (later renamed the Group of Policy Advisers to the European Commission, and now called the Bureau of European Policy Advisers, with a much broader set of participants).[109] The EU further institutionalized the religious dialogue through Article 17 of the Lisbon Treaty, which expanded the official recognition of religious communities codified earlier in the 1997 Amsterdam Treaty by inviting representative groups to join an "open, transparent, and regular dialogue" with the EU. The inclusion of Article 17 was seen by many as a sop to the Catholic Church and the Catholic member states, which had pressed hard for recognition of Christianity in the preamble to the Constitutional Treaty.[110] Secularist and humanist groups have strenuously opposed the article's special treatment of religious organizations—even though secular groups themselves participate in the dialogue as "convictional" bodies. In their view the disturbing influence of the Catholic Church best explains the anomalous Article 17.[111]

Official dialogue began under Delors in the late 1980s. He appointed a body of advisers called the "Lacroix Group" to facilitate contact with the churches. For Protestants working through the CEC, this was the first experience of official contact with the institutions of the EU.[112] In September 1990 Delors appointed Marc Luyckx to lead efforts to facilitate religious dialogue, and subsequent Commission presidents have followed suit with their own facilitators. The Bureau of European Policy Advisers' mandate goes far beyond dialogue with religious bodies, but that remains a key element of its mission.[113]

Is this dialogue important? Measuring the efficacy of a "dialogue" is very difficult. Certainly there is great benefit in bringing religious representatives together for structured discussions. But the dialogue seems to be hampered by several problems. First, the participants are carefully chosen and generally represent liberal religious positions. They are, in Jean-Paul Willaime's telling quip, the "European ecclesiocrats."[114] Few Christian fundamentalists or Islamists attract invitations. Meetings without hard-liners certainly go better, but the full range of religious perspectives, especially conservative viewpoints, is not represented. Second, the agendas are limited. As one observer put it, the meetings seem "set on celebrating religions and showing deference to traditions, more than on instigating a dynamic which can then be carried over on the ground."[115] Third, while Delors provided focused leadership during the early years, such guidance has since been lacking. Without top-flight political leaders behind the dialogue, the meetings attract little media attention and thus have no public impact. Religious groups are much more effective when they are not engaging in official dialogue but are simply lobbying the EU like other Brussels interest groups.

Political Parties

Political parties have evolved in ways similar to the European churches since 1975. Mainstream parties with Catholic roots or large Catholic electoral bases have continued to support integration, usually with enthusiasm. Some Catholics, however, began to drift to new nationalist parties of the far right. Meanwhile, mainstream parties in Protestant countries developed a guarded openness to deeper forms of integration, while Protestant sectarian parties maintained their strong opposition.

The European People's Party

Mainstream parties of the left, right, and center in the Catholic or confessionally mixed EU member states have universally supported the integration process—even if they have differed on details.[116] The Social Democrats, Liberals, and Christian Democrats have backed the community method of integration through supranational institutions as a matter of ideological conviction.[117] Christian Democrats, however, have continued to be most comfortable with the special combination of creeping supranationalism, liberal economic policies, state regulation, and subsidiarity found in the developing EU. Ironically, the Christian Democratic political group in the supranational European Parliament has experienced a more significant confessional struggle than any other political group in the years since the first enlargement.

That division appeared as soon as Britain and Denmark joined the European Community. The Christian Democrats from the Six formed the European People's Party (EPP) in July 1976 to serve in large part as the European parliamentary wing of the European Christian Democratic Union (EUCD), the successor to the Nouvelles Équipes Internationales.[118] These leaders, however, were divided over exactly what the new party was to stand for. The traditional Christian Democrats, mainly from Italy and the Benelux countries, stressed fidelity to Catholic social teaching and its emphasis on social and economic justice. Other Christian Democrats, mainly from Germany, stressed markets and individualistic liberalism over Catholic social teaching. Overlapping—and, in fact, reinforcing—this cleavage was a gap between Christian Democrats from Catholic parties and those from mixed confessional parties (again, primarily Germany). The former tended toward a purist approach to party ideology and drew dark lines between themselves and non–Christian Democratic movements. The latter tended to be more pragmatic, open to joining forces with other conservative parties across the Continent.[119] Tension between the two groups developed over naming the party, with the Catholic Christian Democrats insisting that "Christian Democratic" represented the nature of the party, while their pragmatic German counterparts pushed for a more inclusive label, such as "Democratic Center." At the same time, the two groups clashed over inclusion of the British and Danish Conservative parties (which were not members of the EUCD). The Christian Democratic faction argued that conservatism in these Protestant countries overemphasized individualism and markets while ignoring the social justice elements of Christian Democracy. The Germans, conversely, thought a party that included conservatives would be in a much better position to oppose a unified socialist movement in the European Parliament and elsewhere. A compromise was found with the adoption of the "European People's Party" (a name associated with Christian Democracy, especially in Italy), but no agreement was reached on admitting the conservative parties in Britain and Denmark. These parties remained outside the EPP in their own parliamentary formation, the European Democratic Group.[120] The issue, however, refused to die.

Christian Democrats from German-speaking countries continued to press for an alliance with conservative parties, and they eventually (October 1977) established a new group called the European Democratic Union that brought British and Nordic conservative parties together with a smattering of Christian Democrats. This incensed hard-line Christian Democrats; an alliance with conservative parties clearly opposed to Catholic social policy and European federation was out of the question. In their minds the EPP was designed as a federated party (of member state parties) to operate within the European Community as a harbinger of a new supranational politics. To traditional Christian Democrats the inclusion of Euroskeptical conservatives in a grand coalition of the right would weaken what the EPP's 1989 electoral manifesto called its "most important task": "the further development of the EC to a political union, to a socially responsible economic and monetary union and to a security union."[121] Thus many Christian Democrats initially saw the Bureau of European Policy Advisers as a rival to the EUCD and EPP and demanded that parties and individuals choose sides. Over time, however, emotions cooled and all three organizations found useful roles. All sides simply agreed not to discuss the issues that divided them.[122]

No further movement occurred until the early 1990s, when the end of the Cold War brought the issue of a general alliance of the right again to the fore. A complicated dance ensued as the conservative parties and pragmatic Christian Democrats (led especially by the Belgian Wilfried Martins and German chancellor Helmut Kohl) worked to convince resistant ideologues that an alliance with the conservatives was essential if the EPP was to maintain influence as the EU expanded to areas without traditional Christian Democratic movements. Martins and the chairman of the British Conservative Party, Chris Patten (a Catholic who was ideally suited to the task of dealing with the continental Christian Democrats), conducted talks; but the breakthrough occurred when Margaret Thatcher left 10 Downing Street. British and Danish conservatives in the EP joined the EPP Group in May 1992 (the Spanish conservatives had joined earlier). EPP Group membership in the European Parliament, however, was not the same as party membership in the EPP, which was still denied to the center-right Anglo-Nordic parties. Discussion continued within the EPP regarding the membership of conservative parties and the antifederalist Christian parties of the Nordic region. At the Athens Congress in November 1992 the EPP decided to amend its statutes and to open itself to broader membership. Eventually, the conservative and Christian Democratic parties of Denmark, Finland, Sweden, and even Norway were granted some form of official status (the British Conservatives never officially joined).[123] The alliance clearly benefited the EPP, making it one of the two largest groupings in the European Parliament. But tension between the old-line—mostly Catholic—Christian Democrats and the mostly Protestant conservatives and Nordic Christian Democrats over the federal nature of Europe never disappeared. Although the Nordics and others learned to live and work with the tension, the British Conservatives never did.

For the Tories, membership in the ideologically federal EPP felt uncomfortable. Euroskeptical Conservatives put relentless pressure on the Tory leadership to withdraw from the EPP group in the European Parliament. The Euroskeptical Bruges Group, for instance, addressed the contradictory visions of Europe held by the British Tories and the EPP in a paper written in 1999: "How can a group with the desired objective of opposing a federal Europe and of stopping Britain being run by Europe be part of a larger group whose loudly expressed purpose is the creation of a United States of Europe? The two competing visions are impossible to reconcile."[124]

But the alliance with Christian Democrats gave the Tories influence in the European Parliament that they could never have gained alone, so the party leadership delayed action. In response to continued pressure, however, the Tories formed a group within the EPP called the European Democrats. But pressures continued, and in 2009 Conservative leader David Cameron made good on his pledge to withdraw from the EPP and form a new parliamentary bloc called the European Conservatives and Reformists Group. Joining the Tories were other Euroskeptical conservative parties from Poland (Law and Justice), the Czech Republic (Civic Democracy), Latvia (National Alliance), and the Dutch Protestant Christian Union. In the end, the cultural struggle within the EPP ended in divorce.

The Anglo-Nordic Parties

The political parties in the Protestant-majority countries of the North adjusted to their national situations, but most remained wary of significant moves toward a federal Europe. The Conservative Party in Britain removed Margaret Thatcher from leadership in part because of her intransigent Euroskepticism.[125] Since her departure, however, the Tories have moved inexorably in her direction. When in government, the party has dragged its feet on integration, but generally it has tried to behave responsibly as an EU member. The euro crisis, however, undermined some economic arguments for staying in the EU, making withdrawal a realistic option to many—perhaps most—Conservative Party members. At the other end of the political spectrum, the Labour Party under Tony Blair, Gordon Brown, and Ed Miliband looks Euro-enthusiastic only by comparison. Blair did sign the Constitutional Treaty, but then (after some arm twisting) promised a national referendum that most doubted could be won. The only truly European party in Britain is the small Liberal Democratic party, which was formed by a merger of the Social Democratic and Liberal parties in 1988. The Social Democrats had seceded from Labour in 1981, due in part to the party's lack of enthusiasm for Europe. Led by former Commission president Roy Jenkins, David Owen, Bill Rodgers, and Shirley Williams (a prominent British Catholic[126]), the Social Democrats failed to really break the mold of British politics, but they did raise the profile of the traditional third political force. The hung Parliament of 2010 accorded the Liberal Democrats unusual influence as the junior partner in a Tory-led government. But a dismal showing in the 2014 EP elections underlined the unpopularity of the party's pro-EU position. By contrast, Nigel Farage and the UK Independence Party bolted from the political margins to first place in the 2014 elections on an anti-EU platform. The Independence Party's victory does not guarantee British withdrawal from the EU, but certainly makes it conceivable.

Like the mainstream British parties, the major Nordic parties since 1975 have also been lukewarm in their enthusiasm for Europe. Most have understood that the small countries had limited options and thus were eager to cooperate with their southern neighbors. But the patterns were complex. The conservative parties in the Nordic countries have favored integration, primarily on economic and security grounds, while the Social Democratic parties have split between centrist advocates of intergovernmental integration and left-wing skeptics. The Protestant Christian Democratic parties in the Nordic countries, however, provide us with an interesting picture of Protestant perspectives there. As "moral protest parties" the Christian People's parties (now renamed "Christian Democratic" parties in every country except Norway) have consciously defended conservative religious values in the face of more liberal social trends that accelerated in the 1960s and 1970s. Their countercultural positions on alcohol consumption, abortion, pornography, same-sex relationships, child rearing, religious education, and a host of related social issues have ensured their positions as small, but sometimes influential, ideological parties in multiparty systems. On the question of European integration, these parties have generally opposed cooperation with Europe; but their positions have evolved.[127]

The experience of the Nordic Christian Democrats parallels to some extent the clergy/laity divide observed in the established Protestant churches. Although elites have grown more favorable to integration, the party faithful have remained staunchly opposed. We saw earlier how the Norwegian Christian People's Party divided in the early 1970s over the issue of European Community membership, with the party rank and file voting overwhelmingly against joining over the wishes of several (but not all) party leaders. Over time, the elites fell in line, and now the Norwegian party is united in opposition to institutional ties to the EU. The issue also divided the Danish Christian Democrats. And though party leaders generally favored the arms-length Danish approach to membership, rank-and-file members cared little for integration. Intraparty conflict broke out in the early 1990s over the two Maastricht Treaty referenda, with the parliamentary group arguing for ratification and the Central Committee (representing the members) demanding that the party adhere to its 1986 Statement of Principles call to resist "the development of the EC towards a more extensive form of political-economic cooperation than is laid out in the EC Treaties."[128] The two sides patched up their differences, however, and the party united in opposition to euro zone membership in 2000.

The division between leaders and members was most dramatic in Sweden, where the Christian Democratic Party elites, under the robust leadership of Alf Svensson, strongly supported EU membership in 1994. Svensson argued that the EU had been "brought forth" by Christian Democratic pioneers and was supported by Christian Democratic parties that, in his view, were political "family." Party members were not so sure.[129] To many of the party's faithful, the continental Christian Democrats looked opportunistic, corrupt—and Catholic. One activist warned in a 1993 party congress that "Europe should not come under the papacy."[130] A majority of the Swedish Christian Democrats voted "no" in the 1994 accession referendum, and again in the 2003 referendum on adopting the euro. Finally, in Finland the Christian Democrats have been more unified. The party took a vigorously Euroskeptic stance, going so far as to withdraw from the Esko Aho coalition in 1994 to protest the preparations for membership. The party—even when in government—has continued to oppose EU membership and membership in the euro zone, despite Finland's official commitment to both.

In the Netherlands the mainstream Christian Democratic Appeal, with its Catholic contingent, has remained supportive of integration, but the smaller Reformed parties have taken more skeptical positions.[131] Two small orthodox Calvinist parties merged in 2001 to form the Christian Union (CU), which inched away from the hardline anti-EU approach of its constituent parties to assume a mildly Euroskeptical position. The CU declared its willingness to work within the EU, but continued to resist federalism and (like its Protestant Nordic political cousins) the social liberalism of mainstream Europe. To the right of the CU stands the tiny Reformed Political Party (Staatkundig Gereformeerde Partij), which openly espouses a brand of Calvinist theocracy and consistently takes a hard-line anti-European position.

Finally, as we would expect, the confessional divide runs deeply through Northern Ireland. The Social Democratic and Labour Party (SDLP), the primary party of Catholics, has consistently followed a strong pro-EU line.[132] The SDLP leader John Hume wrote in a 1992 newsletter that Northern Ireland was participating in a process of shared sovereignty "as we move inevitably towards the United States of Europe and . . . rid ourselves of the obsession with Britain and re-build our links with the rest of Europe." In his view, "the only union that matters is the European union."[133] Moreover, the party has favored a progressive approach to EU policy that reflects Catholic social policy: "The SDLP wants to see the EU continue as a frontrunner in advancing peace and sustainable social and economic development worldwide. We do not believe simply in a Europe of economies, but in a Europe of values and a Europe of influence—a real challenge to poverty, disease, and war."[134]

On the other side of the sectarian divide stand the unionist parties: the Ulster Unionist Party (UUP) and the late Ian Paisley's Democratic Unionist Party (DUP). Both Protestant parties have taken strong anti-European positions, but the DUP has always been the more radical. As a member of the European Parliament, Ian Paisley repeatedly denounced the very institution he belonged to in speeches and protests on the floor. During the pope's visit to the Parliament in October 1988, he held up a placard reading: "John Paul II is Anti-Christ."[135] Paisley's antipapal antics—which he continued in retirement until his death in 2014 (as Lord Bannside)—violated the polite norms of the European public sphere; but viewed in historical perspective, he represented the constant in British attitudes toward Europe. As Alex Greer has put it, "Rev. Paisley's defence of Protestant Britain against a Papal-dominated Europe, historically speaking, is in keeping with British religious values since the Reformation."[136] Although the tone and rhetoric of British mainstream opponents of integration are much more muted than Paisley's were, the central message is quite similar: Europe threatens this blessed nation.

The Catholic Nationalists

We saw above how some conservative Catholic elements have grown dissatisfied with the EU, despite the continued support of the Church hierarchy. Catholic Euroskeptical political movements, though still relatively rare, have emerged, but only when mobilized by a right-wing political party.[137] In Ireland Catholic Euroskepticism has materialized politically during referenda, as we saw above, but has not gravitated to a single political party. In contrast, Euroskeptical parties in Hungary (Jobbik) and

Slovakia (Slovak National Party) have been somewhat more successful in mobilizing the Catholics critics of integration. The anti-EU French National Front, the big winner in the 2014 European Parliament elections, has attracted a segment of nominal Catholics since its inception under Jean-Marie Le Pen. Under the leadership of Marine Le Pen, the party has expanded its reach to more observant Catholics as it has moved to solidify a base in the French countryside where opposition to integration, globalization, and neoliberalism runs high. And although the French episcopate is "deeply committed to Europe," increasing numbers of Catholics voted, as they saw it, for France.[138]

Poland, however, provides the most prominent example of successful right-wing Catholic mobilization. Father Tadeusz Rydzyk's Radio Maryja would have remained a fringe voice if it had not ventured into Polish politics (quite against the wishes of the Church hierarchy) and raised the profile of the political far right. Before 2001 Polish right-wing populism made little impact on postcommunist Poland.[139] But in May 2001 Rydzyk forged an alliance of far-right groups called the League of Polish Families to contest—with the vocal backing of Radio Maryja—the parliamentary elections held later that year. According to Rafal Pankowski, "The endorsement by Father Tadeusz Rydzyk was the single most important factor in securing parliamentary seats for the newly established group."[140] The far right campaigned against Polish EU accession but failed to overcome the weighty endorsement of Pope John Paul II. Following the referendum defeat, the relationship between Rydzyk and the League became strained, and by 2005 Radio Maryja had switched its support from the shrinking League to the rising Law and Justice Party of Lech and Jarosław Kaczyński.[141]

While in power from 2005 to 2007, the Kaczyński twins channeled into a single national integration strategy both Catholic approaches to the EU—populist skepticism and cautious support. They favored Polish membership but in an EU defined as an "intergovernmentalist 'Europe of Nations' rooted in Christianity."[142] In contrast to other approaches to a "Europe of Nations," Law and Justice's version remained heavily influenced by Catholic Christian Democratic thinking. Protecting Polish sovereignty was important as a defense against immoral values and free market liberalism, but Poland should encourage more "solidaristic" or collectivist EU policies.[143] This approach was, frankly, "somewhat schizophrenic," as Poland pushed for greater influence in the Council of Ministers and opt-outs from the Lisbon Treaty while calling for a common European army and greater EU support for farmers.[144] For the radical Catholic right, however, Law and Justice's approach went too far to accommodate the EU. Tensions finally erupted in 2011, as the party ejected a small faction of Catholic nationalists who formed a new, more radical party called United Poland.

The European political parties continue to reflect their confessional cultures. Catholic-inspired Christian Democratic parties remain staunch supporters of

European union, although some conservative Catholics (including recent popes) have become disillusioned with the EU's moral direction. The Protestant-inspired Christian Democratic parties in the Netherlands and the Nordic region remain highly skeptical of the EU, despite evidence that increased contact with continental Christian Democrats has moderated their leaders' view on integration.[145] No moderation, of course, has occurred in the antipapist, anti-EU stance of the Northern Irish DUP, which seems intent on dragging the seventeenth century into the twenty-first.

Notes

1. Kenneth R. Himes, OFM, "Vatican II and Contemporary Politics," in *The Catholic Church and the Nation-State: Comparative Perspectives*, ed. Paul Christopher Manuel, Lawrence C. Reardon, and Clyde Wilcox (Washington, DC: Georgetown University Press, 2006), 28.

2. John Paul II, *Ecclesia in Europa*, June 28, 2003, n117, Vatican, www.vatican.va/holy_father /john_paul_ii/apost_exhortations/documents/hf_jp-ii_exh_20030628_ecclesia-in-europa _en.html.

3. For a rational choice assessment of the Catholic Church's role as an interest group, see Carolyn M. Warner, *Confessions of an Interest Group: The Catholic Church and Political Parties in Europe* (Princeton, NJ: Princeton University Press, 2000).

4. John XXIII, "Pope John's Opening Speech to the Council," October 11, 1962, Christus Rex, www.christusrex.org/www1/CDHN/v2.html.

5. Ibid.

6. Paul VI, "Dogmatic Constitution of the Church: *Lumen Gentium*," November 21, 1964, Vatican, www.vatican.va/archive/hist_councils/ii_vatican_council/documents/vat-ii_const_19641 121_lumen-gentium_en.html.

7. Paul VI, *Gaudium et Spes: Pastoral Constitution on the Church in the Modern World*, December 7, 1965, Vatican, www.vatican.va/archive/hist_councils/ii_vatican_council/documents/vat-ii _const_19651207_gaudium-et-spes_en.html. See also Himes, "Vatican II and Contemporary Politics." in *Catholic Church*.

8. Paul VI, *Gaudium et Spes*, para. 42. See also Himes, "Vatican II," 23.

9. Commission of the Bishops Conferences of the European Community, *The Evolution of the European Union and the Responsibility of Catholics*, May 2005, Commission of Bishops' Conferences of the European Community, 52, www.comece.org/content/site/en/publications/pubcomece /index1.html.

10. Warner, *Confessions*, 217.

11. Robert Leonardi and Douglas A. Wertman, *Italian Christian Democracy: The Politics of Dominance* (New York: St. Martin's Press, 1989), 200.

12. Eric O. Hanson, *The Catholic Church in World Politics* (Princeton, NJ: Princeton University Press, 1987), 128–29.

13. Specifically, the pope wrote: "Today the universal common good poses problems of worldwide dimensions, which cannot be adequately tackled or solved except by the efforts of public authorities endowed with a wideness of power, structure and means of the same proportions: that is, of public authorities which are in a position to operate in an effective manner on a world-wide basis. The moral order itself, therefore, demands that such a form of public authority be established." John XXIII, *Pacem in Terris*, April 11, 1963, sec. 137, Vatican, www.vatican.va/holy_father /john_xxiii/encyclicals/documents/hf_j-xxiii_enc_11041963_pacem_en.html.

14. Paul VI, *Gaudium et Spes*.

15. See Blandine Chelini-Pont, "Papal Thought on Europe and the European Union in the Twentieth Century," in *Religion, Politics, and Law in the European Union*, ed. Lucian N. Leustean and John T. S. Madeley (London: Routledge, 2010), 132.

16. The quotations that follow are from the text of the letter "European Unity Based on the Christian Concept of Man," *Catholic Messenger* 80 (August 2, 1962).

17. Chelini-Pont credits Pope Pius XII with supporting specific steps toward integration. In our view, Pius indirectly offered support without naming specific policies. See Chelini-Pont, "Papal Thought," 130–31.

18. See Jo Renee Formicola, *Pope John Paul II: Prophetic Politician* (Washington, DC: Georgetown University Press, 2002).

19. Steven Greenhouse, "Pope, Visiting France, Calls for a United Europe," *New York Times*, October 9, 1988.

20. John Paul II, "Address of John Paul II during the Visit to the European Parliament, Palace of Europe, Strasbourg, France, 11 October 1988," Vatican, www.vatican.va/holy_father/john_paul_ii /speeches/1988/october/documents/hf_jp-ii_spe_19881011_european-parliament_fr.html.

21. Ibid.

22. Ibid.

23. Quoted by George Weigel, *Witness to Hope: The Biography of Pope John Paul II* (New York: Cliff Street Books, 1999), 311.

24. Quoted in ibid., 312.

25. John Paul II, *Ecclesia in Europa*, June 28, 2003, Vatican, www.vatican.va/holy_father /john_paul_ii/apost_exhortations/documents/hf_jp-ii_exh_20030628_ecclesia-in-europa _en.html.

26. Simon Coss, "Holy Orders: Pope John Paul II," *European Voice*, November 7–13, 2002.

27. John Paul II, *Ecclesia in Europa*, n109.

28. Ibid.

29. Ibid., n116.

30. Ibid., n114.

31. Ibid., n117.

32. Ibid., n120.

33. "Text of The Treaty Establishing a Constitution for Europe," Eurotreaties, www.eu rotreaties.com/constitutiontext.html.

34. John Paul II, *Ecclesia in Europa*, n114; John L. Allen Jr., "Pope Bolsters Ailing Spanish Church," *National Catholic Reporter*, May 16, 2003, 6.

35. "Text of The Treaty."

36. See Chelini-Pont, "Papal Thought," 134–36.

37. Quoted by Jonathan Kwitny, *Man of the Century: The Life and Times of Pope John Paul II* (New York: Henry Holt, 1997), 649.

38. Timothy A. Byrnes, "Transnational Religion and Europeanization," in *Religion in an Expanding Europe*, ed. Timothy A. Byrnes and Peter J. Katzenstein (Cambridge: Cambridge University Press, 2006), 290.

39. Quoted by Ray Taras, "Poland's Transition to a Democratic Republic: The Taming of the Sacred?" in *The Secular and the Sacred: Nation, Religion and Politics*, ed. William Safran (London: Frank Cass, 2003), 138.

40. See José Casanova, "Religion, European Secular Identities, and European Integration," in *Religion in an Expanding Europe*, ed. Byrnes and Katzenstein, 68.

41. John Paul II, "Message of John Paul II to the Polish Bishops," June 10, 1997, Vatican, www .vatican.va/holy_father/john_paul_ii/travels/documents/hf_jp-ii_mes_08061997_bishops _en.html. See also Byrnes, "Transnational," 289.

42. Timothy A. Byrnes, "The Polish Church: Catholic Hierarchy and Polish Politics," in *Catholic Church and the Nation-State*, ed. Manuel, Reardon, and Wilcox 109. See also Byrnes, "Transnational," 290.

43. Quoted by Byrnes, "Polish Church," 112.

44. Ibid.

45. Ibid., 113; Taras, "Poland's Transition," 149.

46. A Redemptorist is a member of the Congregation of the Most Holy Redeemer, a Catholic missionary organization formed in the early eighteenth century.

47. Simona Guerra, "Eurosceptic Allies or Euroenthusiastic Friends? The Political Discourse of the Roman Catholic Church in Poland," in *Representing Religion in the European Union: Does God Matter?* ed. Lucian N. Leustean (London: Routledge, 2013), 141.

48. See Zdzisław Mach, "The Roman Catholic Church in Poland and the Dynamics of Social Identity in Polish Society," in *Religion and Politics: East–West Contrasts from Contemporary Europe*, ed. Tom Inglis, Zdzisław Mach, and Rafał Mazanek (Dublin: University College Dublin Press, 2000), 127.

49. See, e.g., Jesuit Centre for Faith and Justice, "The Catholic Vision and the European Community," *Doctrine and Life* 39 (December 1989): 531–36; and Séamus Murphy, "The European Community and Irish Culture," *The Furrow* 42 (June 1991): 355–60.

50. Edward Pentin, "Former Irish Prime Minister Discusses Views on Europe's Future," *National Catholic Register*, October 14–20, 2003.

51. See, e.g., Katy Hayward, "Not a Nice Surprise: An Analysis of the Debate Surrounding the 2001 Referendum on the Treaty of Nice in the Republic of Ireland," *Irish Studies in International Affairs* 13 (2002): 167–86; and Richard Sinnott, "Cleavages, Parties, and Referendums: Relationships between Representative and Direct Democracy in the Republic of Ireland," *European Journal of Political Research* 41 (2002): 811–26.

52. "Will Ireland's Catholic Voters Shoot Down the Treaty of Nice Again?" *National Catholic Register*, October 13–19, 2002.

53. "Entre Nous," *European Voice*, June 14–20, 2001.

54. John Murray Brown, "Ireland Vote on Lisbon Unlikely before Election," *Financial Times*, August 27, 2008.

55. Justin Bell, "Ireland's Pro-Lifers Wary of Treaty," *National Catholic Register*, November 8, 2009.

56. Ibid.

57. Gareth Peoples, "Ireland Challenged on Abortion Law—in European Court," *National Catholic Register*, February 28, 2010.

58. European Court of Human Rights, *A, B and C v. Ireland*, December 16, 2010, 29 BHRC 423 (2011), 3 FCR 244 (2010), ECHR 25579/05 (2011), 53 EHRR 13 (2010), ECHR 2032, www.bailii.org /eu/cases/ECHR/2010/2032.html.

59. See Lucian N. Leustean and John T. S. Madeley, "Religion, Politics, and Law in the European Union: An Introduction," in *Religion, Politics, and Law*, ed. Leustean and Madeley, 1.

60. Joseph Cardinal Ratzinger, *Europe Today and Tomorrow: Addressing the Fundamental Issues*, trans. Michael J. Miller (San Francisco: Ignatius Press, 2007), 21.

61. Ibid., 115.

62. Ibid., 87.

63. Ibid., 23–24.

64. For a sympathetic commentary on Pope Benedict XVI's views on Europe, see George Weigel, *The Cube and the Cathedral: Europe, America, and Politics without God* (New York: Basic Books, 2005).

65. Ratzinger, *Europe Today*, 34.

66. "Our Profession of the Visible Unity of the Church," speech at the Uppsala Jubilee, August 21, 1993, quoted by Susan Sundback, "The Nordic Lutheran Churches and the EU Question in 1994," *Temenos* 37–38 (2001–2): 195.

67. World Council of Churches, "About Us/History," www.oikoumene.org/en/about-us /wcc-history.

68. Philip M. Coupland, "Western Union, 'Spiritual Union,' and European Integration, 1948–1951," *Journal of British Studies* 43, no. 3 (2004): 391.

69. Jean-Paul Willaime, "Protestant Approaches to European Unification," in *Religion in Contemporary Europe*, ed. John Fulton and Peter Gee (Lewiston, NY: Edwin Mellon Press, 1994), 96.

70. Some of these leaders included Jean Rey, an eventual president of the Commission; Gustav Heinemann, the president of West Germany; and Max Kohnstamm, secretary to the High Authority of the European Coal and Steel Community. Leustean, *Representing Religion*, 6.

71. Ibid., 6.

72. Coupland, "Western Union," 372.

73. Ibid., 385.

74. Ibid., 386.

75. British Council of Churches and Conference of British Missionary Societies, *Christians and the Common Market: A Report Presented to the British Council of Churches* (London: SCM Press, 1967), 7.

76. Ibid., 9–15.

77. Ibid., 36–37.

78. Ibid., 40.

79. Ibid., 76.

80. "Resolution Adopted at the Meeting of the British Council of Churches, Held on 25th–26th October, 1967," quoted in *Christians and the Common Market*, 5.

81. See Stephen Plat, "British Methodists and Europe: An Unfinished Story," and David Fergusson, "The Kirk: Scottish, British or European?" in *Unterwegs nach Europa: Perspecktiven evangelisher Kirchen / En Route towards Europe: Perspectives of Protestant Churches*, ed. Hans Jürgen Luibl, Christine-Ruth Müller, and Helmut Zeddies (Frankfurt: Verlag Otto Lembeck, 2001), 211–14, 219–21.

82. Sundback, "Nordic Lutheran Churches," 200.

83. Ibid., 196.

84. Ibid., 196. See also Susan Sundback, "The Position of the National Lutheran Churches in the Process of European Integration," in *The Transformation of Europe: Social Conditions and Consequences*, ed. Matti Alestalo et al. (Warsaw: IFiS Publishers, 1994), 248.

85. Antti Raunio, "The Contribution of the Evangelical Lutheran Church of Finland towards an Ecumenical and Social Europe," in *Unterwegs nach Europa*, ed. Luibl, Müller, and Zeddies, 47.

86. Peder Hørgaard-Højen, "Denmark, Europe and Leuenberg," in ibid., 72.

87. Willaime, "Protestant Approaches," 101–3.

88. Ibid., 103.

89. Ibid.

90. Reinhard Frieling, "Europe: A Challenge to Christians, the Evangelical Churches in Germany, and the European Integration Process," in *Unterwegs nach Europa*, eds. Luibl, Müller, and Zeddies, 123.

91. Ibid., 127.

92. Willaime, "Protestant Approaches," 107.

93. Peter Pavlovic, "Churches in the Process of European Integration," May 2001, Conference of European Churches, http://csc.ceceurope.org/fileadmin/filer/csc/European_Integration/Churches_in_the_process_of_European_unification_final.pdf.

94. Ibid., 15.

95. *"Charta Oecumenica*: Guidelines for the Growing Cooperation among the Churches in Europe," Council of European Churches, April 2001, www.ceceurope.org/fileadmin/filer/cec/CEC_Documents/Charta_Oecumenica.pdf.

96. Sundback, "Nordic Lutheran Churches," 198.

97. Ibid., 204.

98. Willaime, "Protestant Approaches," 107.

99. Ian R. K. Paisley, "May God Save Us from Coming under This Dictatorship Once Again," European Institute of Protestant Studies, www.ianpaisley.org/article.asp?ArtKey=soul.

100. Arthur Noble, "The Conspiracy behind the European Union: What Every Christian Should Know, a Lecture delivered at the Annual Autumn Conference of the United Protestant Council in London on Saturday, November 7, 1998," European Institute of Protestant Studies, www.ianpaisley.org/article.asp?ArtKey=conspiracy; Clive Gillis, "The Popes at War and the Fall of the Papal States," European Institute of Protestant Studies, www.ianpaisley.org/article.asp?ArtKey=papalstates.

101. See Bente Struksnæs and Abel Struksnæs, "Watch Out for a Catholic European Union!" Christian Information Service, www.endtime.net/engelsk/KEU.htm.

102. See Chris Mathieu, *The Moral Life of the Party: Moral Argumentation and the Creation of Meaning in the Europe Policy Debates of the Christian and Left-Socialist Parties in Denmark and Sweden 1990–1996* (Lund: Department of Sociology at Lund University, 1999), 135.

103. Willaime, "Protestant Approaches," 97.

104. Sundback, "Nordic Lutheran Churches," 198.

105. Leustean, *Representing Religion*, 11. For a complete list of religious organizations represented in Brussels and a close analysis of current trends, see ibid., 5–18. See also Frank Turner, "The Roman Catholic Church and the European Institutions: Dialogue and Advocacy at the European Union," in ibid., 77–90.

106. This figure comes from Leustean, *Representing Religion*, 12–13.

107. Mark Hill, "Voices in the Wilderness: The Established Church of England and the European Union," *Religion, State & Society* 37, nos. 1–2 (2009): 174.

108. Quoted by Leustean, *Representing Religion*, 4.

109. See "BEPA: An Overview of Its History," Bureau of European Policy Advisers, http://ec.europa.eu/bepa/about/history/index_en.htm.

110. John T. S. Madeley, "Deus Ex Machina: Representing God on the Stage of the European Union," in *Representing Religion*, ed. Leustean, 48.

111. See David Pollock, "Article 17: Reasons for Concern," in *Representing Religion*, ed. Leustean, 122.

112. Willaime, "Protestant Approaches," 99.

113. See "BEPA Action Programme 2010–2014," Bureau of European Policy Advisers, http://ec.europa.eu/bepa/pdf/about_pdf_see_also/action_programme.pdf, 5.

114. Willaime, "Protestant Approaches," 106.

115. Tariq Ramadan, "Religion and the European Union," in *Representing Religion*, ed. Leustean, 120.

116. See Leonard Ray, "Measuring Party Orientations towards European Integration: Results from an Expert Survey," *European Journal of Political Research* 36 (1999): 283–306.

117. Gary Marks, Carole J. Wilson, and Leonard Ray, "National Political Parties and European Integration," *American Journal of Political Science* 46, no. 3 (2002): 585–94.

118. See David Hanley, "The European People's Party: Towards a New Party Form?" in *Christian Democracy in Europe: A Comparative Perspective*, ed. David Hanley (London: Pinter, 1994), 186–89; and Thomas Jansen, *The European People's Party: Origins and Development* (New York: St. Martin's Press, 1998), 61–70.

119. Hanley, "European People's Party," 191–92.

120. Ibid., 193.

121. Quoted in ibid., 189.

122. For a full discussion of the tensions within the center-right in the 1970s, see Jansen, *European People's Party*, 67–70, 110–13. The EPP merged with the EUCD in 1999 and the EDU in 2002.

123. The EPP absorbed the EDU in 2002. To date, no Icelandic party has joined the EPP.

124. Martin Ball and Jonathan Collett, "Conservative MEPs and the European People's Party: Time for Divorce," Bruges Group, Paper 36 (1 June 1999), www.brugesgroup.com/mediacentre/index.live?article=94.

125. See Geoffrey Howe, *Conflict of Loyalty* (New York: St. Martin's Press, 1994), 643–45.

126. See Shirley Williams, *God and Caesar: Personal Reflections on Politics and Religion* (Notre Dame, IN: University of Notre Dame Press, 2003).

127. See John T. S. Madeley, "Life at the Northern Margin: Christian Democracy in Scandinavia," in *Christian Democratic Parties in Europe since the End of the Cold War*, ed. Steven Van Hecke and Emmanuel Gerard (Leuven: Leuven University Press, 2004), 235–39; and John Madeley, "Reading the Runes: The Religious Factor in Scandinavian Electoral Politics," in *Religion and Mass Electoral Behaviour in Europe*, ed. David Broughton and Hans-Martien ten Napel (London: Routledge, 2000), 28–43.

128. Quoted by Mathieu, *Moral Life*, 126. For a detailed discussion of the intraparty debates in the early 1990s, see ibid., 123–92.

129. For a detailed discussion of the internal debate, see ibid., 247–320.

130. Quoted in ibid., 262.

131. The Christian Democratic Appeal was created in 1977 to combine the Catholic People's Party, the Anti-Revolutionary Party, and the Christian Historical Union.

132. The Alliance Party, a liberal alternative in Northern Ireland, also takes a pro-European stance, but it is not aligned with the Catholics or Protestants in the sectarian rivalry.

133. Alex Greer, "From Maastricht to Dublin and Belfast: The Irish Debate European Union," *Journal of Social, Political, and Economic Studies* 18, no. 2 (1993): 208.

134. "International Affairs," Social Democratic and Labour Party, www.sdlp.ie/issues /international-affairs/.

135. "Ian Paisley Heckles the Pope and Makes a Fool of Himself," October 12, 1988, www.you tube.com/watch?v=7Fm0QOIw8nQ.

136. Greer, "From Maastricht to Dublin," 216.

137. Rafal Pankowski, *The Populist Radical Right in Poland: The Patriots* (London: Routledge, 2010), 120–21.

138. "Catholics to the Rescue of Le Pen," Servizio Informazione Religiosa, May 30, 2014, www.agensir.it/pls/sir/v4_s2doc_b2.europa?tema=Sir+Europa+english&argomento=dettaglio &id_oggetto=288044.

139. Pankowski, *Populist Radical Right*, 78–79.

140. Ibid., 111.

141. Ibid., 156–57.

142. Aleks Szczerbiak, *Poland within the European Union: New Awkward Partner or New Heart of Europe?* (London: Routledge, 2012), 150.

143. Ibid., 149.

144. Ibid., 152–53.

145. Madeley, "Life at the Northern Margin," 238.

10

European Identity

W E TURN FINALLY to European citizens. From the very beginning, integration theorists knew that citizens would be crucial to the construction of a new supranational identity. National leaders might develop a deep mutual sense of community and regional identity through constant interaction and meaningful exchange. They might even join in a conscious effort to create a "European" identity to undergird a federal union. But if leaders could not inspire in ordinary citizens the same sense of community that they were experiencing, union would not be possible. Economic, social, and political integration would only go as far as the sense of common identity allowed. Thus, the key to integration in Europe is "European" identity among citizens.

We have already seen how confessional culture shapes a European sense of community. Catholic and Protestant cultures have constructed different kinds of identity, which make it difficult to extend to the "other" a "we feeling" strong enough to constitute a new identity. It clearly can be done; Catholics and Protestants in Germany, the Netherlands, and Switzerland did so—more or less—in the nineteenth century. But do we see signs of this happening in Europe today? The answer will help us determine whether the EU can move closer toward political union, as still favored by some elites, or if the limits of integration have been reached—at least for now.

We begin by examining the impact of confessional culture on public support for integration. The confessional divide in the electorate confirms that the two visions of Europe that divide the Continent's elites also split its citizens. We then explore efforts by the elites to create a new European identity through socialization and the extent to which confessional cultures have influenced this construction process. Finally, we survey the evidence for an evolving European identity and discuss the implications of recent findings for the future of Europe.

Confessional Culture and Support for Integration

Before 1970, surveys of public support for integration were irregular and were confined to individual countries. The limited evidence points to broad popular support for the Christian Democratic program of reconciliation and integration. The French

320

scholar Alfred Grosser points out that in 1944 the French saw "no enemy but Germany," but by 1960 that had shifted to "no friend but Germany."[1] Only twenty years after Germany's defeat, the French identified West Germany as "the best friend of France."[2] Furthermore, elite support for a united Europe also seems to have trickled down into the streets. As Gillingham observes, "The Schuman Plan announcement moved international cooperation from the domain of diplomats, bureaucrats, and businessmen into the public realm, turning a cherished ambition of policymaking elites into the great hope of the masses."[3] Support for integration was strong and rising throughout the early postwar era. Between 1950 and 1962, European support for integration rose from 50 to 70 percent.[4] Thus, by the early 1960s, a "permissive consensus" (to use Leon Lindberg and Stuart Scheingold's famous term) facilitated elite efforts to build a new Europe.

Systematic surveys of public attitudes toward European integration began when the Commission conducted two surveys of public opinion in the Six in 1970 and 1971. Biannual polls of an enlarged European Community began in late 1973, with the spring 1974 poll the first to be tagged as the "Eurobarometer." The *Eurobarometer* series has made available a wealth of longitudinal data on attitudes toward integration. Unfortunately, for our purposes the surveys do not always include questions on religion. The rare surveys that do, however, allow us to piece together a clear picture of religion's impact on attitudes toward integration.

We would certainly expect such an effect. Confessional cultures permeate the lives of individuals from birth, whether or not they believe, practice, or grow up in religious families. The effects of culture are hard to escape. Moreover, "true believers"—individuals who identify with the beliefs and practices of the religion at the core of a confessional culture—should most readily conform to the patterns of thought and custom characteristic of each confession. Thus, Catholics should favor integration more than Protestants, and observant Catholics should be more supportive than the less devout. Conversely, practicing Protestants should be far less inclined to favor integration than their Catholic or nominally Protestant counterparts.

Eurobarometer data consistently confirm our general hypothesis: Confessional culture (as measured by self-identified religious tradition) has a significant effect on attitudes toward integration, even under rigorous controls for other factors more often identified as determinants of such support (e.g., nationality, party identification, ideology, political engagement, European identity, postmaterial values, economic situation, gender, class, education).[5] From 1973 to 2006 Catholic respondents in the Nine (the Six, plus Britain, Denmark, and Ireland) were significantly more inclined to support the European Community / Union than those of other faiths or no faith. Furthermore, the more devout Catholics—regular church attenders—showed the strongest support. Protestants in these member states demonstrate much weaker support for integration; but in general, greater devotion *increases* support, with nominal Protestants being the most negative. The fact that Protestant church attendance increases support for integration, especially in more recent decades, may seem surprising, but we suspect that exposure to the mainline Protestant ecumenism discussed in Chapter 9 has encouraged more positive views of internationalism. "Cultural" Protestants who do not regularly practice tend to remain skeptical of supranational cooperation.[6] The qualitative evidence strongly suggests that church-attending sectarian Protestants are far less supportive of integration than their mainline coreligionists. *Eurobarometer* affiliation measures are not usually precise enough to identify the small numbers of sectarian Protestants; but where they are, we find them to be fiercely anti-integration.

Religion works slightly differently in the newer member states. Catholicism has no independent effect on attitudes in Portugal or Austria, but does in Spain, which conforms to patterns in the Nine. Protestant identity in the Nordics, however, has a strong negative effect, although religiosity now points in the other direction. In the 2004 new member states, which were mostly Eastern European, only a nominal Catholic affiliation has a positive impact on attitudes, whereas a Catholic commitment has a *negative* sign that just misses statistical significance, perhaps reflecting the skepticism of extremely conservative Catholics. Thus conservative Catholicism in the East is beginning to negatively affect attitudes toward integration.

Using *Eurobarometer* data we can also explore the cultural cleavage in Europe over integration's ultimate goal: the EU's *finalité*. Catholics, we have argued, favor a federalist goal, whereas Protestants resist federalism in favor of a cooperative Europe that jealously guards member state sovereignty. A recent survey (*Eurobarometer 78*, Autumn 2012) asked whether respondents thought that "the EU should develop further into a federation of Nation-States."[7] Because the survey does not include a religion question, we can only examine nationally aggregated data. Still, table 10.1 reveals what looks like a strong relationship between confessional culture and public support for European federation: Citizens in Catholic-majority member states favor a federation, but Protestant-majority states include fewer "federalists." Indeed, the correlation between a Protestant population and support for federation is negative and very strong ($r = -.730$).

As we did in chapter 8, we test this relationship against the most important alternative explanations, the timing of accession and per capita gross domestic product. Presumably, longer experience in the EU and greater wealth should lead to more support for federation. This time, however, we find that neither timing nor wealth is correlated with public support for federation and that neither reduces the impact of Protestantism in a regression analysis (table 10.2). Confessional culture thus remains a strong predictor of aggregate support for the EU developing into a federation of nation-states.

Will the strong relationship between Catholicism and support for integration last? Recent studies indicate that the relationship remains strong in the European Union of the Nine, plus Greece, Spain, Finland, and Sweden (the exceptions are

Table 10.1 EU Public Opinion on Development of a Federation of Nation-States

Country	Percent "Agree"	Country	Percent "Agree"
Poland	63	Greece	44
France	55	Netherlands	43
Czech Republic	55	Estonia	43
Cyprus	54	Italy	42
Austria	54	Bulgaria	40
Slovakia	52	Lithuania	38
Luxembourg	48	Romania	37
Spain	47	Malta	37
Belgium	47	Ireland	35
Latvia	46	United Kingdom	24
Germany	46	Finland	23
Slovenia	44	Sweden	19
Portugal	44	Denmark	18
Hungary	44		

Source: Eurobarometer 78, Autumn 2012.

Table 10.2 Confessional Culture and Support for a Federation of Nation-States
(OLS, standardized coefficients)

Measure	Pearson's r	Beta
Percent Protestant	−.730***	−.722***
Late accession	.038	.016
GDP per capita	−.179	−.054
Adjusted R^2 =		.477
N =	27	27

Source: Eurobarometer 78, Autumn 2012.

Austria and Portugal). Analysis of the links between confessional culture and attitudes toward integration in the newer member states added after 1995 indicates that in these countries economic, political, and identity issues tend to explain more of the variance than religion does—although religion is not completely irrelevant.[8] Even in the older member states, it is not clear that the relationship between confessional culture and public attitudes will hold up much longer. Some decline in Catholic influence has been detected.[9] Although studies of youth support for integration completed in the 1990s showed results similar to those in broader samples,[10] there is more recent evidence that younger Europeans are far less influenced by confessional culture than their elders.[11]

The evolution of the religious landscape in Europe may have a profound effect on support for integration. The decline in Catholic identification and practice and the rise of people identifying as having no religion at all indicate that the overall support for integration across Europe may well decline, even if the relationship between

Catholicism and support for integration remains significant.[12] The EU cannot benefit from Catholic support if the Catholic community continues to evaporate. Just as worrisome to European elites should be growing resistance to integration among the most conservative Catholics in the new member states (and Ireland), despite continued Vatican support for the EU. The Continent's observant Catholics have provided European leaders with a deep well of emotional support for integration. Although other segments of the population have offered support for the EU when they expected material benefits, Catholics have been more likely to base their support on principle. The EU cannot afford to lose too many more principled loyalists.

Constructing a European Identity

Confessional culture influences support for integration. But does it affect European identity? European elites have attempted since the 1950s to construct a new national identity. They have assumed, like the scholars in the stable peace school (see chapter 1), that union required the emergence of a new "we feeling" strong enough to coalesce into a national identity. In this section we examine contemporary elite efforts to construct an identity.

Some scholars have argued that the EU does not need a people with a conscious national identity—a *demos*—to back its claim to democratic legitimacy.[13] Most scholars and political elites, however, have recognized the necessity of a European identity strong enough to bind together peoples divided by language, nationality, class, religion, gender, ethnic identity, and other social markers. According to them, the EU must have the backing of a democratic "people" if it is to make difficult policy choices that will benefit some and harm others—the very decisions it now faces.[14] The elites can construct national identities, but not out of thin air. They need shared cultural materials that carry emotional weight across social cleavages to bind together a new nation—to create "solidarity among strangers."[15] As we saw in chapter 6, the Christian Democratic founders of the European Communities saw themselves as "national identity constructors" and began creating common symbols for the budding European polity, often grounding them in Christian or Carolingian iconography. The passing of that Christian Democratic postwar generation and the dramatic secularization of Europe did not end the elites' attempts to construct a European identity, but it did shift the emphasis away from overtly religious symbolism—although religious elements remained.

The result was the addition of "European" to the multiple identities held by citizens. Whatever metaphors were used to describe the simultaneous identification with several communities, whether nested Russian Matryoshka dolls or marble cakes, the emergence of a European identity across the Continent was undeniable.[16] What is more problematic is the strength of this European identity and the factors contributing to its intensity, especially in relationship to national identity. As Thomas Risse has shown, some national identities are Europeanized by incorporating a European identity into the very content of national identity.[17] For instance, in Germany "a 'good German' equals a 'good European,' supporting a united Europe."[18] But this melding is not apparent in all EU members. Although the German, French, Italian, and Luxembourgish identities may sit easily next to or blend with a European identity, other national identities (e.g., those of Britain and the Nordic region) resist a new regional addition. Some national identities may be weaker than others—Luxembourgers, for example, may not be as emotionally tied to their identity as are the citizens of the other member states—but some strong national identities seem quite compatible with a European identity as well. The French fit this category. Still other national identities remain nearly exclusive; these are found disproportionately in the Protestant-majority countries. Thus the content—not just the presence or strength—of national identity matters.[19] The Protestant national identities still contain notions of "Europe" as the cultural and political "other"—Catholic, undemocratic, and backward. The construction of a Europe-wide identity thus clashes with national identities for some people in some countries, in what amounts to a zero-sum game. The harder Brussels pushes for a new identity, the more the citizens of the Protestant-majority countries have difficulty feeling attached to Europe. Confessional culture makes all the difference.

The Identity Construction Policy

Continental elites naturally led the European identity construction projects. The British and the Danes (and later the Finns and Swedes) signed on to these projects but did not consider them central to the activities of the Community. But to many continental political and bureaucrats, the building of a "People's Europe" was indeed central to integration. Without mass identification with the Community/Union, these leaders would find it impossible to push integration forward.[20]

In December 1973 the Copenhagen European Summit (which included the new members Britain, Denmark, and Ireland) issued a "Declaration on European Identity."[21] This remarkable statement committed the Community to developing a common identity that it could project to the world: "In their external relations, the Nine propose progressively to undertake the definition of their identity in relation to other countries or groups of countries." Such actions would reinforce the "construction of a United Europe thus making easier the proposed transformation of the whole complex of their relations into a European Union." The Nine recognized that supranational institutions and common policies constituted "an essential part of the European Identity," but the "fundamental elements" were the principles of representative democracy, the rule of law, social justice, and respect for human rights. These values were hardly the sole property of Europe. What gave "the European

Identity its originality and its own dynamism" were cultural commonalities: "a common European civilization, the attachment to common values and principles, the increasing convergence of attitudes to life, the awareness of having specific interests in common and the determination to take part in the construction of a United Europe." This declaration did not commit the Nine to a specific course of action, but it assumed that "the European Identity" was emerging out of actions already taken and that further integration would naturally result in a more fully formed identity, firmly grounded in common values and a shared civilization.

The 1980s "relaunch" of Europe, with a new emphasis on a "People's Europe," focused attention once again on constructing a European identity.[22] The introduction of European parliamentary elections in 1979 had already created a Community-wide political event and civic symbol.[23] In addition, the European Council had also accepted in principle the creation of a common European passport. Even more was in the works. In June 1984 the European Council established an ad hoc committee to assist in "adopting measures to strengthen and promote its identity and its image both for its citizens and for the rest of the world."[24] Chaired by Pietro Adonnino, the committee's final report suggested ways to strengthen Community citizens' rights and ensure ease of movement across borders. It also recognized the importance of frequent transnational contact and offered recommendations to broaden and deepen cross-border exchanges through commercial transactions, audiovisual productions, tourism, sports, the pairing of cities, and, most important, education. The committee suggested an increased emphasis on teaching foreign languages, creating cross-border student and apprentice exchanges, and recognizing university diplomas. The intent was clearly to encourage and facilitate the mingling of the people of Europe with the goal of broadening their concept of "us."

Coupled with this indirect approach to European identity construction, the Adonnino committee also proposed the creation of a set of symbols of nationhood designed to bond citizens emotionally to the European Community and to each other as members of the community of Europe. In the committee's words, these symbols would strengthen "the Community's image and identity."[25] Thus the report recommended adoption of the Council of Europe's flag as the Community's; Beethoven's *Ode to Joy* as the Community's anthem; a series of European postal stamps; attractive uniform border signs; the establishment of a new European Academy of Science, Technology, and Art; and even the creation of a "Euro-lottery." In addition, the committee proposed that European citizens should start getting more information on the history and benefits of the "construction of Europe."[26]

Socialization through Education

Europe's leaders did not take the Adonnino committee's recommendations lightly. Starting in the mid-1980s, officials both inside and outside the European institutions expanded efforts to socialize citizens through education and the creation of new symbols.

Neil Fligstein argues that educators have been easy recruits to the European cause because they perceive a close connection between the integration project and the Enlightenment principles at the core of their collective worldview: "democracy, rule of law, respect for differences of others, and the principles of rational discourse and science."[27] Education elites have thus been in "the forefront of trying to create a European society by transforming their curricula and engaging in collective dialogue."[28] Education associations, although not formally sponsored by the European institutions, have rewritten textbooks and reshaped national curricula to reflect a broader European perspective that puts greater emphasis on European values. In these materials, national narratives are not eliminated but are reshaped to place the nation in its European context; students are encouraged "to see themselves more as Europeans and less as citizens just of nation-states."[29] As Fligstein puts it, "The message to students is that there is a kind of trajectory to the history of Europe whereby, if people work together, they can produce a more just society."[30] These efforts are explicitly aimed at creating a European society based on common values, so it should come as no surprise that the British government has "explicitly resisted" the teaching of "Europe."[31]

Other educational programs are also designed to increase the number of "Europeans." School systems have promoted cross-border communication by making the learning of a second language compulsory (except in Ireland) and by beginning language training in primary school. And not satisfied with bilingualism, the EU issued a white paper in 1995 calling for students to speak *three* languages.[32] In higher education, the Community began several student (and faculty) exchange programs in the late 1980s to encourage study across borders. The most important of these has been the Erasmus Programme, overseeing the exchange of more than a million European university students. The most significant policy initiative has been a major effort—the "Bologna process"—to create a European Higher Education Space that will facilitate the easy transfer of credits and credentials across borders. This process, which began in 1999, is not an EU program (it now includes forty-seven countries), but EU elites have viewed Bologna as a vehicle for student and professional mobility and thus have eagerly supported it. These programs have mainly targeted the young in a deliberate attempt to shape a new citizenry by loosening traditional national identities and strengthening a broader European identity.

Socialization through European Symbols

In addition to using education as a tool of socialization, European elites have also sought to manipulate the symbols of a single Europe. Political symbols, if widely disseminated, can transmit meanings from elites to the masses.[33] Mass publics, in turn, can use these symbols in everyday life and imbue them with additional layers of meaning. As we saw in chapters 1 and 4, symbols often draw on the sacred—allusions to the divine, ancient memories, myths of origin, notions of chosen-ness, and collective mission—to elicit emotional responses that can mold a collection of disparate individuals into a single group. Symbols do not need to be overtly religious, but to be effective they need to perform a sacred function through popular interpretation or ritual use. Effective symbols will always be open to interpretation and multiple uses. The best symbols, in fact, are revered by all, but for myriad reasons.[34]

The most obvious evokers of European unity are the EU's official symbols: the flag, anthem, motto ("united in diversity"), the euro (adopted by the euro zone countries in 1999), and Europe Day (May 9, commemorating the Schuman Declaration).[35] All were listed in the rejected Constitution, but they proved controversial for some member states and were omitted from the Lisbon Treaty. Sixteen members, however, attached a declaration to the Lisbon Treaty indicating that for them the flag, anthem, motto, euro, and Europe Day would "continue as symbols to express the sense of community of the people in the European Union and their allegiance to it." Britain, the Nordics, Estonia, Latvia, the Czech Republic, and the Netherlands stayed out—all member states with relatively large numbers of Protestants. But France, Poland, and Ireland also rejected the symbols. These states preferred not to recognize what looked like an attempt to enshrine the EU in the symbolic trappings of statehood.[36]

Beyond the official symbols range a plethora of other icons of European unity. The postwar "founders"—Schuman, Adenauer, Monnet, and de Gasperi—have been elevated to mythical status, and their memories are invoked at every turn in an attempt to shape a common historical narrative.[37] For more contemporary models for emulation, the EU has created no fewer than three presidents and one high representative, each with some right to represent and speak for the EU.[38] The fact that an EU official can speak with authority at a Group of Seven summit (Commission president) or chair a meeting of the European heads of state and government (Council president) carries symbolic weight; but at the same time, the number and obscurity of such high office holders may symbolize the political weakness of the EU, not its strength.

Buildings can also carry much symbolic meaning. None of the official EU structures is architecturally noteworthy, and thus none has become a universally recognized symbol of political power in the manner of Westminster, the Reichstag, or the US Capitol. Their placement in an odd jumble in Brussels around Parc Léopold and Place Schuman at the end of the less-than-grand Rue de la Loi (and on a windswept plain in Luxembourg and in hard-to-reach Strasbourg) also speaks to the ability of the member states to undermine the supranational institutions' pretensions to power. At the same time, the buildings do symbolize Europe's commitment to transparency and democracy with their striking expanses of glass, ubiquitous elliptical tables, and ever-present army of translators. The European elites have also used the opportunity to honor European heritage by naming important edifices after symbols and heroes of unity, including the mythical Europa (European Council), Charlemagne (Commission), Justus Lipsius (Council of Ministers), Paul-Henri Spaak, Altiero Spinelli, Konrad Adenauer, Willy Brandt, and József Antall (Parliament), to name some of the most prominent. Less positively, however, the monthly parliamentary trek from Brussels to Strasbourg, accompanied by phalanxes of rolling metal file boxes, has come to epitomize the waste and inefficiency of the institutions caused by member state intransigence (in this case, France's refusal to allow the European Parliament to permanently locate in Brussels).

The edifices adjacent to the EU institutions' buildings in Brussels have also provided an opportunity to construct a common historical narrative for the EU. In 2007, on the initiative of its president, Hans-Gert Pöttering, the European Parliament committed to creating the "House of European History" in the Parc Léopold. This new museum will explore Europe's history and the development of the European Union, with the latter section guided by "the theme of striving for a better life through a growing united Europe."[39] In describing the purpose of the project in 2013, the secretary-general of the European Parliament, Klaus Welle, explained, "We need to actively engage to support and create the sense of European identity. We need to start thinking of our own history not just as national history but also as joint European history."[40] Thus the project is designed not only as a symbol of Europe's common culture and experience but also as a vehicle for educating the European public to think of itself as one people with a single overarching narrative.

European symbolism is not always exclusive of national symbols. The euro, because the member states mint it, combines common European symbols (mostly architectural) with the chosen symbols of the members.[41] Many EU cultural initiatives also fit into this category—including the European Capitals of Culture, cities chosen to highlight the richness and diversity of European culture; Heritage Days, opening to the public historical sites and cultural events; the European Heritage Label, identifying heritage sites; and the EU Culture Prizes, awards in a number of fields. All are designed to highlight the cultural jewels of the member states while weaving them together into a single European tapestry; the purpose is to "foster a feeling of European citizenship."[42]

European "citizenship" has itself become a symbol of a single Europe. The Maastricht Treaty established EU citizenship, and subsequent treaty revisions refined this concept. Every citizen of a member state is automatically a citizen of the European Union. Citizenship allows an individual to live and work in any other member state and to stand for office and vote in both European and municipal elections. Citizens have the right to petition the European Parliament and the Office of the European Ombudsman and to gain access to documents in any of the EU's twenty-four official languages. They can also ask the Commission to initiate a piece of legislation. When

traveling outside the EU, citizens carry a common passport and are entitled to con-
sular services in any member state's embassy or consulate. EU citizens also enjoy
the protections codified in the Charter of Fundamental Rights.[43] Many EU citizens
do not know they have a supranational citizenship, but its creation was an explicit
attempt to draw a new line around "Europeans" and to differentiate them from all
international "others."

Finally, by calling the draft treaty of 2004 a "Constitution," the elites shrouded
the document with a mystical national aura. Constitutions are written for nation-
states, and Europe's leaders were signaling that it was time to place the EU on a
national footing. With an eye to the symbolic, the signing ceremony occurred in
Rome in the same Capitoline Hill complex where the representatives of the Six had
gathered in 1957 to sign the Treaties of Rome. The heads of government and their
foreign ministers signed the constitutional treaty under a larger-than-life statue of
Pope Innocent X that was only a short stroll from the busts of Julius Caesar and
Constantine the Great.[44] Though this venue dripped with ancient and medieval symbolism, the national publics later decided that the EU was not ready for a nation's
founding.

The official and unofficial symbols of European unity are decidedly secular in
purpose, but do they carry—perhaps unintentional—religious meaning? François
Foret has pointed out that most EU symbols have some connection to the sacred,
or have been interpreted by some Europeans to have religious connotations despite
their secular intent. Religious references seem to float around European symbols,
despite official attempts to define them in nonreligious, or at least non-Christian,
terms.[45] And no symbol of the EU has been quite as controversial for its alleged religious meaning as the European flag.

The origins of the European flag are not particularly mysterious. The Council
of Europe, soon after its establishment in May 1949, following international norms,
launched a search for an appropriate flag design to represent the organization. In June
1950 the council set up a committee to sift through design submissions. A number
of prominent individuals submitted designs, including Count Richard Coudenhove-
Kalergi (a red cross in an orange circle on a blue background), and Salvador de
Madariaga, cofounder of the College of Europe (a constellation of stars on a blue
background). And then there was Arsène Heitz, not a prominent individual but
rather an employee in the council's postal service, who submitted more than twenty
proposals.[46] He had at one time been interested in incorporating into his design the
green standard that Pope Leo III reportedly gave to Charlemagne at his imperial
coronation in 800;[47] another of his designs featured a cross like those found on the
Scandinavian flags.[48] But the design that drew particular attention was "a crown of
12 golden stars with 5 rays, their points not touching" on a blue background.[49] The
Council of Ministers favored the idea of stars on a simple background, so in April
1955 the ministers narrowed the choices to two: Heitz's golden stars and Madariaga's
constellation. The Parliamentary Assembly favored the Heitz design, but increased

the number of stars to fifteen to reflect the current membership. The Council of Ministers, on reviewing the Assembly's choice, rejected the notion that the stars represented member states (a dispute over the Saar region proved a sticking point) and the number was returned to twelve. Paul M. G. Lévy, director of the Council of Europe's Department of Culture, was responsible for the final design, which the Parliamentary Assembly approved on October 25, 1955. The Council of Ministers voted to adopt the flag on December 8, and it was unveiled in Paris five days later.

The Council of Europe intended for its new flag to be used as a symbol of postwar integration and actively lobbied other organizations to adopt it. For many years the institutions of the European Communities formally ignored these encouragements, but that did not prevent an informal process of gradual acceptance. From 1958 to 1999 the Council of Europe's Parliamentary Assembly and the European Communities' European Parliamentary Assembly (later the European Parliament) shared the same buildings (the House of Europe until 1977, followed by the Palace of Europe) in Strasbourg; they also informally shared the Council of Europe's flag. Thus in April 1983 it was natural for a directly elected, newly confident European Parliament to adopt the golden stars flag as its own symbol. In June 1984 the European Communities' heads of government, after accepting the Adonnino committee's report, agreed to work actively to promote a common European identity, which included adopting the symbols shared by the EU's member nation-states. In 1985 the European heads of government adopted the flag as the symbol of the European Community. By 1986 the flag was flying outside the European Commission's building (the Berlaymont) in Brussels.

The flag became, as originally intended, a symbol of an integrated Europe. But it also proved controversial. Several characteristics of the flag seemed to reference Catholic iconography: the shade of blue was often associated with the Madonna, and Catholic artists frequently used shades of yellow or gold to represent eternal glory. But it was the flag's "crown of twelve golden stars" that drew the most attention. The Virgin Mary is often represented encircled by a halo of twelve stars, which refers to a passage in Revelation that Catholics interpret as depicting the Virgin as queen of Heaven: "And a great sign appeared in Heaven: a woman clothed with the sun, and the moon was under her feet, and on her head was a crown of twelve stars" (Rev 12:1).[50] The twelve-star halo also came to be associated with the iconography of the Virgin of the Immaculate Conception, thus figuring prominently in paintings and sculptures across Catholic Europe in the Baroque period and after.[51] For those seeking religious associations, the Council of Europe in 1956 donated to the city of Strasbourg a magnificent stained glass window (*Blessing Madonna*) for the Cathedral, which depicts the Virgin Mary with a circle of twelve stars on a blue background hovering above her like a celestial wheel.

The flag's religious symbolism took on greater meaning for many who examined its origins. Arsène Heitz and Paul Lévy were both devout Catholics. The Belgian Lévy was a Jewish Holocaust survivor who converted to Catholicism after World

War II. Popular histories sometimes attribute the flag's inspiration to a glimpse Lévy once had of the sun reflecting off the star halo of a statue of the Virgin.[52] That may have increased Lévy's support for the circle of stars design, but Heitz was most responsible for the original concept. In interviews later in his life, Heitz—who was, according to one source, a member of the Order of the Medal of the Immaculate Conception[53]—claimed to have taken his inspiration directly from the passage in Revelation.[54] Moreover, the Council of Europe itself seemed to underline the flag's Marian connections. The Council of Ministers voted to adopt the flag one day earlier than originally planned—on December 8, the Feast of the Immaculate Conception.[55]

Symbols, by their nature, are open to interpretation. The contemporary Council of Europe and European Union, without explicitly denying any religious references in the flag, officially point to more secular interpretations.[56] The EU's statement on the flag references the broad unity of Europe that goes beyond the EU itself, but makes no religious reference: "[The flag] is the symbol not only of the European Union but also of Europe's unity and identity in a wider sense. The circle of gold stars represents solidarity and harmony between the peoples of Europe. . . . The number of stars has nothing to do with the number of Member States. There are twelve stars because the number twelve is traditionally the symbol of perfection, completeness, and unity."[57]

However, for people sensitive to religious symbols, the flag took on deep meaning. For many devout Catholics, the flag represented the deep Catholic roots of integration; but for many Protestants in England, Northern Ireland, the Netherlands, and Scandinavia, and for secularists across Europe, it served as veiled proof of a papist conspiracy.[58]

Other official EU symbols also developed religious dimensions. The anthem, adopted without lyrics from a popular symphony (Beethoven's Ninth), seems secular enough, except that many English-speaking Protestants recognize the tune as also that of the early-twentieth-century hymn *Joyful, Joyful We Adore Thee*. The euro, too, may seem completely secular, but Foret argues that all money possesses a religious dimension. To be accepted by the population, a currency must elicit a high degree of collective trust, which can then form the foundation for an identity and polity. Indeed, "the stability of the currency has a sacred status which is constitutive of the political community."[59] People, therefore, must *believe in* the euro and treat it as a sacred trust, thus laying a foundation for an emerging political union. Like the deutschmark, which in important ways created the German postwar state, the euro may be creating the European state. After the European Council adopted the name "euro" for the new currency in 1995, Portuguese prime minister Antonio Guttieres paraphrased Jesus' statement to Peter in Matthew 16:18: "Thou art euro, and on this rock we shall build the European Union."[60] The desperate attempts by euro zone leaders to save the euro in recent years have only underlined its symbolic importance: As goes the euro, so goes the Union.

The euro has become a sacred symbol of European unity, but few notice the prevalence of religious iconography on the currency. The banknotes feature archetypal architectural images for their common sides, but the Romanesque €10 and Gothic €20 notes recall Europe's great cathedrals, if no specific structure. As for the national sides of the currency, religious images abound. The Vatican is not an EU member, but it can produce euro coins with images of the reigning pope. In addition, the Slovakian and Maltese coins display crosses, while the Spanish and Austrian coins picture cathedrals.[61] The Commission's 2013 move to prevent the Slovakian Central Bank from minting commemorative coins picturing Saint Cyril and Saint Methodius, complete with halos and crosses, failed.[62] Thus the sacred remains mixed with the profane.

The several initiatives highlighting Europe's cultural heritage—the Culture Prizes, Heritage Days, and so forth—also necessarily intermingle with Europe's rich legacy of religious architecture, art, music, crafts, festivals, and traditions. In addition, planning for the House of European History has encountered controversy over the role of Catholic Christianity in shaping European culture in general and the European Union specifically. Some observers have objected to perceived bias toward Christianity on the committee charged with developing the narrative for the museum.[63] This conflict echoes the debate over the inclusion of Christianity in the proposed EU Constitution's preamble.

Without a doubt, the European elites have created a constellation of symbols in their campaign to construct a European identity. They have constructed a narrative that puts the EU at the center of the Continent's postwar achievements. The symbols of European unity adopted were not meant to be explicitly religious, but Europe's Christian past has crept in to give some symbols religious meaning for some people. The ceremonies commemorating Franco-German reconciliation are sometimes explicitly religious (1962 and 1997), but according to former French president Nicolas Sarkozy, Franco-German friendship itself must be called "sacred."[64] Moreover, in a solemn ceremony every December, the European Parliament awards the Sakharov Prize for Freedom of Thought to a defender of human rights. This ceremony sacralizes the Enlightenment values that are central to secular European society: rationalism, democracy, the rule of law, equality, inclusion, human rights, social justice, and, more recently, sustainability. Such ceremonies and those accompanying Europe Day (and the awarding of the Charlemagne Prize discussed in chapter 6) indicate that a nascent civil religion has developed in the EU.

In sum, the European elites have consciously attempted to create a European "nation," as Anthony Smith sees it: "a named and self-defined human community whose members cultivate shared myths, memories, symbols, values, and traditions, reside in and identify with a historic homeland, create and disseminate a distinctive public culture, and observe shared customs and common laws."[65] They have written a history of Europe that highlights the EU's role as savior of a now-reconciled and prosperous continent—a narrative taught to schoolchildren and enshrined in museums. And they have also created symbols that have sometimes quite uninten-tionally come to resemble what Smith has called the "sacred foundations" of na-tional identity. Not all the European elites accept this agenda. Confessional culture still divides the EU's elites, making the Protestants less likely to support explicit attempts to create a European identity. Thus it is primarily continental Europeans who have worked to construct European attachments. The total package may look like rather thin gruel next to the rich stew of national ceremonies, symbols, values, memories, myths, and heroes. But, as we shall see in the next section, a European identity is in fact emerging.

European Identity

In exploring the emerging European identity, we start with an elementary question: Are there any Europeans? The short answer seems to be "yes, but not many."[66] The response depends on what "European" means and on how one measures European identity.

Scholars have attempted to assess the growth of European identity in opinion surveys, using a confusing variety of questions, alternative definitions of "Euro-pean," and a different array of options. Some surveys have defined "Europe" as a geographic unit, and others have prompted respondents to think about their national (or other) identity and then whether or not they have the same types of feelings toward Europe.[67] Another common approach has been to ask respondents to com-pare their future attachments with their member state and Europe.[68] Few questions have specifically referred to the European Community/Union, so most researchers have assumed that "Europe" means the EU. Michael Bruter, however, finds evidence for two separate meanings of "Europe": a *civic* meaning attached to the EU, and a *cultural* meaning attached to Europe as a civilization.[69] When confronted with a general query about "Europe," people in France and the Netherlands have tended to equate "Europe" with the "European Union" (civic identity), but in Britain people have been more inclined to identify with "Europe" culturally than civically.[70] Thus, for the British, Europe is a cultural union but not a political or civic one.

Thus, the questions used by researchers have produced somewhat different re-sults. All have seemed to divide the public into what Green calls core, secondary, and non-European identifiers.[71] Surveys requiring respondents to make specific choices of identities (European or national) have found that core-European identifiers (first choice) make up approximately 5 percent, with an additional 12 percent choosing Europe, but listing it second.[72] Thus, approximately 83 percent of Europeans fall into the nonidentifier category. Surveys allowing greater flexibility, however, have yielded higher proportions of core and secondary identifiers. Fuchs and his col-leagues, for instance, used a *Eurobarometer 62* (Autumn 2004) question: "People feel different degrees of attachment to their town or village, to their region, to their country or to Europe. Please tell me how attached you feel to (a) your city/town/ village, (b) your region, (c) your country, and (d) Europe?"[73] About 3 percent identified exclusively with Europe (core identifiers), and 31 percent identified exclusively with their countries or refused to identify with either their country or Europe (non-identifiers). Thus, 66 percent of the respondents identified with Europe to some extent (secondary identifiers), a much higher proportion than the 12 percent cited above. Different questions have thus yielded different results. But after reviewing all the data, Green offered his "best guess" summary: "It would seem reasonable to conclude that something on the order of 15 percent of Europeans (roughly one of every six or seven) strongly identifies with Europe, while perhaps another 35 percent (roughly every third person) also identifies with Europe, but to a lesser extent. This leaves about half of the population for whom a European identity is either irrelevant or actively rejected."[74]

The good news for European elites is that many citizens do consider themselves "European." The bad news is that half do not, and just as significantly, that the European identity that does exist seems quite shallow: Very few citizens see themselves exclusively in European terms. In Risse's telling term, it is "European identity lite."[75]

The news might be better for EU elites if European identifiers were increasing, perhaps in response to identity construction efforts. Some countries—such as France, Belgium, and Luxembourg—have seen slight rises in identification with Europe.[76] But on the whole, the story since the early 1970s has been "stasis, not movement."[77] Nevertheless, Bruter offers evidence that exposure to European institutions and symbols has positively influenced cultural identity;[78] and Risse argues that the growth of a "common communicative space," in which Europeans debate issues of shared concern, has helped to Europeanize identities.[79] The efforts of the European elites to create ceremonies and symbols may have only touched the emotional surface of most Europeans. Deep identification with broader Europe—civic or cultural—takes more than seeing a flag or holding a passport. The emergence of a truly European public sphere may be a better indication of a growing European identity, but the effects of such a development are hard to measure with public opinion surveys. Most scholars suspect that even if such an identity is widening and deepening, it is still fragile and vulnerable to economic and political shocks.

Who are the Europeans—the true believers in Europe and the European Union? At the individual level, our best available data come from the Nine, which have the longest history with the EU. In these countries the "Europeans" tend to be the privileged—upper class and educated, urban, well traveled, male, and competent in a second language They are also likely to hold postmaterialist values, lean to the center-left, think they will benefit from EU membership, believe in European integration—and more likely to be Catholic.[80] They are the movers and shakers; the upwardly mobile and networked; the creative and the politically engaged. Those who identify weakly with Europe (or not at all) tend to struggle economically, and to see no personal benefit from their country's EU membership. They are from smaller towns in rural areas, have modest educations, travel infrequently, probably do not speak a second language well, are politically conservative, and have little interest in the idea of integration. And they are more likely to be female. They are also less likely to be Catholic, which usually (but not always) means they are Protestant or secular. These are only central tendencies, of course; there are many exceptions. Broadly speaking, however, European identifiers are the integration winners, whereas the national identifiers are the less privileged who gain little from the integration process.[81]

Second, European identity is unevenly distributed across the EU's member states, with some states showing a higher proportion of European identifiers than others. *Eurobarometer 61* (Spring 2004) gave respondents four options, ranging from exclusive national identity to exclusive European identity. Table 10.3 shows the proportion in each of the fifteen member states who answered "nationality only." Aside from the few who answered "don't know," most respondents identified to some degree as Europeans, but they are concentrated in the states toward the top of table 10.3. The Catholic countries tend to be grouped at or near the top, whereas the Protestant countries tend to be grouped at or near the bottom. As expected, the bivariate correlation between the proportion of Protestants and "national only" identifiers is substantial ($r = .419$); the more Protestants, the more "national only" identifiers (table 10.4). To extend the analysis, we ran the proportion of Protestants with the timing of accession and per capita gross domestic product in a multivariate analysis, just as we did above with support for the "development of a federation." Once again, we find that the proportion of Protestants is the only significant predictor of exclusive national identity, aggregated by country (see table 10.4).

The *Eurobarometer* does not permit a direct test of the relationship between confessional culture and European identity because no survey includes both religion and identity questions. But *Eurobarometer 65.2* (Spring 2006) offers an indirect method of testing the relationship. This survey asked a multipart question concerning the EU flag. Two of the parts produced significant variations in the responses: "This symbol is the European flag. I have a list of statements concerning it. I would like to have your opinion on each of these. For each of them, could you please tell me if you tend to agree or tend to disagree? (a) I identify with this flag. (b) This flag should be seen on all public buildings in (our country) next to the national flag."[82] These questions can serve as proxies for identity questions and yield interesting results when explored in relation to religion.

In the EU of twenty-five member states, 55 percent of Catholics felt attached to the EU flag, whereas 46 percent of Protestants felt the same way. When asked if their national flag and the EU flag should be flown at the same time, 63 percent of Catholics, but only 40 percent of Protestants, said "yes." If we combine those who

Table 10.3 Identity in the EU Member States (percent "Nationality Only")

Country	Nationality Only	Country	Nationality Only
Luxembourg	27	Bulgaria	45
Italy	28	Portugal	46
France	29	Netherlands	48
Spain	32	Ireland	49
Malta	32	Cyprus	49
Romania	37	Czech Republic	50
Slovakia	38	Austria	50
Germany	38	Lithuania	52
Belgium	39	Greece	55
Latvia	40	Sweden	57
Slovenia	42	Finland	60
Denmark	43	Hungary	61
Estonia	44	United Kingdom	62
Poland	45		

Source: Eurobarometer 61, Spring 2004.

Table 10.4 Confessional Culture and National Only Identity
(OLS, standardized coefficients)

Measure	Pearson's r	Beta
Percent Protestant	.419*	.422*
Late accession	.353	.297
GDP per capita	−.210	−.064
Adjusted R^2 =		.203
N =	27	27

*$p < .05$; **$p < .01$; ***$p < .001$.
Source: Eurobarometer 61, Spring 2004.

both identify with the EU flag and think it should fly alongside their national flag, we find that 46 percent of Catholics but only 29 percent of Protestants fit this category. Clearly the Catholics, on the whole, see the EU flag more favorably than the Protestants do.

A more interesting result emerges, however, when we divide the EU's religious groups according to whether or not respondents are in the religious majority or minority in their member states. When we do this, the effects of confessional culture are more pronounced. Being in the majority or minority does not affect Catholic identification with the EU flag; 55 percent of Catholics feel attached. But in the Catholic-majority countries, 66 percent of Catholics think both flags should fly, compared with 46 percent where Catholics are in a minority. When attachment and flag flying are combined, 47 percent of Catholics when in the majority support both, but only 35 percent of those in a minority context. The Protestant differences are more dramatic. Fully 55 percent of Protestants in a *minority* situation identify with the EU flag (equal to the overall Catholic percentage), but only 36 percent in a Protestant-majority country do. Protestants in a minority situation favor flying both flags more than Catholics do (52 percent vs. 46 percent), but only 27 percent of Protestants in Protestant-majority countries agree. If we combine both measures, a greater proportion of Protestants than Catholics in a minority situation favor both (40 percent vs. 35 percent), but only 16 percent of Protestants in Protestant-majority states do.

What does all this mean? Catholics tend to act as though the EU flag is their flag; they identify with it and want to see it flying—a bit more so when they are in the majority, but pretty much all the time. Protestants, conversely, identify with the EU flag only when they are a religious minority. When in the religious majority, they want nothing to do with it. Why are the Protestants so negative? We can only conjecture, but the flag may act as a symbol of resistance to the dominant national culture when Protestants are in the minority and a symbol of domination by the foreign "other" when they are in the majority. When they are in the minority, they see "Europe" as culturally friendlier to them than "nation" is; but when in the majority, they see "Europe" as a threat to their way of life. Catholics seem to be rather attached to the flag in all contexts, but especially when they are in the majority.

Fortunately, *Eurobarometer 62.5* offers us opportunity to develop a multivariate model to test the strength and durability of religion as a predictor of identification with the EU flag and support for flying both flags, controlling for a variety of other variables, many of which are stressed in other theories about the development of European identity (table 10.5). Although the patterns for the two variables are slightly different, the results confirm the findings of other scholars about the demographic and ideological basis of identification with "Europe." Professionals and business owners, neoliberals, and the "cognitively mobilized" identify with the EU flag and tend to support flying both flags together, but their demographic and ideological counterparts do not. (The negative coefficient for higher education is a residual, appearing because of the powerful positive effect of cognitive mobilization, strongly correlated with education.)

Nevertheless, even after controlling for all these theoretically important factors, confessional culture still matters. Catholics identify with the flag—and committed Catholics identify even more. Protestants are much less willing to identify with the flag, although observant Protestants are now a bit more willing to support the flag as mainline ecumenism again becomes a factor. (As with Protestants, Orthodox believers identify less with the flag, but committed ones are more supportive.) Thus once again, Catholics and Protestants behave differently. If the EU flag is a symbol of identity, then at the individual level Catholicism encourages the development of a European identity, but Protestantism (generally) undermines identity construction efforts.

In sum, the best evidence available indicates that a European identity has emerged across the Continent. But its distribution is decidedly lumpy. Clumps of relatively

Table 10.5 Attitudes toward the EU Flag, 2006
(logistic regression analysis)

Characteristic	Identify with EU Flag B	Should Fly Both Flags B
Confessional culture		
Catholic	.386***	.207***
x commitment	.068***	.067***
Protestant	−.263**	−.860***
x commitment	.141***	.142***
Orthodox	−.481*	.176
x commitment	.200**	.099
Majority religion	−.153***	.313***
Ideology		
Neoliberal ideology	.365***	.328***
Right	−.045***	−.045***
Left	.006	.037***
Cognitive mobilization		
Understand EU	.322***	.187***
Discuss politics often	.103***	.090***
Know about the EU	.077***	.056***
Occupation		
Professional	.195**	.029
Small business	.127*	.006
Clerical	−.105**	−.063
Labor	−.030	−.147***
Demographics		
Male	.118***	.067*
Age	−.006***	−.002*
Education	−.082***	−.026
Constant	−.776***	−.567***
Nagelkerke R^2	.134	.117

*$p < .05$; **$p < .01$; *** $p < .001$.
Sources: Eurobarometer 65.2. For variable coding, see Brent F. Nelsen, James L. Guth, and Brian Highsmith, "Does Religion Still Matter? Religion and Public Attitudes toward Integration in Europe," *Politics and Religion* 4, no. 1 (2011): 1–26.

few European identifiers can be found at the cosmopolitan end of the social spectrum, with national identifiers concentrating on the lower end. "Europeans" are also more likely to be found in EU member states with more Catholics (or Orthodox) than Protestants. And finally, Catholics are more likely to be European identifiers than Protestants, all things being equal. European elites have consciously and creatively attempted to construct a European identity with staying power. But measuring their success has proved difficult. The stability of European identity over time indicates that construction efforts may not have dramatic short-term effects; socialization effects may not show up for a generation or more. What seems clear from our analysis is that despite all the efforts of European elites, Protestant confessional culture limits the number of "Europeans" in a member state and encourages exclusive national identity. Protestantism evidently makes national identity decidedly "stickier."

Divided Europe

Neil Fligstein sees a sharp and pervasive class divide in the European identity data.[83] The educated, the professionals, the managers, the government officials—the middle and upper middle classes—have connected across national borders, and in a Deutschian flurry have come to like and trust each other through frequent contact and communication. A community spirit has developed among the privileged classes that has created a developing, although still shallow, European identity. But this new identity has come at a price, producing a backlash that could prove difficult to manage: "The class aspects of European economic and social integration explain some of the anti-EU national politics that have emerged. On the political right, the EU is viewed as elitist and against the nation. On the political left, the EU's lack of a social policy provides ammunition for the view that the EU is the enemy of the 'average' man."[84] Thus, for Fligstein, capitalism has produced a clash between a pro-Europe economic and social elite and a nationalist underclass; the fundamental forces are economic.

Thomas Risse disagrees. For him, Europe is divided primarily along cultural lines, with a "modern" elite facing a resistant nation. The new European identity constructed by elites is a "postnational identity . . . that emphasizes democracy, human rights, the market economy, the welfare state, and cultural diversity." No European state can join the EU without adhering to these values—as the Yugoslav successor states have painfully discovered. "Europe's political identity," Risse argues, "constitutes a 'sacred' identity construction, . . . insofar as it is seen as superior to other political orders."[85] But this new "Establishment" identity is opposed by a cultural vision of Europe "based on a common historical and religious heritage." This Euroskeptical vision "is constructed as a primordial European identity, one that is based on traditional values, and a particular interpretation of Christianity and other historical traditions."[86] Polish Catholics listening to Radio Maryja, French Catholics voting for the National Front, and Lega Nord's supporters in Italy advocate an exclusively Catholic set of sacred foundations for Europe. But as Risse points out, these "nationalist" movements are sometimes projecting a "distinct *European* identity" to the supranational level.[87] He sees a growing politicization between two competing visions of Europe—"cosmopolitan and modern Europe vs. nationalist and xenophobic Europe." But far from fearing this competition, he welcomes it as necessary to the normalization of democratic politics in the EU.

EUROPEAN IDENTITY · 341

Both Fligstein and Risse argue that these fundamental divides run right through European society as a whole. But this view ignores persistent national differences in citizens' identification with Europe. The Nordics (including Norway and Iceland), for instance, are certainly not filled with economic "losers" and premodern troglodytes; yet they claim a disproportionate number of exclusive national identifiers. And the British elites adhere to Enlightenment values as much as the Belgians or Italians, yet are reluctant to join the federalist vision of their continental counterparts. The divide that Fligstein and Risse perceive may well represent the fundamental cleavage through society on the European Continent, but does it also describe the Anglo-Scandinavian North? Certainly, there are class differences in Britain and the Nordics on attitudes toward European integration, but the division is between those favoring some form of European *cooperation* and the outright anti-Europeans.[88] To exaggerate only a little, class and culture divide the citizens of Protestant countries into two groups: the mildly Euroskeptical, and the rabidly Euroskeptical.

Protestant confessional culture helps us understand why Protestants and the Protestant-majority EU member states lack enthusiasm for the European project that has been embraced by most continental elites. Their national identities were forged in the fires of the Reformation. Their national struggles were fought to protect a special, even chosen, people against a universalist "other" in the form of Catholic Christendom. European identity is difficult enough to hold alongside a French, German, or Polish national identity; but it is even more tenuous when historic national identity centers on a fear of domination from core Europe. Moreover, Protestants may not be the only ones to feel this. Orthodox confessional culture gives rise to uneasiness among Greeks, Cypriots, Romanians, and Bulgarians about how well they fit into the EU. And Turkish Muslims may one day also find adopting a European identity a challenge. Before he was a national leader, Turkish president Recep Tayyip Erdoğan said in 1992 that "the EU's real name is Union of Catholic Christian States."[89] The secular norms of the European institutions make such a statement ridiculous; but to non-Catholic outsiders, the charge has cultural if not religious merit.

The Catholic-majority states and the mixed states of Germany and the Netherlands—certainly most of the elites, and large swaths of their populations—have adopted a vision of an "ever-closer union." When they think of "Europe," they think of core Europe and imagine a supranational (or multilevel) governance structure authoritative enough to solve the economic and financial problems facing their troubled Continent. The Protestant-majority countries, both inside and outside the EU, simply do not accept the federalist assumption behind an "ever-closer union"—and they *never* have. The British and the Nordics—along with many Dutch and German Protestants—see continental Europe as "like us," but not as "one of us." They support and pursue deep cooperation with European partners from Reykjavík to Istanbul as a necessity in a globalized and interdependent world, but they do not see

"Europe" as sufficiently like them to relinquish the privileges of sovereignty. This is not surprising; even the culturally similar Nordic countries have rejected the formation of a Nordic or Scandinavian federal state. It is also not surprising given the resistance to federation even by those EU member states with Catholic confessional cultures, despite the federal vision of so many continental elites. And this may be the point. Political and economic integration is difficult; creating a new supranational identity is even more difficult. The European nation-states and the loyalties they generate are proving hard to demote from their historic positions.

Europe's culture had commonalities enough to support a "we feeling" sufficient for a pluralistic security community on a war-torn continent—a world-historical success in itself. Europe, however, has reached the limits of integration; the two major confessional cultures have produced different visions of unity that are simply incompatible. Further steps will require such sacrifices in sovereignty that utilitarian interests will no longer trump identity. Some of the Protestant countries, such as Finland, may find fiscal union acceptable; but other Protestant countries will resist it. However, sizable proportions of all the traditionally Protestant EU member states (and nonmember states) will fiercely oppose a move to full political union. The Protestant countries will not sign on to a federation; Protestant electorates remain too strongly identified with their nation-states, and too distrustful of the traditional continental "other," to allow much room for a European identity to emerge. In short, no union is possible with Britain, the Nordics, and perhaps the Netherlands as EU members.

Where does this leave the European Union? The EU will need to choose one of two options. First, it could accept its slow-motion disintegration, which in a sense has already begun. The use of "flexibility" to extend the reach of EU law within voluntary groups of its member states in certain areas, the multiple opt outs written into its treaties, and the creation of extra-EU agreements (e.g., the Fiscal Compact) have already led to its legal fragmentation. And Britain's renegotiation of its EU membership or outright secession will only add to the fraying of the EU as others consider taking their cue from the United Kingdom to also demand the repatriation of powers from Brussels.[90] The newly organized Northern Future Forum, a group of mostly Protestant countries (the five Nordic countries, the three Baltic states, and the United Kingdom) could become an incubator for initiatives to renegotiate the terms of EU membership more in line with the Protestant vision for Europe. Moreover, recent gains by nationalist parties in both the European and national elections have put additional pressure on leaders to reverse integration. Rather than watch this demoralizing process play out over two or more decades, the European elite could codify it and ask the European electorate to legitimate the result in a series of referenda. Codification would probably start with a hard core of EU member states centered on Germany embracing a federal Constitution approved in a same-day referendum in the participating states.[91] Those other European states that were not interested in or eligible for union—from Norway to Britain to Kosovo to Turkey—would need to negotiate agreements governing areas of continuing cooperation. An association resembling the European Free Trade Association of non-EU states—led by Britain, Sweden, Norway, and Turkey—might emerge to simplify this process, but it would remain complicated and relatively opaque to ordinary citizens across the Continent.

The second option would be for the whole of Europe to accept the Protestant view of integration by officially enshrining the principle of member state sovereignty in the EU's treaties through a new, legally binding "Luxembourg Compromise." By doing so, the states of Europe would be admitting the lack of an essential legitimating *demos* and the failure of the identity construction project—but also the continued need for cooperation on multiple fronts. One of these "states" of Europe could be a fully constituted federal United States of Europe; but the European Union as a whole would be reconstituted so loosely as to also be acceptable to Norway, Iceland, Turkey, and perhaps even Switzerland. This would not mean the end of the EU; but it would mean the end of an "ever-closer union."

These are options that recognize the deep importance of culture to the European integration process. Though differences in culture can be overcome, this is harder to do when the content of a particular culture—in Europe's case, the Protestant confessional culture—makes union with the "other" too psychologically and philosophically difficult. And if the Protestants and Catholics cannot overcome their cultural differences, what hope is there in the short term for Turkey to unite with the current EU? Turkey will never be drawn into the West if the price to Turkey is the loss of national sovereignty and a new, "thick" European identity.

So far, Europe's "sacred" national identities have proven too strong to overcome. A European identity built on the pillars of Roman law, Charlemagne's sacral kingship, and the Catholic Church's universal mission has not replaced or even significantly joined national identities. European Enlightenment values, though achieving a certain sacred status and offering Europe a universal mission carrying human rights to the ends of the Earth, have not replaced the national myths of chosen peoples, the memories of glorious origins and fallen heroes, and the emotional and practical bonds of a shared language. In fact, if Risse is right, continental Europe (essentially, the euro zone) may soon find itself struggling over the thin European identity that does exist, as traditionalists and xenophobes challenge Enlightenment moderns over what constitutes Europe's common culture.

All of this may, of course, one day change. Cultures are not static. Enlightenment values may eventually prove strong enough to unite the entire European continent, the Anglo-Nordics included. In one sense, they already have; the European elites have maintained their credibility across the Continent by adhering closely to democracy, the rule of law, inclusion, and all the rest. Hungary's Viktor Orban, for instance, has learned how difficult it is to press the limits of democracy and the rule of law at home and still be accorded legitimacy by his EU colleagues. This elite consensus has existed since the fall of the Berlin Wall, but it has not yet extended deeply enough into the European citizenry to loosen their emotional ties to their respective nation-states.

That will not happen soon. If anything, the economic crisis of the early twenty-first century is testing even the limited commitment to the "idea of Europe." The Catholic Christian Democrats had a religious tie to Europe, beyond politics and certainly beyond economics. But in times of trouble, economic utility—the primary basis of support for the European project—is no replacement for religious fervor. As the conservative Catholics across the Continent continue to diminish in numbers and to turn away from the EU as having become a distortion of their original vision of a culturally united Europe, the EU will struggle to find enthusiasts beyond the narrow halls of the Commission and the multiple hemicycles of the European Parliament.

New European patriots may yet emerge, but probably not in culturally Protestant Europe. In the majority-Protestant countries, the European dream of Robert Schuman, Konrad Adenauer, Alcide de Gasperi, and Jean Monnet never achieved the mythical status that it came to be accorded in Catholic Europe. The Reformation still weighs on the collective imagination of Protestant Europe, making "ever-closer union" still a threat, not a dream. The Christian Democratic vision may yet be realized in culturally Catholic Europe; but Protestant Europe—and Orthodox and Muslim Europe, for that matter—should not be expected to participate. It is time for the whole of Europe to recognize that culture matters to the process of integration. And the persistent cultural differences across the Continent make it impossible to achieve a full political union of all the European states. But these cultural differences are not so great as to preclude the survival of a peaceful, prosperous—and realistic—community of sovereign states.

Notes

1. Jennifer Lind, "The Perils of Apology: What Japan Shouldn't Learn from Germany," *Foreign Affairs* 88, no. 3 (2009): 139.

2. Ibid.

3. John Gillingham, *Coal, Steel, and the Rebirth of Europe, 1945–1955: The Germans and French from Ruhr Conflict to Economic Community* (Cambridge: Cambridge University Press, 1991), 372.

4. Leon N. Lindberg and Stuart A. Scheingold, *Europe's Would-Be Polity: Patterns of Change in the European Community* (Englewood Cliffs, NJ: Prentice Hall, 1970), 39.

5. Brent F. Nelsen, James L. Guth, and Brian Highsmith, "Does Religion Still Matter? Religion and Public Attitudes toward Integration in Europe," *Politics and Religion* 4, no. 1 (2011): 1–26; Brent F. Nelsen and James L. Guth, "Religion and Youth Support for the European Union," *Journal of Common Market Studies* 41, no. 1 (2003): 89–112; Brent F. Nelsen, James L. Guth, and Cleveland R. Fraser, "Does Religion Matter? Christianity and Public Support for the European Union," *European Union Politics* 2, no. 2 (2001): 191n217; Brent F. Nelsen and James L. Guth, "Exploring the Gender Gap:

Women, Men, and Public Attitudes toward European Integration," *European Union Politics* 1, no. 3 (2000): 267–91.

6. Nelsen, Guth, and Fraser, "Does Religion Matter?" 199–200; Nelsen, Guth, and Highsmith, "Does Religion Still Matter?" 14.

7. European Commission, "Public Opinion in the European Union: Report," *Standard Eurobarometer* 78 (Autumn 2012): 92, http://ec.europa.eu/public_opinion/archives/eb/eb78/eb78_publ_en.pdf.

8. Nelsen, Guth, and Highsmith, "Does Religion Still Matter?" 12.

9. Nelsen, Guth, and Fraser, "Does Religion Matter?" 199–200.

10. Nelsen and Guth, "Youth Support."

11. Nelsen, Guth, and Highsmith, "Does Religion Still Matter?" 20.

12. There is some indication that more nominal identifiers of any religious tradition and self-identified atheists and agnostics are less supportive of the EU than religious believers as a whole; see Nelsen and Guth, "Youth Support," 99.

13. Joseph H. H. Weiler, "Does Europe Need a Constitution? Reflections on Demos, Telos, and the German Maastricht Decision," *European Law Journal* 1, no. 3 (1995): 219–58.

14. Gerard Delanty, *Inventing Europe: Idea, Identity, Reality* (New York: St. Martin's Press, 1995); Philippe C. Schmitter, *How to Democratize the European Union . . . and Why Bother?* (Lanham, MD: Rowman & Littlefield, 2000); Larry Siedentop, *Democracy in Europe* (New York: Columbia University Press, 2001); Vivien A. Schmidt, *Democracy in Europe: The EU and National Polities* (Oxford: Oxford University Press, 2006); Willem Maas, *Creating European Citizens* (Lanham, MD: Rowman & Littlefield, 2007).

15. Jürgen Habermas, *The Divided West* (Cambridge: Polity Press, 2006).

16. Thomas Risse, "Neofunctionalism, European Identity, and the Puzzles of European Integration," *Journal of European Public Policy* 12, no. 2 (2005): 295–96; Thomas Risse, *A Community of Europeans? Transnational Identities and Public Spheres* (Ithaca, NY: Cornell University Press, 2010), 24–25; Sara Binzer Hobolt, "Multiple Identities in Europe," in *Euromission: Neue Perspektiven für das erweiterte Europa,* ed. Daniel Dettling and Günter Verheugen (Münster: Lit, 2004), 105–17.

17. Risse, *Community,* 38. See also Thomas Risse, "Social Constructivism and European Integration," in *European Integration Theory,* ed. Antje Wiener and Thomas Diez (Oxford: Oxford University Press, 2004), 167–69.

18. Risse, "Social Constructivism," 68. See also Thomas Banchoff, "German Identity and European Integration," *European Journal of International Relations* 5, no. 3 (1999): 271–76.

19. Dieter Fuchs, "Cultural Diversity, European Identity, and Legitimacy of the EU: A Theoretical Framework," in *Cultural Diversity, European Identity and the Legitimacy of the EU,* ed. Dieter Fuchs and Hans-Dieter Klingemann (Cheltenham, UK: Edward Elgar, 2011), 37–38.

20. On the construction of a European identity, see Ioana-Sabina Prisacariu, "The Symbols Role in the Creation of a European Identity" (MA thesis, Centre for European Studies in Regional Development at Alexandru Ioan Cuza University of Iaşi, 2007).

21. "Declaration on European Identity, Copenhagen, 14 December 1973," European Union, 118–22, www.cvce.eu/obj/declaration_on_european_identity_copenhagen_14_december_1973-en-02798dc9-9c69-4b7d-b2c9-f03a8db7da32.html. All quotations here are from this document.

22. See Michael Bruter, *Citizens of Europe? The Emergence of a Mass European Identity* (Houndmills, UK: Palgrave, 2005), 72–75.

23. Bruter, *Citizens of Europe?* 83.

24. Pietro Adonnino, "People's Europe: Report from the Ad Hoc Committee," *Bulletin of the European Communities* (Office for Official Publications of the European Communities, Luxembourg), supplement 7/85 (1985): 4, http://repositori.uji.es/xmlui/bitstream/handle/10234/49877/Suplemento7-85en.pdf?sequence=1.

25. Ibid., 19.

26. Ibid., 22.

27. Neil Fligstein, *Euroclash: The EU, European Identity, and the Future of Europe* (Oxford: Oxford University Press, 2008), 178.

28. Ibid., 179.

29. Ibid., 180.

30. Ibid.

31. Ibid.

32. Ibid., 179.

33. See John Zaller, *The Nature and Origins of Mass Opinion* (Cambridge: Cambridge University Press, 1992).

34. François Foret, *Religion and Politics in the European Union: The Secular Canopy* (Cambridge: Cambridge University Press, 2014), 203–18.

35. Bruter refers to these as "civic" symbols, but he notes that they also carry cultural content; Bruter, *Citizens of Europe?* 85–86.

36. The official symbols are included in the analysis of member state behavior in chapter 9 of the present volume.

37. Hannes Hansen-Magnusson and Jenny Wüstenberg, "Memorializing the Founding Moments of Europe: Promoting a Shared Identity?" paper presented at International Studies Association Annual Meeting, New Orleans, February 17–20, 2010.

38. Thanks to François Foret for pointing this out to us.

39. European Parliament, "Building a House for the European History: Visit by the Secretary-General on the Eastman Building Site," March 2013, www.europarl.europa.eu/the-secretary -general/en/activities/recent_activities/articles/articles-2013/articles-2013-march/articles -2013-march-1.html.

40. Ibid.

41. Risse, *Community*, 58.

42. European Commission, "European Capitals of Culture," http://ec.europa.eu/culture /tools/actions/capitals-culture_en.htm.

43. European Union, "EU Citizenship," http://europa.eu/pol/cit/index_en.htm.

44. Daniel Williams, "European Leaders Sign Constitution: Prospects for Ratification Uncertain," *Washington Post*, October 29, 2004, www.washingtonpost.com/wp-dyn/articles/A8408 -2004Oct29.html.

45. Foret, *Religion*, chap. 6, at 203–4.

46. Centre Virtuel de la Connaissance sur l'Europe, "Proposals for European Flags from Arsène Heitz (1952–1955)," www.cvce.eu/viewer/-/content/3c8f111a-6be6-4111-a433-20f1a7f9fdba/en.

47. "Lettre d'Arsène Heitz à Filippo Caracciolo (Strasbourg, 5 janvier 1952)," Archives of the Council of Europe, December 3, 2012, www.cvce.eu/collections/object-content/-/object /89e56c97-d316-4e41-b362-d0a0171fac77/ca9b3b29-c645-4eae-9d35-ad69f561abf6/6b758d67 -f606-4ac9-90fc-3339fe66a76c/fr.

48. Centre Virtuel de la Connaissance sur l'Europe, "Proposals."

49. Council of Europe, "The European Flag: Questions and Answers (2005)," www.cvce.eu /viewer/-/content/39d51e24-2e68-4497-b81e-7a08e09ee0d7/en.

50. This is from the Catholic Public Domain Version.

51. Wikipedia, "Circle of Stars," http://en.wikipedia.org/wiki/Circle_of_stars.

52. Wikipedia, "Paul Michel Gabriel Lévy," http://en.wikipedia.org/wiki/Paul_Michel _Gabriel_Levy.

53. Wikipedia, "Arsène Heitz," http://en.wikipedia.org/wiki/Arsène_Heitz.

54. "Real Politics, at Last? Finally, There Is a Pan-European Debate—but It May Not Help the EU," *The Economist*, October 28, 2004, www.economist.com/node/3332056/print?Story_ID=3332056.

55. Centre Virtuel de la Connaissance sur l'Europe, "Account by Paul M. G. Lévy on the Creation of the European Flag," www.cvce.eu/obj/en-6d23210b-865d-4f02-b2ca-2c30b9ed0588.

56. Council of Europe, "How the Twelve Stars Were Born," www.coe.int/T/E/Com/Files /events/2005-12-drapeau/avenement.asp.

57. European Union, "The European Flag," http://europa.eu/abc/symbols/emblem/index _en.htm.

58. See, e.g., Wildolive, "Europe," www.wildolive.co.uk/europe.htm. For a dispensational view of the flag (and many other related topics), see Bente Struksnæs and Abel Struksnæs, "Watch Out for a Catholic European Union!" http://www.endtime.net/engelsk/KEU.htm.

59. Foret, *Religion*, 209.

60. Quoted in ibid., 208.

61. Ibid., 212. See also European Commission, "Euro Notes and Coins," http://ec.europa.eu/economy_finance/euro/cash/index_en.htm.

62. Miroslava Germanova, "More Secular Europe, Divided by the Cross," *New York Times*, June 17, 2013, www.nytimes.com/2013/06/18/world/europe/a-more-secular-europe-divided-by-the-cross.html?ref=europe&_r=1&.

63. Foret, *Religion*, 202.

64. Ibid., 215.

65. Anthony D. Smith, *Cultural Foundations of Nations: Hierarchy, Covenant, and Republic* (Malden, MA: Blackwell, 2008), 19.

66. David Michael Green, *The Europeans: Political Identity in an Emerging Polity* (Boulder, CO: Lynne Rienner, 2007), 52.

67. See Green, *Europeans*, 52, 52n2. Green provides an excellent summary of the approaches taken by the major surveys, including *Eurobarometer* and the World Values Survey.

68. European Union, *Eurobarometer 61: Public Opinion in the European Union*, Spring 2004, B94, http://ec.europa.eu/public_opinion/archives/eb/eb61/eb61_en.pdf.

69. Bruter, *Citizens of Europe?* 110–11.

70. Ibid., 114.

71. Green, *Europeans*, 52.

72. Fascinatingly, "country" is usually chosen second behind "town"; Green, *Europeans*, 56.

73. Dieter Fuchs, Isabelle Guinaudeau, and Sophia Schubert, "National Identity, European Identity and Euroscepticism," in *Euroscepticism: Images of Europe among Mass Publics and Political Elites*, ed. Dieter Fuchs, Raul Magni-Berton, and Antoine Roger (Opladen, Germany: Barbara Budrich, 2009), 101.

74. The "future" question is examined by the following, who find similar results: Green, *Europeans*, 54–55; Fligstein, *Euroclash*, 141; and Risse, *Community*, 40–41.

75. Risse, *Community*, 60. See also Fritz Scharpf, *Governing in Europe: Effective and Democratic?* (Oxford: Oxford University Press, 1999).

76. Bruter, *Citizens of Europe?* 74; Green, *Europeans*, 67.

77. Green, *Europeans*, 66.

78. Bruter's conclusion is significant; see Bruter, *Citizens of Europe?* 123–29, 140–41. But Bruter's measure of exposure to symbols requires greater scrutiny. Respondents in his model are "exposed" to a symbol from the time their member states adopt it. Before adoption, a respondent is given a value "0"; after adoption, "1." The sum of the scores is coded as the response for the variable "symbols." Six items included in the measure (flag, anthem, passport, Europe Day, and direct elections to the EP) are exactly the same for each respondent because all member states of the European Community/Union adopted these symbols at the same time. Two additional items—Schengen agreement and the euro—show variation because member states joined these joint policies at different times or not at all (201–3). But including them in the variable "symbols" may introduce a policy dimension that makes it difficult to interpret the impact of exposure to symbols on identity.

79. Risse, *Community*, 5.

80. Green, *Europeans*, 104–5.

81. See Fligstein, *Euroclash*.

82. Antonis Papacostas, *Eurobarometer 65.2: The European Constitution, Social and Economic Quality of Life, Avian Influenza, and Energy Issues*, March–May 2006.

83. Fligstein, *Euroclash*, 21. For an alternative view, see Cécile Leconte, *Understanding Euroscepticism* (Houndmills, UK: Palgrave Macmillan, 2010), 175–78.

84. Fligstein, *Euroclash*, 251. See also Liesbet Hooghe, Gary Marks, and Carole J. Wilson, "Does Left/Right Structure Party Positions on European Integration?" *Comparative Political Studies* 35, no. 8 (2002): 965–90.

85. Risse, *Community*, 51.

86. Ibid., 52.

87. Ibid.

88. See, e.g., Matthew J. Gable, *Interests and Integration: Market Liberalization, Public Opinion and European Union* (Ann Arbor: University of Michigan Press, 1998).

89. Joe Parkinson, "Turkey Leader Tightens Grip, Putting Nation at Crossroads," *Wall Street Journal*, June 27, 2013.

90. Hannah Kuchler, "UK to Unveil First State of Review into EU Powers," *Financial Times*, July 21, 2013.

91. See Nicolas Berggruen and Nathan Gardels, "The Next Europe: Toward a Federal Union," *Foreign Affairs* 92, no. 4 (2013): 134–42.

Index

Page numbers in italics followed by f represent figures (*224f*). Page numbers in italics followed by t represent tables (*171t*).